美国针灸立法汇编

美国西部地区针灸立法汇编

Collection of Acupuncture Laws in the Western United States of America

（汉英对照）

总顾问
刘保延　沈远东
主　编
桑　珍　杨宇洋　宋欣阳　张博源

上海科学技术出版社

内 容 提 要

针灸于19世纪上半叶传入美国，在20世纪70年代"针灸热"的影响之下，开始在美国流行。针灸在美国流行的五十年间，经历了三次热潮，完成了法律本土化、教育本土化、职业本土化和医学属性本土化四个层次的本土化，广泛应用于变态反应性疾病、糖尿病、艾滋病、各种肿瘤、高血压、肥胖症、戒毒、戒酒、戒烟、化疗或手术后发生的恶心和呕吐等领域。美国47个州及华盛顿特区都在州议会法中专章规定了针灸师执业法律制度，广泛涉及针灸与东方医学的概念、针灸师的准入条件、教育培训、执业规范、行业组织管理和惩戒规则等内容。

本书为美国西部地区针灸立法汇编，包括爱达荷州、俄勒冈州、华盛顿州、怀俄明州、加利福尼亚州、科罗拉多州、蒙大拿州、内华达州、犹他州九州，从针灸人员的法律地位、准入与注册、日常管理机构、职业道德、惩戒报告等方面展开介绍。本书的出版可为中医药政策和法律的制定者、中医药政策和法制研究者以及高等院校、科研机构中医药学科的研习者们提供参考和借鉴。

图书在版编目（ＣＩＰ）数据

美国西部地区针灸立法汇编 = Collection of Acupuncture Laws in the Western United States of America：汉英对照 / 桑珍等主编；刘保延，沈远东总顾问. -- 上海：上海科学技术出版社，2025.1
（美国针灸立法汇编）
ISBN 978-7-5478-6231-5

Ⅰ．①美… Ⅱ．①桑… ②刘… ③沈… Ⅲ．①针灸学－立法－汇编－美国－汉、英 Ⅳ．①D937.122.16

中国国家版本馆CIP数据核字（2023）第108965号

美国西部地区针灸立法汇编：Collection of Acupuncture Laws in the Western United States of America（汉英对照）
总顾问　刘保延　沈远东
主　编　桑　珍　杨宇洋　宋欣阳　张博源

上海世纪出版（集团）有限公司
上海科学技术出版社　出版、发行
（上海市闵行区号景路159弄A座9F-10F）
邮政编码 201101　www.sstp.cn
上海颛辉印刷厂有限公司印刷
开本 787×1092　1/16　印张 18.75
字数 350 千字
2025 年 1 月第 1 版　2025 年 1 月第 1 次印刷
ISBN 978－7－5478－6231－5/R・2788
定价：168.00 元

本书如有缺页、错装或坏损等严重质量问题，请向印刷厂联系调换

编委会名单

总顾问

刘保延　沈远东

主编

桑　珍　杨宇洋　宋欣阳　张博源

副主编

（按姓氏笔画排序）

王　硕　石燕红　刘竞元　李　静
范家伟　徐晓婷　黄祎晨　黄奕然

编委

（按姓氏笔画排序）

王志永　朱弇瑞　刘　冉　刘　祎
阮子蓉　杨　杨　张晓晨　周玥彤
高　阳　程　晗　程雅涵

丛书前言

针灸是我国历代劳动人民及医学家在长期与疾病作斗争中创造和发展起来的一种医学,具有悠久的历史。它是以中医理论为指导,运用针刺和艾灸防治疾病的一门临床学科。针灸具有适应证广、疗效明显、操作方便、经济安全等优点,数千年来深受广大劳动人民的欢迎,对中华民族的繁衍昌盛作出了巨大的贡献。

几千年来,针灸不仅对我国人民的保健事业作出重大贡献,而且很早就流传到国外,成为世界医学的重要组成部分,并产生积极而深远的影响。根据世界卫生组织统计,目前有113个成员国认可使用针灸,其中29个成员国设立了相关法律法规,20个成员国将针灸纳入医疗保险体系。针灸的神奇疗效引发全球持续的"针灸热"。针灸推拿等治疗手段成为奥运会运动员们缓解伤痛的新时尚。我国援外医疗队采用针灸、推拿、中药以及中西医结合方法治疗了不少疑难重症,挽救了许多垂危病人的生命,得到受援国政府和人民的充分肯定。不少国家先后对针灸进行了立法,成立了针灸学术团体、针灸教育机构和研究机构。

从20世纪70年代开始,世界卫生组织就积极地向全世界推广针灸,在多国设立针灸培训机构,支持创建世界针灸学会联合会,发布了针灸治疗的适宜病症、针灸经穴定位、从业人员培训指南等一系列国际标准,努力推进针灸的国际化与标准化进程。伴随着针灸的全球化应用,针灸针的国际贸易也逐年增长。2011年5月,国际标准化组织/中医药技术委员会(ISO/TC 249)在第二次荷兰海牙年会上,决议成立专门的工作组承担针灸针的国际标准研制工作,由中国专家担任召集人的职位。《ISO 17218:2014 一次性使用无菌针灸针》于2014年2月3日正式出版,成为首个在传统医药领域内由中国主导发布的ISO国际标准。截至目前,ISO/TC 249已发布了7项针灸针的国际标准,为针灸的国际化推广应用作出了积极的贡献。

针灸于19世纪上半叶传入美国,在20世纪70年代"针灸热"的影响之下,开始在美国流行。针灸在美国流行的五十年间,经历了三次热潮,完成了法律本土化、教育本土化、职业本土化和医学属性本土化四个层次的本土化。起初,针灸在美国主要用于治疗疼痛症状,后来也广泛应用于变态反应性疾病、糖尿病、艾滋病、各种肿瘤、高血压、肥胖症、戒毒、戒酒、戒烟、化疗或手术后发生的恶心和呕吐、不孕症、性功能不全、神经衰弱、紧张综合征、网球肘、肌纤维组织炎、中风后遗症、骨性关节炎、美容、体外受精、血液病、哮喘等领域。针灸在美国的发展并没有昙花一现，而是入乡随俗，遍地开花。美国的医疗改革给低成本针灸提供了全新的发展契机。中医针灸疗法针对很多病症可以采取非手术的保守疗法，成本低廉，疗效显著。迄今为止，美国50个州除了南达科他州、亚拉巴马州、俄克拉何马州3个州没有专门的针灸立法之外，其余47个州及华盛顿特区都在州议会法中专章规定了针灸师执业法律制度，广泛涉及针灸与东方医学的概念、针灸师的准入条件、教育培训、执业规范、行业组织管理和惩戒规则等内容。

"美国针灸立法汇编"丛书编委会经过两年多的信息搜集，资料整理分析，将美国47个州针灸法律英文文本进行了收集、翻译、校对和法律评析，重点展示美国各州现行针灸法律制度的全貌。本丛书共5册，按照新英格兰地区、中西部地区、西部地区、南部地区、西南部地区划分。每一区域立法均从针灸人员的法律地位、准入与注册、日常管理机构、职业道德、惩戒报告等方面展开介绍。希望本丛书的出版能为中医药政策和法律的制定者、中医药政策和法制研究者以及高等院校、科研机构中医药学科的研习者们提供参考和借鉴。由于时间仓促、经验不足，可能存在不严谨之处，望广大读者朋友不吝指正。

编　者

2023年3月

目　录

概述 …………………………………………………………………………………… 1
爱达荷州 ……………………………………………………………………………… 8
　　爱达荷州针灸法 ………………………………………………………………… 8
俄勒冈州 ……………………………………………………………………………… 13
　　俄勒冈州针灸法 ………………………………………………………………… 13
　　俄勒冈州针灸行政法 …………………………………………………………… 15
华盛顿州 ……………………………………………………………………………… 23
　　华盛顿州针灸法 ………………………………………………………………… 23
怀俄明州 ……………………………………………………………………………… 28
　　怀俄明州针刺法 ………………………………………………………………… 28
加利福尼亚州 ………………………………………………………………………… 33
　　加利福尼亚州针灸法 …………………………………………………………… 33
　　加利福尼亚州针灸行政法 ……………………………………………………… 47
科罗拉多州 …………………………………………………………………………… 75
　　科罗拉多州针灸法 ……………………………………………………………… 75
　　科罗拉多州针灸行政法 ………………………………………………………… 81
蒙大拿州 ……………………………………………………………………………… 90
　　蒙大拿州针刺法 ………………………………………………………………… 90
　　蒙大拿州针刺行政法 …………………………………………………………… 92
内华达州 ……………………………………………………………………………… 97
　　内华达州针刺法 ………………………………………………………………… 97
　　内华达州针刺行政法 …………………………………………………………… 108
犹他州 ………………………………………………………………………………… 121
　　犹他州针灸法 …………………………………………………………………… 121
　　犹他州针灸行政法 ……………………………………………………………… 125

IDAHO 128
    IDAHO CODE ANNOTATED 128
OREGON 134
    OREGON REVISED STATUTES ANNOTATED 134
    OREGON ADMINISTRATIVE RULES COMPILATION 136
WASHINGTON 149
    REVISED CODE OF WASHINGTON ANNOTATED 149
WYOMING 155
    WYOMING STATUTES ANNOTATED 155
CALIFORNIA 161
    ANNOTATED CALIFORNIA CODES 161
    CALIFORNIA CODE OF REGULATIONS 179
COLORADO 220
    COLORADO REVISED STATUTES ANNOTATED 220
    COLORADO ADMINISTRATIVE CODE 229
MONTANA 240
    MONTANA CODE ANNOTATED 240
    ADMINISTRATIVE RULES OF MONTANA 243
NEVADA 249
    NEVADA REVISED STATUTES ANNOTATED 249
    NEVADA ADMINISTRATIVE CODE 263
UTAH 283
    UTAH ACUPUNCTURE LICENSING ACT 283
    UTAH ADMINISTRATIVE CODE 287

概 述

美国西部地区九州包括爱达荷州、俄勒冈州、华盛顿州、怀俄明州、加利福尼亚州、科罗拉多州、蒙大拿州、内华达州、犹他州。濒临太平洋的华盛顿州、俄勒冈州、加利福尼亚州三个州,被称为美国西岸,而其中加利福尼亚州是美国针灸立法领航者,是21世纪初期针灸从业者最多的地方,针灸师数量雄踞美国五十个州和华盛顿特区之首。内华达州是针灸立法在美国第一个获得通过的州,内华达州针灸法的成功通过,有力带动了其他州的立法进程。

美国西部九州的针灸立法分为议会制定法(Statute)和行政法律(Administration Rules)两个层级。前者是由立法机关制定的相对完备的法律规范,后者更为具体,更注重政府规制针灸服务的可操作性。纯粹操作性的行业协会(如针灸委员会)规则是更侧重于行业内部治理的"软法"规范。美国西部九个州的针灸立法实际上就是针灸师规制法,更多以针灸师的职业成长逻辑为主线的执业主体法,比较全面地覆盖了针灸师的注册申请、许可程序和执业证照的获得、变更、终止,以及惩戒措施等设计出的相应的制度规范。就立法内容而言,西部九州主要特色如下。

一、以"双向规制"为立法的价值取向

美国西部九州立法均开宗明义地提出立法目的,即发挥针灸在消除疾病、维护民众健康方面的优势,又鉴于其作为一种职业对公众健康、安全和福利的影响,将个人从事针灸服务保健作为行业管制。加利福尼亚州针灸法(简称加州法,下同)第4926条第2款鼓励本州民众有效利用针灸师技能。其立法文本中体现了非常突出的"优先保护公众"的价值取向。内华达州法第634A.010条则明确东方医学及其分支机构属于承载社会公益性的学术性行业。

二、针灸等术语的明确界定

各州法均有明确的关于针灸、针灸师、针刺疗法等重要概念的定义。对于"针灸"存在着"技术说""功能说""理论说""系统说"等多种界定方式。加州法将"针灸"界定为,通过针刺刺激体表的某点或多点,以消除或减轻疼痛,或使生理功能(包括疼痛控制)正常化,以治疗某些疾病或身体功能失调,包括电针、拔火罐及艾灸等技术。内华达州法侧重从功能视角界定,即通过刺穿人体皮肤,将针头插入人体,以控制和调节体内能量的流动和平衡,并治

愈、缓解或减轻疾病。怀俄明州法、蒙大拿州法也均属于此类。爱达荷州法、犹他州法均侧重从疗法进行定义,包括相关辅助治疗(如电磁治疗和运动性治疗)。华盛顿州法"针灸"或"东方医学"是指利用针灸或东方医学诊断和治疗促进健康和治疗器质性或功能性疾病的卫生保健服务,列举了包括气功在内的十五项具体内容。科罗拉多州法把"针灸"定位为一种基于传统和现代东方医学理念,采用东方医学诊断、治疗和辅助治疗方法,旨在促进、维持和恢复健康并预防疾病的卫生保健体系。

值得注意的是,"针灸"是针法(Acupuncture)和灸法(Moxibustion)的总称,而各州对 Acupuncture 一词的范围有着不同界定。部分州将艾灸技术作为 Acupuncture 的治疗手段之一,包括加利福尼亚州、爱达荷州、俄勒冈州、华盛顿州、科罗拉多州、犹他州。而其余各州对 Acupuncture 一词的定义则不含灸法,包括内华达州、蒙大拿州、怀俄明州。为避免混淆,本书对该术语采取了不同译法,前者均译为"针灸",后者均译为"针刺"。

三、获得针灸师执业的法定条件和证照类型

获得针灸师执照除了年龄、品德等方面条件之外,还需要具备相应的学历背景、培训经历,甚至是医疗执业经历。进行相应的培训通常是获得针灸执照的必要条件。

加州法第 4938 条规定,针灸委员会颁发针灸执照的对象,应当符合以下条件:① 年满 18 岁。② 提供下列资质证明中的 1 项:获批的教育及培训计划;在针灸实践中顺利完成委员会批准的指导教学计划;符合教育培训及临床经验的相关标准。③ 通过委员会组织的测试申请人执业能力、素质和知识的笔试。④ 完成经委员会批准的临床实习培训计划。该临床实习培训计划的期限不得超过九个月,培训地点应设在本州一家获批的承担教育培训计划的诊所内。临床实习的时间长短,取决于参加考试前取得的成绩和已完成的临床培训。

内华达州法的执照分为两类:一类是针刺师执照,另一类是穴位注射疗法执照,两种执照为相互衔接关系。东方医学医师执照申请人需要具备的条件是:第一,通过由委员会组织和评定的下列考试:① 国家针灸与东方医学认证委员会(National Certification Commission for Acupuncture and Oriental Medicine)或其继受机构对东方医学认证考试。② 考察申请人对本州健康与安全的法律法规理解的相关考试。第二,东方医学学校或学院中成功完成认可的四年制学习计划或同等学力。第三,在美国认可的学院或大学获得东方医学学士学位或完成了本硕连读学位课程。第四,通过委员会对其背景和个人历史的调查。另外还有两种情形也可以授予执照:一是完成四年制学习计划,且在其他州或者外国合法从事东方医学治疗至少四年;二是完成了东方医学课程学习,在申请日期前八年内,至少有六年在美国其他州或准州(territory)、华盛顿特区或外国合法从事东方医学治疗的申请人。内华达州法还规定了东方医学医师进一步申请穴位注射疗法执照。申请人完成由国家针灸与东方医学认证委员会研究生课程,至少包含二十四学时亲自授课的指导,含至少八学时的实习指导和两学时肾上腺素肌内注射培训。获得或持有职业责任保险的保险单。

爱达荷州法规定执业资格证书申请认证人员应顺利完成美国医学针灸学会正式会员资格、教育和经验要求。① 拥有相应学院或大学颁发的脊椎按摩、牙科、足病医学或自然疗法医学博士学位。② 已顺利完成一项经相关部门批准的学习计划,该计划包括至少一百学时

的针灸现场教学课程。且此课程应由国家针灸与东方医学审核委员会（NCCAOM）认证的针灸师授课，而该针灸师须具备五年或以上实践经验，具有职业资格，且已以针灸技师的身份完成一年的针灸实习和二十五个案例研究。③已顺利完成血液传播病原体课程，并已通过委员会批准的针灸实践综合考试，该考试包括针的清洁技术和职业安全与健康标准（OSHA）所规定的程序与要求。

蒙大拿州针刺法第37-13-302条除了以年满18岁外，还要求申请人应当是东方医学学校和学院认可的针刺学校的毕业生，参与过委员会认可的同等课程至少一千学时的入门级培训。更为重要的条件是已通过由美国国家针灸师认证委员会（NCCA）筹备和管理的考试。

爱达荷州法规定为获得执业资格证或认证所需经验的人员可申请针灸学员许可证。委员会应考虑其在卫生保健方面的学术与其他培训经历与经验，并针对每位针灸学员开展监督、限制特定疗法和手段。许可证的有效期为自颁发之日起一年，只能续期一次，时长一年。

四、针灸师的执业规范

（一）执业范围

各州无一例外地对针灸、针灸疗法、针灸师等重要概念进行了界定，以此进一步明确执业针灸师从业的具体行为方式。东方医学医师是内华达州法的独特概念。内华达州法第634A.025条规定，如下业务内容不适用于该法有关东方医学医师的法律规定：被本州邀请来会诊者；受雇于本州东方医学学校（accredited school of Oriental medicine）的雇员、在其他州取得针灸治疗执照的人；仅限于在临床环境中向学生教授、检查或演示针灸治疗的方法和实践；向患者提供无偿针灸服务者。更不适用于依据《内华达州制定法修订本》第630章[①]或第633章[②]取得执照的医师。但是，内华达州并不禁止在紧急情况下自愿无偿提供的药剂师服务、家庭治疗中的家庭内部给药等行为。内华达州法中，其执业范围也受到严格限定，只允许注射其接受过训练的药物，包括但不限于营养药物、顺势疗法（Homeopathic）药物和草药。

俄勒冈州法规定除了传统针灸治疗之外，俄勒冈州医学委员会（Oregon Medical Board）授权的下列模式：①传统与现代东方医学及针灸技术的诊断与评价。②东方按摩、功法及相关治疗方法。③使用东方药典、维生素、矿物质和饮食建议。第677.761条明确划清了非针灸执业行为的边界，不限制从事针灸治疗以外的卫生保健活动、从事提供东方按摩、功法和相关治疗方法的医疗实践或提供东方药典所列药物、维生素或矿物质或饮食建议，也不限制俄勒冈州以外的从业人员在该州范围内开展针灸治疗演示的短期教学。

（二）头衔和称谓的使用

各州立法均试图严格区分西医师执业与针灸师执业的界限。针灸师可否向公众表明自己是"医师"，被视为一种非常重要的问题。加州法第4936条规定，针灸师在针灸服务中使

[①] 第54卷第630章"医师、医师助手、医疗助理、灌注师、呼吸保健医生"（Physicians, Physician Assistants, Medical Assistants, Perfusionists and Practitioners of Respiratory Care）。

[②] 第54卷第633章"骨科医学"（Osteopathic Medicine）。

用"医生"或缩写"Dr."属违反职业道德的行为。被授权使用"医生"或其缩写"Dr."头衔的针灸师,如果没有进一步说明其被授权使用的执照或学位类型,其行为也属违反职业道德的行为。

爱达荷州法第54-4712条规定,获得许可人员可使用"执业针灸师"的称谓。获得执照或被授予针灸技师证书的人员,或获得针灸学员许可证的人员,可以分别使用"认证针灸师""针灸技师"和"针灸学员"的称谓。未经授权,上述人员不得使用"执业针灸师"或"医师"的称谓及其缩略名称。针灸执业者不得以任何方式自称为内科医师、骨病医师、脊椎按摩师、理疗师或其他卫生保健专业人员,除非其根据法律规定已获得相应授权。犹他州法第58-72-501条对持证针灸师使用的头衔做出限制。持证针灸师不得将"内科医生""内/外科医生"或"医生"等字眼与针灸师的名称一并展示。如获得相应的针灸学位,针灸师可以使用"针灸医生"或"东方医学医师"的称谓。

(三) 强制信息披露制度

科罗拉多州法要求针灸师初次接待患者必须告知如下信息:姓名、业务地址和业务电话号码;价目表;关于治疗方法、技术和疗程的信息;针灸师的信息清单,包括针灸师的学历、经验、学位、专业组织成员资格;声明证照、注册文件的颁发机关;说明是否被吊销或撤销;监管机构以及主管的地址和电话;针灸师在推荐和应用由传统东方医学概念定义的辅助疗法和草药方面的培训和经验等。上述信息在变更后五日内强制性披露。针灸师还应当披露可能受到的纪律处分。该州对信息披露的重视可以从其立法目的阐述中找到依据。其开宗明义地规定,立法的主要目的是允许公民获得其所期望的针灸服务。在寻求针灸服务的过程中,公民拥有充分且确定的信息进行决策。

(四) 跨州执业问题

科罗拉多州法第12-200-103条规定了三种情形之一即属于客座针灸师:① 在另一个司法管辖区获取执照、完成注册、得到许可或受其监管。② 三个月内,在本州从事指导或教学活动不超过七日。③ 在一名科罗拉多州执业针灸师或执业脊椎指压治疗师的直接监督下从事指导或教育活动。加州法第4949条对于来自其他国家或者州的客座针灸师也进行了必要的行为限制;原则上不得禁止其他国家或州的针灸师通过讲座、临床教学或演示等方式参与针灸职业教育。其可以结合上述方式从事针灸实践,最长不得超过六个月,但不得开设诊室,不得在指定地点进行会诊、接听患者电话或以其他方式从事针灸实践。

其他州的法律也存在类似规定。怀俄明州法第33-49-109条规定,针灸委员会可通过背书的方式向在另一州从事针刺疗法的申请人颁发在怀俄明州从事针刺疗法的执照。其条件是该州具有与怀俄明州相当的针刺师执照要求,包括具有与怀俄明州类似的持证人背书许可条款;申请人在申请时不得有任何纪律处分;申请人没有在本州或任何其他州被吊销或撤销过针刺师执照;申请人应遵守委员会制定的继续教育要求和道德标准。

(五) 针灸师教育培训制度

加州针灸法第4945条规定了针灸师继续教育的标准:每名针灸师根据委员会制定的继续教育标准,每两年完成五十学时的继续教育任务,作为其执照续期的条件。在两年期间,与临床或实际向患者提供卫生保健服务无关的事项上,继续教育时间不得超过五学时。继续教育机构应向委员会提出申请,以获得委员会批准开设的继续教育课程学分。如委员会裁定针灸师继续教育学时不足,可将其执照续期。针灸师在其续期内未能补足的,其执照不得续期,直至完成继续教育学分并向委员会提交文件为止。

五、管理模式和职能

"委员会管理制"是美国西部九州针灸师管理体制的共同特点。除了蒙大拿州法规定由州医学考试委员会负责针灸师的申请、考试、培训和发证等管理实务外,其他各州均以针灸委员会作为其行业管理主管机关。九个州的立法均没有局限于简单"宣示"其针灸师管理体制属于何种类型,而是对委员会管理体制做出了相对严谨的制度设计。加州明确提出针灸委员会在许可、监管和行业规制过程中以"保护公众"为优先原则。各州针灸法在委员会组织的内部治理方面均比较健全。行业组织构成、人选、议事方式和外部支持等制度一应俱全。内华达州法甚至规定了每年举行常务会议的最低次数、公章存放、听证记录的保存,以及每个注册东方医师的姓名和营业地址等信息必须向全社会公开。

(一) 委员会的构成

各州均明确规定了本州针灸委员会成员的数量、选任条件、任命方式和决策机制等规范。然而,执业针灸师在委员会中所占比重则各不相同,各具特色。

加州法规定,委员会七名成员中的三人为从业五年以上的针灸师,其余四人均为既非针灸师又非西医师的社会人士。由州长委任三名针灸师成员及两名社会人士成员,均须获参议院的批准。参议院规则委员会和大会议长各自任命一名社会人士成员。如委员会的任何成员有玩忽职守、行为不端或渎职的情况,任命者可免其职务,但须向其提供书面控告书并给予申辩机会。

内华达州规定,州东方医学委员会的七名委员由州长任命,受州长的监督,根据《内华达州宪法》的规定宣誓就职。其中四人的具体要求为:一名成员需要持有本州东方医学执照,在本州从事东方医学治疗满三年;身为本州居民满一年。一名成员根据《内华达州制定法修订本》第630章获得医学考试委员会(Board of Medical Examiners)的医师执照,且不从事东方医学机构或东方医学学校的管理工作。依据《内华达州制定法修订本》第634A.090条一名成员为东方医学学校或学院的代表。另一名委员会成员则无具体的专业条件要求,仅是该州普通居民,不从事东方医学机构或东方医学学校的管理且与东方医学事务无利益关系。

犹他州法第58-72-201条规定,针灸许可委员会采取"4+1"模式,由四名执业针灸师和一名公众人士组成。华盛顿州法第18.06.220条虽然也采取了"4+1"的委员会模式,但是对四名针灸从业者有从业五年的规定,且在任职后两年内要积极尽职。一名社会人士则致力于维护医疗服务接受者权益。

俄勒冈州法规定由州医学委员会任命的六名成员组成针灸咨询委员会。其中,一人应为医学委员会现任成员,两人应为取得该州医师资格的人员,三人为取得针灸师资格的人。在任命这三位针灸师时,委员会可接受俄勒冈州针灸和东方医学协会(Oregon Association of Acupuncture)及其他针灸组织提名。

委员会决策的法定人数各州规定并不一致。加州法还规定委员会决策的法定人数是四名,包括至少一名针灸师。须由出席委员会会议过半数的人投赞成票,方可采取任何行动或通过任何议案。俄勒冈州则没有具体规定。

（二）职权范围

各州针灸管理委员会的职能范围具有明显的趋同性,涉及了证照审批和管理、教育培训和组织日常管理等内容。加州法规定委员会有权决定东方医学医师学位所需的课程。

俄勒冈州法第677.785条规定针灸咨询委员会应当：① 审查州医疗委员会收到的针灸执照或续期针灸执照的申请,并提出建议。② 向医学委员会建议持照针灸师的职业责任和执业标准。③ 向医学委员会建议针对针灸执照申请人进行教学和临床教育培训的标准。④ 向医学委员会建议符合国家认证机构委员会（National Commission for Certifying Agencies）或全国公认的针灸师测试标准的执照考试。

爱达荷州法第54-4705条规定：针灸委员会除了办理执业证照之外,还有权确定可向本州公众提供的适当的针灸执业范围；制定现行职业标准并促进针灸创新与进步的职业行为标准；出台针灸师进修教育规范,作为其获得许可或认证的条件。聘用或任命员工,包括行政主管、调查员、律师、顾问和独立听证审查官。有权开展调查、检查,举行听证会。

怀俄明州法第33-49-106条规定,委员会除了办理证照类事务外,还应当确定执业针灸师的继续教育要求、职业操守标准、伦理标准。建立必要的分级执照,以区分不同等级的耳穴疗法。对涉嫌违反本章和委员会规则的行为进行调查、听证和提起诉讼。保存所有诉讼程序的记录并向申请人和其他有关各方提供委员会诉讼的年度报告。在财务管理方面,委员会收取的所有费用应由国家财政主管部门存入怀俄明州针灸委员会账户。从该账户中支付的款项不得超过已记入的款项。委员会应使用该账户支付管理产生的费用。爱达荷等州法律也具有类似的规定。

（三）采取禁止令措施和行政罚款措施的权力

内华达州法第634A.240条规定,委员会有权在未发生实际损害的情形下提起禁令诉讼。且不因此免除该人的刑事诉讼。第634A.250条规定,委员会有权对违反州法或拒其通过的条例的人处以不超过二千五百美元的行政罚款（administrative fine）。科罗拉多州法也规定委员会可以采取禁令措施。

六、惩戒与法律责任

（一）行业规制与刑法的衔接

（1）大部分州针灸法均规定了比较详尽的针灸师执业责任,一些州法还体现出针灸行业自律机制与司法机制的有机衔接。加州针灸法第4935条规定,没有依据本章执业规定的现行有效针灸执照,或没有根据本章执业或从事针灸执业的资格,即属轻罪,可处不少于一百美元及不多于二千五百美元的罚款,或在县监狱接受不超过一年的监禁,或两项并罚。

（2）任何人以欺诈方式买卖或取得针灸执照,即属轻罪,可处不少于一百美元及不多于二千五百美元的罚款,或在县监狱接受不超过一年的监禁,或两项并罚。

蒙大拿州针灸法第37-13-316条规定,任何人违反法律或蒙大拿州医学考试委员会的规则,即属犯罪,处以不超过六个月的监禁或不超过五百美元的罚款,或两者并罚。科罗拉多州法第12-200-111条规定,针灸师在护理期间与患者发生性接触,即属一级轻罪,应移交刑事诉讼;对患者进行性侵犯或性行为,即属四级重罪,应移交刑事诉讼。

(二)与执照颁发和撤销相关的事由

针对拒绝颁发、吊销或撤销针灸执业证照的事由,各州立法的处理方式各不相同。加州法针对针灸执照的拒绝颁发、吊销和撤销规定了比较严谨的制度,前述三种情形出现之后的直接后果,就是导致针灸师进入察看期(probationary conditions),进而实质性地影响其执业生涯。导致上述三种情形的原因是多方面的:一是违反职业道德。加州法列举了十一种情形,包括但不限于虚假或误导广告、感染控制不利、干扰取证、隐匿名称错误等行为。二是欺诈。包括通过欺诈或欺骗手段取得执照、身份虚假、贪污、制造虚假病历、服务记录不够充分和准确。三是严重过失、多次重复出现过失和不称职。怀俄明州法也规定了对针刺师的不称职行为,委员会可以施加"察看期"条件。

内华达州法第634A.170条规定导致执照拒绝颁发、吊销和撤销的原因多达20项,犯罪是性质最恶劣的原因。与东方医学执业有关的重罪;涉及道德败坏的罪行;违反药品管制法律等均在此列。其次,以欺诈获取执照或执业、严重的或重复的医疗事故、虚假宣传,个人行为不检点例如欺诈、不诚实甚至习惯性醉酒或瘾癖;身体或精神上的残疾、被判定为不称职或者精神错乱;故意泄露保密信息,甚至执照持有人未能以其专业使用名称"东方医学医师"一词指明其执业性质等行为均在列。科罗拉多州法第12-200-109条对针灸师纪律处分的理由也多达十五项,其中未能强制性披露,或在披露中向患者提供虚假、欺骗性或误导性信息,就是一个重要的原因。科罗拉多州法还规定,针灸师的纪律处分除了吊销执照或暂停执业,还包括对针灸师设定"察看处分条款"。或者向针灸师发送警告信。爱达荷州法还规定,基于委托人对针灸师的信任而从事构成虐待或剥削委托人的行为也属于吊销、撤销执业证书的法定事由。

(三)附期限恢复执照或变更处罚制度

加州法第4960.5条还针对受处罚针灸师提供了一定的"察看"制度。规定:委员会还可以根据被撤销执照的针灸师申请,恢复其执照或更改处罚,包括更改或终止增加的察看条件:① 对于执照被撤销的,至少三年后恢复执照。② 增加三年以上察看期的,满两年可申请提前终止察看期。③ 满两年可申请调整察看期。④ 增加三年以下察看期的,满一年可申请提前终止察看期。

(四)"察看期"制度与信息强制披露

针对察看期的法律地位和待遇问题。加州法第4962条规定了详细的披露规则。即委员会应要求持证人根据察看期命令,在患者首次造访之前向患者、患者监护人或医疗代理人(health care surrogate)独立披露相关信息。包括但不限于持证人的察看状态、察看期时长、察看期结束日期、委员会对持证人施加的所有执业限制、委员会的联系电话,以便患者在委员会执照信息网站上获知有关其察看期的更多有用信息。

爱 达 荷 州

爱达荷州针灸法[①]

第 54－4701 条　目的

立法机关认为针灸服务关乎公众健康、安全和福利,为爱达荷州公众提供高质量的针灸服务符合公众利益。基于此目的,本章对于爱达荷州针灸师的执照及其监管做出相关规定。

第 54－4702 条　定义

下列定义适用于本章：

(1)"针灸"系指从传统和现代东方医学哲学发展而来的一种保健理论。该理论通过刺激人体经络上的特定穴位来诊断人体情况、治疗机体,以促进、维持、恢复健康和预防疾病。针灸的治疗方法包括针对特定穴位进行手法治疗、器械治疗、温针治疗、电针治疗以及电磁治疗。此外,针灸的辅助疗法包括但不限于草药和营养疗法、治疗性锻炼和其他基于传统与现代东方医学理论的疗法。

(2)"委员会"系指爱达荷州针灸委员会。

(3)"NCCAOM"系指美国国家针灸及东方医学审核委员会。

(4)"针灸实践"系指根据东方医学的传统与现代理论,将针灸针插入人体皮肤上的特定穴位,并使用类似的装置和疗法,包括艾灸的使用。但"针灸实践"不包括：

(a)外科手术;或

(b)开出、分发或使用《爱达荷州法典》第 54－1705 条(35)款[②]规定的任何处方药。

第 54－4703 条　执照要求

(1)自 1999 年 7 月 1 日起,未根据本章规定取得执照或认证的,任何在本州从事针灸实践的行为均视为违法。但本章规定并不适用于根据《爱达荷州法典》第 54 卷第 18 章[③]取

[①] 根据《爱达荷州法典》第 54 卷第 47 章(West's Idaho Code Annotated, Title 54. Professions, Vocations, and Businesses, Chapter 47. Acupuncture)译出。

[②] 即第 54 卷第 17 章"药剂师"第 54－1705 条"定义"第 35 款"处方药的定义"。

[③] 第 54 卷第 18 章"医师及医师助理"(Physicians and Physician Assistants)由三部法律构成："医事法"(Medical Practice Act)、"残疾人理疗师法"(Disabled Physician Act)以及"州际医疗许可合约"(Interstate Medical Licensure Compact)。

得执照的人员。此类人员可在自愿的基础上根据本章规定申请执照或认证。根据本章规定,持有针灸学员许可证的人员,可按照本章规定、委员会规则以及许可证规定,在监督下从事受限的针灸实践。

(2)任何人不得以任何头衔、名称、文字、字母、缩写或标志、卡片或图案向公众表明其可以任何形式从事针灸实践或表明已根据本章要求获得执照或认证,除非其确实已获得相应执照或认证,且根据委员会规则该执照或认证信誉良好。

第54-4704条　针灸委员会的设立-任命-任期

(1)在自治机构设立一个州针灸委员会,其成员应在本章生效之日起六十日内由州长任命。

(2)委员会应由五名成员构成,其中三人应根据本章之规定持有相应执照,一人应根据本章之规定获得相应认证,另一人应为与针灸服务消费者权利有利益关系的普通民众。

(3)任命针灸委员会成员时,应考虑爱达荷州针灸协会、其他类似专业组织以及居住在该州的任何个人提出的建议。

(4)委员会所有成员应为现居住在爱达荷州的居民,且在任命前已在爱达荷州居住至少三年。

(5)所有任期应为四年,且允许连任。若有成员在任期届满前死亡、辞职或被免职,则该空缺应按原任命方法进行递补。

(6)委员会成员应听从州长指示。

(7)在接受任命之后的三十日内,委员会应召开一次会议,并选举产生委员会主席,且该会议每年至少召开一次。此外,委员会可应主席的要求或应两名成员的书面要求召开额外会议。如有必要,委员会可委任执委会履行其职责。且委员会成员过半数即构成法定人数。

(8)委员会各成员应根据《爱达荷州法典》第59-509条(p)项①的规定获得报酬。

第54-4705条　针灸委员会-权力与职责-资金

(1)委员会有权:

(a)根据本章规定确定申请执照、认证和针灸学员许可证的人员资格,并按照规定确定可向本州公众提供的适当的针灸服务范围。

(b)聘用或任命员工,包括行政主管、调查员、律师、顾问和独立听证审查官。

(c)根据《行政程序法》的规定,制定本章行政管理所需的规则,其中包括反映现行职业标准并促进针灸创新与进步的职业行为标准。

(d)开展调查、检查,举行听证会。

(e)按照本章规定征收费用和其他款项。

(f)在本州起诉或应诉,并处理其他合法事项。

(g)提供并履行为实现其目的所必需的其他服务和职能。

(h)订立规则,要求其成员接受继续教育,以此作为其继续持有执照或认证的条件。

---

① 即第59卷"一般公职人员"第5章"公务员薪水"第59-509条"委员会成员的酬金或报酬"第(p)项。

（2）根据本章规定收取的所有费用应支付给职业执照局并以职业执照基金的名义存入国库，而所发生的所有成本和费用应由上述基金支付。

第 54－4706 条　执照颁发要求

申请执照的人员除需缴纳所需费用之外，还应提交一份由委员会提供且符合其要求的书面申请，证明该人员符合下列规定：

（1）已获得 NCCAOM 认证，或已顺利完成获委员会批准的其他类似要求。

（2）已顺利完成针灸实习或职业前实习计划、协调计划或获得委员会批准的其他同等经验。

（3）已顺利通过委员会针对执照申请人组织的统一考试或能力证明测试。

第 54－4707 条　认证要求

申请认证的人员除需缴纳所需费用之外，还应提交一份由委员会提供的书面申请，证明其已顺利通过委员会统一组织的考试或能力证明测试，且：

（1）已顺利达到美国医学针灸学会正式会员资格要求。

（2）满足下列教育与经历要求：

（a）拥有经认证学院或大学颁发的脊椎按摩、牙科、足科医学或自然疗法医学博士学位。

（b）已顺利完成一项获相关部门批准的计划，该计划包括至少一百学时的针灸现场教学课程，且此课程应由 NCCAOM 认证针灸师教授，该针灸师须具备五年或以上实践经验，持有现行执照，且在一年内以针灸技师或针灸学员身份完成二百学时的针灸实践和二十五个案例研究。

（c）已顺利完成血液传播病原体课程，并已获得委员会批准的针灸实践综合考试，该考试包括洁针技术和职业安全与健康管理局（OSHA）所规定的程序与要求。

第 54－4708 条　针灸学员许可证

（1）想要根据本章规定获得执照或认证的人员可申请针灸学员许可证。此类人员应缴纳所需费用，提交由委员会提供的书面申请，并向委员会证明其具备相应资格且在积极申请获得针灸执照。

（2）在批准针灸学员许可证时，委员会应考虑申请人迄今为止在卫生保健方面的学术与其他培训及经历的范围和程度，并针对每位针灸学员：

（a）实施委员会指定的适当的监督，监督人由根据本章规定获得执照或认证的人员担任。

（b）限制其在针灸实践中只能采用特定的疗法和治疗手段。

（3）针灸学员许可证自颁发之日起一年到期。但在许可证到期之前，若该学员要求委员会续期，且经委员会确定其出于正当理由，则委员会可将其许可证的有效期顺延一年。针灸学员许可证的续期可按委员会所规定的条件办理。但每张许可证续期不得超过一次，且委员会不得向任何人颁发一张以上的许可证。

第 54－4708A 条　针灸技师

2011 年 7 月 1 日前获得针灸技师证书的个人，有权根据《爱达荷州法典》第 54－4710 条和委员会规则所规定的更新条款保留或续期该证书。但 2011 年 7 月 1 日之后不再颁发新的针灸技师证书。

第 54‐4709 条　背书

若申请人向委员会证明其根据美国另一州、准州或司法管辖区的法律获得执照,且委员会认为该申请人的执照要求与本章规定的基本等同,则申请人在支付所需费用并获得批准后,可根据本章通过背书方式获得执照。

第 54‐4710 条　到期与续期—执照恢复

(1) 根据本章规定颁发的所有执照均应每年续期一次。若未能按照委员会就续期申请、继续教育和收费所规定的方式进行续期,则相应执照到期后作废。执照续期和恢复应符合《爱达荷州法典》第 67‐2614 条①之规定。

(2) 委员会应对下列与执照相关的费用进行确定,各项费用的数额应足以支付本章所规定的行政管理所需的一切费用。

(a) 初次颁发执照。

(b) 执照续期费。

(c) 初次认证费。

(d) 初次颁发针灸学员许可证。

(e) 针灸技师证书或针灸学员许可证续期。

(f) 非执业执照费。

(g) 超期续期费。

第 54‐4711 条　吊销与撤销

为保障公众健康、安全与福利,申请人或执照、证书或许可证持有人有下列行为的,委员会可根据《爱达荷州法典》第 67 卷第 52 章②的规定,拒绝颁发特定执照、认证或许可证,或拒绝为其续期换证,或可根据委员会所设定条件,吊销或撤销特定执照、认证或许可证。

(1) 根据《爱达荷州法典》第 67‐9411 条第(1)款③被判有罪(涉及针灸师的资格、职能或义务)。

(2) 以欺诈、谎报或隐瞒重要事实的手段取得或者企图取得根据本章规定颁发或续期的执照、证书和许可证的。

(3) 在爱达荷州以不符合公认针灸从业标准的方式从事针灸实践的。

(4) 除法律要求或授权的情况外,未对可识别客户的相关记录或其他信息进行保密的。

(5) 基于委托人对针灸师的信任而从事构成虐待或剥削委托人的行为的。

(6) 从事违反本章之规定、委员会规则或委员会颁布的任何许可证条款的行为的。

(7) 未能遵守委员会所规定的纪律事项的。

(8) 执照被委员会或其他州、准州或美国或其他国家的司法管辖区的有关当局吊销或撤掉或以其他方式受到纪律处分的。

---

① 即第 67 卷"州政府和州事务"第 26 章"负责自治机构的部门"第 67‐2614 条"许可证的更新或恢复"。
② 即《爱达荷州行政程序法》(*Idaho Administrative Procedure Act*)。
③ 即《职业注册制度改革法》(*Occupational Licensing Reform Act*)第 67‐9411 条"刑事定罪评估"第(1)款。

（9）在爱达荷州或美国或其他国家的其他州、准州或司法管辖区，相关领域的执照或证书被吊销或撤销或以其他方式受到纪律处分的。

第 54－4712 条　头衔

根据本章规定获得执照的人员可使用"执业针灸师"的头衔。根据本章规定获得执照或被授予针灸技师证书的人员，或获得针灸学员许可证的人员，可以分别使用"认证针灸师""针灸技师"和"针灸学员"的头衔。但未经授权许可，上述人员不得使用"执业针灸师"或"医师"的头衔及其缩略名称。根据本章规定，被授权从事针灸实践的人员不得以任何方式自称为内科医师、骨病医生、脊椎按摩师、理疗师或其他卫生保健专业人员，除非其根据相关法律规定已获得相应授权。

第 54－4713 条　处罚

（1）违反本章任何规定的，一经定罪，即属轻罪。

（2）委员会可对违反本章规定从事针灸实践的个人发布禁令，并可对其发布永久禁令；或此人就任何相关刑事案件认罪或法院作出有罪判决的情况下，处以民事罚款，罚款数额应为委员会就该案件提起诉讼而产生的一切费用。

（3）对于某人向他人声明其持有本章规定的执照、证书或许可证的行为，若其声明不真实，则根据《爱达荷州法典》第 48 卷第 6 章①的规定，应视其所采取的方法、行为或实践为违法行为。

---

① 即《消费者保护法》（Consumer Protection Act）。

俄勒冈州

俄勒冈州针灸法①

第 677.757 条　定义

定义适用于《俄勒冈州制定法修订本》第 677.757 条至第 677.770 条：

(1)(a)"针灸"系指一种东方卫生保健服务,通过针刺刺激身体表面的特定穴位,促进健康,治疗神经、器质性或功能性疾病。"针灸"包括艾灸疗法,以及在用针或不用针的情况下通过电针、温针、器械装置或磁性装置刺激穴位和经络,达到麻醉或镇痛效果的方法。

(b) 针灸实践还包括俄勒冈州医学委员会授权的以下方式：

(A) 传统与现代的诊断及评估技术。

(B) 东方按摩、功法及相关治疗方法。

(C) 使用东方药典所列药物、维生素、矿物药及提供膳食建议。

(2) "东方药典"系指经认证东方医学学校常用的传统东方课本中描述的草药名录,该课本获俄勒冈州医学委员会批准。

第 677.759 条　执照；资格；使用特定术语的效果；准则

(1) 除本条(2)款另有规定外,未获得经俄勒冈州医学委员会颁发的医疗及外科手术执照或针灸执照的,任何人不得从事针灸实践。

(2) 尽管本条(1)款另有规定,在美国其他州或准州取得医疗及外科手术执照或针灸执业执照,并获准在美国其他地区从事针灸实践的,委员会仍有权向其颁发针灸执照。若其他地区的要求与本州或准州不同,则委员会不得颁发此类执照。

(3) 委员会应审查申请人的资格,并决定授权从事针灸实践的人员。

(4) 使用"针灸""针灸师""东方医学"或其他表示某人具有针灸执业资格或执照的术语、头衔、名称或缩写,能够初步证明其可以从事针灸实践。

---

① 根据《俄勒冈州制定法修订本》第 52 卷第 677 章(*Oregon Revised Statutes* Annotated, Title 52. Occupations and Professions, Chapter 677. Regulation of Medicine, Podiatry and Acupuncture, Acupuncturists)译出。因 677 章部分条款与针灸服务相关性不强,本文选译了针灸师专门条款 677.757—677.785。

（5）除本章所述委员会享有的权力和职责外，委员会还应采用与《俄勒冈州制定法修订本》第677.757条至第677.770条相一致的准则，以监管针灸执照的颁发过程。

第677.760条　根据《1989年俄勒冈州制定法》第830章第49条废除

第677.761条　不受677.757条至677.770条约束的人员及服务

第677.757条至第677.770条不适用于下列情形：

（1）阻止、限制或干扰获得俄勒冈州医学委员会颁发执照或认证的人员从事针灸治疗以外的卫生保健服务。

（2）限制其他获得执照或认证的卫生保健从业者在许可范围内从事穴位按压或其他疗法。

（3）在无法律明令禁止的情形下，限制开展以下活动：东方按摩、功法及相关治疗方法或提供东方药典所列药物、维生素、矿物药或膳食建议。

（4）根据委员会通过的条例，限制俄勒冈州以外的从业者在该州范围内展示针灸实践，并将其作为公认的限时教学计划、讲座或活动的一部分。

第677.765条　针灸师未经授权从事针灸实践

在未持证或俄勒冈州医学委员会终止执照或未续期执照的情况下，从事针灸实践构成未经授权的医疗行为，应根据《俄勒冈州制定法修订本》第677.990条的规定受到处罚。

第677.770条　费用

获得内/外科医师或其他获得针灸执照的人，均应向俄勒冈州医学委员会支付其根据第677.265条规定的不可退还的费用。

第677.775条　根据《1989年俄勒冈州制定法》第830章第49条废除

第677.780条　针灸咨询委员会；成员；条款

（1）由俄勒冈州医学委员会任命的六名成员组成针灸咨询委员会。医学委员会任命的咨询委员会成员中：

（a）应有一人为现行医学委员会成员。

（b）应有二人为依据《俄勒冈州制定法修订本》第677章获得医师执照的人。

（c）应有三人为依据《俄勒冈州制定法修订本》第677.759条获得针灸执照的人。在任命三位针灸师时，委员会可接受俄勒冈州针灸和东方医学协会以及其他专业针灸组织的提名。

（2）每位委员会成员的任期为三年，但应听从委员会指示。委员会成员不得连任超过两届。在继任者上任并胜任工作之前，委员会成员不得结束任期。若出现空缺，医学委员会应当立即任命候补人员，任期为剩余的未届满任期。

（3）委员会成员有权获得依据第677.235条规定的医学委员会成员的薪酬和开支。

（4）过半数委员会成员构成处理业务的法定人数。

第677.785条　委员会的职责

针灸咨询委员会应：

（1）审查俄勒冈州医疗委员会收到的针灸执照或续期针灸执照的申请，并提出建议。

（2）向医学委员会建议执业针灸师的职业责任和执业标准。

（3）向医学委员会建议针对针灸执照申请人进行教学和临床教育培训的标准。

（4）向医学委员会建议执照考试，该考试应符合国家认证机构委员会标准或国家认可的用于测验针灸师的同等组织标准。

俄勒冈州针灸行政法[①]

第847-070-0005条 定义

下列定义适用于针灸实践管理条例：

（1）（a）"针灸"系指一种东方卫生保健服务，通过针刺刺激身体表面的特定穴位，促进健康，治疗神经、器质性或功能性疾病。"针灸"包括艾灸疗法，以及在用针或不用针的情况下通过电针、温针、器械装置或磁性装置刺激穴位和经络，达到麻醉或镇痛效果的方法。

（b）针灸实践还包括由俄勒冈医学委员会授权的以下方式：

（A）传统与现代东方医学和针灸的诊断和评估技术。

（B）东方按摩、功法及相关治疗方法。

（C）使用东方药典所列药物、维生素、矿物药以及提供膳食建议。

（2）"委员会"系指俄勒冈州医学委员会。

（3）"临床培训"系指受监督的临床培训，包含诊断和临床实操，临床实操包括插入针灸针。

（4）"咨询委员会"系指针灸咨询委员会。

（5）"执业针灸师"系指委员会根据ORS[②]第677章的规定授权从事针灸实践的个人。

（6）（a）"东方按摩"系指一系列手法治疗方法，包括在使用手法工具或不使用手法工具的情况下进行手法松动，手法牵引、挤压、揉搓、揉捏和敲击，该疗法的适应证包括活动范围受限，肌肉痉挛、疼痛、瘢痕组织、收缩组织和软组织肿胀、水肿及炎症，如东方或亚洲卫生保健教学计划和材料所述。

（b）（A）在俄勒冈州实行的东方按摩不包括对脊柱或四肢关节进行小幅度快速按压。

（B）在俄勒冈州实行的东方按摩不包括骨盆内部按摩（阴道内、肛门内或直肠内）或生殖器按摩。

（7）"医师"系指根据ORS第677章的规定取得内科医师或骨科医生行医资格的个人。

第847-070-0007条 针灸实践

（1）任何人不得在未获得俄勒冈州医学委员会颁发的行医执照、手术执照或针灸执照的情况下从事针灸实践。

（2）希望获批成为临床导师的医生必须满足OAR[③]847-070-0015的要求。

---

① 根据《俄勒冈州行政法规汇编》第847章第70节（*Oregon Administrative Rules Compilation*, Chapter 847. Oregon Medical Board Division 70. Acupuncture）译出。

② *Oregon Revised Statute*，即《俄勒冈州制定法修订版》。

③ OAR，*Oregon Administrative Rules*，即《俄勒冈州行政法规》。

第 847－070－0015 条　申请

（1）每名申请人都必须按照委员会要求,正确填写 OAR 第 847－070－0016 条所列的申请和资格证明。完整填写上述申请和文件后,才有资格获得执照。

（2）虚假文件是委员会拒绝颁发执照或采取纪律处分的依据。

（3）申请人若在十二个月的期限内未完成执照申请程序,必须提交新的申请、文件、信件,并支付全额申请费,流程与首次申请相同。

（4）申请人存在下列情形的,无权获得执照：

（a）其执照或证书曾在本州或任何其他州被撤销或吊销,除非该执照或证书已重新颁发或恢复使用,且该申请人的执照或证书在其被撤销的州内信誉良好。

（b）因针灸执照考试不及格而被其他州拒绝颁发执照或证书；或

（c）曾犯有类似于 ORS 第 677.190 条禁止或适用的行为。

第 847－070－0016 条　执业资格

（1）针灸执照申请人须具备以下条件：

（a）毕业于符合以下机构标准的针灸专业：针灸及东方医学教育审核委员会（ACAOM）或其继受机构,或与申请人毕业时具有同等效力的认证机构。提供如下证据可证明该针灸专业符合上述标准：

（A）从针灸专业毕业时获得 ACAOM 的认证或认证候选资格；或

（B）从针灸专业毕业时获得外国政府教育部、卫生部或具有同等效力的外国政府机构的批准。每位申请人均须将其文件提交给具有同等效力的国外认证服务机构,该机构由国家针灸与东方医学审核委员会（NCCAOM）批准,目的是建立与 ACAOM 认证标准的等效性。若该针灸专业与 ACAOM 的认证专业具有同等效力,则申请人须在毕业时满足 ACAOM 的有效课程要求。

（b）NCCAOM 现行的针灸认证。若申请人已通过 NCCAOM 针灸认证考试或通过 NCCAOM 证书文件考试,则视为申请人通过 NCCAOM 针灸认证。

（A）申请人参加 NCCAOM 针灸认证考试的次数不得超过四次。若申请人在四次考试中均未通过 NCCAOM 认证考试,则没有资格获得执照。

（B）已通过 NCCAOM 认证考试,但未在本规定要求的四次考试内通过的申请人,如在五次考试内通过考试,则如符合下列条件,即可申请豁免该要求：

（i）获得针灸和东方医学博士学位；或

（ii）存在由委员会确定的且并不妨碍安全针灸治疗的减责情形。

（2）不符合 OAR 847－070－0016(1)标准的申请人必须具备以下资格：

（a）在美国持证并从事临床针灸实践五年,包括每年对至少五百人次患者实施针灸疗法。文件必须包括：

（A）两份由营业机构合伙人、诊所主管、会计师或其他获委员会批准的人士提交的宣誓书,这些人士对诊所的执业年数及每年的患者求诊次数有亲身了解。

（B）预约簿、病历表和财务记录的公证副本,或委员会要求的其他文件。

（b）在申请俄勒冈州执照之前的过去七年中,有五年在美国作为执业针灸师执业。执业内容包括针灸和东方医学领域的临床实践、临床监督、教学、研究和委员会批准的其他工作。记录这些执业行为的文件需要提交并获得委员会批准。

(c) 于针灸专业毕业时,顺利完成 ACAOM 的西医学要求,除非申请人在 1989 年之前毕业于未经认证的针灸专业。

(d) 获得 NCCAOM 的现行针灸执照。若申请人已通过 NCCAOM 针灸认证考试或已通过 NCCAOM 执照文件考试,则申请人将被 NCCAOM 视为获得针灸执照。

(A) 申请人通过 NCCAOM 针灸认证考试的次数不超过四次。若申请人在四次考试中均未通过 NCCAOM 认证考试,则申请人没有资格获得执照。

(B) 已通过 NCCAOM 认证考试,但未在本规定要求的四次考试内通过的申请人,如在五次考试内通过,且:

(i) 获得针灸和东方医学博士学位;或

(ii) 存在由委员会确定且并不妨碍安全针灸实践的减责情形。

(3) 在外国接受针灸培训并获得文凭的个人,由于目前无法获得所需文件而无法满足本条例第(1)款或(2)款要求,若该申请人具有同等技能,接受过同等培训,并且可以出示证明该申请人已在美国接受一名执业针灸师为期一年的培训或在其监督下从事实践,符合委员会要求,则可视其为有资格获得执照。

(4) 除满足本规定第(1)、(2)或(3)项要求外,所有执照申请人还必须具备以下条件:

(a) 先前和现行的卫生相关执照在本州和各州均信誉良好。

(b) 具有良好品德,这些品质将关系到申请人能否适当地从事针灸实践。

(c) 有能力用英语与患者和医生进行良好的沟通。若申请人通过 NCCAOM 针灸学英语笔试,则符合此要求。若参加其他外语的笔试,必须通过英语水平考试,如托福考试(TOEFL)或英语口语测试(TSE),才符合此要求。申请人的托福笔试成绩必须达到 500 分或以上,托福机考成绩必须达到 173 分或以上。或者 1995 年 7 月之前的 TSE 成绩达到 200 分或以上,1995 年 7 月之后的 TSE 成绩达到 50 分或以上。通过 NCCAOM 证书文件考试认证的申请人也必须通过英语水平考试。

第 847-070-0017 条 临床培训

(1) 临床导师必须满足以下要求:

(a) 是一名积极执业的俄勒冈州执业针灸师,从事针灸实践至少五年,并且在委员会中信誉良好;或

(b) 是一名俄勒冈州执业医师,在委员会中信誉良好,从事针灸实践至少五年,并通过针灸考试;或

(c) 是一名获得其他司法管辖区执照、注册或认证的针灸师或医生,在该司法管辖区信誉良好,从事针灸实践至少五年,并已通过针灸资格考试,或已通过 NCCAOM 的证书文件考试获得针灸认证。若在这五年或更长的执业时间后获得执照、注册或认证,则以前的执业记录应当符合委员会的要求,并采用 NCCAOM 文件认证标准。本条下的临床导师均须获得委员会批准。

(2) 委员会批准的临床导师、针灸师或医师在非正式的私人医疗场合不得监督超过两

名针灸学员。

（3）如满足以下条件，个人应遵守 OAR 第 847-070-0005 条至 847-070-0055 条（如适用）：

（a）就读于俄勒冈州一所获批提供大专临床教育学分的学校；或

（b）在俄勒冈州医学委员会批准的临床培训中注册并获批在其他州或国外从事针灸实践的执业医师。

（4）针灸专业学生只有满足以下条件，才可在培训过程中提供针灸服务（如适用）：

（a）就读于俄勒冈州一所获批提供大专临床教育学分的学校；或

（b）是其他州或国外持有针灸执照的执业医师，并已参加获得俄勒冈州医学委员会批准的临床培训。

（5）针灸专业的学员或学生不得从事任何构成医学实践或针灸实践的行为，除非如第 847-070-0017 条规定所述，在获得委员会批准的临床培训人员的直接监督下进行。

第 847-070-0019 条 面试和笔试

（1）除获得执照的所有其他要求外，委员会可就申请过程中收到的信息要求申请人参加面试。除非事先说明理由，否则申请人未能出席委员会的面试属于违反 ORS 677 190（17）的行为，并可能受到纪律处分。

（2）若有合理理由质疑申请人的资格，委员会可酌情要求申请人采取以下一项或多项措施：

（a）获得 NCCAOM 的针灸或东方医学认证或再认证。

（b）通过书面、口头、实践或以上多种形式的综合评估。

（c）提供现行的 NCCAOM 针灸认证文件。

（d）在申请俄勒冈州执照之前，申请人每年完成十五学时委员会认可的继续教育。符合 NCCAOM 再认证要求的继续教育也能获得委员会认可。

（e）在获委员会批准的导师指导下完成委员会批准的辅导计划，该计划根据申请人的非执业时间而定，导师必须单独监督申请人。辅导计划顺利完成后，导师须报告委员会。

（3）申请人必须通过《医疗实践法》（ORS 第 677 章）和俄勒冈州行政法规（OAR 第 847 章，第 70 部分）的开卷考试。若申请人三次考试不合格，在参加第四次最终考试之前，申请人必须与委员会成员、行政主管、委员会调查员和/或委员会医学主任共同参与非正式会议，讨论申请人未通过考试的情况。如申请人在第四次考试中仍旧没有通过，申请人可能会被拒绝颁发执照。

第 847-070-0020 条 针灸师行为规范

（1）除经委员会授权从事针灸实践的医师外，其他人不得向任何人提供针灸治疗。

（2）如转诊医生有要求，应立即向其报告针灸治疗的方法、结果及转诊医生为保存针灸治疗记录所要求的其他信息。

（3）针灸师必须清楚地向接受治疗的患者表明其针灸师身份。针灸师在有其他卫生保健提供者执业的医院或诊所执业时，必须佩戴标有"针灸师"名称的名牌。在私人诊所中，针灸师不需要佩戴名牌。

(4) 针灸师不得声称自己是医师,或准许他人声称自己是医师。

(5) 根据 ORS 676.110 的规定,如符合以下情况,获得针灸博士学位的针灸师可以使用与针灸服务相关的"医生"(doctor)称号:

(a) 其博士学位课程拥有联邦认可的认证。

(b) 其特定的博士学位已根据 ORS 676.110(2) 的要求在所有专业交流中指定。

第 847－070－0022 条　申请执照需提交的文件

提交的文件必须字迹清晰且不大于 8 1/2 英寸×11 英寸。委员会将永久保存申请人提交的申请文件和照片等材料。如原始文件大于 8 1/2 英寸×11 英寸,副本必须缩小到正确尺寸,并清楚地显示所有的措辞和签名,外文文件需要提供官方译本。材料如下:

(1) 申请:须完整填写由委员会提供的正式申请。日期须包含年、月和日。

(2) 出生证明:出生证明副本,如申请人因法院命令、收养、结婚、离婚等变更姓名,需提供更名文件、结婚证或离婚判决书的副本。

(3) 针灸学校毕业证书:符合 OAR 847－070－0016(1) 规定的申请人需提供一份获批针灸学校的毕业证书副本。

(4) 照片:提交申请前九十日内拍摄的含头部和肩部(非侧面),并具有明显面部特征正面特写的照片,照片质量需与护照照片质量等同。

(5) 针灸专业的院长为符合 OAR 847－070－0016(1) 规定的申请人出具的信函。

(6) NCCAOM 出具的信函,为符合 OAR 847－070－0016(1) 或(2) 资格的申请人提供现行针灸认证情况。

(7) 相关各州出具的信函,证明申请人先前和现行的所有医疗相关执照均信誉良好。

(8) 由主管或其他负责人出具的执业及雇佣信函,其中应包括对过去五年整体表现的评估以及具体的执业及雇佣的起止日期。对于曾经或正在独立执业的针灸师,需提供三封熟悉申请人执业情况并且认识申请人超过六个月的当地针灸师的推荐信。

第 847－070－0024 条　军人配偶或家庭伴侣的执照申请

(1) "军人配偶或家庭伴侣"系指因军事调动转移至俄勒冈州的美国武装部队现役成员的配偶或伴侣。

(2) 根据本规则,军人配偶或家庭伴侣必须具备以下条件才有资格获得执照:

(a) 符合 OAR 847－070－0016 的规定。

(b) 与美国武装部队成员结婚或与其建立家庭伴侣关系,该成员根据正式现役军事命令被分配到位于俄勒冈州的工作地点。

(c) 获得美国其他州或准州的针灸执照。

(d) 信誉良好,在申请人持有执照或曾经持有执照的任何司法管辖区,不存在针对其执照的任何限制、诉讼、调查或未决的纪律处分。

(e) 在申请前的三年内,至少有一年的针灸实践或教学经历,以证明有此能力。

(3) 如军人配偶或家庭伴侣申请针灸执照,委员会可收取:

(a) 针灸学校毕业证书副本,以满足申请人针灸学校院长的信函要求。

(b) 在当前或最近开展针灸服务的司法管辖区具有良好信誉执照的证明,以满足先前和当前所有司法管辖区的医疗相关执照的验证要求。

（4）除本条第（3）款和 OAR 847-070-0022 中要求的文件外,军人配偶或家庭伴侣必须提交以下文件的副本：

（a）带有申请人姓名和美国武装部队现役军人姓名的结婚证或家庭伴侣关系登记证。

（b）根据正式的现役军人命令,将结婚证或家庭伴侣登记中所列的配偶或家庭伴侣分配到位于俄勒冈州的工作地点。

（5）军人配偶或家庭伴侣在满足本条第（2）至（4）款的要求后,可获得临时行医执照。

第 847-070-0025 条　纪律处分程序

委员会可吊销或撤销针灸师从事针灸实践的权限,针对针灸师或任何被指控非法从事针灸实践的个人的任何纪律处分程序,应根据 ORS 第 183 章的规定进行。

第 847-070-0030 条　撤销或吊销从事针灸实践的权限

委员会可吊销或撤销针灸师从事针灸实践的权限,如发现以下情况：

（1）该针灸师声称自己是医师,或准许他人声称自己是医师。

（2）该针灸师在从事针灸实践过程中,违反有关针灸实践管理的法规、规范。

（3）该针灸师在针灸实践中有重大行为过失。

（4）该针灸师不具备从事针灸实践的能力。

（5）该针灸师已违反 ORS 677.190 的任何规定。

第 847-070-0033 条　客座针灸师要求

（1）俄勒冈州医学委员会可批准一位客座针灸师于以下场合进行针刺演示：俄勒冈州学校或其针灸或东方医学课程、针灸专业组织举办的任何研讨会、会议或培训会,或 NCCAOM 批准的研讨会、会议或培训会上,以提供每次为期不超十日,每年不超三次的继续教育培训。如客座针灸师要求超过十日,或在一年内提出超过三次的要求,就必须申请并获得在俄勒冈州执业的执照。俄勒冈州的执业针灸师必须出席研讨会、会议或培训会。

（2）在获批前,客座针灸师必须向俄勒冈州医学委员会提交以下信息：

（a）针灸或东方医学学校或课程的信函,或邀请州外针灸师参加研讨会、会议或培训会的信函,信函需包含以下信息：

（A）客座针灸师演示针刺的研讨会、会议或培训会的日期。

（B）研讨会、会议或培训会的描述。

（C）负责的俄勒冈州针灸师的姓名,且该针灸师已根据 ORS 677 获得执照且在委员会主动登记且信誉良好,其将出席并负责指导研讨会、会议或培训会中客座针灸师的行为。

（D）客座针灸师简历。

（b）如客座针灸师在其执业所在州获得执照、认证或注册为针灸师,则客座针灸师必须提供文件,以证明其执照、认证或注册有效且信誉良好。

（3）在俄勒冈州以客座针灸师身份执业的申请必须于执业开始至少两周前收到。

第 847-070-0037 条　待审查的受限执照

（1）符合俄勒冈州针灸执照的所有要求,但尚未通过 NCCAOM 颁发的针灸认证考试的针灸师,可以获得待审查的受限执照,在获委员会批准的临床导师的监督下,赴俄勒冈州参

加临床培训,如符合以下条件:

(a) 除 NCCAOM 待认证外,申请文件完整,符合委员会要求。

(b) 申请人以前未通过 NCCAOM 考试。

(c) 获批监督申请人的临床导师符合 OAR 847-070-0017 中的资格,并且在申请人接受培训时,可随时在现场进行监督。

(d) 申请人在获得待审查的受限执照之前已提交正确的表格和费用。

(2) 任何通过待审受限执照获得临床培训的人员,必须向患者表明自己是针灸学员,并佩戴学员名牌。

(3) 可以授予为期六个月的待审查的受限执照。

(4) 在收到申请人已通过 NCCAOM 针灸认证考试的证明后,如申请人的申请文件齐全,则予以永久执照。

(5) 如申请人未通过 NCCAOM 针灸认证考试,则待审查的受限执照将自动失效。

第 847-070-0038 条　客座教授的受限执照

(1) 在该州针灸学院获得教学职位的针灸师可获得客座教授的受限执照,如符合以下条件:

(a) 申请人已证明其具备或受过与 OAR 847-070-0016(1) 的规定同等的技能和培训,符合委员会要求。

(b) 有五年以上针灸师工作经验。

(c) 申请人已提交关于客座教授的受限执照的表格和费用。

(2) 申请人即将任教的针灸学校负责人应以书面形式向委员会证明申请人已获得该部门的教学职位,并且不得从事针灸实践,除非该实践是经委员会批准的申请人教学职位的必要组成部分。

(3) 如申请人满足 OAR 847-070-0017 的要求,申请客座教授的受限执照的针灸师也可获批成为临床导师。

(4) 客座教授的受限执照有效期为一年,并可根据学术上的需要,在每年提交书面理由申请后获得两次为期一年的延长期。如要求延长客座教授的受限执照,则必须在年底前三十日提交续期表格和费用。

第 847-070-0039 条　注册

(1) 在委员会批准申请人获得针灸执照后,申请人必须在颁发执照之前支付注册费。

(2) 应在每个偶数年的 6 月 30 日午夜之前提交两年一次的注册续期申请和法定注册费至俄勒冈医学委员会。

(3) 如未能遵守本条第(1)和(2)款,则根据 ORS 677.228,执照将失效。

第 847-070-0045 条　非执业注册及恢复执业

(1) 任何在本州获得执照的针灸师如改变地点到其他州或国家,都应被委员会列为非执业状态。

(2) 如针灸师希望恢复执业状态,则必须提交一份恢复执业宣誓书,支付手续费并顺利完成恢复执业程序,获得委员会的批准,方可在俄勒冈州恢复执业。

(3)如委员会判断针灸师在非执业状态期间的行为可导致申请初始执照时被拒绝颁发执照,则委员会可以拒绝将其注册为执业状态。

(4)如针灸师申请人在申请执照或恢复执业状态之前连续超过十二个月未执业,申请人可能需要完成以下一项或多项要求:

(a)获得NCCAOM的针灸或东方医学认证或再认证。

(b)提供现行NCCAOM针灸或东方医学认证的文件。

(c)申请人停止执业后,每年须完成十五学时委员会认可的继续教育课程。

(d)在获委员会批准的导师指导下完成获得委员会批准的辅导计划,该计划根据申请人的业余时间而定,导师必须单独监督持证人。辅导计划顺利完成后,导师须报告委员会。

(e)委员会规定的其他要求。

(5)已连续超过二十四个月停止执业的针灸师申请人可能需要完成一份符合委员会要求的重新执业计划。在申请人开始重新执业计划之前,该计划必须通过《重新执业同意协议》获得委员会的审核和批准。根据停止执业时间的长短,重新执业计划可包含本条第(4)款所列的一项或多项要求,以及委员会酌情确定的额外要求。

第847-070-0050条　针灸咨询委员会

(1)成立针灸咨询委员会。针灸咨询委员会必须由俄勒冈州医学委员会任命的六名成员组成。俄勒冈州医学委员会必须任命一名成员、两名医生和三名持有执照的针灸师。针灸师成员可以从俄勒冈州针灸和东方医学协会以及其他专业针灸组织的提名中任命。

(2)针灸咨询委员会成员的任期为三年,可以连任,但任期不得超过两届。针灸咨询委员会的空缺必须由俄勒冈州医学委员会委派填补,任期为剩余的未满任期。每名成员在继任者上任并胜任工作之前,不得结束任期。

(3)俄勒冈州医学委员会可解除针灸咨询委员会任何成员的职务。

(4)针灸咨询委员会自行选举主席,其权利和职责由针灸咨询委员会规定。

(5)针灸咨询委员会成员有权获得ORS 677.235中规定的俄勒冈州医学委员会成员的薪酬和费用。

第847-070-0055条　委员会的职责

针灸咨询委员会应:

(1)审查并建议批准或不予批准提交给俄勒冈州医学委员会的所有针灸执照及其续期申请。

(2)向俄勒冈州医学委员会推荐执业针灸师的职业责任和执业标准。

(3)向俄勒冈州医学委员会推荐针灸执照的教学、临床教育和培训标准。

(4)向俄勒冈州医学委员会推荐临床导师和学员的标准。

(5)向俄勒冈州医学委员会推荐执照考试和合适的临时执照。

第847-070-0060条　撤回和拒绝执照申请

(1)如申请人撤回执照申请,且该执照申请中包含违反ORS677.010~677.855任何规定的证据,可在撤回之日起两年后提交新的执照申请。

(2)如申请人的申请被驳回,则可在被驳回之日起两年后提交新的执照申请。

华 盛 顿 州

华盛顿州针灸法①

第18.06.010条　定义

除文意明显另有所指外,本章术语应具有本条规定的如下含义:

(1)"针灸"或"东方医学"系指利用针灸或东方医学诊断和治疗方法,促进人体健康和治疗器质性或功能性疾病的卫生保健服务,包括:

(a) 针灸,包括使用针灸针或刺血针直接和间接刺激穴位和经络。

(b) 使用电针、器械装置或磁性装置刺激穴位和经络。

(c) 艾灸。

(d) 穴位按压。

(e) 拔罐。

(f) 刮痧。

(g) 红外线法。

(h) 音叉疗法。

(i) 激光针疗法。

(j) 穴位注射疗法,由部门按规则界定。穴位注射疗法包括注射药物,仅限于注射生理盐水、无菌水、草药、矿物药、液体维生素、顺势疗法药物和营养药物,与针灸或东方医学实践相一致。穴位注射疗法不包括注射第69.50章《统一管制药物法》附表一至附表五包含的管制药物,以及第69.41.300条规定的类固醇。

(k) 基于针灸或东方医学理论的膳食建议和健康教育,包括推荐和销售草药、维生素、矿物药以及膳食和营养补充剂。

(l) 呼吸疗法,放松疗法和东方功法。

(m) 气功。

---

① 根据《华盛顿州法典修订本》第18卷第18.06章(*Revised Code of Washington* Annotated, Title 18. Businesses and Professions, Chapter 18.06. East Asian Medicine Practitioners)译出。

（n）东方按摩和推拿，属于东方身体疗法，其特征为揉捏、按压、滚压、摇晃和拉伸身体，不包括脊柱推拿。

（o）表层热疗和冷疗。

（2）"针灸师"或"针灸和东方医学医师"系指根据本章获得执照的人。

（3）"部门"系指卫生部门。

（4）"部长"系指卫生部长或其指定人员。

本章的任何规定均不得要求提供本条第（1）（k）至（o）款中规定的技术和服务或销售草药产品的个人获得针灸师或东方医学医师执照。

第18.06.020条　无证的违法实践

（1）不得自称针灸师、执业针灸师、针灸和东方医学医师或可能使公众误认为自己是其他与之相关的类似身份，已根据本章获得执照的除外。

（2）未根据本章获得执照的人不得从事针灸或东方医学。

（3）任何人不得在其姓名后使用L.Ac.、EAMP或者AEMP的字母组合以表示其在针灸或东方医学方面拥有学位或受到正式培训，已根据本章获得执照的除外。

（4）部长可按照规定禁止或规范广告和其他形式的招揽患者活动，此类活动可能会在某人是否根据本章获得执照方面误导或欺骗公众。

（5）根据本章获得执照的人员可以使用针灸和东方医学医师头衔，并且可以使用字母AEMP表明其持有相关执照。但是，本条没有以任何形式禁止或限制其自称针灸师、执业针灸师或东方医学医师，或在其姓名后使用字母L.Ac.或EAMP。

第18.06.045条　章节豁免

本章规定不得禁止或限制如下行为：

（1）根据本州法律获得许可的个人，在其获得授权的执业范围内提供服务的实践。

（2）受雇于美国政府机构的个人履行美国法律规定的职责。

（3）获部长批准的教育计划的正规学生在讲师的监督下，按照常规课程安排或讲师指派的任务进行实践。

（4）任何有资格在其他司法管辖区从事针灸或东方医学执业实践的，在获部长批准的针灸学校、东方医学学校、中医学校或者日本、韩国或其他东亚国家的传统医学学校的常规教学过程中进行针灸或东方医学实践，或在针灸或东方医学专业组织举办的教育研讨会上进行针灸或东方医学实践。但在后一种情况中，该行为受人员的直接监督，该人员根据本章获得执照或获得任何其他疗法执照，且其执业范围为针灸和东方医学。

第18.06.050条　执照-资格申请

任何人拟申请执照，应向部长出示：

（1）根据部长提供的一种或多种格式填写而成的书面申请，并在宣誓书中列出部长可能要求的各项信息。

（2）候选人的相关证明：

（a）在至少两个学年内，已顺利完成经部长认可的基础科学、针灸和东方医学课程的教学培训。培训内容应包括解剖学、生理学、微生物学、生物化学、病理学、卫生学以及西方临床科学概论。基础科学课程必须与大学课程具有同等水准。如申请人为根据第18.25条获得执照的脊椎按摩师或根据第18.36A条获得执照的自然疗法医师,则本条中与基础科学有关的要求可减少至多一年,具体减少时间取决于候选人任职资格,该资格根据部长制定的规则确定。

(b)已顺利完成获部长批准的五百学时针灸培训或东方医学临床培训。

第18.06.060条 教育计划审批

卫生部应考虑批准符合本章要求并提供第18.06.050条规定培训的学校或计划。临床和教学培训可获批成为单独计划或联合计划。审批程序应由部长按规则制定。

第18.06.080条 部长-考试-知情-豁免权

(1)部长有权执行本章各项规定,并每年举办至少两次针灸师或东方医学执照考试,考试时间和地点由部长选定。考试形式应为笔试,可包括实践考试。

(2)部长应对其确定的科目批准执照考试,此类科目在针灸师或针灸和东方医学医师的工作范围内并与其工作相适应,包括但不限于解剖学、生理学、微生物学、生物化学、病理学、卫生学、针灸和东方医学。所有申请文件应统一交由部长保存,并保留至少一年,届时可销毁。

(3)如考试顺利通过,部长应授予该候选人针灸师或东方医学医师的头衔。

第18.06.090条 要求英语流利

在获得执照前,申请人应表现出足够的英语阅读、口语和理解能力,以便申请人能够与其他卫生保健提供者和患者沟通卫生保健和治疗等问题。

第18.06.100条 申请者的背景调查

每位申请人应提供书面同意书,同意卫生部或者其指派人员对其个人背景、专业培训和经历进行调查,此为申请的一部分。

第18.06.110条 《统一纪律法案》的适用

《统一纪律法案》第18.130章已规定未经认证的医疗实践、执照的颁发和拒发以及对持证人的纪律处分。部长享有本章规定的纪律处分权。

第18.06.120条 遵守行政程序-费用

(1)根据本章获得执照的人员,应遵守部长根据第43.70.250、43.70.280条规定的登记和续期执照的行政程序和行政要求。

(2)根据本条和第18.06.070条收取的所有费用,应根据第43.70.320条的规定记入卫生专业人员账户。

第18.06.130条 患者信息表-处罚

(1)部长应制定表格,供根据本章获得执照的持证人使用,告知患者针灸师或针灸和东方医学医师的执业范围和资格。所有持证人应按照部长规定的方式将该表格出示给患者。

(2)违反本条规定的即属轻罪。

第18.06.140条 与其他卫生保健从业者会诊-患者弃权声明-紧急情况-惩罚(有效期至2022年7月1日)

(1)根据本章获得执照的持证人发现患者患有潜在严重疾病(如心脏疾病,急腹症以及其他疾病),应立即要求与根据第18.71、18.57、18.57A、18.36A章,或者第18.71A章或者第18.79.050条获得执照的初级卫生保健提供者进行会诊,或要求其提供最近的书面诊断。如患有此类疾病的患者不同意进行会诊或拒绝提供初级卫生保健提供者的最近诊断,则只有在患者签署书面弃权声明,确认由于不接受初级卫生保健提供者的治疗而带来的相关风险后,才能继续进行针灸或东方药物治疗。弃权声明还必须包括:

(a)对针灸师或针灸和东方医学医师的执业范围的解释,包括针灸师或针灸和东方医学医师获准开展的服务和技术。

(b)声明针灸师或针灸和东方医学医师获得授权提供的服务和技术无法治疗患者潜在的严重疾病。弃权声明的要求应由部长按照规则制定。

(2)在紧急情况下,根据本章获得执照的人应:

(a)拨打911启动急救医疗系统。

(b)呼叫救护车。

(c)在急救到达前,为患者提供支持。

(3)违反本条规定的即属轻罪。

第18.06.160条　出台规则

部长应按照第34.05章规定的方式出台规则,以实现本章之目的。

第18.06.190条　背书许可

如某人在另一司法管辖区持有针灸师或针灸和东方医学医师相关执照,或具有同等资格,并且根据部长判断,该辖区执业要求等同于或高于华盛顿州,部长可以给未经考试者颁发执照。

第18.06.200条　医疗保险福利不具有强制性

本章规定均不得解释为要求保险公司、卫生保健服务承包商或保健组织的个人、团体保单或合同为本章规定的持证人的服务提供福利和保险。

第18.06.210条　未经授权的药物处方和医疗实践

除非经本章授权,本章不得解释为允许给他人用药或开具处方,或以任何形式违反第18.71章或者第18.57章定义的医疗和外科实践。

第18.06.220条　针灸和东方医学咨询委员会

设立华盛顿州针灸和东方医学咨询委员会。

(1)委员会由五名成员组成,且必须是华盛顿州居民。其中四名成员必须是根据本章获得执照的针灸师、针灸和东方医学医师,其在针灸和东方医学领域的实践经验不少于五年,且在任职后的两年内积极从事针灸实践。第五名委员会成员必须从公众中选任,且必须维护卫生服务消费者权益。

(2)部长应任命委员会成员,委员会成员需听从部长指示。部长可任命首届委员会成员,任期交错,可为一至三年,此后每届任期均为三年。成员不得连任超过两届。

(3)委员会应在必要时召开会议,每年至少召开一次。主席和副主席由委员会选举,目前任职人员过半数即构成法定人数。

(4)委员会应当就针灸和东方医学的服务标准向部长提出建议。

（5）委员会须根据第 43.03.240 条补贴成员，包括按照第 43.03.050、43.03.060 条履行职责时的差旅费。

（6）委员会成员可免于因部门纪律处分程序或基于诚信执行的其他官方行为而提起的民事或刑事诉讼。

第 18.06.230 条 穴位注射疗法服务-教育和培训

（1）在提供穴位注射疗法服务前，针灸师或针灸和东方医学医师须具备提供该服务所需的教育和培训经历。

（2）在 2016 年 6 月 9 日前实施穴位注射疗法的针灸师或针灸和东方医学医师，应根据卫生部要求，证明已顺利完成穴位注射疗法的教育和培训。

第 18.06.240 条 继续教育

卫生部应当出台规则，要求针灸师完成继续教育，以此作为针灸执照续期的条件。

怀俄明州

怀俄明州针刺法①

第 33-49-101 条　简称

本章应称为并引用为"怀俄明州针刺执业法"。

第 33-49-102 条　定义

(a)下列定义适用于本章:

(i)"ACAOM"系指针灸及东方医学教育审核委员会,或委员会认定的同等认证机构。

(ii)"针刺"系指将针灸针插入体内(不论是否使用电针或温针),旨在促进、维持和恢复健康,包括治疗与疼痛有关的身体功能障碍的行为。

(iii)"针刺师"系指根据本章在怀俄明州获得针刺执照的任何人。

(iv)"耳穴针刺疗法"系指由国家耳穴针刺疗法方案认可的实践操作,用于治疗精神和情感健康、创伤后应激障碍和急性创伤、药物滥用和化学依赖。

(v)"委员会"系指基于本章设立的怀俄明州针刺委员会。

(vi)"执照"系指根据本章颁发并与持证人执业范围一致的执照。持证人根据其NCCAOM 学历情况、研究生培训、NADA 培训结业证书或委员会其他授权获得此证。

(vii)"持证人"系指被委员会授予执照的人。

(viii)"NADA"系指国家针灸戒毒协会,或委员会认定的同等机构。

(ix)"NCCAOM"系指国家针灸与东方医学审核委员会,或委员会认定的同等机构。

第 33-49-103 条　委员会设立;成员;任命;任期;资格;免职;空缺

(a)怀俄明州针刺委员会为实施和管理本章规定而设立。委员会由五名怀俄明州的合法居民组成。委员会应由一名公众成员、一名获得 NCCAOM 认证的成员、两名在委员会任命前从事针刺实践不少于五年的成员和一名根据本卷而非本章获得执照的卫生保健专业人员组成。

---

① 根据《怀俄明州法典》第 33 卷第 49 章(*Wyoming Statutes* Annotated, Title 33. Professions and Occupations, Chapter 49. Acupuncture Practice Act)译出。

(b) 州长应任命委员会成员。在委员会任命的首届成员中,两名任期为两年,两名任期为四年。此后,任期为四年。每名成员在继任者上任并胜任工作之前,不得结束任期。任何成员不得连任超过两届。

(c) 如委员会出现任何空缺,则州长应填补剩余的未届满任期。

(d) 州长可根据怀俄明州制定法第 9‑1‑202 条将成员从委员会中除名。

第 33‑49‑104 条　委员会会议;选举;法定人数

委员会每年应至少召开一次会议,并在每年的第一次会议上选举一名主席。委员会可应主席要求或委员会决定召开其认为必要的会议。会议可通过电讯方式进行。三名委员会成员构成法定人数。

第 33‑49‑105 条　费用报销及责任豁免

(a) 委员会成员在执行公务时,不应获得服务报酬,但在执行公务期间,应获得怀俄明州制定法第 33‑1‑302 条 a 款第(vii)项规定的按英里支付的旅费和每日津贴。

(b) 按照怀俄明州制定法 1‑39‑104 条的规定,委员会成员在履行本章规定职责而采取行动时,应享有与国家雇员相同的个人责任豁免。

第 33‑49‑106 条　委员会的责任和义务

(a) 委员会应:

(i) 实施本章规定。

(ii) 确定持证人的下列标准:

(A) 继续教育要求。

(B) 职业行为标准。

(C) 执业的伦理标准。

(iii) 批准或不批准执照申请、颁发、续期和恢复执照。

(iv) 建立必要的分级执照,以区分不同等级的耳穴针刺疗法。

(v) 根据本章和怀俄明州行政程序法的规定,对执照进行审查、吊销和撤销。

(vi) 对涉嫌违反本章和委员会规则的行为发起并进行调查、听证及诉讼。

(vii) 保存所有诉讼程序的记录并向持证人和其他有关各方提供委员会诉讼的年度报告。

(viii) 对本章规定的持证人制定缴纳申请费和执照费的要求。

(ix) 按照怀俄明州制定法第 33‑1‑201 条执行本章的费用要求。

(x) 为执行本章规定,颁布必要的规章制度。

(b) 委员会可雇佣其认为必要之人或与之签订合同,以协助其管理事务及提供支持。

(c) 委员会收取的所有费用应由州财政部长存入怀俄明州针刺委员会账户。从该账户中支付的款项不得超过已记入该账户的款项。委员会应使用该账户支付本章管理中产生的费用。

第 33‑49‑107 条　颁发执照的要求;构成要素;豁免;其他持证卫生保健专业人员

(a) 自 2018 年 1 月 1 日起,除非被允许按照本章及其通过的规章制度从事针刺实践,否则任何人不得:

(i) 在怀俄明州从事针刺疗法或向他人自称是一名针刺师或能够从事针刺实践。

(ii) 使用针刺师的头衔或其他类似头衔。

(iii) 使用字母的任意组合,包括 L. Ac.及在其姓名后面标示针刺等级。

(b) 根据本章颁发的任何执照应:

(i) 以执业针刺师的名义颁发。

(ii) 注明执照发放日期和届满日期。

(iii) 长期在从业或受雇地点以显眼的方式展示。

(c) 符合下列要求的,可免于本章规定的执照要求:

(i) 在另一司法管辖区持有执照并从事针刺实践的针刺师在怀俄明州教学或参加教育研讨会期间进行针刺教学、演示或提供针刺治疗。本款规定的任何豁免在一年内累计不得超过六十日。

(ii) 根据怀俄明州制定法第 35－4－115 条 a(i)项的规定,州长宣布在另一州获得执照的针刺师可在发生自然灾害或突发公共卫生情况下在怀俄明州提供针刺服务。

(iii) 经委员会批准,若针刺服务均在本州执业针刺师的直接监督下进行,则学员可以从事针刺实践。

(d) 本章内容均不得解释为禁止或限制该州的任何其他执业卫生保健提供者在其法定执业范围内从事针刺实践。但是,除非根据本章获得执照,任何人不得以任何方式冠以针刺师身份。

第 33－49－108 条　执照的申请、续期和恢复、资格、费用、报告

(a) 申请针刺师执照的申请人应当:

(i) 按照委员会规定的形式和方式向委员会申请执照。

(ii) 支付委员会确定的所需费用。

(iii) 向委员会提供证据证明申请人已:

(A) 毕业于经 ACAOM 认证的专业,并通过 NCCAOM 的考试。

(B) 毕业于经 ACAOM 认证的专业,并于 2018 年 1 月 1 日前在此州连续从事针刺实践至少 10 年。

(C) 完成委员会认为具有实质性资格的其他考试、教育或学徒阶段的考试。

(D) 持有国家 NADA 培训结业证书(如申请耳穴针刺师执照)。

(b) 应根据委员会据本章规定的时间续期或恢复执照。如持证人未能按照委员会规定的时间续期执照,则执照将到期,持证人不得在该情况下从事针刺实践。

(c) 执照申请人或持证人应在申请、续期或恢复执照时,或不迟于持证人获悉此类判决后三十日内,报告其本人涉及针刺实践渎职行为或不当行为的任何未决或最终行政或纪律处分,以及涉及诉讼或判决的和解及处置条款,无论此类诉讼或判决是否发生在怀俄明州或任何其他司法管辖区。

第 33－49－109 条　背书许可

(a) 委员会可通过背书的方式向在另一州从事针刺实践的申请人颁发在怀俄明州从事针刺实践的执照。但须遵守以下规定:

(i) 另一州应与怀俄明州的针刺师执照要求基本同等,包括与怀俄明州类似的持证人背书许可条款。

(ii) 申请人在申请时未受到任何纪律处分。

(iii) 申请人未在本州或任何其他州被吊销或撤销针刺师执照。

(iv) 申请人应遵守委员会制定的继续教育要求及道德标准。

第 33－49－110 条　听证和调查

(a) 在收到持证人或申请人违反本章的投诉后,委员会可进行调查。如委员会认为有合理理由可以证实指控,则应确定听证的时间和地点,并在听证前至少十五个日历日内向持证人或申请人送达听证通知。应直接送达该通知或通过挂号邮件将该通知发送到持证人或申请人的最后所知地址。

(b) 委员会可发布传票要求证人出庭,并在任何听证会中出示必要的证据。应被告或其律师的请求,委员会应代表答辩人发布传票。

(c) 本条规定的听证应依据《怀俄明州行政程序法》举行,对委员会的裁决不满者可根据该法提出上诉。

第 33－49－111 条　纪律处分;吊销执照;申请恢复执照

(a) 在根据本法第 33－49－110 条举行听证之后,如持证人或申请人有违反职业道德的行为,委员会可批准、拒绝、吊销、撤销、拒绝续期执照或将执照列入察看状态。为本条之目的,违反职业道德的行为包括以下任意一项:

(i) 以欺诈、谎报或隐瞒重要事实的方式取得执照。

(ii) 违反委员会通过和颁布的职业行为道德标准或规则。

(iii) 被判犯有与针刺或针刺实践能力有关的重罪。

(iv) 被判定犯有涉及管制药物的罪行。

(v) 在针刺实践中失职。

(vi) 违反委员会做出或通过的任何合法命令、规则或条例。

(vii) 违反本章的任何规定。

(b) 可在吊销执照之日起一年后向委员会提出恢复执照的申请。委员会可接受或拒绝申请,并可举行听证会,考虑恢复执照。对委员会的任何最终判决不满的申请人,可根据《怀俄明州行政程序法》向地区法院提出上诉。

(c) 在收到家庭服务部门有关法院扣留、吊销等方式限制执照的核证副本后,委员会应按照法院的命令,将扣留、吊销或限制情况通知当事人。不得根据《怀俄明州行政程序法》对基于本条款而扣留、吊销或限制执照的行为提出上诉。

第 33－49－112 条　违规行为;处罚;诉讼

(a) 如有任何违反本章规定者,一经定罪,即属轻罪,应根据怀俄明州制定法第 6－10－103 条的规定进行罚款和处罚。如委员会有理由相信任何个人根据本条承担责任,可向罪行发生所在司法管辖区的检察官做出说明。

(b) 总检察长、委员会、任何州或地区检察官或任何公民,可根据申诉人的关系,以怀俄明州的名义获得一项禁令,禁止任何人无证从事针刺实践。犯罪者居住地区的地区法院或拉勒米县的地区法院对任何此类禁令程序具有原始管辖权。有证据表明其存在一项或多项构成无证从事针刺实践的行为,无需证据证明其已造成实际损害,即可发布禁令,任何违反本款的证据标准采取优势证据的原则。

(c)本条规定不得限制本州法律规定的任何附加民事责任或刑事责任。

(d)尽管本章另有规定,《怀俄明州针刺法》不适用于根据怀俄明州制定法第33－25或26章获得执照的人。

加利福尼亚州

加利福尼亚州针灸法[①]

第一节 行政和一般规定

第 4925 条 简称

(a) 本章为《商业与职业法典》中介绍针灸的章节。本章应称为并引用为《针灸执照法案》。任何法规中凡提及《针灸执照法案》，均应按照本章规定解释。

(b) 在本章或与之有关的条例中，凡提及"证书"(certificate)或"认证"(certification)，其后均指"执照"(license/licensure)。凡提及"批准"(certifying)一词均指"颁发执照"(licensing)，"证书持有人"(certificate holder)一词均指"持证人"(licensee)。凡提及"针灸委员会"(Acupuncture Committee)或"委员会"(committee)均指"针灸委员会"(Acupuncture Board)或"委员会"(board)。

第 4926 条 立法意图

立法机构考虑到根治疾病（而不仅是消除症状），以及对患者采取整体治疗的必要性，制定本条例，旨在通过针灸构建亚洲医学艺术和科学实践的框架。

本条旨在鼓励加利福尼亚州公民更有效地利用针灸服务资源，采取整体的治疗方法，并消除现有的法律限制，以避免对有效提供保健服务造成不必要的障碍。此外，由于针灸关系到公众健康、安全和福利，因此有必要将个体针灸实践作为初级卫生保健职业加以管制。

第 4927 条 定义

除文意另有所指外，下列定义适用于本章：

(a) "委员会"系指针灸委员会。

(b) "人"(person)系指任何个人、组织或法人团体，但本章仅有个人可以获得执照的情况除外。

[①] 根据《加利福尼亚州法典》第 2 卷第 12 章(*Annotated California Codes*, Business and Professions Code, Division 2. Healing Arts, Chapter 12. Acupuncture)译出。

(c)"针灸师"系指根据本章获得针灸执照,且执照有效并未被吊销或撤销的个人。

(d)"针灸"系指通过针刺刺激体表的某个穴位或多个穴位,以消除或减轻疼痛,或使生理功能(包括疼痛控制)恢复正常,以治疗某些疾病或身体功能失调,针灸还包括电针、拔罐及艾灸等技术。

第 4927.5 条　对"获批的教育及培训计划"的解释

(a)为本章之目的,"获批的教育及培训计划"系指提供针灸师实践教育及培训的学校或学院,该学校或学院应符合以下规定:

(1)提供至少三千学时的课程,其中至少二千〇五十学时为教学和实验室培训,至少九百五十学时为受监督的临床指导,且已向委员会提交该课程并获得批准。任何提供针灸实践教育及培训的学校,如在 2017 年 1 月 1 日前获得委员会批准且未被撤销且在获批后未改变其课程设置,为本条之目的,该学校或学院的课程视为已获委员会批准。

(2)根据《教育法典》(Education Code)第 3 卷第 10 部第 59 分部第 8 章第 6 节(第 94885 条以下)[1],在传统亚洲医学领域获得完整的机构审批。如该机构位于本州之外,须由相关政府教育部门予以批准并采用与《教育法典》第 3 卷第 10 部第 59 分部第 8 章第 6 节(第 94885 条以下)同等的标准。

(3)符合下列条件之一:

(A)获得针灸及东方医学教育审核委员会(ACAOM)的认证。

(B)已获得 ACAOM 的预认证资格。在根据本款规定获得完整机构批准后三十日内,向 ACAOM 呈交拟申请认证的意向书,并在呈交意向书后三年内获得预认证资格。

(b)在根据第(1)款的规定收到课程后的三十日内,委员会须审核该课程,确定该课程设置是否符合委员会的规定,并须将委员会是否已批准该课程的决定告知学校或学院、ACAOM 以及私立高等教育局。

第 4928 条　针灸委员会

(a)针灸委员会由七名成员组成,负责执行和实施本章规定。

(b)本条有效期至 2023 年 1 月 1 日[2],并自该日起废除。

(c)尽管其他法律另有规定,本条废除后,委员会须接受立法机构有关政策委员会的审核。

第 4928.1 条　优先保护公众

保护公众是针灸委员会行使其颁发执照、监管和惩罚职能的首要任务。在与其他利益相冲突时,应优先维护公众利益。

第 4929 条　委员会的构成;委员会成员的任命

委员会成员中应有三名五年以上针灸从业经验的针灸师,四名不持有内科医师、外科医

---

[1] 即《2009 年加利福尼亚州私立高等教育法案》(California Private Postsecondary Education Act of 2009),载《教育法典》第 3 卷"高等教育"第 10 部"私立高等教育机构"第 59 分部"私立高等教育机构"第 8 章"私立高等教育机构"第 6 节"批准办学"。

[2] 本条最初由加利福尼亚州立法机关于 2006 年制定,为《2005 年加利福尼亚州制定法》第 658 章"参议院法案第 1476 号"第 76 条。立法机关为本条设定并多次延长有效期限,最新规定为《2018 年加利福尼亚州制定法》第 596 章"议会法案第 3142 号"第 2 条。

师或针灸师证书或执照的公众人士。委员会成员中的针灸师应代表执业针灸师职业的不同文化背景。

州长应委任三名针灸师成员及两名公众成员。州长委任的所有委员会成员均须获参议院的批准。参议院规则委员会和议会议长应分别委任一名公众成员。如委员会的任何成员有玩忽职守、行为不端或渎职的情况，任命者可免其职务，但须向其提供书面控告书并给予申辩机会。

第 4929.5 条　根据《2005 年加利福尼亚州制定法》第 659 章（参议院法案第 248 号）第 7 条规定废除

第 4930 条　委员会成员的任命以及任期

委员会成员任期为四年。

第 4931 条　每日津贴以及开支

委员会成员应根据第 103 条①的规定领取每日津贴、报销每日开支。

第 4933 条　职能；条例；法定人数；过半数票

（a）委员会须执行本章规定。

（b）如有必要，委员会可根据《行政程序法》[《政府法典》(Government Code)第 2 卷第 3 部第 1 分部第 3.5 章（第 11340 条以下）]②的规定，通过、修订或废除行政法规，以便实施与针灸实践有关的法律条文。

（c）委员会的四名成员（至少包括一名针灸师）构成开展业务的法定人数。

（d）须由出席委员会会议的过半数成员投赞成票，方可采取行动或通过议案。

第 4933.5 条　行政人员

经主管批准，委员会可聘用有关人员以执行本章的规定。

第 4934 条　行政官员；任命

（a）经主管批准，委员会可委任一名不受《州公务员法》[《政府法典》第 2 卷第 5 部第 2 分部（第 18500 条以下）]③管辖的行政官员。

（b）本条有效期至 2023 年 1 月 1 日④，并自该日起废除。

第 4934.1 条　密尔顿·马克斯"小胡佛"委员会的评估；审查与建议；向立法机关报告

（a）立法机关要求密尔顿·马克斯"小胡佛"委员会对加利福尼亚州政府的组织与经济状况展开全面分析，包括下列审查与评估，并应在 2004 年 9 月 1 日前向立法机关报告其调查结果及建议：

（1）对针灸师执业范围进行审查并提出建议。

---

①　第 1 部"消费者事务部"第 1 章"部门"第 103 条"委员会成员的薪酬与支出"。
②　《行政程序法》(Administrative Procedure Act)，载《政府法典》第 2 卷"加利福尼亚州政府"第 3 部"行政部门"第 1 分部"州行政部门与行政机关"第 3.5 章"行政法规与制定"。
③　《州公务员法》(State Civil Service Act)，载《政府法典》第 2 卷"加利福尼亚州政府"第 5 部"人员"第 2 分部"州公务员"。
④　本条规定类似于第 4928 条，本条最初由加利福尼亚州立法机关于 2006 年制定，载于 2005—2006 年加利福尼亚州法律汇编第 658 章"参议院法案第 1476 号"。立法机关为本条设定并多次延长有效期限，最新规定为 2018 年通过的议会法案第 3142 号，载于 2017—2018 年加利福尼亚州法律汇编第 596 章。

(2) 对针灸师的教育要求进行审查并提出建议。

(3) 评估由国家针灸与东方医学认证委员会(NCCAOM)组织的国家考试,并就是否应在加利福尼亚州举行国家考试以代替本州考试或作为本州考试的一部分提出建议。

(4) 评估 ACAOM 的批准程序、私立高等教育局(the Bureau for Private Postsecondary Education)的批准程序以及针灸委员会的批准程序,并提出建议。

(b) 针灸委员会须支付所有与全面分析相关的费用。该费用共计二十五万美元,在此由针灸基金拨付给针灸委员会。

第 4934.2 条　由针灸委员会开展的研究与审查;报告

针灸委员会须进行下列研究及审查,并须在 2004 年 9 月 1 日之前向行政部门、针灸委员会、密尔顿·马克斯"小胡佛"委员会以及消费者保护联席委员会报告调查结果并提出建议:

(a) 针灸委员会须全面研究未持有执照的针灸师助理的受雇情况以及向其颁发执照并加以管理的必要性。

(b) 针灸委员会须研究并提出建议,以提高其审计的频率及一致性、课程的质量及相关性。

第二节　认证要求

第 4935 条　执照的必要性;违反规定构成轻罪

(a)(1) 任何人未按照本章规定,持有现行有效的针灸执照,并通过广告或其他方式宣称其正在从事针灸实践,即属轻罪,可处一百美元以上,二千五百美元以下罚款,或处县监狱一年以下监禁,或两项并罚。

(2) 任何人以欺诈手段买卖或取得针灸执照,或违反本章规定的,即属轻罪,可处一百美元以上二千五百美元以下罚款,或处县监狱一年以下监禁,或两项并罚。

(b) 尽管其他法律另有规定,任何人未根据本条取得执照但根据第 2 部(第 500 条以下)取得执照(内科医生师、外科医师、牙医或足科医生除外),并从事涉及人体的针灸实践,或实施任何涉及人体的针灸技术或方法,或指导、管理或监督另一人从事涉及人体的针灸实践的,即属轻罪。

(c) 通过广告或以其他方式宣称其正在从事针灸实践,并在头衔或服务说明中使用"针灸""针灸师""认证针灸师""执业针灸师""亚洲医学""东方医学"等字样或此类单词及短语的任意组合或缩写,或表示该人在针灸、亚洲医学或东方医学,或包含中医、日本医学、韩医在内的涉及针灸的补充医学或整合医学领域具有培训经历、从业经验或专业背景,或以其他方式具有执业资格。

(d) 如当事人符合以下条件之一,本条(a)款不得禁止其把针灸治疗作为教育培训的内容:

(1) 参与本章规定的针灸课程或针灸辅导。

(2) 毕业于获批的教育和培训计划,并在获批的教育和培训计划中参加为期不超过一年的研究生评审课程。

第 4936 条　违反职业道德的行为;未经授权使用"医生"或"Dr."缩写头衔

(a) 针灸师在针灸实践中使用"医生"或缩写"Dr."属违反职业道德的行为。以下情形除外：据《教育法典》第 3 卷第 10 部第 59 分部第 8 章(第 94800 条以下)①,该人拥有特许执照,授权其使用由教育机构(获批或获授权)颁发的医生称号,且上述条文中规定的教育机构应在针灸、东方医学、生物科学或其他方面与第 4927 条以及 4937 条所述的针灸师的授权执业有关。

(b) 依据本款(a)项,被授权使用"医生"或其缩写"Dr."头衔的针灸师,如没有进一步说明被授权使用的执照或学位类型,也属违反职业道德的行为。

第 4937 条

持证针灸师享有以下权力：

(a) 可从事针灸实践。

(b) 实施或制定治疗方案,包括运用亚洲推拿、穴位按压、呼吸技巧、功法、热疗、冷疗、磁疗、营养、饮食、草药、植物产品、动物产品、矿物产品及膳食补充剂等治疗方式,以促进、维持及恢复健康。本条不禁止任何未持针灸执照或其他疗法医师执照的人实施本款所列的治疗方式。

(c) 为本条之目的,"磁疗"系指使用不通过电流而产生磁场的矿物或金属进行治疗。

(d) 为本条之目的,"植物产品、动物产品及矿物产品"系指天然存在的植物、动物或矿物,但并不包括第 4021 条②以及第 4022 条③所界定的合成化合物、管制药物或危险药品,亦不包括《健康与安全法典》(Health and Safety Code)第 10 部第 2 章(第 11053 条以下)④所列的管制药物。

(e) 为本条之目的,"膳食补充剂"的涵义与《美国法典》(United States Code)第 21 卷第 321 条第(f)款界定相同,但不包括第 4021 条或 4022 条所界定的管制药物或危险药品,亦不包括《健康与安全法典》(Health and Safety Code)第 10 部第 2 章(第 11053 条以下)所列出的管制药物。

第 4938 条

(a) 凡是提出申请并符合以下条件者,针灸委员会应向其颁发针灸执照：

(1) 年满十八岁。

(2) 应满足以下任一条件,并提供符合要求的证明：

(A)(i) 获批的教育及培训计划。

(ii) 如申请人在学校或学院开始其教育及培训计划,且该学校或学院向 ACAOM 提交了申请认证的意向书,或已获得候选资格,但委员会其后否认其候选资格或评估其不合格,则委员会可复核和评估申请人的教育培训及临床经验,以决定是否为其豁免本条规定。

(B) 在针灸实践中,顺利完成获得委员会批准的辅导计划。

---

① 即《2009 年加利福尼亚州私立高等教育法案》(California Private Postsecondary Education Act of 2009),载《教育法典》第 3 卷"高等教育"第 10 部"私立高等教育机构"第 59 分部"私立高等教育机构"第 8 章"私立高等教育机构"。

② 即管制药物。

③ 即危险药品以及危险医疗设备。

④ 《健康与安全法典》第 10 部为《加利福尼亚统一管制药物法》(California Uniform Controlled Substances Act),第 2 章为"标准与清单"。

（C）如申请人已在美国境外完成教育及培训，需证明其教育培训和临床经验符合第4939条和第4941条规定。

（3）通过委员会组织的测试申请人针灸执业能力、素质和知识的笔试。该笔试由消费者事务部专业考试服务办公室组织。

（4）不得根据第1.5部（第475条以下）①拒绝颁发。

（5）完成获得委员会批准的临床实习培训计划。该临床实习培训计划的期限不得超过九个月，培训地点应设在本州一家获批的承担教育培训计划的诊所内。个人参加临床实习的时间长短，取决于参加考试前取得的成绩和已完成的临床培训。临床实习培训计划的目的是确保申请人达到临床能力的最低水平。

（b）作为颁发执照的先决条件，除其他要求的费用外，每个有资格获得执照的申请人还应支付首年执照年费。

第4938.1条　根据《1994年加利福尼亚州制定法》第1275章（参议院法案第2101号）第36条规定废除，2000年1月1日生效。

第4939条

（a）为本章之目的，"获批的学历评估服务"系指经委员会批准的机构或组织，评估在美国境外完成的教育，并确定该教育是否与美国境内教育具有同等资质。

（b）如申请人在美国境外完成教育，则该申请人须同时满足以下两项要求：

（1）向获得委员会批准的学历评估服务机构提交学历证明文件，以进行评估。

（2）取得由学历评估服务机构直接送交委员会的评估结果。

（c）如委员会获得根据上述（b）项得出的申请人评估结果，委员会须审查该结果，并确定申请人是否符合颁发执照的规定。经评估，如教育达不到执业要求，委员会可为申请人提供额外的教育、培训或标准化考试，以满足教育要求。如申请人已在美国境内完成教育或培训，委员会不得另行要求额外的教育、培训或考试。

（d）委员会须在条例中制定批准学历评估服务的申请程序、标准及流程。该条例应要求学历评估服务至少符合以下要求：

（1）直接向委员会提交英文评估书。

（2）成为国家认可的外国学历评估协会的成员，如美国大学注册和录取管理者协会（American Association of Collegiate Registrars and Admissions Officers，AACRAO）或国家学历评估服务协会（National Association of Credential Evaluation Services，NACES）的成员，但不限于上述协会。

（3）委员会每五年重新进行一次评估。

（4）向委员会证明，学历评估服务机构备有一套由委员会厘定的完整参考资料。

（5）仅基于经过官方验证的真实成绩单和学位。

（6）有识别伪造成绩单的书面程序。

（7）为该报告之目的，在向委员会呈交的评估报告中应包括申请人成绩单、证书、学位

---

① 即第1.5部"拒绝、吊销以及撤销执照"第475条"拒绝颁发执照；原因"。

及其他教育的特定认证方法。

（8）评估报告应包括申请人所持有的每个学位、美国提供的同等学位、授予学位的日期、授予学位的机构、课程名称的英文译本以及每门课程的学期单位要求。

（9）为申请人提供上诉程序。

（10）向委员会提供关于学历评估服务的资料,包括(但不限于)给每名评估师及译者提供其简历或履历,其中包括个人简历、三封来自公共或私人机构的推荐信、过去五年每年处理的有关申请数目的统计资料,以及委员会可能需要的任何其他资料,这些资料用来确定学历评估服务是否符合本款及委员会条例所订标准。

（11）向委员会提供所需的所有资料,包括但不限于以下资料：

（A）其学历评估政策。

（B）用以编制其学历评估的术语及该术语的完整列表。

（C）学历认证所使用的特定方法的详细说明。

第4940条　批准指导方案;对针灸师的监督

（a）委员会须制定符合第4938条规定的标准,以审批针灸实践的教育和培训辅导计划。委员会还应为获批的针灸导师制定标准。

（b）应允许针灸师指导一名针灸学员,针灸导师须具备以下条件：

（1）在本州获得针灸执照,该执照现行有效、未被吊销或撤销,且未受到任何纪律处分。

（2）已向委员会提出申请。

（3）向委员会提交培训或受雇的学员姓名以及满足委员会要求的培训计划。

（4）任何时候,都不得同时培训或雇佣两名以上针灸学员。

（5）至少具有十年针灸师执业经验,并取得本州执照五年以上。

（6）在针灸师执业过程中,委员会认定其具有教育及培训学员所需的知识。

本条根据1993—1994年州法律汇编中1993年部分作出修订,该修订不会影响修正案生效日期前已获批的针灸导师的批准。

第4940.1条　根据《1996年加利福尼亚州制定法》第829章(议会法案第3473号)第82~84条规定废除

第4940.2条　根据《1996年加利福尼亚州制定法》第829章(议会法案第3473号)第82~84条规定废除

第4940.3条　根据《1996年加利福尼亚州制定法》第829章(议会法案第3473号)第82~84条规定废除

第4941条　培训和实习前的学分

委员会规定,在根据针灸辅导计划完成情况,审查执照申请时,如相关的预培训或实习符合委员会规定的标准,可授予学分。

第4944条

（a）委员会有权按照本章条文,对每名针灸执照的申请人进行调查及评估,并有权最终裁定是否允许申请人参加考试或取得执照。

（b）委员会须调查和评估根据第4939条申请批准的每所学校或学院,并可利用顾问或与顾问订立的合约来评估这些培训计划。本款于2017年1月1日废止。

(c) 委员会可根据本条将其常规事宜上的权限转授予委员会的行政官员或其他人员。

第4945条

(a) 委员会须为针灸师订立继续教育标准。

(b) 委员会须规定针灸师每两年完成五十个继续教育学时,以此作为其执照续期的条件。在两年期间,与临床或实际向患者提供卫生保健服务无关的事项上,继续教育不得超过五十个学时。继续教育机构应向委员会提出申请,以获得委员会批准开设的继续教育课程学分,并填写委员会制定的表格,支付审批费用和监督提供者的费用,还应在申请中说明以下信息:

(1) 课程内容。

(2) 测试标准。

(3) 课程要求中,完成继续教育学分的所需学时。

(4) 教师的经验及培训。

(5) 委员会规定的其他资料。

(6) 如有需要,可提供口译员或双语教学。

(c) 居住在其他州或国家的持证人须符合继续教育的规定。

(d) 继续教育机构须由委员会按照其做出的规定予以监督。

(e) 如委员会裁定针灸师未取得所需继续教育学时,则委员会可延长该针灸师的执照期限,并规定在下一个续期内,除了完成该期间所需的继续教育以外,还应补足所缺的继续教育学时数。如针灸师在其续期内未能补上所缺时间并完成当前继续教育所要求的学时,则在完成所有学时并向委员会提交记录之前,其针灸执照不得续期。

第4945.5条 根据《1991年加利福尼亚州制定法》第983章(参议院法案第1195号)第17条规定废除,1994年1月1日生效

第4946条 根据《2002年加利福尼亚州制定法》第405章(议会法案第2973号)第10条规定废除

第4946.5条 根据《1980年加利福尼亚州制定法》第1313章第11.5条规定废除,1985年1月1日生效

第4947条 针灸治疗;牙医或足科医生

(a) 如牙医或足科医生执照持有人已接受针灸方面的课程,则本章不得解释为禁止其在各自的执业范围内从事针灸实践。本课程材料须由对持证人具有管辖权的执照颁发委员会批准。针灸委员会应协助各执照颁发委员会按照要求提供相关信息。

(b) 上述(a)项所列出的课程要求,不适用于在1982年7月1日前已完成针灸课程(包括继续教育课程)并已开始进行针灸执业的足科医生或牙医。

第4948条 对本章的解释;研究活动

根据第2075条[①],本章规定不得解释为参与研究人员的活动违法。

---

① 即第2部第5章"医疗"第2075条"针灸;由有资质的针灸师或其他进行科学研究的持职业执照者开展针灸治疗;监管;由医学院报告"。

第 4949 条　客座针灸师;参与专业教育;限度

本章规定,不得禁止来自其他国家或州的针灸师(在本州未获得执照),作为针灸职业协会或针灸科学基金会、获批的教育和培训计划、根据第 4945 条获批的继续教育提供者的特邀嘉宾,仅通过讲座、临床教学或演示的方式从事针灸职业教育。客座针灸师可以结合上述方式从事针灸实践,最长不得超过六个月,但是不得开设诊室,不得在指定地点进行会诊、接听患者电话或以其他方式从事针灸实践。

第四节　强 制 执 行

第 4955 条　拒绝颁发、吊销或撤销执照;察看期条件(probationary conditions)

对于违反职业道德的针灸师,委员会可以拒绝颁发、吊销或撤销其执照,或将其列入察看期。

违反职业道德的行为包括但不限于下列行为:

(a) 使用或持有《健康与安全法典》第 10 部第 2 章(第 11000 条以下)[①]所界定的管制药物、危险药品或酒精饮料,对本人、他人或公众造成一定程度的危险,且在一定程度上损害其在保证公共安全的情况下从事针灸实践的能力。

(b) 被判与针灸师的资格、职能、职责实质相关的犯罪,且定罪记录中证据确凿。

(c) 发布虚假或误导性广告。

(d) 直接或间接地协助或教唆、违反或共谋违反本章的条款或委员会根据本章通过的任何规定。

(e) 除正当理由外,因未遵守委员会的感染控制指南而未能为患者提供保护,从而导致血源性传染病从持证人传至患者、从患者传至患者以及从患者传至持证人。在进行细分管理时,委员会应依据国家公共卫生部《健康与安全法》第 1250.11 条[②]制定的标准、行政法规以及指导意见和依据《1973 年加利福尼亚州职业安全卫生法》[③][《劳动法典》(Labor Code)第 5 部第 1 分部(第 6300 条以下)]制定的标准、行政法规以及指导意见,预防艾滋病、乙型病毒性肝炎和其他血源性传播病原体在卫生保健机构内传播。必要时,委员会应与本部医学委员会协商,包括但不限于加州医学委员会(Medical Board of California)、加州足病医学委员会(California Board of Podiatric Medicine)、加州牙科委员会(Dental Board of California)、注册护理委员会(Board of Registered Nursing)和职业护理和精神病技术人员委员会(Board of Vocational Nursing and Psychiatric Technicians),以支持在执行本款时保持适当的一致性。

委员会应确保持证人了解其本人以及其他人士遵守感染控制指南的责任,以及最新科学认可的最大程度降低血源性传染病传播风险的防护措施。

(f) 因患者或持证人在纪律处分或其他法律诉讼中提供证据,或在考虑给予纪律处分

[①] 即《加利福尼亚统一管制药物法》。

[②] 即《健康与安全法典》第 2 部"许可规定"第 2 章"健康设施"第 1250.11 条"指导意见以及行政法规;传播血源性传染病的风险"。

[③] 《1973 年加利福尼亚州职业安全卫生法》(California Occupational Safety and Health Act of 1973),载于《劳动法典》第 5 部"就业安全"第 1 分部"职业安全与健康"。

或其他法律诉讼的调查中提供证据,而对其进行威胁或骚扰。

(g)因雇员遵守本章条款而将其解雇。

(h)公共机构对针灸师或任何专业医疗保健持证人(与资格、职能或职责实质相关的行为)采取纪律处分。

(i)任何可导致拒绝颁发针灸执照的行为。

(j)在针灸师的营业场所内,其雇员或其他使用其执照或经营许可证工作的人员如违反任何与针灸师资格、职能或职责实质相关的法律或当地法令,则雇用该个人的针灸师或使用其针灸执照工作的员工将受到纪律处分。

(k)持证人在患者有合理机会接受另一名医师的治疗之前即放弃该患者,且未书面告知患者即将终止治疗。

(l)未能通知委员会使用错误名称、化名或假名的情况,持证人作为个人针灸执业所使用的姓名除外。

第 4955.1 条　欺诈行为;拒绝颁发、吊销或撤销执照,或附加察看期条件

如针灸师有欺诈行为,包括但不限于以下任何一项,则委员会可以拒绝颁发、吊销或撤销,或对其附加察看期条件:

(a)通过欺诈或欺骗手段获得执照。

(b)作为针灸师,实施虚假或不诚信的行为。

(c)在针灸师的资格、职能或职责方面做出任何不诚信或贪污的行为。

(d)出于欺诈意图更改或修改任何人的病历,或制造虚假病历。

(e)向患者提供服务后,未保存足够且准确的记录。

第 4955.2 条　过失行为或不称职行为;拒绝颁发、吊销或撤销执照,或附加察看期条件

如针灸师有下列任何行为,委员会可拒绝颁发、吊销、撤销其执照或对其附加察看期条件:

(a)重大过失行为。

(b)多次过失行为。

(c)不称职行为。

第 4956 条　定罪;委员会采取行动的时限

就与针灸师的资格、职能或职责实质相关的指控作出的认罪答辩、有罪判决或其后的定罪,均视为本章意义上的定罪。

委员会可撤销有罪判决,或驳回指控、申诉、控告或起诉。如上诉期已过或在上诉中确认了定罪判决,或作出了缓刑命令而暂缓执行判决[不管其后是否根据《刑法典》(Penal Code)第 1203.4 条①的规定作出命令,允许该人撤回其认罪答辩并作不认罪答辩],委员会可下令吊销、撤销或拒绝颁发执照,或对其执照附加察看期条件。

---

① 《刑法典》第 2 部"刑事诉讼"第 8 编"判决与执行"第 1 章"执行"第 1203.4 条"在最终作出裁决前满足缓刑或释放条件;改变认罪或撤销判决;诉讼终结并免除处罚和监禁;例外;赦免"(Fulfillment of conditions of probation or discharge prior to termination; change of plea or vacation of verdict; dismissal and release from penalties and disabilities; exceptions; pardon)。

第 4959 条　调查和起诉案件的费用；由持证人付款

（a）委员会可要求行政法官根据其在委员会职业纪律程序决议中拟议的判决，命令任何被认定违反职业道德的持证人向委员会支付一笔款项（不超过调查和起诉案件的实际和合理费用）。

（b）评估的费用应由行政法官确定，任何情况下，均不得由委员会增加。如委员会不通过拟议的判决并将案件发还行政法法官，则行政法官不得增加拟议决定中评估的任何费用。

（c）如持证人未支付委员会命令中要求支付的费用，委员会可在举行行政听证会所在县的高级法院强制执行支付命令。对于被强制要求支付费用的持证人，该强制执行权应作为委员会对其可能拥有的其他权利的补充。

（d）在追讨上述费用的司法诉讼中，委员会出示的判决证明应作为付款命令和付款条款有效性的确证。

（e）根据本条追回的所有费用，须视为已发生费用的补偿，并须存入针灸基金。

第 4960 条　纪律处分程序（disciplinary proceedings）的实施

本节规定的纪律处分程序应根据《行政程序法》[《政府法典》第 2 卷第 3 部第 1 分部第 5 章（第 11500 条以下）]实施。

第 4960.2 条　撤销执照；撤销记录

委员会撤销执照时应向被撤销执照所在的县级或市级经营许可机构提供证明并加盖公章。由县或市法院书记员（county or city clerk）作出的撤销记录，应当作为撤销事宜和委员会在撤销事项中所有程序合法性的充分证据。

第 4960.5 条　恢复执照；处罚的更改；申请；检查

（a）撤销、吊销、注销执照或执照被列入察看期者，可呈请委员会恢复执照或更改处罚，包括调整或终止察看期，但自纪律处分的决定生效之日起不得少于下列期限：

（1）执照被撤销或注销的，满三年可申请恢复执照。

（2）增加三年以上察看期的，满两年可申请提前终止察看期。

（3）满两年可申请调整察看期。

（4）增加三年以下察看期的，满一年可申请提前终止察看期。

（b）委员会可要求对申请恢复执照进行考试。

（c）尽管第 489 条①另有规定，如任何人因违反本章第 1.5 部（第 475 条以下）而被委员会驳回申请，则该人在驳回之日起三年后，可再次向委员会申请执照或注册。

第 4961 条　执业地点的注册；执照的张贴；地点的变更

（a）凡在本州已取得或将取得针灸执照的，须按照针灸委员会订明的格式注册持证人的执业地点，如有一个以上的执业地点，须注册所有执业地点。如持证人没有执业地点，则持证人应如实通知委员会。并须在委员会颁发执照之日起三十日内进行注册。

（b）针灸执照持证人须随时在其执业地点的醒目位置张贴其执照。如针灸师执业地点

---

① 第 1.5 部分"拒绝颁发、中止或撤销执照"第 2 章"拒绝颁发执照"第 489 条"因缺少良好的品格而拒绝颁发执照"。

多于一个,则须为每个额外地点自委员会获取一份执照副本,张贴于每个执业地点。

(c)持证人如更改其执业地点,须在作出该变更后三十日内进行登记。如持证人更改执业地点后,未在本条规定时间内通知委员会,委员会可拒绝为其执照续期。执照续期申请人须在其申请中指明其执业地点是否有更改,如有,须指明更改日期。委员会可接受该声明,并将其作为更改地址的证据。

第 4962 条　披露持证人的状态;例外情形;持证人的个人网络资料;察看期执照

(a)自 2019 年 7 月 1 日起,除(c)款另有规定外,委员会应要求持证人在患者首次治疗之前向患者、患者监护人或医疗代理人单独披露相关信息,披露内容应包括持证人察看期状况、察看期限、察看结束日期、委员会施行的执业规定、电话,以及说明患者如何在委员会执照信息网站上的持证人的个人资料页面上找到有关持证人察看期的更多信息。

(b)根据(a)款需进行披露的持证人应从患者、患者监护人或医疗代理人处取得披露文件的单独签名副本。

(c)如符合以下条件,则无须持证人根据(a)款规定进行披露:

(1)患者失去意识,或患者无法理解披露内容,无法根据(b)款签署披露文件,且监护人或医疗代理人无法理解披露内容并签署副本。

(2)在急诊室或紧急护理机构出诊,或计划外出诊(包括在住院机构进行的会诊)。

(3)患者直至就诊开始前一刻才知悉将要为患者提供治疗的持证人。

(4)持证人与患者无直接治疗关系。

(d)2019 年 7 月 1 日起,委员会应在委员会执照信息网站的持证人简介页面上,明确提供下列有关察看期持证人和持察看期执照人的执业状况的信息。

(1)在根据有关规定达成和解而进入察看期的情形中,需要列明有效指控中所述原因以及持证人所认罪于诉因,以及接受和解并非承认有罪的声明。

(2)对于委员会裁定的察看期,在察看期的最后裁定中说明察看期原因。

(3)持察看期执照人需说明被列入察看期的原因。

(4)察看时长和结束日期。

(5)委员会对察看期执照施加的执业限制。

(e)违反本条规定的行为不得以犯罪论处。

第 4963 条　禁令

凡有违反本章者,经委员会申请,县以上法院可发布禁令或其他适当命令限制该行为。据本条实施的程序应适用《民事诉讼法典》(*Code of Civil Procedure*)第 2 部第 7 卷第 3 章(第 525 条以下)①。委员会可根据本条,自行在上述高等法院提起诉讼,而在委员会展开的诉讼中,无须做出允诺。

第 4964 条　先前法律的延续

本条规定若与先前针灸执照相关法律实质相同,应解释为对该法的重申和延续,而不应解释为新的法律。

---

① 《民事诉讼法典》第 2 部"民事诉讼"第 7 卷"民事诉讼中的其他临时救济"第 3 章"禁制令"。

第五节 续 期

第4965条 执照到期；出生日期续期政策

（a）根据本章颁发的执照，如未续期，则该执照在其两年期限的最后一年中，于持证人出生月份的最后一日到期。

（b）委员会须设立并管理出生日期续期方案。

（c）为了续期未到期的执照，持证人须按照委员会提供的表格申请续期，并支付委员会规定的续期费用。

第4966条 到期的执照；续期时间；费用；有效日期

除第4969条另有规定外，到期的执照可在有效期届满后三年内随时续期，需通过委员会提供的续期表格提交申请，缴付所有应计未付的续期费用，完成规定的继续教育并提供证明。执照到期未续期的，作为续期执照的先决条件，还应当支付规定的逾期费。根据本条规定，续期应在申请提出之日、缴纳续期费之日或缴纳逾期费之日（以较晚发生者为准）生效。如按此方式续期，则该执照应自续费生效日起持续有效，直至第4965条规定的期满之日，如不再续期，该执照将到期并失效。

第4967条 执照到期后续期失败；申请新的执照

未在到期后三年内续期执照的，不得续期，也不得在到期后重新颁发或恢复执照，但符合下列全部条件的，可以申请领取新的执照：

（a）未实施任何第1.5部（第475条以下）规定中可导致拒绝颁发执照的行为或犯罪。

（b）在首次申请执照时，参加并通过考试（如有），或在充分考虑公众利益的情况下，以符合委员会要求的方式证明其有资格作为针灸师执业。

（c）缴纳首次申请执照所需的全部费用。如没有根据本条进行考试而颁发执照，委员会可豁免或退还全部或部分考试费用。

第4969条 吊销或撤销的资质；到期；续期；恢复；费用

（a）吊销的执照到期后，应按照本节规定进行续期，但续期后执照仍处于吊销状态。在执照恢复前，针灸师不得违反吊销命令从事针灸实践。

（b）根据本条规定，撤销的执照到期后不得续期。如原持证人在执照到期后恢复使用，则持证人应支付续期费作为恢复使用的条件，该续期费的金额相当于执照恢复日期前最后一个正常续期日应付的续期费，加上到期时累计的逾期费（如有）。

第六节 费 用

第4970条 收费价目表

除非委员会根据第4972条规定较低的费用，执业针灸师所需缴纳的费用应依照本条规定：

（a）申请费为七十五美元。

（b）考试费及重考费（应为针灸师委员会每次考试组织、出题、批阅和管理的实际支出费用）。

（c）首年执照年费为三百二十五美元，如该执照在发出后一年内到期，则该费用应为原来的50%。

（d）续期费为三百二十五美元，如委员会规定了更低的费用，则该费用应足以支持委员会发挥本章的管理职能。1996年1月1日前续期费应每年评定一次，自该日起，委员会应每两年评定一次续期费。

（e）应按照第163.5条①规定设置逾期费。

（f）根据第4939条，批准一所学校或学院的申请费为三千美元。该项于2017年1月1日废止。

（g）执照副本费是指委员会用于发放执照副本的费用。

（h）副本续期收据费为十美元。

（i）背书费为十美元。

（j）根据第4961条，额外办公地点的执照副本费应为十五美元。

（k）本条仅在2021年1月1日前有效，并自该日起废除。

第4971条　辅导计划；费用

针灸辅导计划须缴纳如下费用：

（a）用于辅导针灸学员的申请及登记费为二百美元。

（b）用于批准辅导针灸学员的年度续期费为五十美元。

（c）针灸学员的申请费为二十五美元。

（d）针灸学员每年的续期费为十美元。

（e）逾期款为续期费的50%。

第4972条　行政法规；费用

由委员会规定的费用应在委员会正式通过的法规中载明。

第4973条　根据《2014年加利福尼亚州制定法》第397章（参议院法案第1246号）第13条规定废除，2017年1月1日生效

第4974条　向主计长报告；向财务部门支付；设立基金

每月月初，委员会应根据本章，向主计长报告上月获得的总收入及其来源，并将全部金额交予财务部长，存入立法机关为执行本章规定而拨款设立的针灸基金。

第4974.5条　根据《1983年加利福尼亚州制定法》第789章第7条规定予以废除

第七节　针　灸　公　司

第4975条　公司的地位；条件；制订规章的管理机构

针灸公司是指经授权提供专业服务的公司（如《公司法》13401条②所界定），前提是该公司及其股东、管理人员、董事和提供专业服务的员工遵守《莫斯科-诺克斯专业公司法》、本条规定以及现在或之后颁布或通过的与公司及其业务开展相关的所有其他法律法规。

---

① 第1部"消费者事务部"第2章"消费者事务主管"第163.5条"逾期费，罚款；评估；恢复执照费用；续签费占比"。

② 《公司法典》第1卷"公司"第3部"专门领域的公司"第4分部"专业公司"第13401条。第4分部即《莫斯科尼-诺克斯专业公司法》（*Moscone-Knox Professional Corporation Act*）。

就针灸公司而言,《莫斯科尼-诺克斯专业公司法》中提到的政府机构为针灸委员会。

第 4976 条　违反职业道德的行为；违反

根据本章规定获取执照者,如违反、试图违反、直接或间接违反、协助或教唆违反、共谋违反《摩根大通-诺克斯专业公司法》中的规定或条款(或根据该法律正式通过的任何法规),即构成违反职业道德的行为,且违反本章规定。

第 4977 条　违反职业道德的行为；治疗行为

针灸公司不得实施第 4 节(第 4955 条以下)中构成违反职业道德的行为。在执业过程中,应与本章规定的持证人同等地遵守法律法规,受到法律法规的约束。

第 4977.1 条　收入；排除无资格的股东

如股东丧失资格,其间针灸公司因提供专业服务而产生的收入(定义见《公司法》第 13401 条),不得以任何方式计入该股东的收益或其在针灸公司的股份。

第 4977.2 条　董事、股东、高级管理人员；执照要求

除《公司法》第 13403 条[①]另有规定外,针灸公司的每名董事、股东及管理人员(除助理秘书及助理财务部长外)应均为《公司法》第 13401 节界定的持证人。

第 4978 条　名称

针灸公司的名称及其提供专业服务的名称,应包括"针灸""针灸师"等字样,以及表示公司存在的用语或者缩写。

第 4979 条　条例

为贯彻本条的宗旨及目标,委员会可通过并施行相关条例,包括但不限于(a)要求针灸公司的章程应包括一项规定,即丧失资格的人员(如《公司法》第 13401 节所界定)或已故人士所拥有的公司股份须在条例规定的时间内出售给该公司或公司其余股东,以及(b)如患者对针灸公司提供的专业服务不满,并对其提出索赔,针灸公司应通过保险或其他方式为患者提供足够保障。

加利福尼亚州针灸行政法[②]

1399.400　引用

本章可引用并称为"针灸条例"。

1399.401　办公室位置[已废除]

1399.402　时态,性别和数字[已废除]

1399.403　定义

为本章所含规定之目的,术语:

[①] 第 13403 条"一般公司法的适用；主管；医疗公司"。
[②] 根据《加利福尼亚州行政法规》第 16 卷 13.7 章(*California Code of Regulations*, Title 16. Professional and Vocational Regulations Division 13.7. Acupuncture Examining Committee of the Board of Medical Quality Assurance)译出。

(a)"委员会"系指针灸委员会。

(b)"法典"系指商业与职业法典。

1399.404　章节管理[已废除]

1399.405　职能下放

除根据《行政法典》中《行政程序法》第11500条等规定专门保留给"机构本身"的权力外,委员会应委派并赋权其行政官员(或其指定人员)在委员会管辖范围内处理调查及行政程序相关事务,上述职能包括但不限于批准撤销、注销或临时吊销执照的和解协议。

1399.406　填写地址

拥有依本章规定授予的执照、注册、批准或任何其他授权者,须向委员会提交其当前使用的正确邮箱地址,并在更改邮箱地址后的三十日内,以书面形式通知委员会,同时述明新旧地址。

1399.407　定义

(a)为本法第901条之目的:

(1)"社区组织"系指代表社区或社区的重要部分,致力于满足人们集会、教育、环境或公共安全社区需求的公共或民间非营利组织。

(2)"州外医师"系指在加利福尼亚州未获执照,但持有美国其他州、地区或准州现行有效且信誉良好的执照或证书,并从事针灸实践的人。

(3)"信誉良好"是指该人:

(A)未因违反任何与获公共机构颁发执照的执业活动实质相关的行为而受到罪行指控。

(B)未签订任何和解协议,也未受到任何涉及申请人职业行为或执业行为的行政处罚(包括非强制注销执照)。

(C)在其执业范围内未曾因委员会掌握证据判定其失职或不称职而受到不利判决。

1399.407.1　赞助方注册和记录保存要求

(a)注册。根据法典第901条规定,在赞助活动中提供或安排提供卫生保健服务的赞助方,应在赞助活动计划举办日前九十个日历日之内,向委员会注册。赞助方进行注册时,应向委员会提交完整的《商业与职业法典第901条赞助方注册》表格901-A(DCA/2016修订版),该表格在此通过引用并入。

(b)确定表格完整性。委员会可通过决议将代表委员会接收和处理901-A表格的权力委托给消费者事务部。委员会或其委托方应在收到表格901-A的十五个日历日内以书面形式通知赞助方,该表格信息完整且登记成功;或表格信息缺失,需提供完成表格及注册程序所需的具体信息及证明文件。在赞助活动开始前三十日内,如委员会或其委托方发现有问题未得到纠正,可驳回登记。

(c)记录保存的要求。无论赞助方位于何处,都应在加利福尼亚州内的实际办公地点保存第901条要求的所有记录的副本,以及委员会向州外医师颁发的参与授权书的副本。赞助方应在赞助活动结束之日起保留这些记录至少五年。记录可以采用纸质或电子形式保存。赞助方应在注册时通知委员会其保存记录的形式。此外,赞助方应将法典第901条要求的所有记录的副本保存于赞助活动的实际举办地点,直至活动结束。如委员会代表有任何要求,这些记录在赞助活动举办期内可供其核查和备份。

(d)州外医师事先获得委员会批准的要求。若州外医师未获委员会书面批准,则赞助方不得允许其参加赞助活动。

(e)报告。赞助方在赞助活动结束后十五个日历日内,应向委员会提交报告,总结赞助活动详情。本报告可由赞助方选择报告形式,但至少应包括以下信息:

(1)赞助活动的日期。

(2)赞助活动的地点。

(3)赞助活动提供的所有保健服务的类型和一般说明。

(4)根据本条获得授权的每个州外医师名单,以及该医师执照号。

1399.407.2　批准州外医师参加赞助活动

(a)申请参加赞助活动。州外医师("申请人")可向委员会申请参加赞助活动。若申请人已获得委员会的批准,则可在赞助活动中提供相应的卫生保健服务。申请人应向委员会提交一份填写完整的《无加州执照者在已备案的免费卫生保健活动中提供医疗服务的申请》表格901-B(CAB/2016)(该表格在此通过引用并入),并附上二十五美元手续费(不可退还)。申请人还须提供全套指纹或现场指纹采集报告,以确定申请人身份,并允许委员会调查其犯罪记录。

(b)申请的答复。委员会应当在收到完整的申请后的二十个日历日内向赞助方作出批准或否决的答复。

(c)驳回申请。

(1)申请人存在下列情形的,委员会须驳回申请:

(A)提交的901-B表格不完整,且申请人未在七个日历日内对委员会提供补充资料的要求作出答复;或

(B)申请人未遵守本条要求,或做出任何导致委员会驳回申请的行为;或

(C)申请人未持有第1399.407条所界定的现行有效且信誉良好的执照。

(2)申请人存在下列情形的,委员会可驳回申请:

(A)在赞助活动开始前二十日内收到申请;或

(B)申请人曾向委员会申请参加赞助活动,但被驳回;或

(C)申请人曾获得授权参加由委员会终止的赞助活动;或

(D)委员会收到当前申请前十二个月内,申请人已参加了四场或以上的赞助活动。

(d)对驳回的申诉。请求参加赞助活动的申请人,如申请被驳回,可以遵照1399.407.3条中规定的程序进行申诉。

1399.407.3　终止授权及申诉

(a)终止原因。委员会可出于以下原因终止州外医师参加赞助活动:

(1)州外医师未能遵守本条的适用条款、适用执业要求或委员会规定。

(2)州外医师为委员会中的持证者,其行为违反委员会纪律。

(3)委员会收到真实可信的投诉,表明州外医师不适合在赞助活动中进行医疗实践,或

曾以其他方式危害其服务对象。

（b）终止通知。委员会应向赞助方和州外医师提供一份书面的终止通知,包括终止协议的依据。如该书面通知于赞助方举办活动期间发出,委员会可向活动赞助方的任一代表发出通知。

（c）终止结果。在收到书面终止通知后,州外医师应立即停止参加赞助活动。该终止命令（终止其参加赞助活动的权力）应视为一项纪律处分并上报国家医师数据库。此外,委员会还应向该州外医师获得执照的司法辖区内的执照颁发机构提供一份书面终止通知的副本。

（d）申诉。州外医师可按照《法典》第901(j)(2)条规定的方式,对委员会终止批准的决定提出上诉。根据《行政诉讼法》第2卷第3部第1部分第4.5章（第11445.10条以下）的规定,上诉请求应被视为非正式听证请求。

（e）非正式会议备选方案。除了要求听证会外,州外医师还可要求与行政官员举行非正式会议,讨论终止批准其参加赞助活动的原因。行政官员应在收到申请后三十日内,与州外医师举行非正式会议。在非正式会议结束时,行政官员可以确认或驳回该终止命令。行政官员应在非正式会议之日起十日内书面说明其判决理由,并将其调查结果和决定的副本邮寄给州外医师。州外医师要求非正式会议,并非放弃其对终止批准的决定要求听证并提出异议的权利。如非正式会议后,终止命令被驳回,则视作撤销听证要求。

1399.410　验证

申请人或其委托人提交所有声明均不应违反伪证罪相关的法律条款。

1399.411　文件认证

申请人或代表申请人提交的文件应由适当的官方或政府盖章或核证。如委员会确定无法谨慎落实该项要求,可酌情豁免该项要求。

1399.412　翻译需要

采用英语以外语言提交的文件,应附有由申请人以外的翻译人员核证的英文译本。翻译人员应证明该译本的准确性,并遵循伪证罪相关的法律条款。

该数据库于2020年10月9日,2020年第41号登记簿发布前有效。

1399.413　申请截止日期

（a）所有新的考试申请均须以委员会提供的表格形式呈交,并须附有所需的声明及文件。此类申请均应在申请考试日期的至少一百二十个日历日前送达萨克拉门托的委员会办公室。

（b）所有重考申请,均须以委员会提供的表格形式（《补考/执照更新申请》,1996年3月修订）呈交,并须附有所需的声明及文件。所有重考申请均应在申请考试日期的至少三十个日历日前送达委员会办公室。

（c）由具有相关资质的教育机构或辅导教师出具的所有成绩单和证明文件均应在申请考试日期的至少三十个日历日前送达委员会办事处。

（d）如在考试或其他方面的管理上存在困难,委员会可宽限上述申请日期。

1399.414　驳回申请

（a）如申请人的申请被驳回,可在驳回之日起十五个日历日内提交书面申请,要求将其申请呈交委员会作进一步评估。

（b）如委员会认为申请人已符合获得针灸执照的条件，则须为该申请人安排考试。

（c）本条规定不得解释为剥夺申请人根据其他法律规定享有的上诉权。

1399.415　培训文件

（a）若申请人参加辅导课程，则每名申请人应完成条例所列的教育或辅导要求，并由该申请人曾就读学校的教务主任或其导师存档。

（b）（1）如考试申请人在 2005 年 1 月 1 日前报名参加获批的针灸及东方医学教育培训计划，须完成第 1399.436 条列出的课程及培训。

（2）如考试申请人在 2005 年 1 月 1 日后（含当日）报名参加获批的针灸及东方医学教育培训计划，须完成第 1399.434 条列出的课程及培训。

（c）所有考试申请人均须在申请审核前至少三十日达到本规例所列出的最低教育或辅导要求。

1399.416　符合执照资格的同等培训和临床经验

为证明教育培训和临床经验符合《法典》第 4938 条第（b）（3）款中对执照资格的要求，申请人须证明其教育和从业经验符合第 1399.436 条（a）、（b）及（c）款的规定，或第 1399.434 条的规定（如适用）。所有接受培训的外国申请人应将其学历证明材料呈交学历评估服务机构审核（该机构为美国国家认证评估服务协会的成员），并向委员会提交报告。该报告应由申请人在申请考试时一并提交。

1399.417　放弃申请

（a）有下列情形之一的，视为放弃考试申请并没收申请费：

（1）申请人未能在递交申请后一百八十个日历日内完成其申请。如确认审查考试资格所需的文件及信息均已呈交委员会，则视作该申请已完成。

（2）申请人自接到委员会通知之日起两年内未参加考试的，应视作放弃；申请人在其申请被视作放弃前，已向委员会提交无法参加考试的书面说明除外。委员会可连续两次延长申请人参加考试的资格。

（3）如申请人未通过考试，且自收到通知之日起两年内未参加重考，在该申请被视作放弃之前，申请人可向委员会提交书面说明，说明其无法参加重考的原因。委员会可连续两次延长申请人参加考试的资格。

（b）放弃原考试申请后提交的申请，视为新申请。

（c）申请人通过考试并被告知获得执照资格后，如三年内未提交完整的执照申请，视作放弃执照申请。放弃原执照申请后提出的申请，应视作新申请，申请人应参加并通过首次申请执照时要求的考试（如有）。

1399.418　未参加考试-撤回申请［已废除］

1399.419　审查及处理考试申请

（a）委员会须在收到考试申请后四十五个日历日内，通知申请人该申请完整、予以受理，或该申请存在遗漏，需要提交完成该申请所需的具体信息或文件。

（b）委员会须在申请人完整申请后四十五个日历日内，通知其是否有资格参加笔试。

（c）委员会须在笔试完成后三十个日历日内，告知考生成绩，如通过，则在其支付指定费用后向其颁发针灸执照。

（d）自收到完整申请之日至委员会就考试结果做出决定之日，最短、中等及最长处理时间如下：

最短——一百三十个日历日

中等——一百五十五个日历日

最长——一百八十个日历日

以上处理时间适用于第一次参加并通过考试，并在第一次申请截止日期前提交完整申请的考生。

（e）除其他执照要求外，如执照申请人患有可能影响其行动能力的精神疾病或身体疾病，从而无法安全履行针灸师职能，委员会可要求申请人接受委员会指定的一名或多名内科医生、外科医生或心理学家的检查。委员会应支付此类检查的全部费用。如申请人无法满足该要求，应视作申请不完整。

应向申请人提供评估报告。

第2.5条　执照续期　适用于印刷商的文件

1399.419.1　对委员会质询的回应

如委员会或其指定人员要求持证人提供犯罪记录信息，持证人须在三十日内对此要求做出回应。持证人应按要求提供所有文件及其他记录，并回复准确信息。

1399.419.2　指纹和执照续期的披露要求

（a）如续期2011年1月1日后（含当日）到期的执照，则在2001年1月1日之前获发执照，或无指纹电子记录的持证人，须向司法部提供一套完整的指纹，以进行犯罪记录检查，并进行州及联邦一级的刑事罪犯记录查册。

（1）持证人须缴付提供指纹和进行调查所需全部费用。

（2）持证人在申请续期时，须证明是否已按照本条规定向司法部提供其指纹。

（3）申请续期时，如执照处于非执业状态，或持证人正在美国境外的军事地区服役，则豁免本规定。

（4）持证人须在续期日期起至少三年内，保留证明其指纹电子传输给司法部的收据或者证明持证人指纹被取走的收据。

（b）作为续期的条件，持证人应披露自其上次申请续期以来，是否因违反本条例或任何其他州、美国或其他国家的法律而被定罪，《法典》第4022条所界定的低于三百美元罚款且不涉及酒精、危险药物或管制药物的交通违法行为除外。

（c）作为续期的条件，持证人应当披露自其上次申请续期以来，是否被本州、其他州、联邦政府的任何机构，或其他发证机构拒绝颁发执照或受到纪律处分。

（d）若持证人未能遵从本条的规定以致续期申请不完整，则该持证人在证明符合所有规定前，不得办理执照续期。

（e）在规定的执照续期日期前（含当日），未能按照本条规定向司法部提供全套指纹，则委员会可据此给予纪律处分。

(f) 执照处在非执业状态下时,持证人须在激活执照前遵从本条规定。在美国境外服兵役的持证人返回美国后须立即遵守本条规定,返回的期限不足三十日除外。

第3条 针灸辅导

1399.420 引用与参考

本条应称为"针灸辅导条例"。

1399.421 定义

本条例中:

(a)"针灸辅导"系指由委员会依据《法典》第4939及4940条批准的针灸辅导课程,申请人顺利完成课程后,可根据《法典》第4938条的规定获得针灸执照。

(b)"针灸导师"或"导师"系指经委员会批准,向学员(依据《法典》第4940条及本条例在委员会注册)提供针灸辅导的执业针灸师。根据第4940条,内科医生、足科医生或牙医不得担任针灸导师,执业针灸师除外。

(c)"学员"系指在委员会注册并在针灸导师指导下参加针灸辅导的人。

1399.422 事先批准作为针灸学员执业

未经委员会事先批准,任何人不得在针灸辅导中从事针灸实践。

1399.423 事先批准辅导一名针灸学员

未经委员会事先批准,针灸师不得开展针灸辅导。

1399.424 申请;预培训资格

(a)应按委员会提供的格式,将针灸学员的申请提交至萨克拉门托办公室,并缴纳第1399.461条规定的申请费。

(b)应按委员会提供的格式,将辅导针灸学员的申请提交至萨克拉门托办公室,并随附必要的文件,包括培训协议和第1399.461条规定的申请费。

(c)若学员在申请之日起十年内,接受过预培训或具备相关经历,且符合委员会标准,可在制定培训计划时予以考虑(理论培训和临床培训的要求学时数可相应减少)。上述预培训和经历证明应与针灸导师和学员的注册申请一并提交委员会审查。

1399.425 批准针灸辅导的要求

(a)针灸辅导课程须向学员提供结构化的学习经验,包含独立练习针灸所需的所有基本技能和知识。

(b)在职培训性质的针灸辅导,其雇佣关系可以是全职或兼职,但该培训计划及拟议指导须在辅导师与学员之间的书面协议范围内进行。针灸导师不应收取学员的学费。

(c)针灸辅导须提供正规临床培训及补充的理论及教学指导。第(e)(8)至(e)(20)款所规定的理论及教学训练,须在获批的针灸学校或其他高等教育机构完成[经《教育法典》第59部第7章第7节(第94900条以下)认证或批准,或经美国教育部授权的地区评审机构认证]。

(d)该临床培训须至少达到二千二百五十学时,包含下列课程:

(1)实践观察。

(2)病史和体格检查。

(3) 治疗计划。

(4) 患者准备工作。

(5) 设备的消毒、使用及维护。

(6) 艾灸。

(7) 电针(交直流电压)。

(8) 身体与耳部针灸。

(9) 急救治疗,包括心肺复苏。

(10) 对患者进行治疗前后的指导。

(11) 禁忌证及注意事项。

(e) 理论及教学训练须至少达到一千五百四十八学时(约一百学期学分),包含下列课程:最低学时。

(1) 传统东方医学——对传统诊疗方法的理论与实践综述的研究。

(2) 针灸解剖学和生理学——针灸基础,包括经络系统、奇经八脉,以及耳针疗法。

(3) 针刺技术——针刺手法、艾灸、电针的操作,包括禁忌证和并发症的说明。学员须在获委员会批准的针灸学校,完成洁针技术考试的课程,该课程以美国全国针灸基金会(National Acupuncture Foundation)出版的最新《洁针技术手册》为主要参考,或者顺利完成由针灸与东方医学行业协会(Council of Colleges of Acupuncture and Oriental Medicine, CCAOM)举办的洁针技术课程。

(4) 穴位按压。

(5) 呼吸技巧——气功入门课程。

(6) 传统东方功法——太极拳入门课程。

(7) 包括植物学在内的传统东方草药学。

(8) 实践管理——专业实践的法律及伦理指导,包括记录保存、专业责任、患者账户和转诊程序。

(9) 与针灸实践相关的伦理学,至少三十学时。

(10) 临床医学——对医学、整骨、牙科、心理学、护理、脊椎按摩疗法、足疗和顺势疗法的临床实践进行的研究,使针灸医师熟悉其他卫生保健从业者的实践。

(11) 医学史——对医学史的研究,包括跨文化治疗实践。

(12) 医学术语——英语医学术语基础。

(13) 普通科学——普通生物学、化学和物理学的概览或课程。

(14) 解剖学——对显微、大体解剖学和神经解剖学的研究。

(15) 普通心理学——包括咨询技巧。

(16) 生理学——基础生理学的研究,包括神经生理学、内分泌学和神经化学。

(17) 病理学——对疾病和病症性质的研究,包括微生物学、免疫学、精神病理学和流行病学。

(18) 临床医学——对内科、药理学、神经学、外科、妇产科、泌尿学、放射学、营养学、维生素和公共卫生的综述。

（19）西方药理学。

（20）提供急救及成人/儿童心肺复苏（CPR）培训的认证课程至少八学时。该课程须在美国红十字会、美国心脏协会或其他经委员会批准具有同等课程的组织学习。

（f）本条中规定的课程工作应持续至少四学年、八学期、十二个季度、九个三学期制或三十六个月。每十二个月完成的临床培训和/或理论及教学培训不超过一千五百学时。

（g）学员须以不危害患者健康和福利的方式提供针灸服务。

未告知患者的情况下，学员不得为任何患者提供针灸服务。每次治疗中，须告知患者学员将在针灸导师的监督下进行针灸治疗，且患者在治疗前已通过书面形式同意学员对其进行针灸治疗。上述规定也适用于学员协助针灸导师提供针灸服务的情况。

（h）针灸辅导培训计划应在导师和学员签署的书面协议中加以说明，该书面协议应包括但不限于培训计划、培训时长、提供理论及教学培训的方法，以及学员提供针灸服务的培训指南。在申请审批时须提交该书面协议的复印件。

（i）作为获得批准或持续批准的条件，所有辅导课程须由委员会的代表进行实地视察，以复核并评估课程的状况。学员和针灸导师应负责承担委员会进行复核和评估所发生的直接费用。

（j）在辅导计划获批前，针灸学员须符合以下条件：

（1）年满十八岁。

（2）顺利完成获批的高中课程或通过标准的同等学力测试。

（k）不论学员性别、种族、宗教、信仰、肤色或身体缺陷情况，均应为其提供针灸辅导。

（l）本条规定不适用于在 1999 年 1 月 1 日前按照第 1399.424 条规定开始接受辅导并在委员会注册的人。此类人员须符合其辅导计划获批时规定的课程和临床培训要求。

1399.426　针灸导师的职责

每名针灸导师均应履行以下职责：

（a）导师须按本条例规定，随时负责并监督学员的工作。

（b）由导师指派给学员的患者，须与学员所接受的训练水平相符，学员可对其进行安全有效的治疗。导师应在学员提供服务时，对其进行持续的指导和即时的监督。导师与学员须在同一场所或邻近场所提供服务，以便随时向学员提供意见、指示及帮助。

（c）必要时，导师须确保取得患者的知情同意书。

（d）导师须确保学员提交并达成其培训计划目标，并确保学员按照第 1399.425 条（c）款获得所需的理论培训。

（e）导师须确保学员符合《针灸条例》第 5 条的执业标准。

（f）导师须按委员会提供的表格，按季度向委员会提交进度报告，该报告应列出对学员进行理论、教学和临床培训的日程安排。

（g）导师须确保学员在提供服务或以其他方式从事专业活动过程中，始终明确其"针灸学员"的身份并佩戴第 1399.427 条规定的身份徽章。

（h）学员不得单独计费。

（i）导师须遵守《针灸法》《针灸条例》及适用的法律法规中涉及雇员或学员工资、报酬、最长工作时间和工作环境的相关规定。学员如需加班,不得干扰或影响其培训计划,也不得损害学员或患者的健康及安全。

1399.427　学员的职责

针灸学员应承担以下职责:

(a) 学员不得在没有按照规定受到监督的情况下自主提供针灸服务,也不得提供其未受训练或不能胜任的任何服务。

(b) 学员须达到向委员会呈交的培训计划中的教学目标,包括所需的理论训练。

(c) 学员须符合《针灸条例》第5条的执业标准。

(d) 学员在提供服务或以其他方式从事专业活动时,须表明其学员身份,并应在外衣上佩戴标识身份的徽章,该徽章须清楚显示学员姓名及"针灸学员"的身份。

(e) 如导师没有向委员会报告针灸辅导的延迟、中断或终止状况,应由学员向委员会报告。

(f) 学员须保留一份其在临床培训期间所见患者的书面日志。该日志应包括患者就诊的日期和时间,以及学员为患者提供针灸服务的描述。该日志须根据要求供委员会查阅。

1399.428　终止或修改辅导

(a) 无论任何原因导致针灸辅导终止,均应在十个日历日内以书面形式告知委员会。委员会收到通知时,应取消导师和学员的注册信息。如导师或学员其后参加针灸辅导,则应按照1399.424条的规定向委员会重新提交注册申请。

(b) 如针灸辅导的培训计划有实质性修改,须向委员会提交修改报告。提交此报告不收取任何费用。

1399.429　考试申请

辅导结束后,学员可申请考试。

1399.430　拒绝、吊销或撤销导师的注册

针灸辅导中,委员会可基于下列原因,拒绝、授予(在符合相关条款及条件的前提下)、吊销、撤销导师的注册,或将其列入察看期:

(a) 未能遵从《法典》第4940条或针灸辅导条例中有关批准针灸辅导的条款。

(b) 违反《针灸执照法案》或《针灸条例》。

(c) 导师已受到纪律处分,或已受到纪律处分的指控。

(d) 通过欺诈、谎报或向有关部门提供关于针灸辅导的虚假或误导性信息的方式注册为导师。

(e) 导师或学员没有遵从有关辅导、护理或知情同意书的条例。

(f) 学员在针灸辅导中提供违反本法的针灸服务,无论针灸导师是否知悉。

1399.431　拒绝、吊销或撤销学员的注册

针灸辅导中,委员会可基于下列原因,拒绝、颁发(在符合相关条款及条件的前提下)、中止、撤销学员的注册,或将其列入察看期:

(a) 未遵守针灸辅导条例,获批并注册为学员。

(b) 违反《针灸执照法案》或《针灸条例》。

(c) 通过欺诈、谎报或向有关部门提供关于针灸辅导的虚假或误导性信息的方式注册

为学员。

（d）未遵从有关监督、患者护理或知情同意书的条例。

（e）在获批的针灸辅导以外提供针灸服务。

（f）未表明针灸学员身份，或在提供针灸服务时未佩戴身份徽章。

（g）在针灸导师的指导下提供针灸服务，而该导师未获委员会批准，或该导师的注册已根据第1399.430条受到纪律处分。

1399.432　诉讼

以违反职业道德为由，吊销、撤销或拒绝针灸导师或学员的注册，应根据《行政程序法》（《政府法典》第11500条及其后条款）执行。

第3.5条　针灸培训计划

1399.434　批准针灸及东方医学课程审批标准（2005年1月1日起生效）

为获得委员会批准，针灸和东方医学教育和培训课程包括至少二千〇五十学时的教学和实验室培训，以及至少九百五十学时的临床教学培训。课程设置应包含下列课程，并符合以下标准：

（a）基础科学——三百五十学时

基础科学的课程设置应为学生进入高等院校生物医学和临床科学课程做好准备，包括至少三百五十学时基础科学课程的教学和实验指导：

（1）普通生物学。

（2）化学，包括有机化学和生物化学。

（3）普通物理学，包括生物物理学概论。

（4）普通心理学，包括心理咨询技能。

（5）解剖学——显微、大体解剖学和神经解剖学的研究。

（6）生理学——对基础生理学的研究，包括神经生理学、内分泌学和神经化学。

（7）病理学和病理生理学——是对疾病和疾病性质，包括微生物学、免疫学、精神病理学和流行病学的研究。

（8）营养和维生素。

（b）针灸及东方医学原理、理论及治疗——一千二百五十五学时

针灸和东方医学原理、理论和治疗的课程设置应包括至少一千二百五十五学时的针灸和东方医学的指导原则、理论、处方和治疗程序的内容：

（1）针灸与东方医学原理与理论

（A）东方医学原理及理论。

（B）针灸原理及理论。

（C）东方按摩（例如，推拿或指压按摩）原理和理论。

（D）中药原理及理论，包括有关植物学概念（本学科范围须包括至少四百五十学时的教学）。

（E）针灸及东方医学诊断。

（F）针灸及东方医学专业，包括皮肤科、妇科、儿科、眼科、骨科、内科、老年病学、家庭医

学、伤科及急诊护理。

（G）古典针灸及东方医学文献,包括《金匮要略》《温病学》《伤寒论》《内经》。

（H）现代针灸及东方医学文献。

（2）针灸与东方医学

（A）综合针灸及东方医学诊疗程序。

（B）针灸技术及治疗程序,包括电针。

（C）东方按摩（例如,推拿或指压按摩）、穴位按压及其他使用手法疗法和器械装置的技术。

（D）功法,包括呼吸、气功及太极拳。

（E）草药处方、咨询及制备。

（F）东西方临床和医学营养、膳食和补充剂处方及咨询。

（G）冷热疗法,包括艾灸及超音波疗法。

（H）生活方式咨询及自我保健建议。

（I）辅助针灸程序,包括放血、拔罐、刮痧及皮钉疗法。

（J）针灸微针疗法,包括耳穴疗法和头针疗法。

（K）卫生标准,包括洁针技术。本课题的洁针技术部分应使用由美国全国针灸基金会出版的《洁针技术手册》第7版（2016年1月修订）,该手册在此通过引用并入。学生在对人体实施针刺技术前,应顺利完成卫生标准中的洁针技术部分。

（L）设备的保养及安全。

（M）辅助穴位刺激装置,包括磁铁及磁珠。

（c）临床医学、患者评估及诊断——二百四十学时

临床医学、患者评估和诊断课程应包括至少二百四十学时的教学指导,使学生具备运用标准体检、实验室和影像学研究以及国际疾病分类诊断原则所需的知识、技能和能力,以提高疗效、安全性、转诊和护理连续性;改善与所有其他医疗提供者的沟通和合作状况;协助评估和记录患者病情;提高针灸师对生化病因病理的认识。临床医学、患者评估和诊断技能课程应包括下列内容:

（1）全面的病史采集。

（2）标准体格检查和评估,包括神经肌肉骨骼、骨科、神经学、腹部、耳鼻喉检查和功能评价。

（3）药理评价,强调副作用和草药相互作用。

（4）医患间的融洽关系、沟通技巧,包括多元文化敏感性。

（5）诊断影像学、放射学和实验室检验的操作流程,整合所得数据及报告。

（6）临床理论和问题处理。

（7）临床印象和可行的诊断流程,包括针灸和东方医学诊断,以及世界卫生组织的国际疾病分类。

（8）对高危人群的认识,包括对性别、年龄、贫困人群和特定疾病患者的认识。

（9）标准医学术语。

（10）临床科学——内科、药理学、神经学、外科、妇产科、泌尿学、放射学、营养学和公共卫生综述。

（11）临床医学——医学、整骨疗法、牙科、心理学、护理学、脊椎按摩疗法、足疗、自然疗法和顺势疗法的临床实践概述，让医师熟悉其他卫生保健从业者的实践经验。

（d）病例管理——九十学时

病例管理课程应包括至少九十学时的教学指导，让学生有能力作为初级卫生保健专业人员参与患者护理，并应包括下列科目的指导：

（1）初级护理职责。

（2）二级及专科护理职责。

（3）社会心理评价。

（4）治疗禁忌证和并发症，包括药物和草药的相互作用。

（5）治疗计划、护理连续性、转诊和协作。

（6）随访、复查和功能性结果测量。

（7）预后和长期卫生保健。

（8）工伤职工和社会化医疗患者的病例管理，包括了解工伤补偿/劳动规范和程序及合格的医学评价。

（9）现行操作和诊断代码的编码程序，包括现行程序术语和国际疾病分类 ICD－10 的诊断代码。

（10）医疗法律报告的撰写、专家医学证明和独立医学审查。

（11）特殊护理/重症患者。

（12）急救程序。

（e）实践管理——四十五学时

实践管理课程应至少包括四十五学时的教学指导，包括下列科目：

（1）病历保存、保险计费、托收。

（2）书面业务交流。

（3）法规遵从性和法理学知识[市政法律、加利福尼亚州法律和联邦法律，包括《职业安全与卫生条例》（OSHA）、《劳动法》、1996 年《美国健康保险流通与责任法案》（*Health Insurance Portability and Accountability Act of 1996*，HIPAA）]。

（4）前台程序。

（5）规划设立专业办公室。

（6）实践成长与发展。

（7）具有在包括医院在内的跨学科医疗环境中执业的能力。

（8）风险管理和保险问题。

（9）伦理与同行评议。

（f）公共卫生——四十学时。

公共卫生课程应包括至少四十学时的教学指导，其中应包括关于公共卫生原则的培训，包括下列科目：

（1）公共与社区卫生及疾病预防。

（2）公共卫生教育。

（3）至少八学时的急救和成人/儿童心肺复苏（CPR），由美国红十字会、美国心脏协会或者其他经委员会批准有同等课程的组织提供。

（4）化学依赖性治疗。

（5）传染病、公共卫生警报和流行病学。

（g）职业发展——三十学时

专业发展课程须包括至少三十学时的教学指导，并须使学生具备不断扩充知识的能力，包括下列科目的教学：

（1）研究与循证医学。

（2）对同行评审过程有一定的了解。

（3）对研究方法的认识和批判。

（4）医学史。

（h）临床实践——九百五十学时

临床实践课程应至少包括九百五十学时的临床指导，其中75%应在由学校所有并经营的诊所内进行，其中包括下列与患者直接接触的情况：

（1）实践观察（最少一百五十学时）——在监督下观察针灸和东方医学临床实践，病例展示及病例讨论。

（2）诊断与评价（最少二百七十五学时）——中西医结合的诊断方法在患者评价中的应用。

（3）受监督的实践（最少二百七十五学时）——《商业与职业法典》第4927（d）及4937（b）条所列针灸及东方医学治疗模式下患者的临床治疗。

（4）在诊断、评估和临床实践的最初二百七十五学时内，临床导师在患者的诊断和治疗过程中应始终在场。在随后二百七十五学时内，临床导师应在患者接受针灸治疗时始终在场。此后，在进行临床指导期间，临床导师应在患者接受治疗的地点附近。学生也应在每次治疗前和治疗后，请教临床导师。

1399.435　针灸和东方医学培训计划标准

获委员会批准的针灸和东方医学培训计划，自2005年1月1日起，采用下列程序：

（a）入学申请人须顺利完成至少两学年（六十个学期学分/九十个季度学分）的学士学位教育，为攻读研究生课程做好准备。或在美国教育部长指定机构认可的院校完成同等学力课程。

（b）培训计划应在依据《教育法典》第59部第7章第4节（第94770条以下）批准的教育机构内进行，若培训计划在加利福尼亚州外进行，则举办机构须获得相关政府认证机构或美国教育部指定认证机构批准。

（c）该培训计划须制定自学评估方案，以确定其理论及临床培训计划的有效性。

（d）课程应设有学分。

（e）该培训计划中，负责临床部分的主管及导师应为教育机构所在州的执业针灸师，且具有五年以上的针灸和东方医学临床实践经验。

（f）所有导师均应有能力凭借其教育、培训及经验教授指定课程。所有教师资格证等级应与所教授的课程和学位水平同等。

（g）每个培训计划均应制定政策和程序，以评估学生的课程学习和经验，并授予学生与

当前课程和临床指导所同等的转学分。该政策和程序应在学校目录中加以规定,并应包括以下内容:

(1)只对实际的课程授予学分。

(2)若申请人的课程学习及临床教学在未获委员会批准的针灸学校完成,则对申请人的评估应包括由该学校组织并留存的考试,考试范围为可授予转学分的学科。

(3)在委员会批准的另一所针灸学校或学院顺利完成课程学习和临床教学,最高可获得100%的转学分。

(4)在根据《教育法典》第59分部第7章第4节(第94770条以下)批准的学校或由美国教育部指定认证机构批准的学校,顺利修完基础科学、临床医学、病例管理、实践管理、公共卫生和专业发展的课程,最高可获得100%的转学分。

(5)在未获委员会批准的学校内,若顺利完成针灸和东方医学原理、理论和治疗方法的临床实习课程,可通过转学考试或挑战考试获得经委员会批准学校授予的50%学分,前提是在委员会批准的学校内顺利完成至少50%的课程学时。

(6)评估及授予学生转学分的完整记录,应归入学生的学业档案,并作为该学生成绩单的正式部分,按要求提交委员会存档。

(7)所有学生入学时,应收到学校关于评估及授予转学分相关政策及程序的副本。

1399.436　批准针灸培训计划的标准[已废除]

1399.437　委员会批准课程的要求

(a)每项教育和培训计划在申请委员会批准其课程时,应提交"委员会批准课程申请"(第4/15号修订版),在此通过引用并入。申请时应附有以下资料和文件:

(1)教育培训计划法定名称、当前地址、电话号码、网站、联系人以及需要委员会审批的课程。

(2)符合委员会课程要求的完整课程清单,包括课程编号、课程学时和课程单元,以证明课程符合第1399.434条的要求。

(3)申请委员会批准的计划中的所有课程清单,包括课程学时、课程单元、课程编号和课程标题。

(4)申请委员会课程审批的所有课程大纲副本。

(5)当前课程目录的副本。

根据本条提交的所有信息和文件均应以英文书写。

(b)根据《商业与职业法典》第4927.5(b)条规定,如委员会收到一份完整的申请,包括表格、所有信息和文件时(如本条a款所界定),则视为委员会收到并完成了"委员会批准课程申请"。

(c)如教育和培训计划的"委员会批准课程申请"不完整,应书面通知其申请不完整及其原因,并说明如何处理不完整申请。如教育和培训计划的申请不完整,在收到申请不完整的书面通知后三十日内,未向委员会提交完整的申请,则视为放弃该申请。

(d)在放弃先前的申请后提交的"委员会批准课程申请"应视为新的申请。

(e)1399.434条中所列课程在获委员会批准后,如出现任何变更,均视为新课程,此类课程需根据《商业与职业法典》第4927.5条规定,在开课前获委员会批准。

1399.438　吊销或撤销批准

对于任何未能遵守本条规定、《针灸条例》或《针灸执照法案》的针灸培训计划,委员会可对该计划的批准予以否决、吊销、撤销或将其列入察看期。

1399.439　学校监督;记录;报告

(a) 每所获批的针灸学校须在该学校财政年度结束后六十日内,向委员会呈交一份现行课程目录,并附上一封信,述明以下事项：1) 增加/删除的课程或与上一年课程相比有重大变化的课程;2) 教职员工、行政部门或管理机构的变更;3) 学校设施的重大变更;4) 关于学校财务状况的声明,委员会可借此评估学校是否有足够资源保证其招生能力。

(b) 如有需要,委员会将派代表到学校进行实地考察,以审查和评估学校的状况。学校应承担委员会进行审查和评估所需的直接费用。

(c) 所有学生记录须至少以英文备存。

(d) 各获批针灸学校应在三十日内,向委员会报告其设施和/或诊所及本条规定的课程设置的重大变化。

第 4 条　能力考试与示范

1399.440　地点

考试须在委员会指定的时间及地点进行。如同一考试有多个考点,应同时进行考试。

1399.441　语言

考试应以英文、中文和韩文开展。申请人应在申请考试或执照时,将要求使用的语言告知委员会。如获批申请人总数中,有百分之五以上申请人正式要求委员会提供另一种语言的译本,则委员会应提供相应翻译及翻译人员。否则,申请人应选择上述一种语言参加考试。

1399.442　考试委员

(a) 修正案于8-22-77日提交;此后第30日生效(登记号77,第35号)。

(b) 废除者于5-5-81日提交;此后第30日生效(登记号81,第19号)。

注：引用的权威：第4933条,《商业与职业法典》。

1399.443　考试内容

(a) 该考试应测试申请人在针灸实践方面的知识和能力。

(b) 为通过考试,申请人应按要求考取及格分数,该分数是依照标准参照法确定,此法确定了考试各部分的及格分数。

1399.444　到期执照;考试

执照有效期届满超过三年并根据本法第4967条的规定申请换发新证的针灸师,须参加笔试并合格,方可获发新证。

第 5 条　执业标准

1399.450　诊室条件

每个针灸诊所应时刻保持清洁卫生,并按照《建筑标准法典》(*Building Standards Code*)第2部分第24卷第494A.1条和1994年《统一建筑规范》(*Uniform Building Code*)第2902.3条,设置无障碍洗手间。

1399.451　治疗程序

针灸师治疗患者,应遵守下列程序:

(a) 在检查患者、操作针灸针和其他器械,以及治疗患者之前,针灸师应使用肥皂和温水清洗双手。

(b) 所有器械在使用前以及使用间期均应进行完全灭菌(破坏所有微生物)。所有装有无菌针头的针盘也应处于无菌状态。每次对器械进行灭菌时,针灸师应使用指示胶带或指示卡,指示灭菌过程已完成。

(c) 在进针前,应用适当的消毒剂清洗需要进针的穴位。

(d) 如刺入患者皮下的针灸针断裂,提供治疗的针灸师应立即咨询医生。针灸师不得切断或穿透组织取针。

(e) 任何由针灸治疗引起的并发症,包括但不限于血肿、腹膜炎、气胸,如需立即就医,应立即交由内科医生、牙医或足科医生进行处理(如适用)。

(f) 不得使用皮下注射针进行针灸。

(g) 所有将要丢弃的器械均须安全处置。

(h) 针头应放置在标有"有害垃圾"的密封且不易破碎的容器中,并按照州和地方法律进行处置。

1399.452　诊室外治疗

(a) 针灸师如在诊室外提供针灸治疗,应将所需的无菌针及其他器械放入无菌密闭容器内。

(b) 提供治疗的针灸师应遵守所有适用于诊室外治疗的执业标准。

1399.453　记录保存

针灸师应对每一位接受针灸疗法的患者进行完整和准确的记录,包括但不限于针灸治疗的方法及针灸治疗取得的进展。

1399.454　一次性针具

针灸师应使用符合联邦条例21CFR第880.5580部分(61FR64617,1996年12月6日)规定且注有一次性使用标签的针具。针灸师多次使用同一针头构成违反职业道德的行为。

1399.455　广告

(a) 执业针灸师可采用《法典》第651条所授权的方式为针灸服务进行广告宣传,前提是此类广告不会促成过度或不必要的针灸服务。

(b) 根据《法典》第4955条的规定,广告中以任何方法表示针灸师可以治愈任何类型疾病、状况或症状,均属违法广告。

(c) 根据《法典》第4955条的规定,广告中发布任何不在针灸执业范围内(如《医疗保险法》第4927条和第4937条所界定)的操作、技术或程序,均属违规广告。

1399.456　"医生"头衔的使用

针灸师在针灸实践相关情境中使用"医生"或缩写"Dr."属违反职业道德的行为,除非其持有授权使用该头衔的执照或证书,或具有第59分部第7章第4节(第94760条以下)项下规定的,从经认可、批准或授权的教育机构获得的博士学位,且该学位为针灸、东方医学、生物科学或法典第 4927 条和第 4937 条中规定的与针灸师的执业授权相关的专业。

获得以上授权的针灸师,在没有对授权其使用此类头衔的执照、证书或学位的类型进一步说明的情况下,使用"医生"或缩写"Dr.",也属违反职业道德的行为。

第 6 条 其他规定

1399.460 费用

(a) 申请费用为七十五美元。

(b) 考试及重考费用为五百五十美元,另加申请提交时有效适用的指纹识别费。

(c) 为设立和管理出生日期续期方案,首年针灸执照年费须以执照发出日期及申请人的出生月份为基准。不颁发少于十二个月的执照。首年执照年费须按照以下附表缴付:

出生月份对应的收取的费用

申请人出生月份 \ 执照发出月份	1月	2月	3月	4月	5月	6月	7月	8月	9月	10月	11月	12月
1月	176美元	325美元	312美元	298美元	285美元	271美元	257美元	244美元	230美元	217美元	203美元	190美元
2月	190美元	176美元	325美元	312美元	298美元	285美元	271美元	257美元	244美元	230美元	217美元	203美元
3月	203美元	190美元	176美元	325美元	312美元	298美元	285美元	271美元	257美元	244美元	230美元	217美元
4月	217美元	203美元	190美元	176美元	325美元	312美元	298美元	285美元	271美元	257美元	244美元	230美元
5月	230美元	217美元	203美元	190美元	176美元	325美元	312美元	298美元	285美元	271美元	257美元	244美元
6月	244美元	230美元	217美元	203美元	190美元	176美元	325美元	312美元	298美元	285美元	271美元	257美元
7月	257美元	244美元	230美元	217美元	203美元	190美元	176美元	325美元	312美元	298美元	285美元	271美元
8月	271美元	257美元	244美元	230美元	217美元	203美元	190美元	176美元	325美元	312美元	298美元	285美元
9月	285美元	271美元	257美元	244美元	230美元	217美元	203美元	190美元	176美元	325美元	312美元	298美元
10月	298美元	285美元	271美元	257美元	244美元	230美元	217美元	203美元	190美元	176美元	325美元	312美元
11月	312美元	298美元	285美元	271美元	257美元	244美元	230美元	217美元	203美元	190美元	176美元	325美元
12月	325美元	312美元	298美元	285美元	271美元	257美元	244美元	230美元	217美元	203美元	190美元	176美元

(d) 自1996年1月1日起,执业针灸师的每两年续期费用为三百二十五美元。

(e) 执照可在有效期届满后三年内的任何时间续期。持证人须缴付所有应计及未付的续期费用以及所有逾期费。

(f) 逾期费为二十五美元。

(g) 申请批准院校的费用为一千五百美元。

(h) 复制或更换刻墙执照的费用为十五美元。

(i) 续期收据/口袋执照的复本或补本的费用为十美元。

(j) 背书函的费用为十美元。

1399.461　针灸辅导

每年的续期费用应在完成获批的针灸辅导(一年)后的三十日内支付。

1399.462　继续教育费

继续教育机构的审批费用为一百五十美元。

1399.463　发布传票和罚款的权力

(a) 委员会行政官员有权就持证人违反《针灸执照法》(《商业与职业法典》第4925条以下)或委员会通过的法规的行为发布传票,其中包括颁发禁止令或处以行政罚款。为本条以及第1399.464,1399.466,1399.467和1399.468条之目的,"持证人"一词指加利福尼亚州持牌针灸师或委员会批准的继续教育提供者。

(b) 每项传票均应采用书面形式,并须特别描述该项违规行为的性质及事实,包括提述涉嫌违反的法律法规。传票须亲自或以核证邮件送达持证人。

1399.464　免责条款

有下列情形之一的,不得发布传票:

(a) 该违规行为性质恶劣和/或情节严重,为保护消费者,有必要撤销或限制其执照。

(b) 持证人的行为显示出对患者和/或患者权利的漠视,包括但不限于人身虐待、忽视、放弃、信任滥用[如《福利和制度法典》(Welfare and Institution Code)第15610条所界定]。

(c) 持证人未能遵从先前传唤的任何要求,包括任何禁止令或处以罚款。

(d) 违规行为包含与管制药物或危险药品有关的违反职业道德的行为。

(e) 该违规行为包含对患者进行性虐待或与其产生不当关系、性关系等违反职业道德的行为。

(f) 持证人被认定犯有与针灸师的资格、职能及职责实质关系的罪行,但复权证据不充分。

1399.465　引用;罚款评定

(a) 任何由行政官员收取的行政罚款的金额不得低于一百美元,不得高于二千五百美元。

在评估罚款金额时,行政官员应在确定罚款金额时考虑下列因素:

(1) 违规的严重性。

(2) 被传唤人表现出的善意或恶意。

(3) 故意犯罪的证据。

（4）委员会调查中被传唤人的配合程度。

（5）被传唤人减轻或试图减轻因其违规行为造成的任何损害的程度。

（6）其他影响公正的因素。

（b）尽管第(a)款中已写明行政罚款的金额，但如存在下列一种或多种情况，则传票可包含二千五百〇一美元至五千美元的罚款：

（1）该项传唤涉及与他人健康及安全有直接关系的违法行为。

（2）被传唤人有两次或两次以上相同或类似违法行为。

（3）多次违反规定，故意无视法律。

（4）传唤涉及对老年人、残疾人实施的违法行为。

1399.466 遵从禁止令

（a）若被传唤人收到禁止令后，经过适当勤勉，情况仍不受其控制，因此无法在规定的时间内完成整改，则被传唤人可要求行政官员延长整改时间。该请求应以书面形式在规定的时间内提出。

（b）如被传唤人未对禁止令提出异议，或对禁止令提出上诉却败诉，且未在规定时间内进行整改，则视作违法且未遵从禁止令，委员会可给予其纪律处分或采取适当的司法救济措施。

1399.467 对未获批的针灸实践发出的传票

委员会行政官员有权决定何时针对何人发布传票，并有权针对现在或曾经从事针灸服务并依照《针灸执照法案》获得针灸执照的相关人士发出含禁止令和罚款的传票。每份针对未获批活动发出的传票，应包含一份禁止令，适当情况下，行政官员应根据本条例第1399.465条的规定，对此类未获批活动收取罚款。第1399.463，1399.465，1399.466和1399.468条的规定适用于根据本条发布的针对未获批的执业活动发出的传票。根据本条发出的传票应独立于任何其他民事或刑事救济措施，并作为其他民事或刑事救济措施的补充。

1399.468 对传票有异议

（a）除根据《法典》第125.9节(b)(4)款的规定要求听证会外，被传唤人可在传票送达或收到传票后十日内书面通知行政官员，要求就传票中指控的行为与行政官员举行非正式会议。

（b）行政官员须在接到请求后六十日内，与被传唤人举行非正式会议。非正式会议结束时，行政官员应批准、修改或驳回该传票，包括收取的罚款或发出的禁止令。行政官员应以书面或邮件的形式说明其采取行动的理由，并按照第1399.463条(b)款的规定，在非正式会议日期起十日内将其调查结果和判决的副本送达或邮寄给被传唤人。本判决应视作关于传票的最终命令，包括征收的罚款和禁止令。

（c）行政官员在非正式会议中维持传票原判后，被传唤人仍未放弃要求召开非正式会议举行听证并提出质疑。如非正式会议后传票被驳回，应视作撤回该传票的听证请求。如传票（包括征收的罚款和禁止令）有所变更，应视作撤回原传票，并应发出新的传票。如要求对随后的传票举行听证会，应在三十日内按照第125.9条(b)(4)款的规定提出。

1399.469 纪律规定

根据《行政程序法》（《行政法典》第11400条及其后各条）作出纪律处分决定时，针灸委员会应考虑题为《1996年针灸委员会消费者事务部〈纪律规定〉》的纪律规定,该规定在此通过引用并入。若基于某些特殊案件的事实情况(例如：从轻处罚的因素;案件的时效;证据问题),针灸委员会可酌情决定偏离这些规定及命令,包括察看期的标准条款。

1399.469.1　针对登记在册的性犯罪者的必要措施

(a) 除另有规定外,如根据《刑法》第290条或其他州或准州的同等法律或军事或联邦法律要求将某人登记为性犯罪者,则委员会应：

(1) 根据《行政法典》第2篇第3部第1部第5章(第11500条以下)中规定的程序,拒绝其提出的执业申请。

(2) 根据《行政法典》第2编第3部第1部第5章(第11500条以下)中规定的程序,立即撤销其执照,且不得暂缓撤销执照或提供察看期执照。

(3) 拒绝其任何恢复或重新颁发执照的呈请。

(b) 本条不适用于以下情形：

(1) 根据《刑法》第290.5条,已免除该人登记为性罪犯者的义务,或根据加利福尼亚州法律或要求登记的司法管辖区法律,由于其他原因已正式终止其登记义务。

(2) 该人仅根据《刑法》第314条被判轻罪,而根据《刑法》第290条要求登记为性犯罪者。但是,本款中的任何规定均不得禁止委员会行使酌处权,基于《刑法》第314条对持证人的定罪,根据州法律的其他规定对持证人进行纪律处分。

(3) 在本条生效日前经过充分裁定的行政程序。为本款之目的,呈请恢复被撤销或吊销的执照应视为新的程序,并应以(a)款中禁止恢复执照的规定为准。

1399.469.2　违反职业道德的行为

除《商业与职业法典》第4955条所述的行为外,"违反职业道德的行为"还包括但不限于以下行为：

(a) 因持证人的执业行为而引起的民事纠纷中,持证人已列为当事人或将列为当事人。为解决该纠纷,持证人在诉讼前或诉讼后签订的协议中包含(或准许包含)以下任一条款。

(1) 禁止纠纷的另一方与委员会联系,合作或向委员会提出申诉。

(2) 要求纠纷的另一方尝试撤回已向委员会提出的申诉。

(b) 在收到请求后的十五日内,或在请求中指定的时间内(以较晚的日期为准),未按指示向委员会提供依法要求的文件副本。除非持证人由于正当理由无法在上述期限内提供文件,理由包括但不限于,由于生病或旅行等客观原因无法在指定的时间内获取医疗记录。本款不适用于无权获取并使用医疗记录的持证人。

(c) 委员会针对持证人展开调查时,持证人拒不配合。本款不得解释为剥夺持证人受《美国宪法第五修正案》保障的任何权利以及任何其他宪法或法定权利。本款不得解释为要求持证人放弃其宪法或法定权利以配合调查,或根据持证人的执业时间限制,要求持证人在不合理的期限内提供信息或遵从其他事项。持证人不得在监管或纪律处分程序中行使任何宪法和法定权利。

(d) 存在以下任一情形,且未在三十日内向委员会报告：

(1) 持证人被指控(或起诉)犯有重罪。

(2) 持证人受到逮捕。

(3) 持证人被定罪,包括任何重罪或轻罪的有罪判决,认罪答辩或不抗辩。

(4) 持证人受到本州或另一个州的其他授权机构或官方、联邦政府或美国军方的机构采取的任何纪律处分。

(e) 法院在发布传票时发出命令,要求持证人向委员会公布记录,而持证人不遵守或拒绝遵守这一命令①。

1399.469.3　针灸委员会致消费者的告知书

(a) 从事针灸实践的执业针灸师须告知每位患者,自己由加利福尼亚州针灸委员会颁发执照并受其监管。该告知书须张贴在持证人提供服务的各个地点。该告知书应包括以下声明和信息:

"消费者告知书

针灸师由加利福尼亚州针灸委员会批准并监管

(916)515-5200

http://www.acupuncture.ca.gov/"

(b) 本条规定的告知书须张贴在针灸师执业场所的显眼位置,以供公众阅览,该告知书须采用48号以上字体。

第7条　针灸公司

1399.470　引用与授权

本条例可引用并称为《针灸公司条例》。

1399.471　职业关系和职责不受影响[已废除]

1399.472　办公备案[已废除]

1399.473　应用[已废除]

1399.474　证书的批准和颁发[已废除]

1399.475　对针灸公司的要求

针灸公司应遵守下列规定:

(a) 公司依据《公司法》组织和存在,是《公司法典》第1卷第3部第4分部所指的专业公司。

(b) 每名股东、董事及管理人员(除《公司法典》第13403条及该《法典》第4977.2条另有规定外)持有有效的针灸执照。针灸师可担任多家针灸公司的股东。

(c) 公司内,每位从事针灸工作的专业人员(不论其是否为董事、管理人员或股东),均需持有有效的针灸证书。

1399.476　铭牌

公司名称以及公司提供专业服务时所使用的任何名称中,应包含表明公司主体的词语或缩写,但仅限下列表述:"Professional Corporation""Prof. Corp.""Corporation""Corp.""Incorporated"或"Inc."。

---

① 注意:引用的机构为《商业和行业法典》第4933节。参考《业务和职业法典》第4928.1和4955节。

1399.477　股份：所有权与转让

（a）如针灸公司有两名或两名以上股东，其中一名股东：

（1）死亡，或

（2）成为《公司法典》第13401(d)条所界定的丧失资格的人员，其股份须按照议定的条款出售并转让给公司、公司股东或其他符合资格的持证人。这种出售或转让不得迟于股东死亡后六个月，也不得迟于股东丧失资格之日后九十日。本条款应在针灸公司的公司章程或附例中列明。

（b）如一个人丧失资格后，再次成为符合条件的股东，那么公司及公司股东可以（但不必）同意售回其售出的股份。

（c）针灸公司的股份证书须附有一份恰当的文字说明，列明(a)款的限制。

（d）本条例的任何规定均不得解释为禁止针灸公司持有非专业公司的股份。

1399.478　信托

对专业公司股份所有权的限制，应同时适用于该等股份的法律所有权和衡平法所有权。

1399.479　公司活动

（a）针灸公司可以执行公司章程或内部规章细则中授权的任何行为，只要该行为不被本条例、《针灸认证法》或根据其制定的条例禁止且不相冲突。

（b）针灸公司可与个体执业、团体执业或与其他针灸公司合作的针灸师签订合作协议。

第8条　继续教育

1399.480　定义

（a）为本条之目的：

（1）"继续教育提供者"系指经委员会批准提供继续教育的个人或组织。

（2）"课程"系指时长至少为一学时的系统学习，旨在掌握与针灸实践相关的知识、技能和信息。

（3）"学时"系指至少五十分钟有组织的学习时间。

1399.481　继续教育提供者的批准标准

（a）希望获批成为继续教育提供者的个人、组织、学校或其他单位，须向委员会提交一份继续教育提供者申请（Rev 5/08）（该申请在此通过引用并入），并连同第1399.462条规定的费用一并提交。提交委员会的所有继续教育提供者申请和文件均应采用英文打印稿。

（b）继续教育提供者获委员会批准后，有效期为两年，到期后可提交所需的申请和费用进行续期。

1399.482　获批的继续教育提供者

（a）为本节之目的，只有个人或组织已提交提供者申请、缴纳相应费用、获得委员会批准及提供者编号，才可以使用"提供者"这一名称。

（b）任何人或组织只可获得一个提供者编号。当两个或两个以上的继续教育提供者共同主办课程时，只能由一个提供者的编号标识该课程，该提供者应负责记录保存、广告宣传、证书颁发、讲师资格以及其他要求。

（c）继续教育提供者须在指定地点将下列记录保存四年：

（1）每门获批课程的课程大纲。

（2）每门获批课程的时间及地点记录。

（3）任课讲师的个人简历。

（4）每门课程的出勤记录（包括参加该课程的针灸师姓名、签字及执照编号）以及给该课程学员颁发证书的记录。

（5）每门获批课程的学员评价表。

（d）继续教育提供者须在获批课程结束后六十日内，向每名完成课程的学员发出一份包含以下信息的结业证书（可打字或印刷）：

（1）继续教育提供者的名称及编号。

（2）课程名称。

（3）学员姓名及其针灸执照编号（如有）。

（4）课程的日期和地点。

（5）已完成的继续教育学时。

（6）要求针灸师自课程完成之日起将证书保留至少四年的声明。

（e）继续教育提供者的组织架构或负责人发生更改（包括姓名、地址或电话号码）后，须在三十日内通知委员会。

（f）继续教育提供者的批准不可转让。

（g）委员会保留旁听或监督任一提供者所开课程的权利及权限。

（h）根据委员会要求，继续教育提供者须向委员会呈交已获批课程的出勤记录（包括参加该课程针灸师的姓名、签字及执照编号）以及学员填写的课程评价表格，以评估课程的质量及有效性。

1399.483　批准继续教育课程

（a）只有继续教育提供者可获批提供继续教育课程。

（b）呈交委员会批准的所有继续教育课程的相关内容，须与针灸和亚洲医学实践有关，并应属以下两类：

（1）一类课程是关于临床事务或向患者提供实际医疗服务的课程。例如，一类课程包括但不限于以下课程：

（A）针灸及亚洲医学。

（B）西方生物医学及生物科学。

（C）对患者护理、社区或公共卫生或预防医学的质量有直接影响的科学或临床内容。

（D）有关法律、道德及卫生设施标准的课程。

（E）旨在培养持证人患者教育技巧的课程，包括但不限于治疗性运动技巧、营养咨询和生物力学方面的患者教育。

（F）旨在提高持证人与其他执业医师有效沟通能力的课程。

（G）针灸在个人和公众健康方面（例如紧急情况及灾害）如何发挥作用的课程。

（H）行为科学、患者咨询和患者管理及动机方面的课程，此类课程旨在改善患者健康状况。

（I）与针灸及亚洲医学有关的研究及循证医学。

（2）二类课程是与临床事项或实际医疗服务无关的课程，包括但不限于：

（A）与临床事项及直接患者护理无关的实践管理课程，包括但不限于行政档案管理、与临床医学无关的法律法规、保险报销与记录、业务组织与管理等。

（B）呼吸及其他功法，如气功及太极拳（有益于持证人而非患者）。

（C）提供者应对其开设的每门课程提供一种评价途径，供学员对以下内容进行评价：

（Ⅰ）该课程达到其所述教学目标的程度。

（Ⅱ）教师对该课程了解的充分程度。

（Ⅲ）相应教学方法的运用程度。

（Ⅳ）课程资料的适用性或实用性。

（Ⅴ）其他相关意见。

（c）通过个人独立学习或居家学习的方式修毕的课程，不得超过所需继续教育学时的50%。

（1）需要实践或实操技术的课程，不得批准独立或居家学习。

（2）获批可独立或在家学习的课程，应包括持证人在完成课程后进行的自我评估，以测试学员对课程材料的掌握程度。

（d）提供者不得在课程进行期间销售、宣传或推广任何品牌产品或服务。提供者应确保客观选择和展示关于品牌产品或服务的信息，包括其有利和不利信息，并客观阐述关于产品、竞品、替代疗法或服务的主要信息。提供者应确保在宣传过程中，通过书面形式向观众披露所讨论的任何品牌产品或服务与提供者之间的关系，或任何此类产品或服务与个人讲师、主讲人、讨论小组成员或讨论主持人之间的关系。然而，只要提供者让所有学员知悉，其没有义务留下来参加产品演示或购买任何产品，那么提供者则可以在课程结束后提供销售产品或服务。本款中的任何内容不得解释为限制提供者在课程中讨论非商标产品。

1399.484　课程批准申请书

（a）未经委员会事先批准，提供者不得提供继续教育学时的课程。为获得课程批准，提供者须在课程首次开办前至少四十五日，向委员会提交一份英文的课程批准申请，即"继续教育课程批准申请表"（Rev.5/08），该表格在此通过引用并入。

（b）如需重复开设先前获批的课程，提供者须在课程开始前至少三十日，以书面形式通知委员会新的开课日期及地点。

（c）如提供者对已获批课程的日期或地点做出任何更改，须通知委员会。更改后的日期不得早于最初批准的日期。

（d）如获批课程被延后，提供者须在四十八小时内将课程日期通知委员会。提供者须书面通知委员会延期课程的新日期及地点。若在原定课程日期的三个月内，未教授延后课程，提供者须重新申请批准。

（e）如获批课程的内容或讲师有任何更改，须在课程开始前至少四十五日提出新的课程申请。

1399.485　讲师

（a）各提供者有责任聘用合格的讲师。

(b)教授获批继续教育课程的讲师,须至少具备以下资格:
(1)针灸讲师,应
(A)持有现行有效的针灸执照,或根据《法典》第4949条授权为客座针灸师。"现行有效的执照"是指未被委员会撤销、吊销、列入察看期、非强制注销或以其他方式受到处分的执照,以及
(B)对该课程的主题内容具备丰富、前沿且熟练的学识,依据为:
1. 持有学院或大学学士学位或更高学位,以及具备相关经验的书面证明;或
2. 在该课程前的五年内,具备两年以上教授类似课程内容的经验;或
3. 过去五年内,在其任教的专业领域有两年以上工作经验。
(2)非针灸讲师,须
(A)在其专业领域获得现行执照或证书。
(B)出示专业培训的书面证明,包括但不限于特定学科领域的培训证书或高级学位。
(C)过去五年内,在其所任教的专业领域有两年以上的教学经验。

1399.486 广告

(a)继续教育提供者传播的信息应真实、无误导性,并包括以下内容:
(1)课程名称应反映课程内容,不得包含营销性质的语言。
(2)清晰简明的课程内容和/或目标描述。
(3)该课程是否被批准为一类或二类课程。
(4)课程日期和授课地点。
(5)提供者的名称、编号、电话号码。
(6)声明"本课程经加利福尼亚州针灸委员会批准,提供者编号____,为期____学时的____类继续教育"。
(7)提供者针对缺勤、取消课程情况的退款政策。
(8)课程结束后,对售出的所有课程进行书面披露。
(b)提供者在收到委员会的书面确认前,不得声称其课程已获委员会批准。如提供者正在等待委员会的批准决定,可在广告中表明其课程处于待批准状态。如提供者表明其课程处在待批准状态,而委员会随后拒绝批准该课程,则提供者应承担全部责任。

1399.487 拒绝、撤回和请求批准

(a)委员会可驳回提供者申请,或撤回对提供者的批准,包括但不限于下列事由:
(1)提供者或申请人被判与提供者或持证人的执业活动实质相关的罪。
(2)提供者或申请人未遵守《商业与职业法典》第2部第12章或《加利福尼亚州法规》第16卷第13.7部的条文。
(3)委员会撤销、吊销或非强制注销提供者或申请人执照,或将其执照列入察看期以及给予其他纪律处分。
(4)如针对申请人执照的行政诉讼还未判决,委员会可暂停该申请的审查和批准。
(b)在需提交至委员会的信息中,如提供者或申请人对事实做出重大谎报,即构成撤回或驳回申请的理由。

（c）在向提供者发出书面通知说明撤销理由，并给予其合理机会向委员会或委员会指定人员陈词后，委员会可撤销对提供者或课程的批准。

（d）如委员会驳回提供者或课程申请，申请人可向委员会递交上诉书说明上诉理由，并提出上诉。上诉书须在委员会驳回申请通知发出后十日内由委员会备案。该上诉须由委员会或其指定人员进一步商议。如委员会或其指定人员于课程开始日期后方批准其上诉，则委员会将认可该提供者持证人已完成课程的继续教育学时。

1399.488　提供者和课程申请适用的处理时间

（a）委员会应在收到完整申请和所需费用后三十日内，通知申请提供者该申请是否获批。

（b）委员会应在收到完整申请及所有必要的信息及文件后三十日内，通知课程申请提供者该课程是否获批。

（c）如申请提供者在提交初始提供者申请时一并提交课程申请，则提供者申请获批前，课程申请不得视作获批。在这种情况下，委员会处理课程申请的时间应遵照第 1399.488（b）节的规定。

1399.489　继续教育合规

（a）除持有非执业状态执照的人员，持证人对颁发时间不足两年的初始执照进行续期时，应完成以下经委员会批准的继续教育学时：

初始执照继续教育所需学时：

13—16 个月，三十五

17—20 个月，四十

21—23 个月，四十五

此后，作为续期的条件，所有持证人应每两年完成五十学时的继续教育。每两年的继续教育中，二类课程不得超过五学时。

（b）持证人每两年的继续教育所需学时中，独立或居家学习课程只得占 50%。

（c）在执照续期时，每名持证人应签署一份声明，说明其是否遵从继续教育规定，该声明须遵循伪证相关的法律条款。任何持证人虚报所需继续教育的完成情况，应构成违反职业道德的行为。

（d）委员会可对按照继续教育要求报告的持证人进行随机审查。

（e）被选中接受审查的持证人应提交其参加和完成的继续教育课程文件或记录。

（f）每位持证人应将其参加过的所有继续教育计划的记录保留至少四年，记录中应注明提供者的名称、课程或计划名称、课程日期、课程地点以及已获得的继续教育学时。

（g）对于获批的继续教育课程的授课讲师，每完成一节课堂教学，可获得一学时的继续教育学分，无论讲授多少学时或课程，每年最多可获得六学时的继续教育学分。参加获批课程的专题讨论时，参加人员无法获得与相应类别课程专题讨论实际时间相同的继续教育学时。

（h）参与职业分析发展、考试发展会议、项目审查会议或及格讲习班的持证人，每参加上述活动两小时，应获得一继续教育学时。

1399.489.1　非执业状态执照

（a）任何未积极从事针灸实践的持证人，如希望根据《法典》第 2 部第 1 章第 9 节（第 700 条以下）的规定取得非执业执照，或将非执业状态执照恢复为执业状态，应提交一份完整的"执业/非执业执照申请"（参考 5/08），该申请在此通过引用并入。申请人无须将其证书或证书副本连同申请书一并呈交委员会。

（b）要将非执业执照恢复为执业状态，持证人应按照本条规定在过去两年内完成至少五十学时获批的继续教育。其中，至少四十五学时的继续教育须为获批的一类课程。如执照有效期少于一年，则需至少接受二十五学时的继续教育，其中至少二十二学时的课程须为获批的一类课程。

（c）持证人的执照处于非执业状态时，委员会依然有权根据法律规定给予持证人纪律处分，或维持其纪律处分，或根据任何此类规定下达吊销或撤销其执照的命令，或给予其他纪律处分。

1399.489.2　继续教育：实践管理和医学伦理课程

科罗拉多州

科罗拉多州针灸法[①]

第 12-200-101 条　立法说明

传统的西医实践并不包含针灸服务,本法旨在使公民能够合法获得针灸服务。公民在寻求针灸服务时,可获得确切信息,以便在知情的情况下做出选择。此外,根据全体大会目的,针灸服务提供者或医师不得提供虚假资格,损害患者利益,以不良方式执业,或以其他方式欺骗保险公司或接受针灸服务的患者。

第 12-200-102 条　一般规定的适用性

第 12 章第 1、20 和 30 节规定适用于本第 200 节。

第 12-200-103 条　定义

除文意另有所指外,下列定义适用于本第 200 节:

(1)"针灸"系指一种基于传统和现代东方医学理念,采用东方医学诊断、治疗和辅助治疗方法,旨在促进、维持和恢复健康并预防疾病的卫生保健体系。

(2)"针灸师"系指有偿或公开提供针灸服务的人。

(3)"客座针灸师"系指该针灸师:

(a) 在另一司法管辖区内获取执照、完成注册、得到认证或受其监管。

(b) 三个月内,在本州从事指导或教学活动不超过七日。

(c) 在一名科罗拉多州执业针灸师或执业脊椎按摩师的直接监督下,从事指导或教学活动。

(4)"注射疗法"系指采用主要用于治疗肌肉骨骼疼痛的皮下注射针,将无菌草药、维生素、矿物药、顺势疗法药物或其他类似的非静脉注射药注射到穴位。获批的药物包括生理盐水、葡萄糖、利多卡因、普鲁卡因、东方草药、维生素 B_{12}、顺势止痛软膏[②]、沙拉平[③]和顺势疗

[①] 根据《科罗拉多州法典》第 12 章第 200 节(*Colorado Revised Statutes* Annotated, Title 12. Professions and Occupations, Health Care Professions and Occupations, Article 200. Acupuncturists)译出。

[②] 顺势疗法的一种止痛药物,包括颠茄、山金车、圣约翰草和紫锥花成分。

[③] 沙拉平(sarapin)是一种猪笼草提取物,主要用于注射治疗脊椎病变。

法药物。"注射疗法"包括根据患者护理和安全需要使用肾上腺素和氧气,且需要妥善应对注射药物的过敏反应风险。

(5)(a)"针灸实践"系指进针和出针、注射疗法、应用于人体特定区域的热疗以及辅助疗法。针灸范围内的辅助疗法包括手法治疗、器械治疗、温针治疗、电针治疗以及电磁治疗,治疗性运动建议,以及在遵守联邦法律的前提下提供草药和膳食指导。"针灸实践"基于传统和现代东方医学理念,不包括使用西方医学诊断检测和程序,如磁共振成像、X线片、计算机断层扫描(CT)和超声检查。

(b)除特别规定外,第200节条款均未授权针灸师进行医疗实践、手术、脊柱矫正、脊柱推拿、脊柱松动术以及任何其他形式的治疗。

第12-200-104条　注射疗法-培训-药物-规则

(1)根据主管规定,持证人在实施注射疗法前应接受必要的培训。

(2)尽管第12-280-305条另有规定,接受过必要的注射疗法培训的持证人可从已注册的处方药销售点、制造商或批发商处获取用于注射疗法的药物。如机构根据本章规定向持证人提供任何药物,并信任持证人所提供的执照信息,则不对提供药物承担责任。

(3)主管应颁布实施本条的细则,包括持证人实施注射治疗所需的必要培训,以及持证人可获得的用于注射疗法的药物清单。主管在颁布细则时应咨询有经验的医学专业人士和药剂师。

第12-200-105条　强制向患者披露信息-保留披露记录

(1)每名针灸师在与患者初次接触时应当以书面形式提供以下信息:

(a)针灸师的姓名、营业地址和业务电话号码。

(b)费用表。

(c)关于以下内容的声明:(Ⅰ)患者有权获取关于治疗方法、所用技术和疗程的已知信息;(Ⅱ)患者可以寻求其他卫生保健专业人员的不同意见或随时终止治疗;(Ⅲ)在职业关系中,不宜发生性亲密行为,如有此类行为应报告主管。

(d)针灸师的信息清单,包括针灸师的学历、经验、学位、专业组织成员资格(至少三分之一的成员为本第200节规定的持证人员)、该组织颁发的与针灸有关的证书或证件、获得学位或证件所需时间及经验。

(e)关于以下内容的声明:由地方、州或国家卫生局颁发给针灸师的执照、证书或与针灸或其他卫生保健行业相关的注册文件,并说明此类执照、证书或注册文书是否被吊销或撤销。

(f)关于以下内容的声明:针灸师遵守由公共卫生和环境部就第200节颁布的规定,包括针灸实践中所用针灸针的正确清洁和消毒方式以及针灸诊所卫生情况的相关规定。

(g)关于以下内容的声明:针灸实践由美国司法部监管,并注明监管机构以及主管的地址和电话。

(h)关于以下内容的声明:在推荐和应用根据传统东方医学概念界定的辅助疗法和草药方面,针灸师的相关培训及经验。

(2)若本条第(1)(a)至(1)(f)项所要求的信息出现任何变更,均应在变更后五日内进行强制披露。

(3)针灸师应保留本条第(1)款所规定书面信息的副本,该副本应注明日期并由患者签字。从初步评估至治疗终止后至少保留三年。

第12-200-106条 部门颁发执照要求-年费-披露要求

(1)每名针灸师应以主管规定的格式向部门申请执照。该申请应包括第12-200-105条第(1)(a)及(1)(d)至(1)(g)项所述的信息,还应包括对于下述行为的披露:根据第200节规定,构成对执业针灸师采取纪律处分的行为。

(2)若本条第(1)款的规定有所变更,应在变更后三十日内,以主管规定的格式向部门报告。

(3)为满足获取执照的资格,针灸师应:

(a)顺利完成符合主管审批标准的针灸师课程,课程标准可由专业组织协助建立,该组织至少三分之一的成员为第200节规定的持证人员;或

(b)符合教育、经验或培训的相关资格[类似于第(3)(a)款规定],按照主管要求的格式准备证明文件并得到主管认可后,可代替教育课程。

(4)每名执照申请人应支付由主管根据第12-20-105条规定的颁发、续期和恢复执照的费用。根据第200节颁发的执照应遵从第12-20-202(1)和(2)款执照续期、到期、恢复和逾期费的相关规定。执照到期者应遵从第200节或第12-20-202(1)款的处罚规定。

(5)如针灸师涉及针灸实践渎职行为及不当行为,均应向主管报告关于该行为的判决、行政诉讼、判决及诉讼的和解及处置条款,无论此类诉讼或判决是否发生在科罗拉多州或任何其他司法管辖区。针灸师应当在判决或诉讼后三十日内或申请及恢复执照时(以较早者为准)提交报告。

(6)作为获取执照的条件,每名针灸师应向获授权在本州开展业务的保险公司购买并保有商业职业责任险,最低赔偿金额如下:

(a)个人独资企业或普通合伙企业,每次事故赔偿金额为五万美元,每年赔偿金额为五万美元。

(b)有限责任公司或股份有限公司,每次事故赔偿金额为三十万美元,每年赔偿金额为三十万美元。

第12-200-107条 通过背书方式颁发执照-规则-定义

(1)若申请人向主管提供充分证据,证明其通过背书方式申请执照时,持有与第200节申请执照及资格基本同等的执照及资格,且根据其他司法管辖区法律,该申请人信誉良好,则主管应通过背书方式向其颁发执照,允许其在本州从事针灸实践。

(2)主管应按照规定指明何为本章所称的"基本同等的执照及资格"。

(3)为本章之目的,"信誉良好"系指执照未被撤销或吊销,或者无纪律处分或不良行为。

第12-200-108条 违法行为-例外情况-定义

(1)第200节的规定均不得干涉,或被解释为干涉或阻止任何其他持证卫生保健专业人员在其执业范围内从事第12章规定的执业活动。

(2)(a)任何人在未持有经本部门备案的现行有效的执照的情况下从事针灸实践均属违法行为,除非该针灸师根据第12-240-107(3)(Ⅰ)条的规定执业,或符合本条第(3)款

的要求。

(b) 以下情形均属违法行为：

(Ⅰ) 未持证则从事针灸实践；或

(Ⅱ) 使用"执业针灸师""注册针灸师"或"针灸专科医师"头衔，或使用"L.Ac""R.Ac"或"Dipl.Ac"称号，除非该针灸师根据第 12－240－107(3)款规定进行执业。

(3) 尽管本条有相反规定，接受培训的人员可在部门尚未颁发现行有效执照的情况下从事针灸实践，该实践须在真实的培训计划过程中进行，并受到执业针灸师的现场直接监督。执业针灸师应对所有此类行为和服务负责，如本人所为。

(4)(a) 尽管第 200 节中有相反规定，如精神卫生保健专业人员提供证明文件，证明其已接受本条第(4)(d)款规定的耳穴针灸戒毒培训，则该精神卫生保健专业人员可在当前执业范围内从事耳穴针灸戒毒，该精神卫生保健专业人员应符合如下条件：

(Ⅰ) 根据第 12 章第 245 节获得执照。

(Ⅱ) 根据第 12 章第 245 节第 8 条获得三级成瘾咨询师认证。

(Ⅲ) 根据第 245 节第 7 条注册为心理治疗师。

(b) 根据本条第(4)款进行耳穴针灸戒毒疗法的精神卫生保健专业人员不得使用"针灸师"头衔，也不得声称自己有资格开展除本条第(4)款以外的针灸治疗。

(c) 在本条第(4)款中，"耳穴针灸戒毒"系指在预先确定的以下五个部位皮下插入无菌一次性针灸针，双侧位置保持一致：

(Ⅰ) 交感 AH6a。

(Ⅱ) 神门 HT7。

(Ⅲ) 肾 BL23。

(Ⅳ) 肝 BL18。

(Ⅴ) 肺 BL13。

(d) 希望根据第(4)款从事耳穴针灸戒毒的精神卫生保健专业人员，须顺利完成培训计划，培训内容为用耳穴针灸戒毒治疗药物滥用，该培训计划应达到或超过国家针灸戒毒协会或经主管批准的其他组织制定的培训标准。

第 12－200－109 条　纪律处分的理由

(1) 如针灸师有下列行为之一，主管可根据第 12－20－403、12－20－404 和 24－4－105 条拒绝向针灸师颁发执照或对针灸师采取纪律处分：

(a) 违反第 12－200－108 条的规定。

(b) 未能提供第 12－200－105 条要求的强制性披露，或在披露中向患者提供虚假、欺骗性或误导性信息。

(c) 未能提供第 12－200－106(1)款要求的信息，或向部门提供虚假、欺骗性或误导性信息。

(d) 实施或宣称即将实施第 18－13－119 条禁止的健康保险滥用的行为或 10－1－128 条界定的骗保行为。

(e) 患者的病情超出针灸师的培训、经验或能力范围，而未能将患者转诊至合适的医师。

（f）为转诊患者至其他专业人士而收取佣金、回扣或其他形式的报酬。

（g）为转诊患者开出或给予佣金、回扣或其他形式的报酬；除此之外，尽管第(1)(g)款另有规定，针灸师可为独立广告代理人或营销代理人提供的广告或营销服务支付报酬，包括按患者数计算的绩效工资。

（h）未能遵守、配合，或教唆他人不遵守第200节的规定或公共卫生和环境部行政主管通过的法律条例，包括针灸针正确清洁和消毒方式、针灸诊所卫生规范、公共卫生和环境部及法院的任何合法命令。

（i）未能遵守、配合，或教唆他人不遵守第200节的要求或任何主管制定的针灸实践法律条例、第12章第20或30节的适用条款，或主管和法院的合法命令。

（j）自患者评估至治疗终止，与患者发生第18-3401条所界定的性接触、性侵犯和性侵入行为。

（k）违反或未能遵守类似医师在相同或类似情况下的最低护理标准，无论其是否对患者造成实际伤害。

（Ⅰ）未能将身体疾病、身体状况、行为及精神健康或药物滥用的情况通知主管，从而影响其在保证患者安全的情况下采取合理手段为患者提供针灸服务。

（Ⅱ）未能在身体疾病、身体状况、行为及精神健康或药物滥用造成的限制内行动，导致其无法在保证患者安全的情况下采取合理手段为患者提供针灸服务；或

（Ⅲ）未能遵守保密协议中约定的限制。

（l）根据第18-18-102(5)条的规定，在滥用、习惯性或过度使用酒精、成瘾药物或管制药物的情况下继续从事针灸实践。

（m）被判犯有重罪、对重罪作认罪答辩或不抗辩。

（n）直接或间接发布或传播任何与针灸或针灸师的实践、能力、服务、方法或资格相关的具有欺诈性、虚假性、欺骗性或误导性的声明或陈述。

（2）主管可接受另一司法管辖区对针灸执照或其他执业授权采取纪律处分的证据，作为犯有本条第(1)款所列行为的初步证据，但受到该纪律处分的行为须与本条第(1)款所列行为或做法基本相似。

第12-200-110条　纪律处分和程序

（1）主管有合理理由相信持证人已实施第12-200-109(1)款所禁止的行为时，可以对其启动纪律处分程序。

（2）纪律处分应包括以下内容：

（a）吊销或撤销执照。

（b）将持证人列入察看期，并设定察看期条款。

（c）根据第12-20-404(4)款规定，通过普通邮件向持证人发送警告信。

（3）根据第12-20-404(5)款规定，主管可向持证人发送保密信件。

（4）在调查期间至驳回投诉或听证通知书及指控通知送达持证人之前，主管存档的投诉记录及调查结果不得公开查阅。主管的记录和文件应遵守第24-72-203、24-72-204条规定。

(5)根据第12-20-405条规定的情形和程序,主管可以发布停止令。

第12-200-111条 未经授权的行为-处罚

(1)未持有根据第200节颁发的执业状态执照,而从事、提供或试图从事针灸实践,将根据第12-20-407(1)(a)项进行处罚。

(2)违反第12-200-109(1)(j)项规定,在护理期间与患者进行性接触,即属一级轻罪,应当移交刑事诉讼。

(3)违反第12-200-109(1)(j)项规定,在护理期间对患者进行性侵犯或性侵入,即属4级重罪,应当被移交刑事诉讼。

第12-200-112条 限制服务的保密协议

(1)除本条第(2)款规定的情形外,第12-30-108条限制执业的保密协议适用于第200节的规定。

(2)本条和第12-30-108条不适用于根据第12-200-109(1)(m)条受到纪律处分的持证人。

第12-200-113条 民事处罚

(1)如针灸师对接受针灸服务的患者实施第12-200-109(1)条禁止的行为,由于未按照合同要求提供针灸服务,该针灸师不得对患者提起违约诉讼。

(2)如患者、患者保险人、患者的法定监护人或代表已向针灸师支付针灸服务费,而针灸师对患者实施第12-200-109(1)条所禁止的行为,无论患者是否知悉该行为属于非法,患者、患者保险人或患者的法定监护人可通过法律诉讼追回用于支付针灸服务的所有费用及合理的律师费。

(3)第200节规定的刑事和民事处罚具有累积性而非排他性,是对患者依法享有的其他诉讼理由、权利、救济的补充。

第12-200-114条 主管-权力和职责-条例

(1)除第200节授予的其他权力和职责外,主管具有以下权力和职责:

(a)根据第12-20-204条通过的条例。

(b)接受或拒绝执照申请,收取第200节审定的执照年费。

(c)根据投诉内容,检查提供针灸服务的场所,以确保其符合第200节规定和据此通过的条例。

(d)根据需要,委托公共卫生和环境部或其他部门提供相应服务,对针具的正确清洁、消毒以及针灸诊室卫生情况进行检查。

(e)根据第12-20-403条的规定,如主管收到投诉,并有合理理由认为持证人违反第200节的规定,可对该投诉开展调查、举行听证会并取证。

(f)为执行第200节的规定,举行其他必要的会议或听证会。

(g)在向监管机构拨款的情况下,通过监管机构雇佣全职或兼职的行政法官举行第200节要求的听证会。

(h)为执行第12-20-406条发布的禁令,禁止任何人实施第200节所禁止的行为。

(i)如主管有合理理由认为针灸师患有身体或精神疾病,致使针灸师无法在保证患者安全的情况下采用适当方法治疗患者,可能危及患者的健康或安全,主管可责令对其进行身体或精神检查;也可要求患者进行检查,以确定是否已经对患者造成实际伤害。

(j)根据适用的联邦法律法规,向美国卫生和公众服务部报告针对针灸执照采取的不利措施。

第 12-200-115 条　公共卫生和环境部行政主管的权力和职责-规则

公共卫生和环境部行政主管应就针灸实践中所用针具的正确清洁、消毒方式以及针灸诊所卫生情况颁布相关条例。

第 12-200-116 条　保险范围-不受影响

第 200 节的内容不得解释为影响与针灸保险和保险范围相关的现行或未来法律规定、合同及协议。

第 12-200-117 条　法案范围

第 200 节的规定不适用于根据本第 12 章以其他形式获得科罗拉多州执照,并在其执照范围内提供针灸服务的人员。其意图不是,也不得解释为针灸实践构成第 12 章第 240 节"科罗拉多州医疗实践法案"范围内的医学实践。

第 12-200-118 条　条款的废止-职能的审查

自 2022 年 9 月 1 日起废止第 200 节。在废止之前,根据第 24-34-104 条的规定,对主管颁发执照的职能进行审查。

科罗拉多州针灸行政法[①]

第 1 条　执照颁发要求

本条的目的是根据 C.R.S.[②]第 12-200-106(3)和 12-20-202(4)款的规定,确立针灸执照的资格。

A. 为取得执照资格,第 12-200-106(3)款规定申请人须顺利完成经专业和职业部(Division of Professions and Occupations)主管批准的符合标准的教育计划,或提供与此类教育计划基本相似的资格文件。主管批准的教育计划包括任何针灸及东方医学教育审核委员会(ACAOM)或其继受机构认可的针灸和东方医学文凭课程。

B. 为满足第 12-200-106(3)款规定的执照要求,主管要求申请人在首次申请执照时,须持有国家针灸与东方医学审核委员会(NCCAOM)或其继受机构提供的现行证书。申请人须按主管规定的方式,就现行证书提供证明。

C. 根据 C.R.S.第 12-20-202(4)款所列,在军事服务中获得相关教育、培训或服务经历,如需获得认可并将其用于获取执照,须由主管确定其与接受申请时适用的资格基本同

---

① 根据《科罗拉多州行政法规》第 700 卷第 738 章(Colorado Administrative Code, Title 700. Department of Regulatory Agencies, 738. Office of Acupuncture Licensure, 4 CCR 738-1, Acupuncture Licensure Rules and Regulations)译出。

② 指 Colorado Revised Statutes。

等。申请人有责任及时提供完整的证据,以供审查和考虑。该类有关教育、培训或服务的证明,如符合要求,将逐一进行评估。

第2条 通过背书方式颁发执照

本条的目的是根据 C.R.S.第 12-200-107(2)款的规定,通过背书方式确定与针灸执照基本同等的资格。

A. 申请人如需根据第 12-200-107(2)款取得"实基本同等的认证及资格",主管须要求申请人提交由 NCCAOM 或其继受机构出具的证书。该证书的认证应以主管规定的方式由 NCCAOM 或继受机构直接提供。

B. 应以主管规定的方式对另一州的执照进行核查。

第3条 恢复执照要求

本条的目的是根据 C.R.S.第 12-200-106(4)款规定,陈述恢复到期执照的要求。

A. 申请人希望恢复到期执照的,应填写一份恢复申请,缴纳恢复费用,并证明已按照法律规定的金额缴纳医疗事故保险。

B. 如执照自收到恢复申请之日起已到期两年以上,但少于五年,申请人须根据 C.R.S.第 12-20-202(2)(c)(Ⅱ)目及 C.R.S.第 12-20-105 条规定,通过证明以下事项之一,证明其具备执业能力:

1. 在申请恢复执照之日起前五年内,有来自其他州的信誉良好的执照,以及在该州积极执业两年的证明。

2. 在申请恢复执照前的两年内,完成与针灸实践相关的三十学时继续教育课程。继续教育课程必须获得主管的批准,并以主管规定的方式予以证明。

3. NCCAOM 或其继受机构出具的有效认证。

4. 以主管批准的任何其他方式证明其执业能力。

C. 申请恢复已到期超过五年执照的申请人,须按 C.R.S.第 12-20-202(2)(c)(Ⅱ)目的规定,通过证明以下事项之一,证明其具备执业能力:

1. 从申请恢复执照之日起的前五年内,在其他州有信誉良好的执照,并有在该州积极执业两年的证明。

2. 从事不少于六个月的受监督的实践,但须受主管所订条款规限。

3. 以主管批准的任何其他方式证明其执业能力。

第4条 无证人士参加针灸培训计划

本条的目的是确定在何种情况和条件下,学员不具备根据 C.R.S.第 12-200-108(3)款规定的在专业和职业部门存档的现行有效执照,仍可以从事针灸实践。

A. 如在真实的培训计划中从事针灸实践,则无需专业和职业部门颁发的现行有效执照,学员即可开展针灸治疗。真实有效的培训计划是指在经认证的针灸学校开展的培训或学徒计划。

B. 学员须受持有有效且无限制的科罗拉多州针灸执照的针灸师监督。

C. C.R.S.第 12-200-108(3)款要求针灸导师对学员提供直接、现场监督。直接监督,系指在该等学员的执业场所和同一建筑物内对其进行监督。

D. 学员可从事 C.R.S.第 12-200-103(5)(a)项所界定的全部范围的针灸实践。

E. 在培训计划中,针灸导师负责保存详述真实培训计划起止日期的文件,并确保针灸导师保存所有学员的姓名和当前地址,按照主管或其指定人员的要求随时准备接受检查。

第5条　头衔使用和限制

本条的目的是明确"执业针灸师"和"资深针灸从业者"头衔用法,以及根据 C.R.S.第 12-200-108(2)(b)(Ⅱ)目,"L.Ac."或"Dipl.Ac."称呼的用法。

A. 取得针灸执照并不自动授予持证人使用"Dr."或"博士"头衔的权利。

B. 执业针灸师只有在实际获得针灸或东方医学学术/教育机构授予的博士学位和满足 C.R.S.第 6-1-707 条的要求时才可以使用"博士"或"Dr."的头衔。

C. 如持证人符合使用"博士"或"Dr."头衔的资格,针灸师只有在附有"针灸博士"或字母"D.Ac.""东方医学博士"或"OMD""针灸和东方医学博士"或"D.Ac.OM""中医博士"或"DTCM""针灸与东方医学博士"或"DAOM"等字样,或获主管认可和批准的任何其他博士学位时,方可使用"博士"或"Dr."的头衔。

第6条　宣告令

本条的目的是制定相关程序,以处理根据《科罗拉多州行政程序法》C.R.S.第 24-4-105(11)款提交的宣告令的请求。

A. 任何人或机构可向主管呈请宣告令,要求就任何法定条文或主管的任何规则或命令的适用性终止争议或消除不确定性。

B. 主管可酌情决定是否就该呈请做出裁定,而无须通知呈请人。如主管决定不就该呈请做出裁定,主管须立即将其行动通知呈请人,并说明做出决定的理由。

C. 在决定是否对根据本条提出的呈请作出裁定时,主管将审议下列事项:

1. 在任何法定条文或主管的任何规则或命令的适用性方面,对该呈请做出的裁定是否会终止其争议或消除其不确定性。

2. 呈请是否涉及任何主题、问题或事件,该主题、问题或事件当前正由主管或法院审理,涉及一个或多个呈请人的正式或非正式事项或调查的主题。

3. 呈请是否涉及当前正由主管或法院审理,但并不涉及任何呈请人的正式或非正式事项或调查的主题、问题或事件。

4. 呈请是寻求就尚待讨论的或假设的问题做出裁定,还是将产生一项建议性的裁决或意见。

5. 除根据《科罗拉多州民事诉讼程序规则》57 条提出宣告性救济诉讼外,呈请人是否有其他适当的法律救济,在所涉法令、规则或命令对呈请人的适用性方面,这些法律救济将终止其争议或消除其不确定性。

D. 任何根据本条提出的呈请,须列明下列事项:

1. 呈请人的姓名和地址以及申请人是否根据第 12 章第 200 节取得执照。

2. 与呈请有关的法规、规则或命令。

3. 简明陈述所有必要的事实,以表明争议或不确定性的性质,以及所述法规、规则或命令适用于或可能适用于呈请人的方式。

E. 如主管决定就呈请作出裁定,则适用下列程序:

1. 主管可根据呈请书中陈述的事实,就呈请做出裁定。在该种情况下:

a. 主管的任何裁定的适用范围限于呈请书所陈述的事实以及对呈请书的任何修改。

b. 主管可命令呈请人提交一份书面简介、备忘录或立场声明。

c. 主管可在向呈请人发出适当通知后,将呈请定为非证据性听证。

d. 主管可仅根据呈请书中所列事项处理该呈请。

e. 主管可要求呈请人以书面形式提交补充事实。在这种情况下,这些补充事实将视为对呈请书的修改。

f. 主管可根据《科罗拉多州行政程序法》C.R.S.第24-4-105(8)款就相关事实发出行政通知,并可利用主管的经验、技术能力及专业知识处理呈请。

2. 如主管在不举行听证的情况下就呈请做出裁定,主管应迅速将其决定通知呈请人。

3. 为获得补充事实或信息,或确定呈请中所述任何事实的真实性,或听取对呈请的口头辩论,主管在向呈请人发出适当通知后,可酌情决定安排听证会。应在向呈请人发出的听证会通知中,列明已知范围内主管拟调查的事实或其他事宜。

为进行上述听证,在必要范围内,呈请人负有举证责任,以证明呈请书中所述的所有事实;表明争议或不确定性的性质的所有必要事实;以及有关法规、规则或命令对呈请人适用或可能适用的方式,以及呈请人希望主管考虑的任何其他事实。

F. 根据本规则进行的任何法律程序的当事人应为主管和呈请人。任何其他人可寻求主管批准介入该等法律程序,主管可酌情决定是否准许介入。申请介入的事项应与本条 D 款规定的事项相同。本条中"呈请人"也指获得主管批准介入的任何人。

G. 任何根据本条处理呈请的宣告令或其他命令,应构成根据《科罗拉多州行政程序法》C.R.S.第24-4-106条进行司法审查的机关行为。

第7条 报告定罪、判决及行政程序

本条的目的是明确定罪和其他不利诉讼的程序,包括根据 C.R.S.第12-200-105条、第12-200-106条和第12-200-109条作出的判决和行政程序。

根据 C.R.S.第12-29.5-102条定义的持证人应以主管规定的方式,在下述任何事件发生后三十日内通知主管:

A. 根据任何州或美国的法律,持证人被判犯有重罪,即违反 C.R.S.第12-200-109(1)(n)项的规定。有罪判决、认罪答辩或不抗辩答辩都将视为有罪。

B. 授予针灸执照的其他司法管辖区对持证人施加纪律处分,而该等违纪行为已违反 C.R.S.第12-200-109条的规定,处分包括但不限于传票、制裁、缓刑、民事处罚或拒绝颁发、吊销、撤销或更改执照,无论是以同意令、命令或其他决议对执照施加的处分,而如未能在到期日前缴纳执照费或未能满足继续专业教育要求除外。

C. 其他州委员会、市、联邦或州政府机构颁发的任何与医疗服务有关的执照被撤销或吊销,但 C.R.S.第12-200-109条所述的失效针灸执照除外。

D. 因针灸医疗事故而对持证人作出民事诉讼或仲裁的判决(judgement)、裁决(award)或和解(settlement),并获最终判决或达成和解。

E. 向主管发出的通知应包含以下资料:

1. 如该事件系政府机构提起的诉讼(如上所述),则持证人需提供该机构的名称、管辖权、案件名称、法院记录、法律程序或案件编号,以及同意令、命令或决议的副本。

2. 如该事件属重罪定罪,则持证人需提供法院名称及其司法管辖权范围、案件名称及编号、事件描述或起诉书或指控的副本,以及法院作出的任何陈述与裁决。持证人须向主管提供一份刑罚与判决实施的副本(无论是延期的还是立即的),其中包括重罪定罪以及诉讼发生三十日内该等刑罚或判决的所有条款的完成情况。

3. 如该事件涉及民事诉讼或仲裁程序,持证人需提供法院名称或仲裁人、司法管辖权、案件名称、案件编号、法庭记录、事件描述或起诉书副本、判决书副本以及法院或仲裁决定,如已达成和解,需提供和解协议和法院的撤诉令。

F. 持证人通知主管时可提交一份书面声明,与通知一并纳入执照记录。

第8条 已废除

第9条 自我报告某些医疗状况的义务

A. 如持证人的身体或精神疾病或状况影响其以合理技巧和安全方式提供针灸服务的能力,则持证人须在出现此状况的三十日内,以书面形式向主管提供下列资料:

1. 疾病或状况的诊断和描述。

2. 首次诊断疾病或状况的日期。

3. 现任治疗师的姓名,以及由现任治疗师开具的文件,文件中须确认疾病诊断、发病日期和治疗方案。

4. 针灸师的执业活动说明,以及由于疾病或状况而对该执业所做的任何修改、限定或限制。

B. 如持证人的疾病或状况发生任何恶化或发生任何重大变化,并影响持证人以合理技能安全执业的能力,则在疾病或状况发生变化后三十日内,针灸师须以书面形式向主管提供下列资料:

1. 现任治疗师的姓名以及由现任治疗师开具的文件,文件中须确认疾病或状况发生的变化、疾病或状况发生变化的日期、疾病或状况变化的性质以及现行治疗计划。

2. 持证人的执业活动说明,以及由于病情变化而对该执业所做的任何修改、限定或限制。

C. 遵守本规则为有资格根据 C.R.S 第 12－200－112(1)款与主管签订保密协议之先决条件。但是,不能据此要求主管签订保密协议。相反,主管应评估所有事实和情形,以确定保密协议是否适当。

D. 如主管发现持证人患有影响其合理技能和安全执业能力的精神或身体疾病或状况,而持证人未及时通知主管该疾病或状况,则该持证人可根据 C.R.S.第 12－200－109(1)(1)项受到纪律处分。

第10条 注射疗法

A. 定义。仅为本条之目的:

1. 主管认为,"注射疗法"系指通过皮下注射生理盐水、无菌草药、维生素、矿物药、顺势疗法药物、葡萄糖、利多卡因、普鲁卡因、萨拉平或其他类似物质来刺激穴位,包括激痛点(历史上称为阿是穴),这些药物专门用于非静脉注射。

B. 除本条(C)款所限制的情况外,持有有效执照的针灸师可对其护理的患者实施注射疗法。

C. 实施注射疗法的要求。针灸师应:

1. 持有科罗拉多针灸执照,信誉良好。

2. 通过 NCCAOM(或其继受机构)取得现行洁针技术证书。

3. 当前正在接受美国心脏协会或美国红十字会基本生命支持(BLS)或心肺复苏(CPR)的审批。

4. 完成 D 款所涵盖的教育课程。

D. 针灸师实施注射疗法时,只能使用经过培训的注射药物和注射技术。培训内容应当包括:

1. 解剖学和生理学。

2. 针灸体格检查及鉴别诊断。

3. 针灸穴位,包括基础解剖。

4. 针灸技术。

5. 常规注射安全。

6. [FN1]针灸穴位注射疗法。

7. 药理学。

8. 洁针技术。

9. 使用东方草药制剂的注射药物,需完成中草药和中草药注射剂注射的培训。

为证明其符合中草药和中草药注射剂的培训要求,主管将接受 NCCAOM 或其继受机构的中草药学认证和/或东方医学认证。

10. 使用(E)(3)(a)(12)—(17)所列药物,需要关于紧急使用吸入式氧气和 IM 肾上腺素的使用说明。

E. 允许使用的药物。

1. 针灸师应遵守关于获取、持有和使用任何药品的联邦和州法律。

2. 遵照所有联邦和州法律采购的药物方可被批准使用。

3. 下列药品按照联邦或州法律规定的管理方式进行授权,联邦或州法律另有规定的除外:

a. 针灸师可根据 C.R.S 第 12-200-103(4)款规定和主管的许可,获取用于注射疗法的物质:

(1) 右旋糖。

(2) D-葡萄糖。

(3) 酶,但尿激酶除外。

(4) 葡萄糖。

(5) [FN2]顺势疗法药物(仅包括在美国药典中的物质)。

(6) 透明质酸。

(7) 矿物。

(8) 盐水。

(9) 萨拉平。

(10) 氯化钠。

(11) 无菌水。

(12) 顺势疗法止疼消炎片。

(13) 维生素。

(14) 氰钴维生素。

(15) 利多卡因。

(16) 带或不带肾上腺素的马卡因(盐酸布比卡因)。

(17) 东方草药。

(18) 普鲁卡因。

(19) 维生素 B_{12}。

F. 患者安全。

1. 针灸师应制定不良事件/应急处理方案。

2. 使用(E)(3)(a)(14)-(19)所列药物实施注射疗法的针灸师须配备氧气和肾上腺素,并接受过使用氧气和肾上腺素治疗患者的培训。在使用可能有过敏副作用的药物实施注射疗法时,应配备氧气和紧急肾上腺素包。

3. 经授权实施注射疗法的针灸师不得静脉注射任何药物。

G. 针灸师应出示该程序当前的医疗事故保险,并续保该保险。

1. 针灸师的责任是仅注射 E 款中所列的药物,且这些药物明确包括在其按照 C.R.S.第 12-200-106(6)款获得的保险单中。

第 11 条 关于卫生保健提供者向消费者披露从网络外提供者处获取紧急或非紧急服务的潜在影响

本条由专业和职业部主管("主管")根据 C.R.S.第 12-20-204 条,第 12-200-114(1)(a)项和 24-34-113(3)款的规章制定权颁布并通过,根据 C.R.S.第 24-34-113(2)款的授权,与保险专员和州卫生局协商。

本条的目的是制定相关要求,要求卫生保健提供者按照 C.R.S 第 24-34 113(2)款的规定,向消费者披露从网络外提供者处获取紧急或非紧急服务的潜在影响。

本条适用于 C.R.S.第 24-34-113(1)(f)和 10-16-102(56)款所界定的卫生保健提供者。

A. 披露要求。根据 C.R.S.第 24-34-113 条,卫生保健提供者应向所有客户提供附录 A 中所述信息,即从网络外设施或机构,或在网络内设施或机构提供服务的网络外提供者处获取紧急或非紧急服务的潜在影响。在下列所有情况下,卫生保健提供者均应提供附录 A 中的披露:

1. 紧急服务:经过适当的筛查,确定客户没有紧急医疗状况,或紧急医疗状况经过治疗趋于稳定后,由客户或其指定代表签署披露文件后方可出院。

2. 如客户同意由卫生保健提供者提供非紧急护理或治疗，在服务开始前，客户或其指定代表应签署该披露文件。

3. 关于卫生保健提供者出具的账单报表和账单通知。

4. 与根据保险范围提供的服务有关的其他表格或通信。

B. 不遵守本条规定可能导致实施 C.R.S 第 12-200-109(1)(i), 12-200-110 条和第 12-200-110 条规定的任何处罚。

附录 A

意外账单——了解您的权利

从 2020 年 1 月 1 日起，科罗拉多州法律保护您免于"意外账单"（也称为"差额账单"）。这些保护适用于以下情况：

- 您从科罗拉多州的网络外提供者处接受其紧急服务，救护车服务除外，和/或
- 您无意中从科罗拉多州网络内设施的网络外提供者处接受其服务。

什么是意外/差额账单，何时发生？

如您在卫生保健提供者处就诊，或在您的医疗保险计划提供者网络之外的（有时称为"网络外"）设施或机构中接受服务，您可能会收到与该医疗服务相关的额外费用账单。网络外卫生保健提供者通常会向您收取保险商决定的合格费用和网络外提供者收取的总费用之间的差额。这称为"意外"或"差额"账单。

当无法结算时：

紧急服务

如您正在接收紧急服务，则最多只能向您收取您的保险计划的网络内分摊费用，即共付额、免赔额和/或共同保险。不能因其他费用向您收取差额。这包括您接受紧急服务的应急设施以及任何为您提供紧急护理的服务提供者。

网络内或网络外卫生保健提供者的非紧急服务

卫生保健提供者必须告诉您是位于网络外位置，还是网络外提供者的网络内位置。他们还必须告诉您，使用哪些类型的服务可能由任何网络外提供者提供。

您有权要求网络内提供者提供所有涵盖的医疗服务。但是，如网络内提供者服务不可用，您可能需要从网络外提供者处接受医疗服务。在这种情况下，最多只能向您收取您的保险计划的网络内分摊费用，即共付款、免赔额和/或共同保险。这些提供者不能因其他费用向您收取差额。

其他保护

- 您的保险公司将直接支付网络外提供者和设施的费用。
- 您的保险公司必须将您支付的紧急服务或某些网络外服务（如上所述）的任何金额计入您的网络内免赔额和自付限额。
- 您的提供者、设施、医院或机构必须在收到通知后六十日内退还您多付的任何款项。
- 任何个人（包括提供者、医院或保险公司）都无法要求您限制或放弃这些权利。

如您在其他情况下从网络外提供者或设施或代理机构接受服务，您可能仍需要支付差

额费用,或者您可能要负责整个账单。如您有意从网络外提供者或设施接受非紧急服务,则可能还需要支付差额账单。

如您想对您的卫生保健提供者提出投诉,您可以通过访问本网站提交在线投诉:https://www.colorado.gov/pacific/dora/DPO_File_Complaint。

如您认为已收到共付款、免赔额和/或共同保险以外的其他金额的账单,请致电 303-894-7490 或 1-800-930-3745 联系账单部门或科罗拉多保险部门。

如您有任何问题,请通过您的健康保险 ID 卡上的号码或科罗拉多州保险部门联系您的健康保险计划。

蒙 大 拿 州

蒙大拿州针刺法[①]

第一节 总 则

第 37－13－101 条 章节引用

本章应称为并引用为"1974 年针刺法案"。

第 37－13－102 条 立法机构的决定和目的

本州针刺实践会影响公共健康、安全和福利,为维护公众利益,应对针刺实践进行监管,以保护公众免受未经获授权的、不合格的针刺实践的伤害,以及持证人违反职业道德的行为的侵害。

第 37－13－103 条 定义

下列定义适用于本章:

(1)"针刺"系指通过插入实心针而产生的器械,温针或电针刺激来诊断、治疗或纠正人体状况、病痛、疾病、伤痛或体弱。该术语包括使用穴位按压以及使用东方食品疗法和草药。

(2)"针刺师"系指经针灸医学考试委员会颁发执照的自然人。

(3)"委员会"系指蒙大拿州医学考试委员会。

(4)"针刺学校"系指经医学考试委员会认可和指定的教授针刺疗法的学校。

第 37－13－104 条 部分豁免

(1)(a) 本章不得解释为要求蒙大拿州执业内科医生、骨病医生、脊椎按摩师、牙科医生或足科医生另行参加解剖学、生理学、化学、皮肤学、诊断学、细菌学、药物学或在其各自专业领域获得执照所需的其他科目的考试。

(b) 内科医生、骨病医生、脊椎按摩师、牙科医生或足科医生不得在本州从事针刺实践,除非该医生已完成本章要求的针刺课程且通过本章要求的针刺考试。

[①] 根据《蒙大拿州法典》第 37 卷第 13 章(*Montana Code* Annotated, Title 37 Professions and Occupations, Chapter 13 Acupuncture Practice Act)译出。

（2）除第 37-13-301 条规定，特别是关于实心针针刺操作的规定之外，本章无意限制、干涉或阻止执业卫生专业人员在其执照范围内执业。

（3）未公开表明根据本章获得执照的个人不受本章规定的限制。

第二节 医学考试委员会

第 37-13-201 条 权力和职责

除本章赋予的其他权力和职责外，委员会应具有的权力和履行的职责如下：

（1）根据《蒙大拿州行政程序法》的适用条款，为执行本章条款制定规则。

（2）采用不违反本章条款的最低教育要求。

（3）制定用于考试和执照申请的表格。

（4）筹备并监督申请人的针刺师执照考试。

（5）采用外部的专业考试机构提供的考试服务，代替自行筹备的考试。

（6）按照下列规定颁发、撤销和吊销执照。

（7）举行听证会，发布传票，主持宣誓，并就其管辖范围内的所有事项进行证言和证据收集。

（8）组建委员会，接受生病或州外证人的证词。

（9）盖章，并加盖委员会发行的所有执照和其他官方文件。

第三节 执 照

第 37-13-301 条 执业所需执照

（1）除非根据本章获得执照，任何人不得在本州从事针刺实践。

（2）除非根据本章获得执照，任何人不得意图从事针刺实践或使用"针刺师"头衔或任何类似的头衔。

第 37-13-302 条 执照申请-费用-资格

（1）拟从事针刺实践的，应向委员会申请执照。申请中须附有委员会规定的费用。

（2）申请人应向委员会提供以下证据，证明该申请人：

（a）年满 18 岁。

（b）经委员会认定具有良好品德。

（c）毕业于获得美国国家针灸及东方医学院校审核委员会（NACSCAOM）批准的针刺学校，该校须在公认的针刺疗法分支学科领域提供至少一千学时的入门级培训课程或经委员会认可的同等课程。

（d）已通过由国家针灸师认证委员会（NCCA）或其继受机构筹备和管理的考试。

第 37-13-303 条 根据《1987 年蒙大拿州制定法汇编》第 307 章第 2 条废除。

第 37-13-304 条 颁发执业资格证书-执照费

所有成功通过本章要求考试的申请人，应在委员会名册中注册为执业针刺师，并在缴纳委员会规定的执照费后，以委员会规定的形式获得执业资格证书。证书应加盖委员会公章。

第 37-13-305 条 根据《1995 年蒙大拿州制定法汇编》第 429 章第 128 条废除。

第 37-13-306 条 根据《2005 年蒙大拿州制定法汇编》第 467 章第 127 条废除。

第37-13-307条　根据《2005年蒙大拿州制定法汇编》第467章第127条废除。

第3节：执照

保留第37卷第13章308条至第37卷第13章310条。

第37-13-311条　根据《1995年蒙大拿州制定法汇编》第429章第128条废除。

第37-13-312条　根据《1995年蒙大拿州制定法汇编》第429章第128条废除。

第37-13-313条　根据《1995年蒙大拿州制定法汇编》第429章第128条废除。

第37-13-314条　根据《1995年蒙大拿州制定法汇编》第429章第128条废除。

第37-13-315条　禁止违法行为

除本章所规定的方式外,地方法院可根据委员会的起诉,禁止任何其他方式的针刺实践。在诉讼中,无需证明任何人因受到起诉的行为而受到伤害。如发现被告人不当实践行为,法院应禁止被告人从事针刺实践,直到被告人取得执照为止。这些案件的程序与任何其他禁令诉讼的程序相同。禁令所采取的补偿办法可作为刑事诉讼和惩罚的补充。

第37-13-316条　处罚

违反本章任何规定或蒙大拿州医学考试委员会规则的,即属轻罪,可处六个月以下的监禁或五百美元以下的罚款,或两罪并罚。

蒙大拿州针刺行政法[①]

24.156.1401　定义

（1）"考试"系指国家针灸与东方医学审核委员会（NCCAOM）或其继受机构批准的针灸认证所需的考试。

（2）NCCAOM是1997年前称为国家针灸师认证委员会（NCCA）的组织。

（3）"针灸与东方医学学院委员会（CCAOM）"系指负责管理洁针技术考试的组织。

（4）"针灸及东方医学教育审核委员会（ACAOM）"系指1997年前称为美国国家针灸及东方医学院校审核委员会（NACSCAOM）的组织。

24.156.1402　费用

（1）执照申请人须在申请时,缴纳六十五美元执照费。

（2）针刺师执照的续期费为一百美元。

（3）额外标准化费用在ARM[②]第24卷第101章第403节中规定。

24.156.1403　执照颁发要求

（1）执照申请人须满足NCCAOM或其继受机构进行针刺认证的先决条件并通过所需考试。

---

①　根据《蒙大拿州行政法规》第24卷第156章第14节（*Administrative Rules of Montana*, Title 24. Labor and Industry, Chapter 156. Montana State Board of Medical Examiners, Sub-Chapter 14. Acupuncture）译出。

②　译文中ARM代表Administrative Rules of Montana,即《蒙大拿州行政法规》。

（2）执照申请人须通过由 CCAOM 或其继受机构所管理的洁针技术考试。

24.156.1404　执照申请

（1）申请针刺师执照的,应提交申请书、相应费用,及:

(a) 申请人的正式成绩单,该成绩单来自经 ACAOM 认证的学校。

(b) 申请人的洁针技术考试结果,该结果来自 CCAOM 或其继受机构。

(c) NCCAOM 提供的针刺认证考试结果。

（2）委员会或其指定人员将通过国家执业人员资料库对每个申请人进行查询。

（3）如申请人在其他州或司法管辖区持有执照,申请人应要求颁发执照的州及司法管辖区代表申请人直接向委员会呈交一份执照核实证明。

（4）申请人可在被列入委员会议程之前,向委员会提交书面请求,自愿撤回申请。

24.156.1405　学校批准（已废除）

迁移及废除表

作　用	从	到	生　效　日　期
废除	**2.21.1401**		1984 年 3 月 16 日
废除	**2.21.1402**		1984 年 2 月 16 日
废除	**2.21.1403**		1984 年 3 月 16 日
废除	**2.21.1404**		1984 年 3 月 16 日
废除	**2.21.1405**		1984 年 3 月 16 日
废除	**2.21.1406**		1984 年 3 月 16 日
废除	**2.21.1407**		1984 年 3 月 16 日
废除	**2.21.1408**		1984 年 3 月 16 日
废除	**2.21.1411**		1984 年 3 月 16 日

24.156.1406　课程

委员会将把现有的自学可接受课程作为评估指南,逐个审查 MCA 第 37-13-302 条中规定的任何同等课程。

24.156.1407　向委员会报告的义务

（1）在作出最终判决、终审裁定或最终纪律处分的三个月内,根据本章获得执照的针刺师应向委员会报告与其涉及的渎职行为、不端行为、刑事处罚或纪律处分有关的一切信息。

（2）针刺师存在疑似或已知损伤的,须自行向委员会报告,或者自行向委员会认可的专业援助计划报告,以代替向委员会报告。

（3）针刺师有义务向适当的执照委员会、机构报告其他卫生保健提供者的疑似或已知损伤,也可向经认可的专业辅助计划报告,以代替向委员会或机构报告。

24.156.1408　针刺师继续教育

(1)医学考试委员会的每名执业针刺师每年应接受十五学时经认证的针刺疗法继续教育。学时数或面授学时数应为授课的实际学时数。

(2)首次参加与增强针刺实践、价值观、技能与知识相关的新课程、在职培训会或研讨会,最多可给予八学时的学分;或者,首次在公认的专业期刊上发表针刺疗法专业论文的作者,或首次在州或全国专业会议上发表针刺疗法专业论文的作者,最多可给予八学时的学分。

(3)如持证人在两年执照颁发期内完成超过三十学时的继续教育,则可将不超过十五学时的超出时数结转至下一个两年执照颁发期。

(4)持证人可本着诚信的原则向委员会提交声明,说明其不能遵从本规则的理由,申请免除本规定中有关针灸继续教育的要求,委员会可批准此种豁免。

(5)持证人首次续期执照,无须接受继续教育。

24.156.1409　认证、批准和标准

(1)委员会须委任一个继续教育审核委员会,协助委员会批准旨在满足执业针刺师继续教育要求的课程、论文、研讨会及其他活动。

(2)继续教育审核委员会应批准符合下列标准的针刺疗法继续教育课程、论文、研讨会及其他活动:

(a)具有较强知识性或实践性的内容,以提高针刺师专业能力为主要目的。

(b)制定有组织的学习计划,以处理与针刺师的针刺服务、专业责任或道德义务直接相关的事项。

(c)针刺疗法继续教育的提供者及发表论文的作者,应按部门规定的格式递交申请书,向委员会申请批准课程或发表论文。申请书须填写完整并附有适当文件。

(d)申请人须证明所提供的课程符合该标准。

(e)委员会可酌情决定任何继续教育学分可接受的学时数。

(f)经 NCCAOM 认证的课程,应事先获得委员会批准。

(g)由国家针灸协会或针灸学校主办的课程,应事先获得委员会批准。

(h)在经认证的学术会议或继续教育课程中教授针刺疗法,应视为继续教育。

(3)申请人可要求五学时的自学以满足 ARM 第 24 卷第 156 章第 1408 节的要求。

24.156.1410　报告要求

(1)每名持证人须以委员会批准的格式保存课程记录,以证明每年完成的经认证的继续教育学时。

24.156.1411　续期(已废除)

24.156.1412　违反职业道德的行为

(1)除 MCA 第 37-1-316 条所界定的违反职业道德的行为外,以下行为构成 MCA 第 37 卷第 13 章规定的持证人或执照申请人违反职业道德的行为:

(a)实施性虐待、不端性行为或性剥削行为,不论是否与持证人的针刺实践有关。

(b)未能按照 NCCAOM 或其继受机构的要求使用洁针技术。

（c）做出可能欺骗、欺诈或伤害公众的行为。

（d）在治疗疾病或其他身体、精神状况的过程中，就持证人或经其指示开具药品、采取治疗或疗法的技能、有效性或价值，做出具有虚假性或误导性的陈述。

（e）在对患者进行检查和治疗时，或在开账单、给予或收取与专业服务有关的费用时，或在向个人、公司、机构或组织报告时，采取欺诈、谎报或欺骗行为；包括 MCA 第 39 卷第 71 章或第 72 章规定的在利益要求中的欺诈、谎报和欺骗行为。

（f）在与针刺实践有关的文件中使用具有虚假性、欺诈性或欺骗性的陈述。

（g）持证人因其行为或表现受到其他州或司法管辖区针对针刺师执照或其他执业授权的纪律处分，而该行为或表现与 MCA 第 37 卷第 13 章或本细则构成纪律处分理由的行为或表现类似。其他州或司法管辖区所采取的纪律处分的核证副本，可作为其违反职业道德的行为的证据。

（h）故意不服从委员会通过的规则或委员会强制执行对持证人实施纪律处分的命令。

（i）未向委员会或其调查人员或代表提供委员会合法要求的资料。

（j）未配合委员会进行合法调查。

（k）谎称可以治愈某人明显不可治愈的疾病、伤痛或疾病，从而直接或间接获取费用或其他补偿。

（l）滥开账单。

（m）在紧急情况下出庭作证。

（n）共谋误报或故意误报病情，以促成或阻碍和解（settlement）、裁决（award）、裁定（verdict）及判决（judgement）。

（o）除本款规定的情形外，作为在本州内未持有针刺师执照的人员的合伙人、代理人或雇员，或与其合资经营的人，从事针刺实践；但是，这并不禁止：

（i）根据 MCA 第 35 卷第 4 章，单个持证人或多个持证人成立专业服务公司。

（ii）根据 MCA 第 35 卷第 8 章成立专业有限责任公司，提供 MCA 第 35 卷第 8 章所界定的专业服务。

（iii）作为医院、医疗援助机构或其他持牌卫生保健提供者的合伙人、代理人或雇员，或与之合资，从事针刺实践；但是，

（A）合伙、代理、雇用或合资必须由书面协议予以证明，其中应包含相应措辞，大意为该协议所建立的关系不会影响该针刺师在其针刺实践过程中进行独立判断。

（B）针刺师在针刺实践中的独立判断，须事实上不受该关系影响。

（C）不得要求针刺师将任何患者转诊给特定的医疗服务提供者，或采取其认为不符合患者最佳利益的任何其他行动。

（p）未按患者或患者法定指定代表的要求，将相关和必要的患者记录转交给另一名持证医疗保健提供者、患者或患者代表。

（q）伪造专业资历（即教育、培训、经验、能力水平、技能和/或认证状态）。

（s）所从事行为表明其不具备知识和能力，或未能运用已获认证的专业现行原则和/或技能。

(t) 在变更执业地点、终止医患关系或针刺服务之前、期间、之后,未将病历资料妥善保管;或者明知他人未获批准接收病历资料,仍交与其保管;或

(u) 任何事实上构成违反职业道德的其他行为,不论是否具体列举。

24.156.1413　感染废物管理

(1) 每名获委员会执照的针刺师,须根据 MCA 第 75－10－1005 条的要求,按照 MCA 第 75－10－1003 条的规定贮存、运输及处置感染废物。

(2) 根据职业安全与健康管理局(OSHA)的要求,使用过的锐器须妥为包装,并根据 MCA 第 75－10－1005 条中的规定加上标签。

24.156.1414　继续教育审查

(1) 委员会须对每次续期之后的继续教育进行随机审查。

(2) 被选定进行审查的持证人须按照规则报告要求提交文件,以证明其已完成继续教育学时。

(3) 未能遵从继续教育的规定可作为纪律处分的理由。

内 华 达 州

内华达州针刺法[①]

第一节 一般规定

总则

第 634A.010 条　立法声明

兹声明东方医学及其分支机构的实践活动为专业职业,影响公众安全及福利,承担社会公众利益,因此受本州法律的保护和监管。

第 634A.020 条　定义

除文意另有所指外,下列定义适用于本章:

1."针刺"系指通过刺穿人体皮肤将针刺入人体,控制和调节体内能量的流动和平衡,以达到治愈、缓解或减轻身体不适的目的,包括但不限于:

(a)任何精神或身体疾病。

(b)任何伤口、身体损伤或畸形。

2."委员会"系指内华达州东方医学委员会。

3."东方医学医师"系指根据本章规定获得执照,作为东方医学医师执业的人。

4."干针疗法":

(a)系指限于治疗肌筋膜痛的一种先进针刺技能或技术,使用一次性的无菌针灸针单手进针,不使用温针、热针或任何其他方式及药物,将其刺入皮肤或皮下组织以刺激痛点。

(b)不包括:

(1)刺激耳穴。

(2)利用远端或非局部穴位。

(3)留针。

[①] 根据《内华达州制定法修订本》第 54 卷第 634A 章(*Nevada Revised Statutes* Annotated, Title 54. Professions, Occupations and Businesses, Chapter 634A. Doctors of Oriental Medicine)译出。

（4）使用固定的电刺激导线；或

（5）其他针灸理论的教学或应用。

5."草药"和"草药治疗"系指建议、推荐、规定或指导患者使用草药来治疗、减轻或缓解精神或身体疾病，以及治疗或减轻伤口、身体损伤或畸形。

6."草药"系指未被美国或本州法律禁止使用的植物全株或部分植株，可用于东方医学实践中的检验或检查。

7."东方医学"系指一种医疗体系，主要强调体内能量的流动和平衡，并将能量作为维持机体健康和预防疾病最为重要的一种因素。该术语包括但不限于针刺疗法、草药、艾灸、干针疗法以及获得委员会批准的其他服务。

第634A.025条 本章适用范围

1.本章不适用于存在下列情形的东方医学医师：

（a）临时调入本州参加会诊。

（b）根据《内华达州制定法修订本》第634A.163条暂时豁免执照，并在豁免范围内从事东方医学实践。

2.本章不适用于下列针刺疗法医师：

（a）州内经认证东方医学学校的雇员。

（b）在其他州或司法管辖区内取得针刺疗法执照的人员。

（c）在本州从事针刺疗法实践的人员：

（1）仅限于在临床向学生教授、指导或演示针刺疗法的方法和实践。

（2）在从事针刺疗法实践相关服务时不向患者收取费用。

3.本章不适用于根据《内华达州制定法修订本》第630章[①]或第633章[②]取得执照的医师。

4.本章不禁止：

（a）药剂师或其他人员在紧急情况下提供无偿服务。

（b）在家庭内部治疗中施药。

（c）任何人协助根据本章取得执照的人员从事相关疗法，但不得将针刺入皮肤或者开具草药处方。

5.为本条之目的，"经认证东方医学学校"系指至少已从针灸及东方医学教育审核委员会（ACAOM）或其继受机构获得候选资格的学校。

内华达州东方医学委员会

第634A.030条 创立；成员职务与人数；宣誓

1.特此设立内华达州东方医学委员会，该委员会由州长任命的七名委员组成。

2.委员会的每位成员在履行职务之前，应在规定的宣誓负责人面前履行宪法规定的就职宣誓。

---

① 第54卷第630章"医师、医师助手、医疗助理、灌注师、呼吸保健医生"（Physicians, Physician Assistants, Medical Assistants, Perfusionists and Practitioners of Respiratory Care）。

② 第54卷第633章"骨科医学"（Osteopathic Medicine）。

3. 委员会成员听从州长指示。

第 634A.040 条　成员任职资格

1. 州长须委任四名委员会成员,这四名委员会成员应:

(a) 持有根据本章规定颁发的执照。

(b) 目前在本州从事东方医学实践,被任命为委员会成员前已在本州进行至少三年的东方医学实践。

(c) 是美国公民。

(d) 现居内华达州,且在被任命为委员会成员前在内华达州定居一年以上。

2. 州长须委任一名委员会成员,该成员应:

(a) 根据《内华达州制定法修订本》第 630 章获得医学考试委员会的医师执照。

(b) 不从事东方医学机构或东方医学学校的管理工作。

(c) 除作为患者或潜在患者外,与东方医学有关的任何事项均无利益相关。

(d) 是美国公民。

(e) 现居内华达州,且在被任命为委员会成员前在内华达州定居一年以上。

3. 州长须委任一名委员会成员,该成员应:

(a) 不从事东方医学机构或东方医学学校的管理工作。

(b) 除作为患者或潜在患者外,与东方医学有关的任何事项均无利益相关。

(c) 是美国公民。

(d) 现居内华达州,且在被任命为委员会成员前在内华达州定居一年以上。

4. 州长应任命一名委员会成员,代表根据《内华达州制定法修订本》第 634A.090 条建立的东方医学学校或学院。

第 634A.050 条　委员会成员的薪酬;委员会成员和雇员的每日津贴和差旅费

1. 负责委员会事务期间,委员会成员有权获得:

(a) 委员会规定的日薪,该日薪不得超过一百五十美元。

(b) 委员会规定的每日津贴和差旅费用,该费用不得超过州政府工作人员和雇员的工资标准。

2. 负责委员会事务期间,委员会的每位雇员均有权按照委员会规定的费用获得每日津贴和差旅费。该费用不得超过州政府工作人员和雇员的工资标准。

第 634A.060 条　官员

委员会应每年从其成员中选出一位主席、副主席和财务部长。

第 634A.070 条　雇员;办事处;相关规定;传票

委员会可:

1. 聘用律师、调查员、其他专业顾问及文书人员履行相应职责。为开展遴选工作,委员会可召集在东方医学方面声望较高且能力受到认可的人进行协助。

2. 尽可能在州内多设立办事处,以贯彻本章规定。

3. 通过不与本章规定相悖的规章。该规章可包含规范持证人职业行为的道德准则。

4. 通过传票强制证人出庭并出示证据。

第 643A.080 条　会议;公章;存放和使用委员会收到的款项;财政年度;记录

委员会应:

1. 每年至少举行一次会议,会议可在主席或过半数成员要求的任意时间举行。

2. 持有并使用公章。

3. 将根据本章规定收到的所有款项存入内华达州的计息账户,这些款项必须用于支付委员会费用。

4. 以每年 7 月 1 日起至第二年 6 月 30 日止的财政年度为基础开展工作。

5. 保存相关程序记录,该记录必须保持公开,且必须载明每名持证人的姓名和州内营业地址。

第 634A.083 条　委员会检查场地

委员会的成员或代理人,应进入符合本章规定的持证人在本州从事东方医学实践的营业场所进行检查,以确定其是否存在违反本章规定的情况,包括但不限于检查该营业场所是否有人在未持有根据本章规定颁发的执业资格证的情况下从事东方医学实践。

第 634A.085 条　委员会关于书面投诉的职责;委员会可聘请总检察长对重要投诉进行调查;委员会要求迅速裁决;保留投诉;总检察长可收取服务费

1. 若有人向委员会提交有关东方医学医师的书面投诉,委员会应审查该投诉。投诉可以匿名方式提交。若投诉以匿名方式提交,委员会应受理该投诉,但若该投诉的匿名性质导致委员会无法处理该投诉或对投诉对象不公平,则委员会可以拒绝受理该投诉。若从该投诉或其他记录来看,该投诉并非无关紧要,则委员会应:

(a) 聘请州总检察长调查该投诉。

(b) 若委员会聘请州总检察长,则应将投诉信原件及从审查中获得的所有事实或资料移交总检察长。

2. 若委员会已聘请总检察长,总检察长应对移交的投诉进行调查,以确定是否对执照内容进行变更、吊销或撤销执照等处理。若总检察长认为有必要进一步审理,则应向委员会报告调查结果及所有建议。

3. 针对总检察长报告的每项投诉,委员会应立即做出决定。委员会应:

(a) 驳回投诉;或

(b) 采取适当的纪律处分。

4. 委员会应将所有根据本条收到的投诉保留至少十年,包括但不限于所有未处理的投诉。

5. 若委员会已聘请总检察长,总检察长应根据《内华达州制定法修订本》第 228.113 条①第 2 款规定就调查投诉相关服务向委员会收取费用。

第 634A.090 条　在本州创办和维持东方医学学校或学院的要求;委员会有权规定取得学位所需的学习课程

1. 仅在下列情况下,可在本州创办和维持东方医学学校或学院:

(a) 获委员会批准。

---

① 第 18 卷"州行政部门"第 228 章"总检察长"第 228.113 条(服务费用)。

（b）已获得针灸及东方医学教育审核委员会（ACAOM）或其继受机构的认证或机构认定的候选资格。

（c）持有由高等教育委员会（Commission on Postsecondary Education）颁发的现行执照。

2. 委员会可规定东方医学博士学位的所需课程。

执照

第 634A.110 条　申请；指纹；费用

1. 申请东方医学执照考试或其分科考试的申请人，应：

（a）按委员会提供的格式向委员会提交申请。

（b）提交符合要求的证明，证明申请人已满二十一岁，并满足相应的教育要求。

（c）提交一套完整的指纹，与申请书一同提交，委员会可将其转交内华达州犯罪历史记录中央储存库（Central Repository for Nevada Records of Criminal History），以向联邦调查局（Federal Bureau of Investigation）提交报告。

（d）交纳委员会规定的费用（该费用不得超过一千美元）。

（e）交纳委员会要求的申请人调查或翻译服务的所有费用（如申请人进行考试时需要翻译）。

2. 根据第 1 款向委员会提交的申请必须包含完成申请所需的全部信息。

第 634A.115 条　支付抚养费：申请人提交相应信息；拒绝颁发执照的理由；委员会的职责[①]

1. 除本章规定的其他要求外：

（a）根据本章规定，在申请颁发执照时，申请人应在提交给委员会的申请中提供其社会安全号码。

（b）根据本章规定获发或续期执照的申请人，应根据《内华达州制定法修订本》第 425.520 条规定向委员会提交州卫生与公众服务部社会福利局规定的声明。该声明必须由申请人填写并签名。

2. 委员会应将第 1 款规定的声明写入：

（a）获发或续期执照须提交的申请书或其他表格。

（b）委员会另行规定的表格。

3. 根据本章规定，申请人存在下列情形的，委员会不得为其颁发或续期执照：

（a）未提交第 1 款规定的声明。

（b）在第 1 款规定的声明中表明，其受限于法院要求抚养子女的命令，但未遵从该命令，或未遵从经执行该命令的地方检察官或其他公共机构批准的还款计划，以偿还根据该命令所欠的款项。

---

① 内华达州立法机关官网上对该条做出注明："有效期至《美国法典》第 42 章第 666 节废除之日，联邦法律要求各州制定程序，扣留、暂停和限制拖欠儿童抚养费以及不遵守与亲子抚养或儿童抚养程序的专业、职业和娱乐执照。"另外，立法机关制定了废除《美国法典》第 42 章第 666 条之后对应的条文并规定其效力于该条文通过 2 年后到期。

资料来源于内华达州立法机关官网，https://www.leg.state.nv.us/Division/Legal/LawLibrary/NRS/NRS-634A.html，访问日期：2020 年 8 月 24 日。《美国法典》第 42 章第 666 节规定"通过法定程序提高儿童抚养费执法的有效性"。

4. 如申请人在第1款规定的声明中表明,其受限于法院要求抚养子女的命令,但未遵从该命令,或未遵从经执行该命令的地方检察官或其他公共机构批准的还款计划,以偿还根据该命令所欠的款项,委员会应通知申请人联系执行该命令的地方检察官或其他公共机构,以确定申请人清偿欠款的方式。

第634A.120条 考试:国家考试;委员会批准的考试;相关规定

1. 每位申请东方医学医师执照的申请人须通过:

(a) 国家针灸与东方医学审核委员会(NCCAOM)或其继受机构对东方医学认证所要求及举办的各项考试。

(b) 经委员会批准,考察申请人是否了解并认识本州东方医学实践中与健康和安全相关法律法规的考试。

2. 在根据第1款(b)项要求的考试中,委员会可制定考试规定:

(a) 增加的考试科目范围。

(b) 举办考试的具体方式,包括但不限于笔试、口试、演示、实操或多种形式结合的考试。

3. 根据第1款(b)项,委员会应制定与考试准备、管理及评定相关的要求。

4. 除第5款另有规定外,委员会应在其规定的时间和地点举行第1款(b)项所要求的考试,一年至少举行两次。

5. 若委员会在考试前六十日内未收到参加考试的申请,即可取消第1款(b)项要求的考试。

6. 未通过第1款(b)项要求的考试者,可以重新参加考试。

第634A.140条 向东方医学医师颁发执照

1. 申请人符合下列要求的,委员会应向其颁发东方医学医师执照:

(a) 申请人已:

(1) 在东方医学学校或学院顺利完成四年制学习计划或同等学力课程,该学校或学院经美国针灸及东方医学审核委员会或其继受机构认可,且符合《内华达州制定法修订本》第634A.090条规定的要求。包括但不限于有关临床和教学部分的要求。

(2) 在美国认证的院校获得东方医学学士学位或已完成本硕连读学位课程。

(3) 通过委员会对其背景及个人经历的调查。

(4) 通过《内华达州制定法修订本》第634A.120条要求的考试。

(b) 持有由NCCAOM或其继受机构颁发的现行东方医学执照。

2. 除第3款另有规定外,委员会可以向符合以下条件的申请人颁发东方医学医师执照:

(a) 申请人已:

(1) 在东方医学学校顺利完成四年制学习计划或同等学力课程,该院校经NCCAOM或其继受机构批准,且符合根据《内华达州制定法修订本》第634A.090条规定的要求。包括但不限于有关临床和教学部分的要求。

(2) 在其他州或国家合法从事东方医学实践至少四年。

(3) 通过委员会对其背景及个人经历的调查。

(4)通过《内华达州制定法修订本》第634A.120条要求的考试。

(b)持有由NCCAOM或其继受机构颁发的有效东方医学执照。

3.委员会可向以下人员颁发东方医学医师执照：

(a)申请人已：

(1)在2008年1月1日之前,顺利完成经ACAOM或其继受机构认证的东方医学学校或学院的东方医学课程学习,其中包括草药学。

(2)在申请日期前八年内,至少有六年在美国其他州或准州、华盛顿特区或外国合法从事东方医学实践。

(3)通过委员会对其背景和个人经历的调查。

(4)通过《内华达州制定法修订本》第634A.120条要求的考试。

(b)持有由NCCAOM或其继受机构颁发的有效东方医学执照。

第634A.142条　实施穴位注射疗法的批准

1.根据本章获得东方医学医师执照的医师,可向委员会申请,获得实施穴位注射疗法的批准。申请人须提交以下证明：

(a)顺利完成由NCCAOM或继受机构认证的研究生课程,该课程至少提供二十四学时的授课指导,包括但不限于至少八学时的实习指导和两学时的肌注肾上腺素训练。

(b)已投保或以其他方式持有职业责任保险保单,该保单承保申请人免受因提供穴位注射疗法而产生的任何责任。

2.委员会应批准符合第1款要求的申请人实施穴位注射疗法。

3.获批实施穴位注射疗法的持证人只允许注射其接受过培训的药物,包括但不限于营养药物、顺势疗法药物和草药。

4.本条所称"穴位注射疗法"系指通过皮下、肌内和皮内注射药物,以刺激穴位、阿是穴(ashi points)和激痛点来减轻疼痛并预防疾病。

第634A.144条　废除

第634A.150条　废除

第634A.160条　执照展示

每张执照必须在持证人的办公室、营业地点或工作地点展示。

第634A.163条　临时豁免东方医学医师向来访本州的运动队或运动员提供治疗；豁免范围的扩大；条件和局限性

1.除第5款另有规定外,若东方医学医师在美国其他州、准州或其他国家持有有效且不受限的执照并从事东方医学实践,且签署书面协议或达成口头协议,向来访的运动队或组织成员提供治疗,则该医师可暂时豁免执照要求,可以向来访本州参加比赛或训练的运动队或组织成员提供东方医学治疗。

2.除第5款另有规定外,若东方医学医师在美国其他州、准州或其他国家持有有效且不受限的执照并从事东方医学实践,且受到国家组织管理机构邀请,则该医生可暂时豁免执照要求,可以向参加该组织批准或承办的体育赛事或训练的运动员提供治疗,并可在为此类人员提供服务的同时,在本州从事东方医学实践。

3. 除本款和第 4 款另有规定外,本条所述的豁免在每次比赛或训练期内有效,有效期不超过十日。委员会可根据东方医学医师的申请,在每次比赛或训练期内批准额外的不超过二十日的豁免期。

4. 获得本条所述豁免的东方医学医师不得:

(a) 在医疗机构中从事东方医学实践。

(b) 向第 1 款或第 2 款所述以外的人提供服务。

(c) 于一个日历年内利用该豁免从事东方医学实践六十日以上。

5. 本条规定不适用于根据《内华达州制定法修订本》第 467 章规定的任何徒手格斗的竞赛或表演赛。

6. 在本条中,"来访的运动队或组织"系指主要以本州之外地点为训练基地的运动队或组织。

第 634A.165 条　为讲座或教育研讨会颁发临时证书;保险;费用;相关规定

1. 委员会可制定相关规定,向未根据本章规定获得执照的人员颁发临时执照。在下列情形中可颁发临时证书,如该证书:

(a) 与东方医学或针灸的合法教育研讨会有关;或

(b) 旨在授权某人短期内在本州从事关于东方医学或针灸的讲座或教学。

2. 委员会颁发临时执照可收取相应费用。该费用不得超出委员会在以下方面的总花费:

(a) 根据本条规定调查申请人的费用。

(b) 监督研讨会的费用,如委员会认为有此必要。

第 634A.167　续期规定;委员会为续期或恢复执照而要求继续教育的职责;自动到期和恢复

1. 根据本章颁发的执照,续期须在每年 2 月 1 日或之前:

(a) 向委员会申请续期。

(b) 向委员会支付规定的执照年费,该年费不得超过一千美元。

(c) 向委员会提交完成继续教育的证明。

(d) 提交完成续期所需的所有资料。

2. 作为执照续期或恢复的先决条件,委员会应要求每位持证人均须遵守委员会规定的继续教育要求。

3. 若持证人未能在每年 2 月 1 日前支付费用或提交所有必需的信息,则执照将自动到期。根据本款,在执照到期后九十日内,可以通过支付所需费用并提交所需信息来恢复执照效力。

第 634A.170 条　吊销、撒销或拒绝颁发执照:理由

委员会可因以下任何一种或多种原因拒绝颁发、吊销或撒销任何执照:

1. 持照者犯有以下罪行:

(a) 与东方医学实践有关的重罪。

(b) 任何涉及违反道德的罪行。

（c）如法院记录的核证副本所示，违反任何州或联邦关于持有、分销或使用管制药物的法律；或

（d）违反《内华达州制定法修订本》第 616D.200 条①、616D.220 条②、616D.240 条③或 616D.300 条至 616D.440 条的任何规定。

2. 持照者通过欺诈性的谎报，以金钱或任何其他贵重物品来获取或企图获取该职业的执照或执业资格。

3. 执照者出现严重的医疗事故或反复出现医疗事故，该事故可由医师的医疗事故索赔证明。

4. 故意以具有虚假性或欺骗性的陈述进行广告宣传。

5. 以他人名义进行广告宣传、执业或者企图执业。

6. 习惯性醉酒或习惯性管制药物成瘾。

7. 使用任何具有虚假性、欺诈性或伪造而成的声明或文件，或从事与本章执照要求有关的任何具有欺诈性、欺骗性、误导性或不道德的治疗。

8. 有身体或精神上的残疾，进一步治疗存在危险。

9. 参与任何可能欺骗、诈骗或损害公众的不光彩、不道德或违反职业道德的行为，或做出不符合本章规定的行为。

10. 使用关于东方医学或其分科治疗的具有虚假性或欺诈性的陈述。

11. 违反或企图违反、协助或教唆违反或共谋违反本章任何规定。

12. 被判定为不称职或者精神失常。

13. 以不道德或违反职业道德的方式做广告。

14. 利用欺诈性的诊断、疗法或治疗方式来获取费用或经济利益。

15. 故意泄露保密信息。

16. 持证人在执业过程中展示其姓名时，未以"东方医学医师"的头衔标明其执业性质。

17. 故意违反有关公众健康、安全或福利的法律或国家卫生委员会通过的条例。

18. 除了预防、减轻、治疗疾病或减轻痛苦的药物外，施用、配发任何管制药物。

19. 亲自、协助或建议向人体内注射任何液态硅酮药物。

20. 违反本法第 1 条规定进行或指导盆腔检查。

21. 根据《内华达州制定法修订本》449.0151 条的规定，在以下时期经营医疗机构：

（a）机构的营业执照被吊销或撤销时。

（b）根据《内华达州制定法修订本》第 449.160 条，出现可导致执照吊销或撤销的作为或不作为情况。

本款适用于负责机构运营的机构所有人或其他负责人。

---

① 第 53 卷"劳资关系"第 616D 章"劳工保险：禁止行为；处罚；起诉"第 616D.200 条"雇主未提供、保证和维持赔偿：决定和申诉程序；罚款"。

② 第 616D.220 条"虚假陈述或未报告与工资额有关的重大事实的责任，或与工资额有关的员工分类或职责的不实陈述；上诉；罚款"。

③ 第 616D.300 条至第 616D.440 条涉及禁止行为（prohibited acts）以及欺诈性行为（fraudulent practices）。

第 634A.175 条　因未能支付子女抚养费或未遵守传票或命令而吊销执照；恢复执照①

1. 若委员会收到根据《内华达州制定法修订本》第 425.540 条发布的法院命令副本，规定吊销所有专业执照、职业执照、业余执照、证书、许可证及持证人根据本章获发的执照，则委员会应在法院发出命令之日后第三十日，将颁发给该持证人的执照视为吊销状态，除非委员会收到地方检察官或其他公共机构根据《内华达州制定法修订本》第 425.550 条②的规定发给持证人的信函，声明该持证人已根据《内华达州制定法修订本》第 425.560 条遵守传票、命令或③清偿欠款。

2. 若委员会收到地方检察官或其他公共机构根据《内华达州制定法修订本》第 425.550 条向执照吊销者签发的信函，信函声明该持证人已根据《内华达州制定法修订本》第 425.560 条遵守传票、命令或④清偿欠款，则应恢复根据本章颁发而又根据《内华达州制定法修订本》第 425.540 条吊销的执照效力。

第 634A.180 条　对某些违反《劳工保险法》的行为展开纪律处分程序

尽管《内华达州制定法修订本》第 622A 章另有规定，若委员会收到《内华达州制定法修订本》第 228.420⑤条第 5 款规定的报告，则必须在其收到报告后三十日内展开纪律处分程序。

第 634A.185 条　委员会某些记录的保密性；免责条款

1. 除本条和《内华达州制定法修订本》第 239.0115 条⑥另有规定外，向委员会提交的投诉、与投诉一并提交的所有文件和其他信息，以及为确定是否采取纪律处分而进行的调查，汇编的所有文件和其他信息均为机密，除非向委员会提交书面声明要求将这些文件和资料作为公开记录。

2. 根据《内华达州制定法修订本》第 622A 章规定，向委员会提交的采取纪律处分的指控文件，以及委员会在决定是否采取纪律处分时参考的所有文件和信息，均为公开记录。

3. 强制执行纪律处分的命令，以及支持该命令的事实和法律结论均为公开记录。

4. 委员会应在可行范围内，与任何其他执照颁发部门或正在调查某人的其他机构（包括但不限于执法机构）沟通、合作或向其提供文件或其他信息。

其他规定

第 634A.190 条　不受《内华达州制定法修订本》第 630 章约束的持证人；持证人为东方医学医师

1. 根据本章获得执照的人不受《内华达州制定法修订本》第 630 章规定的约束。

---

① 内华达州立法机关官网上对该条做出注明：有效期至《美国法典》第 42 章第 666 节废除之日后 2 年，联邦法律要求各州制定程序，扣留、暂停和限制儿童抚养欠费和不遵守与亲子鉴定或儿童抚养程序有关程序的专业、职业和娱乐执照。资料来源于内华达州立法机关官网，https://www.leg.state.nv.us/Division/Legal/LawLibrary/NRS/NRS-634A.html，访问日期：2020 年 8 月 24 日。
② 第 425.550 条"发出和散发表明该人已遵守传票或令状或清偿欠款的信"。
③ 第 425.560 条"确定该人拖欠了抚养费；清偿欠款"。
④ 第 425.560 条"确定该人拖欠了抚养费；清偿欠款"。
⑤ 第 18 卷"州行政部门"第 228 章"总检察长"第 228.420 条"涉及劳工保险欺诈的案件的总检察长的管辖权；建立劳工保险欺诈控制单位；职责和权力"。
⑥ 第 19 卷"与政府和公共事务有关的其他事项"第 239 章"政府档案"第 239.0115 条"向法院申请命令以允许检查或复制至少 30 年的公共书籍或由政府实体控制的记录；可反驳的推定；例外情况"。

2. 根据本章获得东方医学医师执照的人可以自称为东方医学医师。

第634A.200条　第634A.025条替换对第634A.200条的修改

第634A.210条　人口动态统计报告

东方医学医师应遵守所有与此相关的州、市规定并受其约束,报告所有与公共卫生相关的出生与死亡事件。

违法行为;处罚;强制执行

第634A.225条　禁止举办不符合委员会规定的培训会;处罚

1. 在本州,除按照委员会的规定举办合法的教育研讨会外,不得举办有关东方医学和针灸的研讨会。

2. 任何人违反第1款,即属轻罪。

第634A.226条　第634A.083条代替第634A.226条的修订版

第634A.228条　无证情况下执业或企图执业：委员会的报告要求

若有人未经本章规定获发执照,而从事或企图从事东方医学,则除去确定存在可减轻罪行的情况外,委员会应将所有关于该人且得到证实的信息转交给适当的执法机构。

第634A.230条　禁止无证执业;处罚

1. 任何在本州自称为东方医学或其分科医师,或从事东方医学或其分科实践的人,而并未持有委员会颁发的有效执照,即属严重轻罪。除非《内华达州制定法修订本》第200.830条①或第200.840条②已规定更高级别的处罚。

2. 除法律另有规定外,若委员会裁定某人已实施第1款所述的任何行为,则委员会可：

(a) 向该人发出停止违法行为的命令,直至该人从委员会获得正规执照,或以其他方式证明不再违反第1款规定。停止违法行为的命令必须包含该人与委员会联系的电话号码。

(b) 向该人发布传票。根据本款,传票必须以书面形式发出,并详细说明违法行为的性质,且告知当事人本款的规定。若该人从事的每项活动均构成单独的罪行,可分别对其发布传票。若该人要对传票提出申诉,则必须在传票发布之日起三十日内向委员会提交书面的听证会请求。

(c) 根据《内华达州制定法修订本》第634A.250条的规定,对该人处以行政罚款。

(d) 对(a)、(b)和(c)项规定的处罚进行任意组合。

第634A.240条　禁令救济

1. 委员会可在任何有管辖权的法院对违反本章任何规定的人发布禁令。

2. 该类禁令：

(a) 可在没有证据显示任何人遭受实际损害的情况下发布,本规定作为一项预防性和惩罚性措施。

(b) 不得免除该人因违法行为而受到的刑事诉讼。

---

① 第15卷"犯罪与惩罚"第200章"针对个人的犯罪"第200.830条"没有执照实施卫生保健活动;处罚"。
② 第200.840条"没有执照实施手术活动;处罚"。

第 634A.250 条　行政罚款

除法律规定的任何其他处罚外,委员会可根据法律要求,在发出通知和举行听证会后,对违反本章规定或根据本章通过的条例的人,处以二千五百美元以下的行政罚款。

内华达州针刺行政法[①]

总则

第 634A.001 条　定义

除文意另有所指外,下列定义适用于本章。NAC 第 634A.002 至 634A.008 条中定义的词汇和术语具有上述条款中赋予其的含义。

第 634A.002 条　"委员会"定义

"委员会"系指州东方医学委员会。

第 634A.003 条　"东方医学医师"定义

"东方医学医师"系指根据 NRS 第 634A 章获得东方医学医师执照的人。

第 634A.004 条　"行政主管"定义

"行政主管"系指委员会的行政主管。

第 634A.007 条　"持证人"定义

"持证人"系指东方医学医师。

第 634A.008 条　"东方医学"定义

"东方医学"具有 NRS 第 34A.020 条赋予的含义。

第 634A.010 条　行政主管;主要办公场所

委员会将指定一人担任委员会行政主管。

委员会的主要办公场所是行政主管的办公室。

第 634A.020 条　会议

委员会将于指定时间在其主要办公场所或指定的其他地点举行定期会议。

第 634A.025 条　工作人员工资限制

主席、副主席及财务部长无权获得除薪水外的其他薪酬,该薪水由委员会依照 NRS 第 634A.050 条审定。委员会不必遵照 NRS 第 634A.060 条支付薪酬。

第 634A.035 条　东方医学学校或学院学习计划的课程设置审批

为 NRS 第 634A.090 条第 1 款(b)项之目的,若东方医学学校或学院向委员会提交证据,证明其已向 ACAOM 或其继受机构缴纳年度持续认证及预认证费用,则其学习计划的课程设置将获委员会批准。委员会不必进行其他课程审查。

第 634A.071 条　申请:一般要求

若想获得委员会颁发的东方医学医师执照,申请人须在计划参加实践考试开始前至少

---

① 根据《内华达州行政法规》第 634A 章(*Nevada Administrative Code*, Chapter 634A. Oriental Medicine)译出。

三个月：

（a）向行政主管提出申请。

（b）在提交申请时,向委员会支付第 634A.165 条规定的申请费用。

（c）提交委员会可能要求的其他文件或证明。

2. 申请须：

（a）按委员会提供的格式填写。

（b）用英文打印或书写。

3. 申请须包括：

（a）申请人的社会安全号码。

（b）申请人的全套指纹以及申请人的书面同意书,同意委员会将指纹提交给相关执法机构。

（c）申请人的书面同意书,同意委员会或委员会代表对其个人背景、专业培训和经验进行调查。

（d）申请人资格证明,证明申请人根据本章和 NRS 第 634A 章规定,具备东方医学医师执照的申请资格。

第 634A.075 条　申请：委员会驳回申请

1. 申请人存在下列情形的,委员会可驳回其东方医学医师执照申请：

（a）申请人不具备执照申请资格或不具备良好品德及声誉。

（b）提交虚假资历。

（c）申请格式不当或存在其他问题；或

（d）未在六个月内完成申请。

2. 若申请人用于支付申请费用的支票由于资金不足被退回,委员会将驳回该申请。

第 634A.080 条　申请人资格证明；学习计划的批准

1. 申请东方医学医师执照的申请人,须在提交申请的同时,一并提交其已在获得委员会批准的东方医学学校或学院顺利完成四年东方医学课程或同等课程的证明。

2. 如根据 NRS 第 634A.140 条第 1 款提交申请,则申请人须提交证据,证明其已获得经美国认证的学院或大学学士学位。

3. 如根据 NRS 第 634A.140 条第 2 款通过背书形式提交执照申请,则申请人须提交证据,证明其：

（a）在其他州或国家合法从事东方医学四年以上。

（b）持有 NCCAOM 或其继受机构颁发的东方医学认证。

4. 为第 1 款之目的,在核实下列情况后,委员会可批准东方医学学校或学院开设四年制东方医学课程或同等课程：

（a）东方医学学校或学院须：

（1）经 ACAOM 或其继受机构认证；或

（2）处于 ACAOM 或其继受机构的预认证状态,并满足（b）项的要求。

（b）学习计划包括针刺、艾灸、草药学、东方生理学、东方病理学、东方诊断、推拿或气功、生物学、化学或生物化学、解剖学、西方生理学、西方病理学、西方诊断、药理学、实验室和放射学等科目的培训和教学。

（c）学习计划：

（1）2002年11月25日前毕业的学生，须至少完成二千八百学时的教学，其中讲授课程不少于二千五百学时；或

（2）2002年11月25日或之后毕业的学生，须至少完成三千学时的教学，其中讲授课程不少于二千五百学时。

5. 为第1款之目的，如硕士学位的学习计划符合第4款（b）项和（c）项的要求，则委员会将认定该学位相当于四年制的学习计划。

6. 为第2款和第3款之目的，申请人具备东方医学医师执照获取资格的证明材料，须包括申请人取得的文凭、成绩单、执照及证书的核证副本。如有可能，所有正式文凭、成绩单、执照或证书的核证副本应由签发机构直接送交行政主管而非由申请人转交。

第634A.085条　符合国家机关规定的考试合格要求

根据NRS第634A.120条，为达到由委员会批准的国家机关规定的东方医学考试合格要求，东方医学医师执照申请人须：

1. 申请执照之日前十二个月内，已通过NCCAOM或其继受机构规定的东方医学认证考试；或

2. 获得NCCAOM或其继受机构的认证。

第634A.090条　申请人调查；实践考试的前提

1. 委员会或其代表人对申请人的背景和培训情况进行调查，调查内容须包含：

核查联邦调查局的无犯罪记录证明。

核实申请人是否从委员会批准的学校或学院毕业。

如申请人有其他州或国家的执照，应对其进行核实。

核实申请人是否正确回答与其背景相关的问题。

视情况需要，对曾经在国外院校就读，或者在其他州或国家从事东方医学实践的申请做进一步调查。

2. 在背景及培训调查完成前，申请人不得参加其申请的实践考试。

第634A.095条　申请人的英语水平

1. 除第2款另有规定外，东方医学执照的申请人须：

（a）在参加实践考试前：

（1）通过托福纸考，总成绩不低于550分；或

（2）通过托福网考，总成绩不低于80分。

（b）在实践考试中通过口试证明自己熟练掌握英语。

2. 第1款不适用于美国高中或大学毕业的申请人。

第634A.100条　申请人的实践考试；考试科目

1. 委员会启动线上实践考试管理程序前：

（a）实践考试安排在每年的6月和12月。

（b）申请人通过第634A.085条要求的考试后，方可参加实践考试。行政主管应在安排的实践考试日期前二十日，将考试的时间和地点通知申请人。

（c）在实践考试期间，只允许考试顾问和申请人进入考场。

2. 线上实践考试管理程序启动后：

（a）考试将在委员会规定的时间和地点举行，依照NRS第634A.120条的规定每年至少举行两次。

（b）委员会将通知申请人获得参加线上实践考试的资格。获得委员会通知后九十日内，申请人须在委员会指定的考点参加线上考试。

3. 作为实践考试的一部分，委员会应考核申请人以下科目的基本知识：

（a）解剖学、生理学、病理学、细菌学和传染病等基础医学。

（b）洁针技术。参照CCAOM洁针技术课程的现行指南。

（c）东方医学理论，草药学和针刺疗法。

（d）东方草药的安全性及草药与药物之间的相互作用。

（e）健康与安全的相关法律法规。

4. 实践考试为笔试。每位申请人应使用英语参加考试。

5. 申请人取得实践考试总分的70%，并取得每章或每节总分的65%，方可通过考试。

第634A.105条　委员会成员与申请人之间特定关系的披露

如申请人与委员会成员是三代以内血亲、姻亲关系或两人有重大利益关系，则该委员会成员不得参与考试准备、审查、评分工作或与申请人有关的其他决策。如存在此类关系，委员会成员和申请人须在申请时表明。

第634A.110条　未通过实践考试的申请人参加重考

申请人未通过东方医学执照的实践考试，可在下一个考试日重新参加考试。申请重考时，申请人须填写委员会规定的表格，并缴纳第634A.165条中规定的费用，使行政主管获悉。

若申请人在实践考试中仅有一部分不合格，则只重考该部分。若申请人在实践考试中有两个或两个以上的部分不合格，则须重考实践考试的全部内容。

第634A.116条　外籍人士获得的执照：非执业状态；必要声明

1. 如外籍人士丧失在美居留权和工作权，其执照自动转为非执业状态。

2. 2008年6月17日后颁发给外籍人士的执照须以显著方式注明：

本执照的颁发受美国国土安全部所属美国公民及移民服务局相关规定的限制。持证人在美国合法居留和工作权限终止后，其执照立即转为非执业状态。

第634A.121条　以假名执业；禁止一人多证及多次注册

1. 除非持证人符合NRS第602章规定，向委员会提交由县书记员签发的证书核证副本，否则持证人不得以假名经营。

2. 如持证人意欲用假名执业，须使用委员会提供的表格向委员会提交申请，并随附五十美元。

委员会不得在同一人名下颁发一个以上的执照或注册一个以上的持证人。

第 634A.125 条　研讨会、讲座或教学临时执照的颁发

如符合以下条件,可根据 NRS 第 634A.165 条向非持证人颁发临时证书:

1. 申请人使用委员会提供的表格向委员会提交申请,其中包括:

(a) 申请人简历。

(b) 与东方医学或针刺疗法相关的特定主题,作为研讨会、讲座或教学的主题。

(c) 申请办理临时执照的具体日期。

(d) 相关证明材料,证明申请人有能力就东方医学或针刺疗法相关主题开展研讨会、讲座或教学活动。

2. 申请人根据第 634A.165 条缴纳颁发临时证书的费用。

3. 委员会以会议形式批准该申请。

第 634A.130 条　口袋执照

1. 在颁发及续期执照时,每名持证人将获得一张标有执照到期日或续期到期日的口袋执照。在执业期间,持证人应随身携带该执照。

2. 应患者、潜在患者、委员会成员及治安官的要求,持证人应准许检查其口袋执照,以证明所有现行费用均已缴纳。

第 634A.133 条　持有 2018 年 12 月 31 日以后颁发的执照,需要维持国家认证;执业证明

2018 年 12 月 31 日之后首次获得新执照的持证人(包括但不限于根据 NRS 第 634A 章第 2 条通过背书形式获得执照的持证人),应:

维持 NCCAOM 或其继受机构的东方医学认证;且

下列情形须向行政主管提供认证证明:

(a) 认证。

(b) 再认证。

(c) 将其执照类别由非执业状态改为执业状态。

第 634A.135 条　继续教育;执照;恢复到执业状态

1. 除本条另有规定外,持证人应在每个自然年度内完成至少十学时的继续教育。

2. 根据第 634A.137 条,持证人只能从经委员会批准的继续教育课程学时中获得学分。

3. 自 2003 日历年起,持证人在某年获得超过十学时继续教育学分的,可结转超出十学时的学分并将该超额学分用于满足下一年的继续教育要求。持证人根据 NRS 第 634A.167 条提交续期执照的表格时应以书面形式表明结转超额学分的意向。

4. 未在本州执业的持证人可要求委员会将其执照划为非执业状态。非执业执照的持证人不受本条规定中有关继续教育要求的约束。

5. 申请人向委员会申请将其执照从非执业状态改为执业状态,须:

(a) 在该申请人试图重新分类其执照的当年,满足继续教育要求。

(b) 向委员会提交证明材料,证明申请人已满足申请要求。

(c) 缴纳第 634A.165 条规定的费用。

第 634A.137 条　继续教育课程的批准;申请;免除批准及批准费的课程;批准到期

1. 除第 2 款另有规定外,个人或机构不得在本州为持证人提供继续教育课程,除非该个人或机构已根据本条事先获得委员会批准。

2. 经 NCCAOM 批准再认证的针灸与东方医学与生物医学(AOM-BIO)核心能力课程,可在本州作为面向持证人的继续教育课程,且无需获得委员会批准,根据第 634A.165 条可免除其继续教育课程的批准费用。

3. 个人或机构可向委员会提交以下文件,申请批准其继续教育课程:

在委员会提供的表格上填写的申请须包含以下信息:

(a)拟定课程的具体主题或题目,每位拟定讲师的姓名。

(b)与课程有关的所有材料,包括但不限于向参加课程的持证人提供的书面材料。

(c)根据第 634A.165 条要求的费用。

4. 如委员会根据本条批准继续教育课程,则委员会将确定持证人参加该课程应获得的继续教育学时数。

5. 继续教育课程将于委员会批准四年后到期,第 2 款所述课程除外。

第 634A.140 条　年度续期费的支付;首次续期费用的分配比例

除本条另有规定外,东方医学执照持有人应按照第 634A.165 条的要求向委员会支付执照年度续期费,不论其执照为执业状态还是非执业状态。处于执业状态或非执业状态下的东方医学执照首次续期时,委员会将按月分摊年费。

第 634A.150 条　恢复因未支付年费而作废的执照;重新申请新执照

1. 凡是根据 NRS 第 634A.160 条执照作废的,如需恢复其执照,应满足下列条件:

(a)执照作废未满一年:

(1)申请人向委员会缴纳执照作废期间所有应缴费用,以及第 634A.165 条中规定的滞纳金。

(2)申请人提交证明材料,证明其遵守继续教育的相关要求。

(b)委员会在例会上恢复此人执照。

2. 凡是根据 NRS 第 634A.160 条执照作废,且未能遵守第 1 条第(a)款规定的,如需获得执照,须重新申请新的执照。

第 634A.160 条　执照和口袋执照吊销或撤销时将其交回;丢失、被盗或被毁执照或口袋执照的换发

1. 如执照被撤销,持证人应在收到撤销通知后的五日内,将委员会先前颁发的执照和口袋执照交回行政主管处。

2. 如执照被吊销一段时间,持证人应在收到吊销通知后的五日内,将委员会先前颁发的执照和口袋执照交回行政主管处。

3. 如根据第 1 款或第 2 款的规定,必须收回执照或口袋执照,但执照已丢失、被盗或销毁,则持证人必须填写一份宣誓书并交予委员会,说明执照或口袋执照已丢失、被盗,或被毁,持证人重新找到时会立即将其归还。

4. 如持证人的执照或口袋执照丢失、被盗或被销毁,持证人必须:

(a)填写一份宣誓书并交予委员会,说明执照或口袋执照已丢失、被盗或被毁,持证人重新找回时会立即将其归还。

(b) 支付第634A.165条中规定的费用,以更换执照或口袋执照。

第634A.165条　委员会费用

委员会将收取以下费用:

初次申请东方医学医师执照	1 000美元
2月1日续期有效执照	700美元
2月1日之前续期非执业执照	500美元
2月1日后逾期九十日内续期执照的罚款	100美元
2月1日后逾期超过九十日续期执照的罚款	200美元
恢复作废执照的罚款	200美元
初次申请使用假名	100美元
换发口袋执照	100美元
换发执照	200美元
初次实践考试的费用	1 000美元
实践考试补考费	500美元
执照从执业状态转为非执业状态	200美元
执照从非执业状态转为执业状态	500美元
继续教育课程批准	100美元
讲座或培训临时证书	100美元
金额不足退回支票	25美元
本章和NRS的第634A章的副本	10美元
其他副本,每页	0.25美元
以光盘或磁带格式录制的其他副本	20美元
东方医学院或学院的初次申请费	2 000美元
2月1日之前批准课程的年费	1 000美元

第634A.170条　纪律处分的理由

委员会认为以下行为属于违反职业道德的行为,应予以适当的纪律处分:

1. 与另一位持证人分配或"分割"费用,除非另一位持证人事实上为该持证人的患者提供了相关服务(转诊除外)。持证人不应:

(a) 雇佣他人或给他人支付酬金,为持证人招揽或获取专业工作。

(b) 直接或间接与无证人员分享由专业工作产生或附带的报酬。

(c) 直接或间接协助或教唆无证人员从事东方医学、针刺疗法或草药相关工作或从中获取报酬。

2. 使用付费推荐的方式招揽或鼓励公众选用持证人的服务。

3. 制作、发布或让他人制作、发布任何广告、要约、声明或其他形式的书面或口头陈述,且该陈述中存在直接的或暗示性的具有虚假性、误导性或欺骗性的信息。只要广告中存在欺骗、误导或有害公众的倾向,即使公众没有真正被广告欺骗、误导或伤害,均足以导致违反本条款的相关处分程序。本款所述"广告"包括但不限于:

（a）名片、室内或室外标志、信笺、记入电话号码簿或其他名录中的文字。

（b）报纸或杂志上的广告。

（c）通过电子方式制作的广告，包括但不限于在互联网上登出的广告。

4. 使用未获委员会批准的假名。

第 634A.210 条　规定的范围、解释和适用

1. 除委员会另有指示外，第 634A.210 至 634A.570 条的规定（含本条）适用于委员会的所有惯例和程序。

2. 第 634A.210 至 634A.570 条的规定（含本条）可被宽松解释，以确保公正、迅速并简化地解决交予委员会的所有问题。

3. 如第 634A.210 至 634A.570 条的规定（含本条）或该等规定对任何人、物或情势的适用被认定为无效，委员会认为该等失效规定不影响余下条款的效力或其适用，余下条款的效力或其适用不受无效条款的影响。

第 634A.220 条　通信

所有正式的书面通信和文件须发送给州立东方医学委员会，而不是委员会的成员或工作人员。

第 634A.230 条　支付费用和汇款；退还申请费

费用和汇款须以汇票、银行汇票或支票的形式支付给委员会，抬头为"州立东方医学委员会"。以纸币或硬币形式汇款的风险完全由汇款人承担，委员会对其损失不承担任何责任。邮票不予汇寄。

申请人存在下列情形的，申请费不予退回：

（a）未能在实际递交表格后六个月内提交表格要求的所有文件以完成其申请。

（b）撤回其申请；或

（c）在委员会颁发执照之前死亡。

第 634A.240 条　时间的计算

第 634A.210 至 634A.570 条授权的任何行为相应的完成时限均不包含首日，包含最后一日。如遇周末及法定节假日，则顺延至下一个正常工作日。

第 634A.245 条　要求委员会在会上就某事项审议或采取行动

要求委员会在会上就某事项审议或采取行动的申请，务必于会议日期前至少十五个工作日内送交委员会。

第 634A.250 条　要求委员会提供更多信息

在委员会主要办公场所向行政主管提出申请，即可获得有关委员会审议程序或事项状态的补充信息。

第 634A.260 条　当事人的类型

1. 根据诉讼程序的性质和当事人之间的关系，委员会诉讼程序的一方应称为申请人、呈请人、申诉人、答辩人、介入第三人或利害关系人。

2. 向委员会申请或请求任何权利或授权的人应称为"申请人"。

3. 请求肯定性救济的人（申诉人除外）应称为"呈请人"。

4. 向委员会投诉任何个人或行为的人应称为"申诉人"。在委员会自行提起的诉讼中,委员会应称为"申诉人"。

5. 被投诉或调查的人应称为"答辩人"。

6. 除程序的主要当事人外,可能受该程序直接及实质影响的人,在取得委员会或审裁官的命令许可介入后,应称为"介入第三人"。经委员会许可,或以其他类似方式介入事项或程序,并不意味着委员会决定赋予介入第三人以认为其合法权益受到委员会裁决、命令或决定的损害而提起司法审查或起诉的当事人主体资格。认为自己可能受程序影响,但未参与程序者应称为"利害关系人"。

第634A.270条 委员会工作人员作为当事人

委员会的工作人员可以出席听证会,并有权以当事人身份参与程序。

第634A.280条 当事人的权利

在听证会上,除利害关系人外,第634A.260条中指名的所有当事人均可出庭、引进证据、审查和盘问证人、提出异议并参与诉讼程序。利害关系人可能会被要求陈述其潜在利益。

第634A.290条 出席听证会

当事人应在听证会开始时或在审裁官指定时间出席,向审裁官提供其姓名和地址并陈述其立场或利益。这些信息将记录在听证会笔录中。

第634A.300条 各方代表;律师资格

当事人可亲自、委托律师或委托其他代表人参加听证会。

以当事人代理人身份出席听证程序的律师必须具有律师资格,并经任一州最高法院许可以律师身份执业,且信誉良好。如该律师未经内华达最高法院许可执业,则须关联一位已被认可并有权执业的律师。

第634A.310条 向律师送达文件

在律师代表某一方出席听证会后,其后所需送达的所有通知、法律文书和命令必须送达该律师。为被代表的当事人之目的,该送达视为有效送达。

第634A.320条 律师退出

任何经备案的律师欲退出委员会程序,须以书面形式及时通知委员会或审裁官、其所代表的当事人以及其他程序当事人。

第634A.330条 行为要求

出席委员会程序者应遵守道德及行为标准。

第634A.340条 法律文书的标题,修改和解释

1. 提交给委员会的法律文书包括申请书、呈请书、申诉书和答辩书。

2. 除委员会自己发起的申诉外,所有法律文书均须经过核实。

3. 在不侵犯当事人实体权利的情况下,委员会可允许修改或更正法律文书,或补充遗漏内容。

4. 所有法律文书均可宽松解释为实现双方当事人之间的公正,而在诉讼程序的每个阶段,如法律文书或诉讼程序中的错误或缺陷不影响各方当事人实体权利,委员会或审裁官将不予理会。

第634A.350条　申请书

1. 要求委员会提供特权、许可或授权的所有法律文书应称为"申请书"。

2. 申请书须写明申请人的全名和地址,由申请人签字。

第634A.360条　呈请书

所有申请肯定性救济(申请书、申诉书或答辩书除外)的法律文书,包括申请获得宣言命令或咨询意见以及请求通过、备案、修改或废除规定的请求,应称为"呈请书"。

所有呈请书须写明呈请人的全名和地址,并且必须由呈请人签字。

第634A.370条　申诉书;答辩人通知;通知后获取证据之使用

1. 根据任何利害关系人或者委员会任何成员的提议,可根据NRS第634A章,就一个或多个理由提起申诉。

2. 如两名或多名申诉人的理由针对同一人,并处理实质上相同的违反法律、法规或委员会命令的行为,则可合并为同一程序。

3. 所有程序须以书面形式交予委员会的行政主管。

4. 除非委员会收到通知,表明该申诉已通过答辩人答复或以其他类似形式获得解决,委员会将在方便时尽快安排听证会。

5. 在听证会召开至少三十日前,委员会将通知答辩人听证会的日期、时间和地点,并将通知副本以及委员会目前所掌握的与程序相关的通讯、报告、书面陈述或证人证言一并提供给答辩人。根据本款,在向答辩人提供通知和相关材料副本之日后,新获得的证据不得提交给委员会,除非能够证明在该日之前无法通过委员会审慎调查获得该证据,并在获得该证据后立即将其交予答辩人。

第634A.380条　答辩书;未递交回复时的缺席登记

1. 根据第634A.370条第5款,答辩人应在通知和相关材料送达后二十日内提交答辩书。答辩书中须对申诉书中的每项事实陈述予以承认或否认。

2. 答辩书可亲自送达,也可通过挂号邮件发送到委员会总办事处。

3. 一经证据证明,答辩人收到申诉书和听证会通知后未按照本条规定的时间给予答复,即可视作答辩人缺席,并可根据申诉书中的指控作出判决。

第634A.390条　动议:内容;反对;答复;口头辩论

1. 动议系指针对委员会授权,就特定主体采取行动的程序。

2. 除非在听证会期间提出,所有动议均须采用书面形式。

3. 所有书面动议都必须陈述所寻求救济的性质及其理由。

4. 反对动议的一方可在收到动议后十日内送达并提交对动议的书面答复。

5. 只有在动议的反对意见送达并提交后,动议方才可在五日内送达并提交书面答复。

6. 除非委员会要求口头辩论,否则无需经过口头辩论即可做出动议决定。如有要求,委员会将安排听证会的日期和时间。

第634A.400条　存档

当事人须向委员会提交所有法律文书、动议或其他文件的原件和两份清晰的副本。如委员会认为其他人可能受诉讼影响,或有其他人希望获得法律文书副本,委员会可要求当事人向其提供一份法律文书副本。

第634A.410条 送达

除特定法规或条例另有规定外,要求委员会送达的所有通知、意见和文件(裁决或命令除外)以及当事人提交的所有文件须按照《内华达州民事诉讼规则》第4条的规定送达。

第634A.430条 委员会召开听证会:地点;通知

听证会将在委员会通知中指定的州内地点举行。

先前已举行的听证会欲重新举行,须至少提前十日发送通知。

第634A.440条 延期听证

委员会可在听证会举行前或听证会举行期间,基于申请人的诚信,同意听证会延期申请,以供申请人提交与听证会任何主题相关的进一步证据或补充证据。

听证会召开前的延期申请须在听证会计划日期前的七个工作日内提出。

第634A.450条 当事人缺席

1. 如一方未能出席委员会安排的听证会,且未请求延期或未获得延期批准,委员会应听取已出庭证人的证词,且可根据之前所获得的证据进行审议和处理。

2. 由于意外、疾病或其他合理原因,当事人未能出席委员会安排的听证会或请求延期未能通过者,则可在不超过十五日的合理期限内,向行政主管申请重启听证程序,经调查当事人具有充分且合理的理由后,委员会将立即确定听证会的时间和地点,并向当事人发出通知。在确定时间和地点后,当事人可为自己作证,或提交对其有利的其他证据。除非委员会提出要求,否则先前作证的证人无需再次出席听证会。

第634A.460条 传票

1. 委员会可根据书面申请发出要求证人出席听证的传票。

2. 除非委员会自行发布传票,要求出示文件、账簿或其他记录的传票只有在提出书面申请后才会发出。申请书需尽可能清楚地指明所需文件、账簿或其他记录。

3. 在传票规定的时间或之前,委员会应:

4. 如传票不合理或不公平,撤销传票;或

5. 被传唤人预付所需文件、账簿或其他记录的合理费用,方可拒绝动议。

第634A.470条 证词必须经过宣誓

在正式听证会上委员会审议的所有证词必须经过宣誓,正式通知或规定事项除外。在证人席上作证前,每个证人都应当宣誓或肯定自己在听证会上所作的证词都是事实,绝无虚言。

第634A.480条 初步程序

委员会主管人员应宣布程序或听证会就位,出席并解决未决动议。此后双方可以进行开场陈述。

第634A.490条 出示证据

1. 申请人、呈请人或申诉人可出示证据,然后答辩人也可提交证据。委员会主管人员应确定介入诉讼人出示证据的顺序。通常按照以下顺序收取各方提供的证据:

(a) 申请和呈请:

(1) 申请人或呈请人。

（2）委员会的工作人员。

（3）介入第三人。

（4）申请人或呈请人的反驳。

（b）申诉：

（1）申诉人。

（2）答辩人。

（3）委员会的工作人员。

（4）申诉人反驳。

（c）委员会的申诉：

（1）委员会。

（2）答辩人。

（3）委员会工作人员反驳。

2. 本程序可由委员会或主管人员酌情修改。

3. 委员会或主持成员可酌情决定是否允许当事人作最后陈述。

第634A.500条　合并

1. 如不同事项实质上相同并且合并审理不会损害各方的利益,则委员会可在听证会上合并两个或两个以上的审理程序。

2. 在合并审理的听证会上,委员会主管人员应确定当事人提交证据及开庭陈述和最后陈述的顺序。

第634A.510条　约定

1. 经委员会主管人员同意,当事各方可以就任何争议事实作出约定,或通过引入证据的书面约定,或通过记录在案的口头陈述。

2. 规定对各方均有约束力,委员会可将其视作听证会的证据。尽管当事各方另有规定,委员会可要求提供证据对规定的事实加以证明。

第634A.520条　委员会正式通知

委员会可对其专业知识范围内司法认定的事实以及公认的技术或科学事实作出正式通知,包括：

1. 委员会或本州其他监管机构的法规、官方报告、决议和命令。

2. 内华达州修订法规。

3. 委员会颁发的证书和许可证。

4. 常识问题以及得到确定的技术或科学事实。

5. 正式文件,如：

（a）这些文件与本听证相关,并在此通过引用并入该记录。

（b）提供文件的一方适当、明确地引用此类文件。

（c）这些文件公开并广泛传播,以便参加听证会的所有利害关系人进行审查并提出反证。

第634A.530条　听证记录

1. 在听证会上,委员会可要求在规定时间内将听证记录存档。

2. 须向委员会提交三份要求的听证记录副本,并随附送达确认书或邮寄给其他当事人的证明书。

3. 听证记录归档后,或动议存在争议时,委员会应就此进行口头辩论。该等事项应提前十日通知所有记录在案的相关方,除非委员会认为应缩短该时间。

第634A.540条　决议和命令

1. 在取证,提交听证记录或进行委员会允许的口头辩论后,将程序交由委员会决议。

2. 命令或决议将在听证会结束后九十日内宣布。

3. 经书面申请,可取得额外的命令副本。

第634A.550条　听证会记录

1. 听证会记录将由机械设备或电子设备保存。

2. 如有要求,任何人均可索取该记录的副本,费用自理。

第634A.560条　呈请书;颁布命令或意见

宣告性命令或咨询意见的呈请只能由执照或证书的持有人或申请人提出。

呈请书的原件和七份副本,必须在委员会下一次定期会议前至少十日交予行政主管。呈请书须在会上交予委员会。会议后三十日内,委员会将发布宣告性命令或咨询意见。

第634A.570条　呈请书

要求通过、提交、修改或废除规定的呈请书须采用书面形式。

必须将呈请书的原件和七份副本交予委员会。

犹 他 州

犹他州针灸法①

第一节 一般规定

第 58-72-101 条　标题

本章为"针灸许可法"。

第 58-72-102 条　针灸执业许可-定义

除了第 58-1-102 条②中所涉及的定义，下列定义适用于本章：

(1)"委员会"系指根据第 58-72-201 条设立的针灸许可委员会。

(2)(a)"注射疗法"系指已获得国家针灸与东方医学审核委员会(NCCAOM)洁针技术资格的执业针灸师使用皮下注射针头，将下列液态无菌物质皮下或肌内注射到身体的针刺穴位：

(i) 营养药物。

(ii) 局部麻醉剂。

(iii) 自体血液，如持证人持有现行有效的血液采集静脉切开术认证资格。

(iv) 无菌水。

(v) 葡萄糖。

(vi) 碳酸氢钠。

(vii) 无菌生理盐水。

(b)"注射疗法"包括使用超声引导以确保注射仅为皮下注射或肌内注射。

(c)"注射疗法"不包括向静脉、关节、动脉、血管、神经、肌腱、深层器官或脊柱注射药物。

(d) 不得向孕妇或八岁以下儿童实施"注射疗法"。

(3)"执业针灸师"，即"L. Ac."，系指根据本章规定取得针灸执照的人。

---

① 根据《犹他州法典》第 58 卷第 72 章(Utah Code Annotated, Title 58. Occupations and Professions, Chapter 72. Acupuncture Licensing Act)译出。

② 《职业证照管理部门法》(Division of Occupational and Professional Licensing Act)第 58-1-102 条"定义"。

(4)"艾灸"系指使用草本艾灸来加热身体穴位的热疗法。

(5)(a)"针灸实践"系指在传统东方医学诊断和现代研究基础上,在人体特定部位实施针刺、注射疗法或灸法为主的治疗方法。

(b)针灸执业范围内的辅助疗法包括:

(i)基于传统东方医学诊断和现代研究的手法治疗、器械治疗、温针治疗、电针治疗以及电磁治疗。

(ii)根据从业培训,基于传统的东方医学诊断和现代研究,推荐、管理或提供膳食指南、草药、补品、顺势疗法和治疗性运动。

(iii)本条第(5)款(a)项和(b)项中所述针灸实践在以下规定允许的范围内在动物身上进行。

(A)第58-28-307条(12)款①。

(B)本章的规定。

(C)部门规章。

(c)"针灸疗法"不包括:

(i)超出弹性范围的人体关节手法或关节调整。

(ii)第58-73-102条②中定义的"脊柱关节手法"。

(6)第58-1-501条③和第58-72-503条中所定义的"违反职业道德的行为",将由部门规章进一步界定。

第58-72-103条 规章制定

相关部门行使本章项下的规章制定权时,应遵守第63G卷第3章《犹他州行政规章制定法》的有关规定。

第二节 委 员 会

第58-72-201条 针灸许可委员会

(1)设立的针灸许可委员会由以下成员组成:

(a)四名执业针灸师。

(b)一名公众人士。

(2)委员会的任命和就职应符合第58-1-201条④的规定。

(a)委员会的义务与责任应符合第58-1-202条⑤和第58-1-203条⑥的规定。

---

① 《兽医执业法》(Veterinary Practice Act)第58-28-307条"本章的豁免条款"(12)款。
② 《整脊医师执业法》(Chiropractic Physician Practice Act)第58-73-102条"定义"。
③ 《职业证照管理部门法》第58-1-501条"违法和违反职业道德的行为"。
④ 《职业证照管理部门法》第58-1-201条"委员会-任命-成员资格-任期-职位空缺-法定人数-每日津贴和费用-委员会主席-财务利益或在禁止教授继续教育的专业学校中担任的教职"(Boards-Appointment-Membership-Terms-Vacancies-Quorum-Per diem and expenses-Chair-Financial interest or faculty position in professional school that teaches continuing education prohibited)。
⑤ 《职业证照管理部门法》第58-1-202条"委员会-义务、职能与责任"。
⑥ 《职业证照管理部门法》第58-1-203条"与委员会合作的部门的义务、职能与责任-建设服务委员会"(Construction Services Commission)。

(b)此外,委员会应指定一名成员作为为常任委员,负责下列工作:
(i)协助行政部门审查关于持证人违法行为或违反职业道德的行为的投诉。
(ii)在调查投诉过程中向该部门提供建议。
(4)根据第(3)款,审查投诉或向其提供调查建议的委员会成员,无法在委员会关于该投诉的裁决程序中担任审裁官。

第三节 执　　照

第58-72-301条　执照要求-执照分类
(1)除第58-1-307条①或第58-72-304条中规定的情形外,需要持有执照才能从事针灸实践。
(2)部门须向符合本章要求的人颁发执业针灸执照。

第58-72-302条　取得执照的条件
申请针灸执照应当具备以下条件:
(1)按照行政部门规定的格式提交申请。
(2)根据第63J-1-504条②的规定支付费用。
(3)通过现行有效的认证或其他适当的文件,证明其根据NCCAOM的制定的指南,符合现行针灸执业证书的要求。
(4)通过行政部门根据相关规定组织的考试。
(5)按照相关规定制定程序,使患者能够针对此治疗做出知情同意书。
(6)如接到要求,与委员会当面评估申请人的执业资格。

第58-72-303条　执照-到期-续期条款
(1)(a)根据本章颁发的每份执照应按照两年续期周期的规定颁发。
(b)续期期限可延长或缩短最多一年,以维持或更改既定的续期周期。
(2)除非持证人按照第58-1-308条③的规定续期执照,否则执照将在执照到期日自动失效。
(3)续期执照应具备以下资格:
(a)现行有效的NCCAOM认证文件;或
(b)达到与根据本章取得执照的人员相同的专业发展要求。

第58-72-304条　获得执照的豁免
除了第58-1-307条规定的执照豁免外,下列人员可在规定的情况和限制条件下从事针灸实践,而无需根据本章获得执照:
(1)根据第67章《犹他州医疗实践法》和第68章《犹他州骨科医疗服务法》获得内科医师、外科医师、骨科内科医师或骨科外科医师的人。

---

① 《职业证照管理部门法》第58-1-307条"执照的豁免"。
② 《预算程序法》(*Budgetary Procedures Act*)第63J-1-504条"费用-采纳、程序和批准-未经立法机关批准而确定和评估的费用"。
③ 《职业证照管理部门法》第58-1-308条"执照期限-执照到期-执照更新-执照恢复-申请程序"。

（2）在美国或其他联邦机构的武装部队服役的特派医生或外科医生。

（3）根据第73章《整脊医师执业法》获得整脊医师执照的人。如没有针灸执照，整脊医师不得自称"执业针灸师"。

第四节　拒绝颁发执照以及纪律处分

第58-72-401条　拒绝颁发执照-纪律处分程序-恢复执业的理由

如拒绝向申请人颁发执照，拒绝续期持证人执照，撤销、吊销、限制执照或将执照列入察看期，向持证人进行公开或私下谴责，以及向持证人发出停止和终止执照的命令，此类程序的理由应符合第58-1-401条①的规定。

第五节　违法行为和违反职业道德的行为——处罚

第58-72-501条　执业针灸师-对使用头衔的限制

（1）（a）执业针灸师除使用"执业针灸师"或者"L.Ac."的字样以外，不得将任何头衔、字词或标识与本人姓名或工作一并展示或以任何方式使用。

（b）如与该针灸师的实践结合使用时，"执业针灸师""L.AC."的字样，应当紧邻该执业针灸师姓名显示。

（2）（a）执业针灸师不得将"内科医生""内/外科医生"或"医生"等字眼与针灸师的名称或工作一并展示。

（b）如获得相应的针灸学位，针灸师可使用"针灸医生"或"东方医学医师"的头衔。

（3）内科医生或脊椎按摩师选择从事针灸实践，应以内科医生或脊椎按摩师而非执业针灸师的身份从事针灸实践。

第58-72-502条　对违法行为的处罚

（1）任何人违反第58-1-501条（1）款（a）项违法行为规定的，即属三级重罪。

（2）任何人违反第58-1-501条（1）款（b）至（e）项违法行为规定的，即属A类轻罪。

第58-72-503条　违反职业道德的行为

违反职业道德的行为包括未按要求将英文记录传送给有关行政部门、患者的全科医生或第三方保险支付人。

第六节　针灸师治疗-保险支付

第58-72-601条　针灸执照未授权开展医疗实践-保险支付

本章任何内容均不得解释为允许开展医疗活动，而且不得要求第三方保险公司直接向从事针灸实践的人员支付款项。

---

① 即《职业证照管理部门法》第58-1-401条"拒绝颁发执照的理由-纪律处分程序-时间限制-制裁"。

第七节 采购与施用权限

第58-72-701条 采购与施用权限

(1) 已接受实施注射疗法的必要培训的持证人,包括已经获得NCCAOM的洁针技术证书的持证人:

(a) 有权采购和施用第58-72-102条(2)款(a)项和(b)项中所规定的药物,并且仅允许在诊所内使用。

(b) 可从已登记的处方药商店、注册制造商或注册批发商处获得第58-72-102条(2)款所规定的药物。

(2) 如机构根据本章规定向持证人提供药物,并信任持证人所提供的执照信息,则不对提供药物承担责任。

犹他州针灸行政法[①]

第156-72-101条 标题

本条称为"针灸许可法细则"。

第156-72-102条 定义

除了第58卷第1章《职业证照管理部门法》和第58卷第72章《针灸许可法》中的定义外,下列定义补充了法定定义:

(1) "ACAOM"系指针灸及东方医学教育审核委员会(Accreditation Commission for Acupuncture And Oriental Medicine, ACAOM)。

(2)《针灸许可法》第58-72-102(5)(b)(ii)目中的"根据从业者培训"系指持证人已完成ACAOM认证或认可的教育计划中关于推荐、使用或提供膳食指南、草药、补充剂、顺势疗法和治疗性运动的教育和培训。

(3)《针灸许可法》第58-72-102(5)(b)(ii)目中的"使用"系指通过下列方式对患者身体直接应用草药、顺势疗法或补充剂:

(a) 摄入。

(b) 局部应用。

(c) 吸入;或

(d) 穴位注射疗法(PIT)。

(4)《针灸许可法》第58-72-102(5)(b)(ii)目中使用的"草药"和"顺势疗法"可包括:

(a) 维生素。

[①] 根据《犹他州行政法规》第156卷第72章(Utah Administrative Code Commerce, Title R156. Commerce, Occupational and Professional Licensing. Rule R156-72. Acupuncture Licensing Act Rule)译出。

（b）矿物药。

（c）氨基酸。

（d）蛋白质。

（e）酶。

（5）《针灸许可法》第 58－72－102（5）（a）项中的"针灸针刺入穴位"系指针灸和东方医学中的一种治疗方法，包括肌筋膜激痛点治疗、肌内注射疗法、穴位注射疗法（PIT）、增生疗法、感受刺激、阿是穴或干针治疗。

（6）《针灸许可法》第 58－72－102（5）（b）（ii）目中的"现代研究"系指根据经 NCCAOM 认可的针灸和东方医学教育和培训进行执业。

（7）"NCCAOM"系指美国国家针灸与东方医学审核委员会（National Certification Commission for Acupuncture and Oriental Medicine，NCCAOM），原名国家针灸师审核委员会（NCCA）。

第 156－72－103 条　权限-目的

本条由行政部门根据《职业证照管理部门法》第 58－1－106（1）（a）项的规定通过，以便其能够根据第 58 卷第 72 章开展管理。

第 156－72－104 条　组织-与第 156 卷第 1 章的关系

本条中的组织及其与第 156 卷第 1 章的关系如第 156－1－107 条所述。

第 156－72－302A 条　持证人的资格条件-认证和考试要求

根据《针灸许可法》第 58－72－302（3）和（4）款的规定，为满足 NCCAOM 指南中有关现行有效针灸认证的要求，以及通过针灸师考试的要求，申请执照应提交下列文件：

（1）现行有效的 NCCAOM 认证。

（2）根据《职业证照管理部门法》第 58－1－302（1）款的规定，申请者在申请前至少一年内，在美国的任何州、地区或准州从事针灸师的工作，且信誉良好。

第 156－72－302B 条　颁发执照的资格-动物针灸

根据第 58－28－307（12）（d）项和《针灸许可法》第 58－72－102（5）（b）（iii）目的规定，从事动物针灸执业的执业针灸师应完成一百学时的动物针灸培训和教育，其中包括：

（1）在执业兽医的督导下完成五十学时的在职培训。

（2）完成动物解剖学训练。

（3）完成动物继续教育剩余学时。

第 156－72－302C 条　知情同意书

（1）根据《针灸许可法》第 58－72－302（5）款的规定，为使患者能够对治疗作出知情同意书，执业针灸师应为每位患者制作一份病历，其内容包括：

（a）对症状的书面审查。

（b）患者签署的同意接受针灸治疗的声明。

（c）如患者正在接受《针灸许可法》第 58－72－102（5）款所定义的辅助治疗，则需提供一份由患者签署的关于执业针灸师进行该治疗所接受的教育和培训的书面披露。

（2）根据《针灸许可法》第 58－72－503 条的规定，应保存七年患者记录，其中包括知情同意书的记录。

第 156‑72‑302D 条　重新编号

曾被引为 UT ADC 第 156‑72 章

第 156‑72‑303 条　续期周期‑程序

(1) 根据《职业证照管理部门法》第 58‑1‑308(1) 款的规定,第 58 卷第 72 章中持证人两年续期周期的续期日由第 156‑1‑308A 条规定。

(2) 续期程序按照第 156‑1‑308B 至第 156‑1‑308L 条执行。

(3) 根据第 58‑1‑308 (3)(b) 项和《针灸许可法》第 58‑72‑303 (3) 款的规定,未持有现行有效的 NCCAOM 认证的持证人应当:

(a) 在两年续期周期内至少完成三十个继续教育学分(CEU)或三十个专业教学活动(PDA)。

(b) 维持现行的基本生命支持(BLS)及心肺复苏术(CPR)认证。

第 156‑72‑503 条　违反职业道德的行为

根据《针灸许可法》第 58‑72‑102(6) 款的规定,"违反职业道德的行为"包括:

(1) 未保持办公室、仪器、设备、器具、用品的安全卫生。

(2) 违反《针灸许可法》第 58‑72‑303(3) 款有关续期资格的规定:

(a) 未能维持现行有效的 NCCAOM 认证。

(b) 未能完成本规则第 156‑72‑303(3) 款要求的继续教育学分(CEUs);或

(c) 未能维持基本生命支持(BLS)及心肺复苏术(CPR)有效认证。

(3) 未能遵守 2016 年 1 月 1 日修订后的 NCCAOM《道德准则》,该准则在此通过引用并入。

(4) 未按规定保存七年患者记录的。

(5) 在未完成《针灸许可法》第 58‑72‑102(5)(b)(ⅱ) 目和本规则第 156‑72‑102(2) 款规定的从业者培训的情况下,推荐、使用或提供饮食指南、草药、补充剂、顺势疗法或治疗性运动;或

(6) 给予静脉注射、免疫接种或使用管制药物。

IDAHO

IDAHO CODE ANNOTATED

54-4701 PURPOSE

The legislature finds and declares that the provision of acupuncture services affects the public health, safety and welfare. The legislature further finds that it is in the public interest to aid in the provision of acupuncture services of high quality to the people of Idaho. To aid in fulfilling these purposes, this chapter provides for the licensure and regulation of acupuncturists within the state of Idaho.

54-4702 DEFINITIONS

As used in this chapter:

(1) "Acupuncture" means that theory of health care developed from traditional and modern Oriental medical philosophies that employs diagnosis and treatment of conditions of the human body based upon stimulation of specific acupuncture points on meridians of the human body for the promotion, maintenance, and restoration of health and for the prevention of disease. Therapies within the scope of acupuncture include manual, mechanical, thermal, electrical and electromagnetic treatment of such specific indicated points. Adjunctive therapies included in, but not exclusive to, acupuncture include herbal and nutritional treatments, therapeutic exercise and other therapies based on traditional and modern Oriental medical theory.

(2) "Board" means the Idaho state board of acupuncture.

(3) "NCCAOM" means "National Certification Commission for Acupuncture and Oriental Medicine".

(4) "Practice of acupuncture" means the insertion of acupuncture needles and use of similar devices and therapies, including application of moxibustion, to specific indicated points on the skin of the human body as indicated pursuant to traditional and modern theories of Oriental medicine. The "practice of acupuncture" does not include:

(a) Surgery; or

(b) Prescribing, dispensing or administering any prescription drug or legend drug as defined in section 54-1705 (35), Idaho Code.

54-4703 LICENSE REQUIRED

(1) From and after the 1st day of July, 1999, it is unlawful for any person to practice acupuncture in this state without, at such time being licensed or certified pursuant to this chapter; provided however, the provisions of this chapter shall not apply to persons licensed pursuant to chapter 18, title 54, Idaho Code, but such persons may seek licensure or certification pursuant to this chapter on a voluntary basis. Persons holding an acupuncture trainee permit pursuant to this chapter may practice acupuncture on a supervised, limited basis as prescribed by this chapter, the board's rules and the permit.

(2) No person shall use any title, designation, words, letters, abbreviations, or sign, card or device which indicates to the public that such person may practice acupuncture in any form or has been issued a license or been certified pursuant to this chapter unless the person is so licensed or certified, has been issued such license or certification, and the license or certification is in good standing pursuant to rules of the board.

54-4704 BOARD OF ACUPUNCTURE CREATED-APPOINTMENT-TERMS

(1) There is hereby established in the department of self-governing agencies a state board of acupuncture and the members thereof shall be appointed by the governor within sixty (60) days following the effective date of this chapter.

(2) The board shall consist of five (5) members, three (3) of whom shall be licensed pursuant to this chapter, one (1) of whom shall be certified pursuant to this chapter, and one (1) of whom shall be a member of the public with an interest in the rights of the consumers of acupuncture services.

(3) In making appointments to the board of acupuncture, consideration shall be given to recommendations made by the Idaho acupuncture association, other similar professional organizations and any individual residing in this state.

(4) All members of the board shall be current residents of the state of Idaho and have been residents of the state of Idaho for a minimum of three (3) years immediately preceding appointment.

(5) All terms shall be four (4) years, and a member may be reappointed. In the event of death, resignation, or removal of any member before the expiration of the term to which appointed, the vacancy shall be filled for the unexpired portion of the term in the same manner as the original appointment.

(6) Board members shall serve at the pleasure of the governor.

(7) The board shall, within thirty (30) days after its appointment, and at least annually thereafter, hold a meeting and elect a chairman. The board may hold additional meetings on the call of the chairman or at the written request of any two (2) members of the board. The board

may appoint such committees as it considers necessary to carry out its duties. A majority of the members of the board shall constitute a quorum.

(8) Each member of the board shall be compensated as provided in section 59 – 509 (p), Idaho Code.

54 – 4705 BOARD OF ACUPUNCTURE-POWERS AND DUTIES-FUNDS

(1) The board shall have the authority to:

(a) Determine the qualifications of persons applying for licensure, certification and acupuncture trainee permits pursuant to this chapter and define, by rule, the appropriate scope of acupuncture services that may be rendered to the public in this state;

(b) Hire or appoint employees, including an executive director, investigators, attorneys, consultants and independent hearing examiners;

(c) Establish, pursuant to the administrative procedure act, such rules as are necessary for the administration of this chapter, including standards for professional conduct that reflect current practice standards and promote inclusion of innovations and advances in acupuncture;

(d) Conduct investigations and examinations and hold hearings;

(e) Collect fees and other funds as prescribed by this chapter;

(f) Contract, sue and be sued, and pursue other matters lawful in this state;

(g) Provide such other services and perform such other functions as are necessary and desirable to fulfill its purposes;

(h) Adopt rules requiring continuing education as a condition of continued licensure or certification.

(2) All fees received under the provisions of this chapter shall be paid to the bureau of occupational licenses and deposited in the state treasury to the credit of the occupational licenses fund and all costs and expenses incurred under the provisions of this chapter shall be a charge against and paid from said fund.

54 – 4706 REQUIREMENTS FOR LICENSURE

A person applying for a license shall, in addition to paying all required fees, submit a written application provided by the board showing to the satisfaction of the board that such person meets the following requirements:

(1) Has received certification from NCCAOM, or has successfully completed other similar requirements as have been approved by the board; and

(2) Has successfully completed an acupuncture internship or pre-professional practice program, coordinated program, or such other equivalent experience as may be approved by the board; and

(3) Has passed an examination or other demonstration of proficiency as may be uniformly required by the board for other similarly qualified applicants for licensure.

54 – 4707 REQUIREMENTS FOR CERTIFICATION

A person applying for a certification shall, in addition to paying all required fees, submit a written application provided by the board showing that such person has successfully passed an examination or other demonstration of proficiency as may be uniformly required by the board and:

(1) Has successfully completed the requirements for full membership in the American academy of medical acupuncture; or

(2) Has met each of the following education and experience requirements:

(a) Possesses from an accredited college or university a doctoral degree in chiropractic, dentistry, podiatric medicine, or naturopathic medicine;

(b) Has successfully completed an approved program consisting of a minimum of one hundred (100) hours of on-site didactic coursework in acupuncture taught by an NCCAOM certified acupuncturist who has been practicing acupuncture for at least five (5) years and is currently licensed, two hundred (200) hours of practice as a certified technicia or as an acupuncture trainee over a one (1) year period and twenty-five (25) case studies; and

(c) Has successfully passed a blood-borne pathogen course and comprehensive examination concerning the practice of acupuncture approved by the board that incorporates clean needle techniques and OSHA procedures and requirements.

54-4708 ACUPUNCTURE TRAINEE PERMIT

(1) A person seeking the experience needed to obtain licensure or certification pursuant to this chapter may apply for an acupuncture trainee permit. Such person shall pay all required fees, submit a written application provided by the board and show to the satisfaction of the board that such person is qualified and actively pursuing an acupuncture license or certification.

(2) In approving an acupuncture trainee permit the board shall consider the scope and extent of the applicant's academic and other training and experience in health care to date and may, for each individual acupuncture trainee:

(a) Require such supervision, as the board may deem appropriate, by a person licensed or certified pursuant to this chapter;

(b) Restrict the practice of acupuncture for the acupuncture trainee to specified therapies or treatments.

(3) A person's acupuncture trainee permit expires one (1) year from the date of issuance. However, the board may renew the permit for up to one (1) year if, before the permit expires, the person asks the board for an extension and establishes to the board's satisfaction that good cause exists for the board to renew the permit. The renewal of any acupuncture trainee permit may be upon such conditions as the board may require. The board may not renew a permit more than once and the board may not issue more than one (1) permit to any person.

54-4708A ACUPUNCTURE TECHNICIAN

Individuals who have been granted an acupuncture technician certificate before July 1, 2011, shall be entitled to retain and renew such certificate under the renewal terms as provided in section 54 – 4710, Idaho Code, and the board's rules, but no new technician certificates shall be issued on and after July 1, 2011.

54 – 4709 ENDORSEMENT LICENSURE

An applicant who proves to the satisfaction of the board that he is licensed or registered under the laws of another state, territory, or jurisdiction of the United States that, in the opinion of the board, imposes substantially equivalent licensing requirements as this chapter may, upon the payment of the required fee and the approval of the application, be licensed by endorsement pursuant to this chapter.

54 – 4710 EXPIRATION AND RENEWAL-REINSTATEMENT

(1) All licenses and certifications issued under the provisions of this chapter shall be subject to annual renewal and shall expire unless renewed in the manner prescribed by the board regarding applications for renewal, continuing education and fees. License renewal and reinstatement shall be in accordance with section 67 – 2614, Idaho Code.

(2) The board shall establish the following fees relating to licensing, which fees shall be established in an amount that is sufficient to defray all costs necessary for the administration of this chapter:

(a) Initial license;

(b) Renewal of license fee;

(c) Initial fee for certification;

(d) Initial acupuncture trainee permit;

(e) Renewal acupuncture technician certificate or acupuncture trainee permit;

(f) Inactive license and certification fees;

(g) Late renewal fees.

54 – 4711 SUSPENSION AND REVOCATION

To protect the health, safety and welfare of the public, the board, in accordance with the requirements of chapter 52, title 67, Idaho Code, may refuse to issue or may refuse to renew a license, certification or permit, or may suspend or revoke a license, certification or permit, under such conditions as the board may require, if the applicant or holder of the license, certification or permit has:

(1) Been convicted of a crime that is deemed relevant in accordance with section 67 – 9411 (1), Idaho Code; [that reflects on the qualifications, functions, or duties of an acupuncturist]

(2) Obtained or attempted to obtain the issuance or renewal of a license, certification or permit pursuant to this chapter by means of fraud, misrepresentation or concealment of material facts;

(3) Engaged in the practice of acupuncture in a manner that does not meet the generally accepted standards for the practice of acupuncture within the state of Idaho;

(4) Failed to maintain the confidentiality of records or other information pertaining to an

identifiable client, except as required or authorized by law;

(5) Engaged in any conduct that constitutes an abuse or exploitation of a client arising out of the trust and confidence placed in the acupuncturist by the client;

(6) Engaged in conduct that violates the provisions of this chapter, the rules of the board or the terms of any permit issued by the board;

(7) Failed to comply with a board order entered in a disciplinary matter;

(8) Had a license revoked or suspended or has been otherwise disciplined by the board or the proper authorities of another state, territory, or jurisdiction of the United States or another country; or

(9) Had a license or certification in a related field revoked or suspended or has been otherwise disciplined in Idaho or another state, territory, or jurisdiction of the United States or another country.

54-4712 TITLES

Persons licensed pursuant to this chapter may use the title "licensed acupuncturist". Persons certified or granted an acupuncture technician certificate, or an acupuncture trainee permit pursuant to this chapter, may use the title "certified acupuncturist", "acupuncture technician" or "acupuncture trainee", respectively, but may not use the title "licensed acupuncturist" or "doctor", or any abbreviation thereof, unless the acupuncturist is otherwise authorized to use such title. No person authorized to practice acupuncture pursuant to this chapter may hold himself out in any way as a medical physician, doctor of osteopathy, chiropractor, physical therapist or other health care professional unless the person is properly authorized for such practice pursuant to law.

54-4713 PENALTIES

(1) A person who violates any provision of this chapter shall, upon conviction, be guilty of a misdemeanor.

(2) The board may seek injunction against any person who practices acupuncture in violation of this chapter and may, in the event a permanent injunction is entered against such person or plea or verdict of guilty is entered in any criminal matter, impose a civil penalty in the amount of all costs and fees incurred by the board in prosecuting the matter.

(3) The representation to another person that a person holds a license, certification or permit pursuant to this chapter, when such representation is untrue, constitutes the using of a method, act or practice which is declared to be unlawful under the provisions of chapter 6, title 48, Idaho Code.

OREGON

OREGON REVISED STATUTES ANNOTATED

677.757 DEFINITIONS FOR ORS 677.757 TO 677.770

As used in ORS 677.757 to 677.770:

(1)(a) "Acupuncture" means an Oriental health care practice used to promote health and to treat neurological, organic or functional disorders by the stimulation of specific points on the surface of the body by the insertion of needles. "Acupuncture" includes the treatment method of moxibustion, as well as the use of electrical, thermal, mechanical or magnetic devices, with or without needles, to stimulate acupuncture points and acupuncture meridians and to induce acupuncture anesthesia or analgesia.

(b) The practice of acupuncture also includes the following modalities as authorized by the Oregon Medical Board:

(A) Traditional and modern techniques of diagnosis and evaluation;

(B) Oriental massage, exercise and related therapeutic methods; and

(C) The use of Oriental pharmacopoeia, vitamins, minerals and dietary advice.

(2) "Oriental pharmacopoeia" means a list of herbs described in traditional Oriental texts commonly used in accredited schools of Oriental medicine if the texts are approved by the Oregon Medical Board.

677.759 LICENSE REQUIRED; QUALIFICATIONS; EFFECT OF USING CERTAIN TERMS; RULES

(1) No person shall practice acupuncture without first obtaining a license to practice medicine and surgery or a license to practice acupuncture from the Oregon Medical Board except as provided in subsection (2) of this section.

(2) Notwithstanding subsection (1) of this section, the board may issue a license to practice acupuncture to an individual licensed to practice acupuncture in another state or territory of the United States if the individual is licensed to practice medicine and surgery or acupuncture

in the other state or territory. The board shall not issue such a license unless the requirements of the other state or territory are similar to the requirements of this state.

(3) The board shall examine the qualifications of an applicant and determine who shall be authorized to practice acupuncture.

(4) Using the term "acupuncture", "acupuncturist", "Oriental medicine" or any other term, title, name or abbreviation indicating that an individual is qualified or licensed to practice acupuncture is prima facie evidence of practicing acupuncture. In addition to the powers and duties of the board described in this chapter, the board shall adopt rules consistent with ORS 677.757 to 677.770 governing the issuance of a license to practice acupuncture.

677.760

677.761 PERSONS AND PRACTICES NOT WITHIN SCOPE OF ORS 677.757 TO 677.770

Nothing in ORS 677.757 to 677.770 is intended to:

(1) Prevent, limit or interfere with an individual licensed or certified by the Oregon Medical Board from practicing health care other than acupuncture within the scope of the license or certification of the individual.

(2) Limit any other licensed or certified health care practitioner from practicing acupressure or other therapy within the scope of the license or certification of the individual.

(3) Limit the activities of any person who engages in the business of providing Oriental massage, exercise and related therapeutic methods or who provides substances listed in an Oriental pharmacopoeia, or vitamins or minerals or dietary advice, so long as the activities of the person are not otherwise prohibited by law.

(4) Limit the ability of practitioners from outside Oregon to demonstrate the practice of acupuncture as part of a recognized and limited duration educational program, lecture or event within this state under rules adopted by the board.

NOTE: 677.761 was enacted into law by the Legislative Assembly but was not added to or made a part of ORS chapter 677. See Preface to Oregon Revised Statutes for further explanation.

677.765 UNAUTHORIZED PRACTICE BY ACUPUNCTURIST

Performance of acupuncture without licensure or after the termination of licensure by the Oregon Medical Board or in the absence of renewal of licensure constitutes the unauthorized practice of medicine and subjects the person to the penalties provided by ORS 677.990.

677.770 FEES

Every physician or surgeon or other person licensed as an acupuncturist shall pay to the Oregon Medical Board nonrefundable fees as determined by the board pursuant to ORS 677.265.

677.775

677.780 ACUPUNCTURE ADVISORY COMMITTEE; MEMBERSHIP; TERMS

(1) There is established an Acupuncture Advisory Committee consisting of six members

appointed by the Oregon Medical Board. Of the committee members appointed by the board:

(a) One shall be a person who is a current member of the board.

(b) Two shall be physicians licensed under ORS chapter 677.

(c) Three shall be acupuncturists licensed under ORS 677.759. In appointing the three acupuncturists, the board may receive nominations from the Oregon Association of Acupuncture and Oriental Medicine and other professional acupuncture organizations.

(2) The term of office of each committee member is three years, but a committee member serves at the pleasure of the board. A committee member may not serve more than two consecutive terms. A committee member serves until a successor is appointed and qualified. If there is a vacancy for any cause, the board shall make an appointment to become immediately effective for the unexpired term.

(3) A committee member is entitled to compensation and expenses as provided for board members in ORS 677.235.

(4) A majority of the members of the committee constitutes a quorum for the transaction of business.

677.785 DUTIES OF COMMITTEE

The Acupuncture Advisory Committee shall:

(1) Review and make recommendations concerning all applications to the Oregon Medical Board for acupuncture licensing or acupuncture license renewal.

(2) Recommend to the board standards of professional responsibility and practice for licensed acupuncturists.

(3) Recommend to the board standards of didactic and clinical education and training for acupuncture license applicants.

(4) Recommend to the board a licensing examination that meets the standards of the National Commission for Certifying Agencies or an equivalent organization nationally recognized for testing acupuncturists.

NOTE: See NOTE under 677.780.

OREGON ADMINISTRATIVE RULES COMPILATION

847 - 070 - 0005 DEFINITIONS

As used in the rules regulating the practice of acupuncture:

(1)(a) "Acupuncture" means an Oriental health care practice used to promote health and to treat neurological, organic or functional disorders by the stimulation of specific points on the surface of the body by the insertion of needles. "Acupuncture" includes the treatment method of moxibustion, as well as the use of electrical, thermal, mechanical or magnetic devices, with or without needles, to stimulate acupuncture points and acupuncture meridians and to induce acupuncture anesthesia or analgesia.

(b) The practice of acupuncture also includes the following modalities as authorized by the Oregon Medical Board:

(A) Traditional and modern Oriental Medical and acupuncture techniques of diagnosis and evaluation;

(B) Oriental massage, exercise and related therapeutic methods; and

(C) The use of Oriental pharmacopoeia, vitamins, minerals and dietary advice.

(2) "Board" means the Oregon Medical Board for the State of Oregon.

(3) "Clinical training" means supervised clinical training which consists of diagnosis and actual patient treatment which includes insertion of acupuncture needles.

(4) "Committee" means the Acupuncture Advisory Committee.

(5) "Licensed Acupuncturist" means an individual authorized by the Board to practice acupuncture pursuant to ORS Chapter 677.

(6)(a) "Oriental massage" means methods of manual therapy, including manual mobilization, manual traction, compression, rubbing, kneading and percussion, with or without manual implements, for indications including limited range of motion, muscle spasm, pain, scar tissue, contracted tissue and soft tissue swelling, edema and inflammation, as described in instructional programs and materials of Oriental or Asian health care.

(b)(A) Oriental massage as practiced in Oregon does not include high-velocity, short-amplitude, manipulative thrusting procedures to the articulations of the spine or extremities.

(B) Oriental massage as practiced in Oregon does not include internal pelvic massage (intravaginal, intra-anal, or intra-rectal) or genital massage.

(7) "Physician" means an individual licensed to practice medicine as a medical doctor or doctor of osteopathic medicine pursuant to ORS Chapter 677.

847-070-0007 PRACTICE OF ACUPUNCTURE

(1) No person may practice acupuncture without first obtaining a license to practice medicine and surgery or a license to practice acupuncture from the Oregon Medical Board.

(2) A physician who desires to be approved as a clinical supervisor must meet the requirements of OAR 847-070-0015.

847-070-0015 APPLICATION

(1) Every applicant must satisfactorily complete an application and document evidence of qualifications listed in OAR 847-070-0016 to the satisfaction of the Board. Such application and documentation must be complete before an applicant may be considered eligible for licensure.

(2) False documentation is grounds for denial of licensure or disciplinary action by the Board.

(3) An applicant applying for licensure under these rules who has not completed the

licensure process within a 12 month consecutive period must file a new application, documents, letters and pay a full filing fee as if filing for the first time.

(4) No applicant is entitled to licensure who:

(a) Has had his/her license or certificate revoked or suspended in this or any other state unless the said license or certificate has been restored or reinstated and the applicant's license or certificate is in good standing in the state which had revoked the same;

(b) Has been refused a license or certificate in any other state on any grounds other than failure in an acupuncture licensure examination; or

(c) Has been guilty of conduct similar to that which would be prohibited by or to which ORS 677.190 would apply.

847 – 070 – 0016 QUALIFICATIONS

(1) An applicant for licensure as an acupuncturist must have:

(a) Graduated from an acupuncture program that satisfies the standards of the Accreditation Commission for Acupuncture and Oriental Medicine (ACAOM), or its successor organization, or an equivalent accreditation body that are in effect at the time of the applicant's graduation. An acupuncture program may be established as having satisfied those standards by demonstration of one of the following:

(A) Accreditation, or candidacy for accreditation by ACAOM at the time of graduation from the acupuncture program; or

(B) Approval by a foreign government's Ministry of Education, or Ministry of Health, or equivalent foreign government agency at the time of graduation from the acupuncture program. Each applicant must submit their documents to a foreign credential equivalency service, which is approved by the National Certification Commission for Acupuncture and Oriental Medicine (NCCAOM) for the purpose of establishing equivalency to the ACAOM accreditation standard. Acupuncture programs that wish to be considered equivalent to an ACAOM accredited program must also meet the curricular requirements of ACAOM in effect at the time of graduation.

(b) Current certification in acupuncture by the NCCAOM. An applicant will be deemed certified by the NCCAOM in Acupuncture if the applicant has passed the NCCAOM Acupuncture Certification Examinations or has been certified through the NCCAOM Credentials Documentation Examination.

(A) The applicant has no more than four attempts to pass the NCCAOM Acupuncture Certification Examinations. If the applicant does not pass the NCCAOM Certification Examinations within four attempts, the applicant is not eligible for licensure.

(B) An applicant who has passed the NCCAOM Certification Examinations but not within the four attempts required by this rule may request a waiver of this requirement if the applicant passed the examination within five attempts and:

(i) Has obtained a Doctor of Acupuncture and Oriental Medicine degree; or

(ii) Experienced extenuating circumstances that do not indicate an inability to safely practice acupuncture as determined by the Board.

(2) An applicant who does not meet the criteria in OAR 847-070-0016(1) must have the following qualifications:

(a) Five years of licensed clinical acupuncture practice in the United States. This practice must include a minimum of 500 acupuncture patient visits per year. Documentation must include:

(A) Two affidavits from office partners, clinic supervisors, accountants, or others approved by the Board, who have personal knowledge of the years of practice and number of patient visits per year; and

(B) Notarized copies of samples of appointment books, patient charts and financial records, or other documentation as required by the Board; and

(b) Practice as a licensed acupuncturist in the U.S. during five of the last seven years prior to application for Oregon licensure. Licensed practice includes clinical practice, clinical supervision, teaching, research, and other work as approved by the Board within the field of acupuncture and oriental medicine. Documentation of this practice will be required and is subject to Board approval; and

(c) Successful completion of the ACAOM western medicine requirements in effect at the time of graduation from the acupuncture program, unless the applicant graduated from a non-accredited acupuncture program prior to 1989; and

(d) Current certification in acupuncture by the NCCAOM. An applicant will be deemed certified in Acupuncture by the NCCAOM if the applicant has passed the NCCAOM Acupuncture Certification Examinations or has been certified through the NCCAOM Credentials Documentation Examination.

(A) The applicant has no more than four attempts to pass the NCCAOM Acupuncture Certification Examinations. If the applicant does not pass the NCCAOM Certification Examinations within four attempts, the applicant is not eligible for licensure.

(B) An applicant who has passed the NCCAOM Certification Examinations but not within the four attempts required by this rule may request a waiver of this requirement if the applicant passed the examinations within five attempts and:

(i) Has obtained a Doctor of Acupuncture and Oriental Medicine degree; or

(ii) Experienced extenuating circumstances that do not indicate an inability to safely practice acupuncture as determined by the Board.

(3) An individual whose acupuncture training and diploma were obtained in a foreign country and who cannot document the requirements of subsections (1) or (2) of this rule because the required documentation is now unobtainable, may be considered eligible for licensure if it is established to the satisfaction of the Board that the applicant has equivalent skills and training and can document one year of training or supervised practice under a licensed acupuncturist in

the United States.

(4) In addition to meeting the requirements in (1), (2) or (3) of this rule, all applicants for licensure must have the following qualifications:

(a) Licensure in good standing from the state or states of all prior and current health related licensure; and

(b) Have good moral character as those traits would relate to the applicant's ability properly engage in the practice of acupuncture; and

(c) Have the ability to communicate in the English language well enough to be understood by patients and physicians. This requirement is met if the applicant passes the NCCAOM written acupuncture examination in English, or if in a foreign language, must also have passed an English language proficiency examination, such as TOEFL (Test of English as a Foreign Language), or TSE (Test of Spoken English). An applicant must obtain a TOEFL score of 500 or more for the written TOEFL exam and 173 or more for the computer based TOEFL exam, or a TSE score of 200 or more prior to July 1995, and a score of 50 or more after July 1995. An applicant who is certified through the NCCAOM Credentials Documentation Examination must also have passed an English proficiency examination.

847-070-0017 CLINICAL TRAINING

(1) A clinical supervisor must meet the following requirements:

(a) Be an actively licensed Oregon acupuncturist who has practiced as an acupuncturist for a period of at least five years, and is in good standing with the Board; or

(b) Be an actively licensed Oregon physician who is in good standing with the Board, who has been practicing acupuncture for a period of at least five years, and has passed the examination for acupuncture; or

(c) Be an acupuncturist or physician licensed, registered, or certified by another jurisdiction, who is in good standing with such jurisdiction, who has been practicing acupuncture for a period of a least five years and has passed a qualifying examination for acupuncture, or been certified in acupuncture by the National Certification Commission for Acupuncture and Oriental Medicine (N.C.C.A.O.M.) through its Credentials Documentation Examination. If a portion of those five or more years was prior to licensing, registration, or certification, then prior practice must be documented to the Board's satisfaction. The N.C.C.A.O.M. Certification Standards for Documentation will be used. All clinical supervisors under this section are subject to Board approval.

(2) Board approved clinical supervisors, acupuncturists or physicians shall supervise no more than two acupuncture trainees in an informal private clinical setting.

(3) Where applicable, an individual shall comply with OAR 847-070-0005 to 847-070-0055 if they are:

(a) Enrolled in a school approved to offer credit for post-secondary clinical education in

Oregon; or

(b) A practitioner licensed to practice acupuncture in another state or foreign country who is enrolled in clinical training approved by the Oregon Medical Board.

(4) Where applicable, an individual may perform acupuncture in a training situation only when such services are rendered by an acupuncture student:

(a) Who is enrolled in a school approved to offer credit for post-secondary clinical education in Oregon; or

(b) Who is a practitioner licensed to practice acupuncture in another state or foreign country who is enrolled in clinical training approved by the Oregon Medical Board.

(5) An individual who is a trainee or student of acupuncture may not perform any act that constitutes the practice of medicine or the practice of acupuncture, except under direct supervision of a person approved by the Board to provide clinical training as described in rule 847-070-0017.

847-070-0019 INTERVIEW AND EXAMINATION

(1) In addition to all other requirements for licensure, the Board may require an applicant to appear for a personal interview regarding information received in the application process. Unless excused in advance, failure to appear before a Committee of the Board for a personal interview violates ORS 677.190(17) and may subject the applicant to disciplinary action.

(2) If there is reasonable cause to question the qualifications of an applicant, the Board in its discretion may require the applicant to do one or more of the following:

(a) Obtain certification or re-certification in Acupuncture or Oriental Medicine by the National Certification Commission for Acupuncture and Oriental Medicine (NCCAOM);

(b) Pass an evaluation which may be written, oral, practical, or any combination thereof;

(c) Provide documentation of current NCCAOM Acupuncture certification;

(d) Complete 15 hours of continuing education acceptable to the Board for every year the applicant has ceased practice prior to application for Oregon licensure. Continuing education that meets NCCAOM's recertification requirements would qualify as Board-approved continuing education;

(e) Complete a Board-approved mentorship tailored to the applicant's time out of practice under a Board-approved mentor who must individually supervise the applicant. The mentor must report the successful completion of the mentorship to the Board.

(3) An applicant must pass an open-book examination on the Medical Practice Act (ORS Chapter 677) and Oregon Administrative Rules (OAR chapter 847, division 70). If an applicant fails the examination three times, the applicant must attend an informal meeting with a Board member, the Executive Director, a Board investigator and/or the Medical Director of the Board to discuss the applicant's failure of the examination before being given a fourth and final attempt to pass the examination. If the applicant does not pass the examination on the fourth attempt, the

applicant may be denied licensure.

847 – 070 – 0020   REGULATION OF ACTIVITIES OF ACUPUNCTURISTS

(1) An individual other than a physician who is not authorized by the Board to engage in the practice of acupuncture shall not administer acupuncture treatment to any other individual.

(2) An acupuncturist shall report promptly to the referring physician, if requested, the method of acupuncture treatment and the results of such treatment together with such other information as the referring physician requires to maintain the records regarding acupuncture treatment.

(3) An acupuncturist must clearly indicate that he/she is an acupuncturist to individuals being treated. The acupuncturist must wear a name tag with the designation "Acupuncturist" thereon when practicing in a hospital or clinic setting where other health care providers practice. Acupuncturists are not required to wear name tags in a private practice setting.

(4) An acupuncturist shall not represent him/herself as a physician or permit another to so represent him/her.

(5) As provided in ORS 676.110, an acupuncturist who has earned a doctoral degree in acupuncture may use the title "doctor" in connection with the practice of acupuncture if:

(a) The doctoral degree program holds federally recognized accreditation, and

(b) The specific doctoral degree is designated in all professional communications as required by ORS 676.110(2).

847 – 070 – 0022   DOCUMENTS TO BE SUBMITTED FOR LICENSURE

The documents submitted must be legible and no larger than 8 1/2″ x 11″. All documents and photographs will be retained by the Board as a permanent part of the application file. If original documents are larger than 8 1/2″ x 11″, the copies must be reduced to the correct size with all wording and signatures clearly shown. Official translations are required for documents issued in a foreign language. The following documents are required:

(1) Application: Completed formal application provided by the Board. Required dates must include month, day and year.

(2) Birth Certificate: A copy of birth certificate and a copy of Change of Name documentation, Marriage Certificate, or Divorce Decree if the applicant's name has been changed by court order, adoption, marriage, divorce, etc.

(3) Acupuncture School Diploma: A copy of a diploma showing graduation from an approved school of acupuncture for those applicants who qualify under OAR 847 – 070 – 0016(1).

(4) Photograph: A close-up, passport-quality photograph, front view, head and shoulders (not profile), with features distinct, taken within 90 days preceding the filing of the application.

(5) A letter from the Dean of the applicant's program of acupuncture for those applicants who qualify under OAR 847 – 070 – 0016(1).

(6) A letter from the National Certification Commission for Acupuncture and Oriental

Medicine (NCCAOM) verifying current certification in acupuncture by the NCCAOM for those applicants who qualify under OAR 847-070-0016(1) or (2).

(7) A letter verifying licensure in good standing from the state or states of all prior and current health-related licensure.

(8) A letter from the Director or other official for practice and employment to include an evaluation of overall performance and specific beginning and ending dates of practice and employment, for the past five(5) years only. For acupuncturists who have been or are in solo practice, three reference letters from acupuncturists in the local treatment community who are familiar with the applicant's practice and who have known the applicant for more than six months.

847-070-0024 APPLICATION FOR LICENSURE BY MILITARY SPOUSE OR DOMESTIC PARTNER

(1) "Military spouse or domestic partner" means a spouse or domestic partner of an active member of the Armed Forces of the United States who is the subject of a military transfer to Oregon.

(2) To qualify for licensure under this rule, the military spouse or domestic partner must:

(a) Meet the qualifications for licensure as stated in OAR 847-070-0016;

(b) Be married to, or in a domestic partnership with, a member of the Armed Forces of the United States who is assigned to a duty station located in Oregon by official active duty military order;

(c) Be licensed to practice acupuncture in another state or territory of the United States;

(d) Be in good standing, with no restrictions or limitations upon, actions taken against, or investigation or disciplinary action pending against his or her license in any jurisdiction where the applicant is or has been licensed; and

(e) Demonstrate competency by having at least one year of active practice or teaching of acupuncture during the three years immediately preceding the application.

(3) If a military spouse or domestic partner applies for a license to practice acupuncture, the Board may accept:

(a) A copy of the acupuncture school diploma to fulfill the requirement for a letter from the Dean of the applicant's acupuncture school; and

(b) Verification of licensure in good standing from the jurisdiction of current or most recent practice of acupuncture to fulfill the requirement of verifications of licensure from all jurisdictions of prior and current health related licensure.

(4) In addition to the documents required in section (3) of this rule and in OAR 847-070-0022, the military spouse or domestic partner must submit a copy of the:

(a) Marriage certificate or domestic partnership registration with the name of the applicant and the name of the active duty member of the Armed Forces of the United States; and

(b) Assignment to a duty station located in Oregon by official active duty military order for the spouse or domestic partner named in the marriage certificate or domestic partnership registration.

(5) A military spouse or domestic partner may obtain a temporary authorization for a license to practice medicine after satisfying sections (2) through (4) of this rule.

847 – 070 – 0025 DISCIPLINARY PROCEEDINGS

The Board may suspend or revoke the authority of an acupuncturist to engage in the practice of acupuncture and any disciplinary proceedings against an acupuncturist or any individual charged with the unlawful practice of acupuncture shall be in accordance with ORS Chapter 183.

847 – 070 – 0030 REVOCATION OR SUSPENSION OF AUTHORITY TO ENGAGE IN THE PRACTICE OF ACUPUNCTURE

The Board may suspend or revoke the authority of an acupuncturist to engage in the practice of acupuncture if the Board finds that:

(1) The acupuncturist has represented him/herself as a physician or permitted another to so represent him/her.

(2) The acupuncturist has performed any act involving the practice of acupuncture in violation of any applicable law or rules regulating the practice of acupuncture.

(3) The acupuncturist has engaged in conduct constituting gross negligence in the practice of acupuncture.

(4) The acupuncturist is manifestly incapable to engage in the practice of acupuncture.

(5) The acupuncturist has violated any of the provisions of ORS 677.190.

847 – 070 – 0033 VISITING ACUPUNCTURIST REQUIREMENTS

(1) The Oregon Medical Board may grant approval for a visiting acupuncturist to demonstrate acupuncture needling as part of a seminar, conference, or workshop sponsored by an Oregon school or an Oregon school's program of acupuncture or oriental medicine, or professional organization of acupuncture, or any seminar, conference, or workshop approved by the National Certification Commission for Acupuncture and Oriental Medicine (NCCAOM) to provide continuing education training for a period up to ten days no more than three times a year. The visiting acupuncturist who requests additional time beyond the ten days, or submits more than three requests in a year, must apply for and obtain a license to practice in the state of Oregon. An Oregon licensed acupuncturist must be in attendance at the seminar, conference or workshop.

(2) Prior to being granted approval, the following information must be submitted to the Oregon Medical Board:

(a) A letter from the school or program of acupuncture or oriental medicine, or organization which will have an out-of-state acupuncturist demonstrate needling as part of a seminar, conference, or workshop with the following information:

(A) Dates of the seminar, conference, or workshop in which the visiting acupuncturist will be demonstrating acupuncture needling;

(B) Description of the seminar, conference or workshop;

(C) Name of the responsible Oregon acupuncturist, licensed under ORS 677, actively registered and in good standing with the Board, who will be in attendance and responsible for the conduct of the visiting acupuncturist at the seminar, conference or workshop.

(D) A curriculum vitae for the visiting acupuncturist; and

(b) If the visiting acupuncturist is licensed, certified or registered to practice as an acupuncturist in the state in which the acupuncturist is practicing, the visiting acupuncturist must provide documentation that their license, certificate, or registration is active and in good standing.

(3) The request for approval to practice in the state of Oregon as a visiting acupuncturist must be received at least two weeks prior to the beginning date of such practice.

847-070-0037   LIMITED LICENSE, PENDING EXAMINATION

(1) An acupuncturist who meets all requirements for Oregon acupuncture licensure but has not yet passed the acupuncture certification examination given by the National Certification Commission on Acupuncture and Oriental Medicine (NCCAOM) may be issued a Limited License, Pending Examination for the purpose of obtaining clinical training in Oregon under the supervision of a Board approved clinical supervisor if the following criteria are met:

(a) The application file is complete to the satisfaction of the Board with the exception of pending certification by the NCCAOM;

(b) The applicant has not previously failed the NCCAOM examination;

(c) The clinical supervisor approved to supervise the applicant meets the qualifications in OAR 847-070-0017 and is on-site and available to supervise at all times when the applicant is training; and

(d) The applicant has submitted the appropriate form and fee prior to being issued a Limited License, Pending Examination.

(2) Any person obtaining clinical training under a Limited License, Pending Examination must identify themselves to patients as an acupuncture trainee and wear a name tag identifying themselves as a trainee.

(3) A Limited License, Pending Examination may be granted for a period of six months.

(4) Upon receipt of verification that the applicant has passed the acupuncture certification examination given by the NCCAOM, and if the applicant's application file is otherwise satisfactorily complete, the applicant shall be scheduled for approval of permanent licensure.

(5) The Limited License, Pending Examination will automatically expire if the applicant fails the acupuncture certification examination given by the NCCAOM.

847-070-0038   LIMITED LICENSE, VISITING PROFESSOR

(1) An acupuncturist who has received a teaching position in a school of acupuncture in this state may be issued a Limited License, Visiting Professor if the following criteria are met:

(a) The applicant has established to the satisfaction of the Board that he/she has the skills and training equivalent to OAR 847-070-0016 (1);

(b) The applicant has at least five years experience as an acupuncturist; and

(c) The applicant has submitted the appropriate form and fee for a Limited License, Visiting Professor.

(2) The head of the acupuncture school in which the applicant will be teaching shall certify in writing to the Board that the applicant has been offered a teaching position which will be under the direction of the head of the department and will not be permitted to practice acupuncture unless as a necessary part of the applicant's teaching position as approved by the Board.

(3) An acupuncturist who is applying for a Limited License, Visiting Professor may also be approved as a clinical supervisor if the applicant meets the requirements of OAR 847-070-0017.

(4) The Limited License, Visiting Professor may be granted for one year and may be granted a total of two one-year extensions upon annual review of the written justification of the need based upon academic necessity. The renewal form and fee must be submitted 30 days before the end of the year if an extension of the Limited License, Visiting Professor is requested.

847-070-0039 REGISTRATION

(1) Upon Board approval of an applicant to be licensed to practice acupuncture, the applicant must pay the registration fee before being issued a certificate.

(2) An application for renewal of the biennial registration and the statutory registration fee shall be submitted to the Oregon Medical Board prior to midnight June 30 of every even-numbered year.

(3) Upon failure to comply with section (1) and (2) of this rule, the license shall lapse as per ORS 677.228.

847-070-0045 INACTIVE REGISTRATION AND RE-ENTRY TO PRACTICE

(1) Any acupuncturist licensed in this state who changes location to some other state or country shall be listed by the Board as inactive.

(2) If the acupuncturist wishes to resume active status, the acupuncturist must file an Affidavit of Reactivation and pay a processing fee, satisfactorily complete the reactivation process and be approved by the Board before beginning active practice in Oregon.

(3) The Board may deny active registration if it judges the conduct of the acupuncturist during the period of inactive registration to be such that the acupuncturist would have been denied a license if applying for an initial license.

(4) If an acupuncturist applicant has ceased practice for a period of 12 or more consecutive months immediately preceding the application for licensure or reactivation, the applicant may be required to do one or more of the following:

(a) Obtain certification or re-certification in Acupuncture or Oriental Medicine by the National Certification Commission for Acupuncture and Oriental Medicine (NCCAOM);

(b) Provide documentation of current NCCAOM Acupuncture or Oriental Medicine certification;

(c) Complete 15 hours of continuing education acceptable to the Board for every year the applicant has ceased practice;

(d) Complete a Board-approved mentorship tailored to the applicant's time out of practice under a Board-approved mentor who must individually supervise the licensee. The mentor must report the successful completion of the mentorship to the Board; and

(e) Additional requirements as determined appropriate by the Board.

(5) The acupuncturist applicant who has ceased practice for a period of 24 or more consecutive months may be required to complete a re-entry plan to the satisfaction of the Board. The re-entry plan must be reviewed and approved through a Consent Agreement for Re-entry to Practice prior to the applicant beginning the re-entry plan. Depending on the amount of time out of practice, the re-entry plan may contain one or more of the requirements listed in section (4) of this rule and such additional requirements as determined appropriate by the Board.

847-070-0050 ACUPUNCTURE ADVISORY COMMITTEE

(1) An Acupuncture Advisory Committee is established. The committee must consist of six members appointed by the Board. The Board must appoint one of its members, two physicians, and three acupuncturists licensed by the Board. The acupuncture members may be appointed from nominations of the Oregon Association of Acupuncture and Oriental Medicine and other professional acupuncture organizations.

(2) The term of office of a member of the committee is three years, and members may be reappointed to serve not more than two terms. Vacancies in the committee must be filled by appointment by the Board for the balance of the unexpired term, and each member must serve until a successor is appointed and qualified.

(3) The Board may remove any member from the committee.

(4) The committee elects its own chairperson with such powers and duties as fixed by the committee.

(5) The committee members are entitled to compensation and expenses as provided for Board members in ORS 677.235.

847-070-0055 DUTIES OF THE COMMITTEE

The Acupuncture Advisory Committee shall:

(1) Review and recommend approval or disapproval of all applications submitted to the Board for acupuncture licensing and for renewal thereof.

(2) Recommend to the Board standards of professional responsibility and practice for licensed acupuncturists.

(3) Recommend to the Board standards of didactic and clinical education and training for acupuncture licensing.

(4) Recommend to the Board standards for clinical supervisors and trainees.

(5) Recommend to the Board licensing examinations, and temporary licenses as considered appropriate.

847 - 070 - 0060　LICENSE APPLICATION WITHDRAWALS AND DENIALS

(1) An applicant who withdraws an application for licensure that may contain evidence of a violation of any provision of ORS 677.010 - 677.855 may submit a new application for licensure two years after the date of withdrawal.

(2) An applicant whose application has been denied may submit a new application for licensure two years after the date of denial.

WASHINGTON

REVISED CODE OF WASHINGTON ANNOTATED

RCW 18.06.010 DEFINITIONS

The following terms in this chapter shall have the meanings set forth in this section unless the context clearly indicates otherwise:

(1) "Acupuncture" or "Eastern medicine" means a health care service utilizing acupuncture or Eastern medicine diagnosis and treatment to promote health and treat organic or functional disorders and includes the following:

(a) Acupuncture, including the use of acupuncture needles or lancets to directly and indirectly stimulate acupuncture points and meridians;

(b) Use of electrical, mechanical, or magnetic devices to stimulate acupuncture points and meridians;

(c) Moxibustion;

(d) Acupressure;

(e) Cupping;

(f) Dermal friction technique;

(g) Infra-red;

(h) Sonopuncture;

(i) Laserpuncture;

(j) Point injection therapy, as defined in rule by the department. Point injection therapy includes injection of substances, limited to saline, sterile water, herbs, minerals, vitamins in liquid form, and homeopathic and nutritional substances, consistent with the practice of acupuncture or Eastern medicine. Point injection therapy does not include injection of controlled substances contained in Schedules I through V of the uniform controlled substances act, chapter 69.50 RCW or steroids as defined in RCW 69.41.300;

(k) Dietary advice and health education based on acupuncture or Eastern medical theory, including the recommendation and sale of herbs, vitamins, minerals, and dietary and nutritional supplements;

(l) Breathing, relaxation, and Eastern exercise techniques;

(m) Qi gong;

(n) Eastern massage and Tui na, which is a method of Eastern bodywork, characterized by the kneading, pressing, rolling, shaking, and stretching of the body and does not include spinal manipulation; and

(o) Superficial heat and cold therapies.

(2) "Acupuncturist" or "acupuncture and Eastern medicine practitioner" means a person licensed under this chapter.

(3) "Department" means the department of health.

(4) "Secretary" means the secretary of health or the secretary's designee.

Nothing in this chapter requires individuals to be licensed as an acupuncturist or Eastern medicine practitioner in order to provide the techniques and services in subsection (1)(k) through (o) of this section or to sell herbal products.

RCW 18.06.020　PRACTICE WITHOUT LICENSE UNLAWFUL

(1) No one may hold themselves out to the public as an acupuncturist, licensed acupuncturist, acupuncture and Eastern medicine practitioner, or any derivative thereof which is intended to or is likely to lead the public to believe such a person is an acupuncturist, licensed acupuncturist[,] or acupuncture and Eastern medicine practitioner, unless licensed as provided for in this chapter.

(2) A person may not practice acupuncture or Eastern medicine if the person is not licensed under this chapter.

(3) No one may use any configuration of letters after their name (including L. Ac., EAMP, or AEMP) which indicates a degree or formal training in acupuncture or Eastern medicine unless licensed as provided for in this chapter.

(4) The secretary may by rule proscribe or regulate advertising and other forms of patient solicitation which are likely to mislead or deceive the public as to whether someone is licensed under this chapter.

(5) A person licensed under this chapter may use the title acupuncture and Eastern medicine practitioner and may use the letters AEMP indicating such license. However, nothing in this section prohibits or limits in any way a practitioner licensed under this chapter from alternatively holding himself or herself out as an acupuncturist, licensed acupuncturist, or East Asian medicine practitioner or from using the letters L. Ac. or EAMP after his or her name.

RCW 18.06.045　EXEMPTIONS FROM CHAPTER

Nothing in this chapter shall be construed to prohibit or restrict:

(1) The practice by an individual credentialed under the laws of this state and performing services within such individual's authorized scope of practice;

(2) The practice by an individual employed by the government of the United States while engaged in the performance of duties prescribed by the laws of the United States;

(3) The practice by a person who is a regular student in an educational program approved by the secretary, and whose performance of services is pursuant to a regular course of instruction or assignments from an instructor and under the general supervision of the instructor;

(4) The practice of acupuncture or Eastern medicine by any person credentialed to perform acupuncture or Eastern medicine in any other jurisdiction where such person is doing so in the course of regular instruction of a school of acupuncture, Eastern medicine, traditional Chinese medicine, or medical traditions from Japan, Korea, or other East Asian countries, approved by the secretary or in an educational seminar by a professional organization of acupuncture or Eastern medicine, provided that in the latter case, the practice is supervised directly by a person licensed under this chapter or licensed under any other healing art whose scope of practice is acupuncture and Eastern medicine.

RCW 18.06.050 APPLICATIONS FOR LICENSURE-QUALIFICATIONS

Any person seeking to be licensed shall present to the secretary:

(1) A written application on a form or forms provided by the secretary setting forth under affidavit such information as the secretary may require; and

(2) Proof that the candidate has:

(a) Successfully completed a course, approved by the secretary, of didactic training in basic sciences and acupuncture and Eastern medicine over a minimum period of two academic years. The training shall include such subjects as anatomy, physiology, microbiology, biochemistry, pathology, hygiene, and a survey of western clinical sciences. The basic science classes must be equivalent to those offered at the collegiate level. However, if the applicant is a licensed chiropractor under chapter 18.25 RCW or a naturopath licensed under chapter 18.36A RCW, the requirements of this subsection relating to basic sciences may be reduced by up to one year depending upon the extent of the candidate's qualifications as determined under rules adopted by the secretary;

(b) Successfully completed five hundred hours of clinical training in acupuncture or Eastern medicine that is approved by the secretary.

RCW 18.06.060 APPROVAL OF EDUCATIONAL PROGRAMS

The department shall consider for approval any school or program that meets the requirements outlined in this chapter and provides the training required under RCW 18.06.050. Clinical and didactic training may be approved as separate programs or as a joint program. The process for approval shall be established by the secretary by rule.

RCW 18.06.080 AUTHORITY OF SECRETARY-EXAMINATION-CONTENTS-IMMUNITY

(1) The secretary is hereby authorized and empowered to execute the provisions of this chapter and shall offer examinations in order to become a licensed acupuncturist or acupuncture

and Eastern medicine practitioner at least twice a year at such times and places as the secretary may select. The examination shall be a written examination and may include a practical examination.

(2) The secretary shall approve a licensure examination in the subjects that the secretary determines are within the scope of and commensurate with the work performed by an acupuncturist or acupuncture and Eastern medicine practitioner and shall include but not necessarily be limited to anatomy, physiology, microbiology, biochemistry, pathology, hygiene, acupuncture, and Eastern medicine. All application papers shall be deposited with the secretary and there retained for at least one year, when they may be destroyed.

(3) If the examination is successfully passed, the secretary shall confer on such candidate the title of acupuncturist or acupuncture and Eastern medicine practitioner.

RCW 18.06.090 FLUENCY IN ENGLISH REQUIRED

Before licensure, each applicant shall demonstrate sufficient fluency in reading, speaking, and understanding the English language to enable the applicant to communicate with other health care providers and patients concerning health care problems and treatment.

RCW 18.06.100 INVESTIGATION OF APPLICANT'S BACKGROUND

Each applicant shall, as part of his or her application, furnish written consent to an investigation of his or her personal background, professional training, and experience by the department or any person acting on its behalf.

RCW 18.06.110 APPLICATION OF UNIFORM DISCIPLINARY ACT

The Uniform Disciplinary Act, chapter 18.130 RCW, governs uncertified practice, the issuance and denial of licenses, and the disciplining of license holders under this chapter. The secretary shall be the disciplining authority under this chapter.

RCW 18.06.120 COMPLIANCE WITH ADMINISTRATIVE PROCEDURES-FEES

(1) Every person licensed under this chapter shall comply with the administrative procedures and administrative requirements for registration and renewal set by the secretary under RCW 43.70.250 and 43.70.280.

(2) All fees collected under this section and RCW 18.06.070 shall be credited to the health professions account as required under RCW 43.70.320.

RCW 18.06.130 PATIENT INFORMATION FORM-PENALTY

(1) The secretary shall develop a form to be used by a person licensed under this chapter to inform the patient of the scope of practice and qualifications of an acupuncturist or acupuncture and Eastern medicine practitioner. All license holders shall bring the form to the attention of the patients in whatever manner the secretary, by rule, provides.

(2) A person violating this section is guilty of a misdemeanor.

RCW 18.06.140 CONSULTATION WITH OTHER HEALTH CARE PRACTITIONERS-PATIENT WAIVER-EMERGENCIES-PENALTY (EFFECTIVE UNTIL JULY 1, 2022)

(1) When a person licensed under this chapter sees patients with potentially serious disorders

such as cardiac conditions, acute abdominal symptoms, and such other conditions, the practitioner shall immediately request a consultation or recent written diagnosis from a primary health care provider licensed under chapter 18.71, 18.57, 18.57A, 18.36A, or 18.71A RCW or RCW 18.79.050. In the event that the patient with the disorder refuses to authorize such consultation or provide a recent diagnosis from such primary health care provider, acupuncture or Eastern medicine treatments may only be continued after the patient signs a written waiver acknowledging the risks associated with the failure to pursue treatment from a primary health care provider. The waiver must also include: (a) An explanation of an acupuncturist's or acupuncture and Eastern medicine practitioner's scope of practice, including the services and techniques acupuncturists or acupuncture and Eastern medicine practitioners are authorized to provide and (b) a statement that the services and techniques that an acupuncturist or acupuncture and Eastern medicine practitioner is authorized to provide will not resolve the patient's underlying potentially serious disorder. The requirements of the waiver shall be established by the secretary in rule.

(2) In an emergency, a person licensed under this chapter shall: (a) Initiate the emergency medical system by calling 911; (b) request an ambulance; and (c) provide patient support until emergency response arrives.

(3) A person violating this section is guilty of a misdemeanor.

RCW 18.06.160   ADOPTION OF RULES

The secretary shall adopt rules in the manner provided by chapter 34.05 RCW as are necessary to carry out the purposes of this chapter.

RCW 18.06.190   LICENSING BY ENDORSEMENT

The secretary may license a person without examination if such person is credentialed as an acupuncturist or acupuncture and Eastern medicine practitioner, or equivalent, in another jurisdiction if, in the secretary's judgment, the requirements of that jurisdiction are equivalent to or greater than those of Washington state.

RCW 18.06.200   HEALTH CARE INSURANCE BENEFITS NOT MANDATORY

Nothing in this chapter may be construed to require that individual or group policies or contracts of an insurance carrier, health care service contractor, or health maintenance organization provide benefits or coverage for services and supplies provided by a person licensed under this chapter.

RCW 18.06.210   PRESCRIPTION OF DRUGS AND PRACTICE OF MEDICINE NOT AUTHORIZED

This chapter shall not be construed as permitting the administration or prescription of drugs or in any way infringing upon the practice of medicine and surgery as defined in chapter 18.71 or 18.57 RCW, except as authorized in this chapter.

RCW 18.06.220   ACUPUNCTURE AND EASTERN MEDICINE ADVISORY COMMITTEE

The Washington state acupuncture and Eastern medicine advisory committee is established.

(1) The committee consists of five members, each of whom must be a resident of the state of Washington. Four committee members must be acupuncturists or acupuncture and Eastern medicine practitioners licensed under this chapter who have not less than five years' experience in the practice of acupuncture and Eastern medicine and who have been actively engaged in practice within two years of appointment. The fifth committee member must be appointed from the public at large and must have an interest in the rights of consumers of health services.

(2) The secretary shall appoint the committee members. Committee members serve at the pleasure of the secretary. The secretary may appoint members of the initial committee to staggered terms of one to three years, and thereafter all terms are for three years. No member may serve more than two consecutive full terms.

(3) The committee shall meet as necessary, but no less often than once per year. The committee shall elect a chair and a vice chair. A majority of the members currently serving constitutes a quorum.

(4) The committee shall advise and make recommendations to the secretary on standards for the practice of acupuncture and Eastern medicine.

(5) Committee members must be compensated in accordance with RCW 43.03.240, including travel expenses in carrying out his or her authorized duties in accordance with RCW 43.03.050 and 43.03.060.

(6) Committee members are immune from suit in an action, civil or criminal, based on the department's disciplinary proceedings or other official acts performed in good faith.

RCW 18.06.230 POINT INJECTION THERAPY SERVICES-EDUCATION AND TRAINING

(1) Prior to providing point injection therapy services, an acupuncturist or acupuncture and Eastern medicine practitioner must obtain the education and training necessary to provide the service.

(2) Any acupuncturist or acupuncture and Eastern medicine practitioner performing point injection therapy prior to June 9, 2016, must be able to demonstrate, upon request of the department of health, successful completion of education and training in point injection therapy.

RCW 18.06.240 CONTINUING EDUCATION

The department shall adopt a rule requiring completion of continuing education for acupuncturists as a condition of license renewal.

WYOMING

WYOMING STATUTES ANNOTATED

33-49-101 SHORT TITLE

This chapter shall be known and may be cited as the "Wyoming Acupuncture Practice Act".

33-49-102 DEFINITIONS

(a) As used in this chapter:

(i) "ACAOM" means the accreditation commission for acupuncture and oriental medicine educational institutions, or its equivalent as determined by the board;

(ii) "Acupuncture" means the insertion of acupuncture needles into the body, with or without the application of electric current or heat to the needles, for the therapeutic purpose of promoting, maintaining and restoring health, including the treatment of dysfunctions of the body involving pain;

(iii) "Acupuncturist" means any person to whom a license to practice acupuncture in this state has been issued under this chapter;

(iv) "Auricular acupuncture" means a practice trained by a nationally recognized auricular acupuncture program for the purpose of treating mental and emotional health, post and acute trauma, substance abuse and chemical dependency;

(v) "Board" means the Wyoming board of acupuncture created under this chapter;

(vi) "License" means a license to practice acupuncture in this state issued by the board pursuant to this chapter and consistent with the scope of practice a person is qualified to perform as a result of their NCCAOM diplomate status, post graduate training, NADA certificate of training completion or as otherwise authorized by the board;

(vii) "Licensee" means a person licensed by the board under this chapter;

(viii) "NADA" means the national acupuncture detoxification association, or its equivalent as determined by the board;

(ix) "NCCAOM" means the national certification commission for acupuncture and oriental medicine, or its equivalent as determined by the board.

33 – 49 – 103   BOARD CREATED; MEMBERS; APPOINTMENT; TERMS; QUALIFICATION; REMOVAL; VACANCIES

(a) The Wyoming board of acupuncture is created to implement and administer the provisions of this chapter. The board shall consist of five(5) members who are legal residents of Wyoming. The board shall consist of one(1) member of the public, one(1) member who is NCCAOM certified, two(2) members who have been engaged in the practice of acupuncture for a period of not less than five(5) years immediately preceding appointment to the initial board and one(1) member who is a health care professional licensed pursuant to this title other than this chapter.

(b) The governor shall appoint the members of the board. Of the initial members appointed to the board, two(2) members shall be appointed for a term of two(2) years and three(3) members shall be appointed for a term of four(4) years. Thereafter, the terms of office shall be four(4) years. Each member shall serve until the member's successor is appointed and qualified. No member shall serve more than two(2) consecutive full terms.

(c) Any vacancy on the board shall be filled by the governor for the balance of the unexpired term.

(d) The governor may remove any member from the board pursuant to W. S. 9 – 1 – 202.

33 – 49 – 104   BOARD MEETINGS; ELECTIONS; QUORUM

The board shall meet at least once each year and elect a chairman at the first meeting each year. The board may convene at the request of the chairman or as determined by the board for any other meeting as may be deemed necessary to transact its business. Meetings may be carried out via telecommunications. Three (3) board members shall constitute a quorum.

33 – 49 – 105   REIMBURSEMENT OF EXPENSES AND IMMUNITY

(a) Members of the board shall not receive compensation for their services but shall receive mileage and per diem as provided in W. S. 33 – 1 – 302(a)(vii) while engaged in the discharge of official duties.

(b) Members of the board shall have the same immunities from personal liability as state employees for actions taken in the performance of their duties under this chapter, as provided in W. S. 1 – 39 – 104.

33 – 49 – 106   BOARD RESPONSIBILITIES AND DUTIES

(a) The board shall:

(i) Administer this chapter;

(ii) Determine the following standards for licensees:

(A) Continuing education requirements;

(B) Professional conduct standards;

(C) Ethical standards of practice.

(iii) Approve or disapprove applications for licensure and issue licenses, renewals and reinstatements;

(vi) Establish tiered licensing as necessary for the purpose of differentiating auricular acupuncture;

(v) Censure, suspend or revoke licenses as provided in this chapter and the Wyoming Administrative Procedure Act;

(vi) Initiate and conduct investigations, hearings and proceedings concerning alleged violations of this chapter and board rules;

(vii) Keep a record of all proceedings and make available to licensees and other concerned parties an annual report of all board action;

(viii) Establish application and licensure fee requirements for licensees regulated under this chapter;

(ix) Prescribe fees in accordance with W. S. 33-1-201 for implementing this chapter;

(x) Promulgate rules and regulations as necessary to carry out this chapter.

(b) The board may employ or contract with individuals it determines necessary to administer its affairs and provide support services.

(c) All fees collected by the board shall be deposited by the state treasurer to the credit of the Wyoming board of acupuncture account. Disbursements from the account shall not exceed the monies credited to it. The account shall be used by the board to defray costs incurred in the administration of this chapter.

33-49-107 LICENSURE REQUIRED; COMPONENTS; EXEMPTIONS; OTHER LICENSED HEALTH CARE PROFESSIONALS

(a) Beginning January 1, 2018, unless the person is licensed to practice acupuncture in compliance with this chapter and the rules and regulations adopted pursuant thereto, no person shall:

(i) Practice acupuncture or hold himself out as an acupuncturist or as being able to practice acupuncture in Wyoming;

(ii) Use the title of acupuncturist or any variant thereof; or

(iii) Use any configuration of letters, including L. Ac., after his name indicating a degree in acupuncture.

(b) Any license issued under this chapter shall:

(i) Be issued in the name of the licensed acupuncturist;

(ii) State the licensing and expiration dates; and

(iii) Be displayed at all times in a conspicuous manner in the place of business or employment of the licensee.

(c) The following persons are exempt from this chapter's licensure requirements:

(i) acupuncturist licensed to practice acupuncture in another jurisdiction while teaching or demonstrating or providing acupuncture in connection with teaching or participating in an educational seminar in Wyoming. Any exemption under this paragraph shall not exceed sixty (60) days cumulatively in a calendar year;

(ii) An acupuncturist licensed in another jurisdiction who enters this state to provide acupuncture during a natural disaster or a public health emergency, as declared by the governor pursuant to W. S. 35-4-115(a)(i);

(iii) With board approval, a person in training may practice acupuncture provided all services are performed under the direct supervision of an acupuncturist licensed in this state.

(d) Nothing in this chapter shall be construed to prohibit or restrict any other licensed health care provider in this state from practicing acupuncture within their statutory scope of practice. However, no person may represent themselves as an acupuncturist in any manner unless licensed in accordance with this chapter.

33-49-108 APPLICATION FOR LICENSE; RENEWAL AND REINSTATEMENT; QUALIFICATIONS; FEES; REPORTING

(a) An applicant for licensure to practice acupuncture under this chapter shall:

(i) Apply for licensure with the board by providing an application in the form and manner prescribed by the board;

(ii) Pay the required fees established by the board; and

(iii) Furnish to the board evidence that the applicant has:

(A) Graduated from an accredited ACAOM program and passed NCCAOM examination;

(B) Graduated from an accredited ACAOM program and continuously practiced acupuncture in this state for at least ten (10) years before January 1, 2018;

(C) Completed other examination, education or apprenticeship processes the board considers substantively qualifying; or

(D) NADA certificate of training completion, if applying for an auricular acupuncturist license.

(b) Licenses shall be renewed or reinstated according to a schedule established by the board pursuant to this chapter. If a licensee fails to renew a license pursuant to the schedule established by the board, the license shall expire and the licensee shall not practice acupuncture in this state.

(c) An applicant for licensure or licensee shall report any pending or final administrative or disciplinary actions, or other judgments, as well as the terms of any settlement or other disposition of an action or judgment, against the applicant or licensee involving malpractice or improper practice of acupuncture, whether occurring in Wyoming or in any other jurisdiction upon application for licensure, renewal or reinstatement, or not later than thirty (30) days after the licensee becomes aware of such actions or judgments.

33-49-109 LICENSURE BY ENDORSEMENT

(a) The board may issue a license by endorsement to practice acupuncture in Wyoming to an applicant who is licensed to practice acupuncture in another state subject to the following:

(i) The other state shall have substantially equivalent acupuncture licensure requirements as Wyoming, including similar licensure by endorsement provisions for licensees of this state;

(ii) The applicant shall not have any disciplinary actions pending at the time of application;

(iii) The applicant shall not have had a license to practice acupuncture suspended or revoked in this state or any other; and

(iv) The person shall adhere to all requirements of continuing education and ethical standards established by the board.

33-49-110 HEARINGS AND INVESTIGATIONS

(a) Upon receiving a complaint charging a licensee or applicant with any act prohibited by this chapter, the board may conduct an investigation. If the board finds reasonable grounds to substantiate the allegations of the complaint, a time and place for a hearing shall be set, notice of which shall be served on the licensee or applicant at least fifteen (15) calendar days prior to the hearing. The notice shall be by personal service or by certified or registered mail sent to the last known address of the licensee or applicant.

(b) The board may issue subpoenas for the attendance of witnesses and the production of necessary evidence in any hearing before it. Upon request of the respondent or his counsel, the board shall issue subpoenas on behalf of the respondent.

(c) Hearings under this section shall be held in accordance with, and a person aggrieved by a decision of the board may take an appeal pursuant to, the Wyoming Administrative Procedure Act.

33-49-111 DISCIPLINARY ACTION; SUSPENSION AND REVOCATION OF LICENSE; APPLICATION FOR REINSTATEMENT

(a) After any hearing conducted pursuant to W. S.33-49-110, the board may approve, deny, suspend, revoke or refuse to renew a license or impose probationary conditions on the license if the licensee or applicant has engaged in unprofessional conduct. For purposes of this section, unprofessional conduct includes any of the following:

(i) Obtaining a license by means of fraud, misrepresentation or concealment of material facts;

(ii) Violating the ethical standards of practice or rules of professional conduct as adopted and published by the board;

(iii) Being convicted of a felony that relates to the practice of acupuncture or to the ability to practice acupuncture;

(iv) Being convicted of an offense involving a controlled substance;

(v) Being negligent in the practice of acupuncture;

(vi) Violating any lawful order, rule or regulation rendered or adopted by the board;

(vii) Violating any provision of this chapter.

(b) An application for reinstatement may be made to the board not earlier than one (1) year after the date of the revocation of the license. The board may accept or reject an application for reinstatement and may hold a hearing to consider reinstatement. An applicant for reinstatement aggrieved by any final action of the board may appeal to the district court pursuant to the Wyoming Administrative Procedure Act.

(c) Upon receipt from the department of family services of a certified copy of an order from a court to withhold, suspend or otherwise restrict a license issued by the board, the board shall notify the party named in the court order of the withholding, suspension or restriction of the license in accordance with the terms of the court order. No appeal under the Wyoming Administrative Procedure Act shall be allowed for a license withheld, suspended or restricted under this subsection.

33-49-112 VIOLATIONS; PENALTIES; PROCEEDINGS

(a) Any person who violates any provision of this chapter is guilty of a misdemeanor and upon conviction shall be subject to the fines and penalties prescribed in W.S. 6-10-103. If the board has reason to believe that any individual is liable under this section, it may certify the facts to the prosecuting attorney of the jurisdiction in which the offense was committed.

(b) The attorney general, the board, any county or district attorney or any citizen may obtain an injunction in the name of the state of Wyoming upon the relation of a complainant enjoining any person from engaging in the practice of acupuncture without a license. The district court of the district in which the offending person resides or the district court of Laramie county has original jurisdiction of any such injunction proceedings. An injunction may be issued without proof of actual damage sustained and upon proof of one (1) or more acts constituting the practice of acupuncture without a license. The standard of proof of any violation of this subsection shall be by a preponderance of the evidence.

(c) Nothing in this section shall limit any additional civil or criminal liability under the laws of this state.

(d) Notwithstanding any other provision of this chapter, the Wyoming Acupuncture Practice Act shall not apply to persons licensed under title 33, chapter 25 or chapter 26 of the Wyoming statutes.

CALIFORNIA

ANNOTATED CALIFORNIA CODES

ARTICLE 1 ADMINISTRATION AND GENERAL PROVISIONS

4925

(a) This chapter constitutes the chapter on acupuncture of the Business and Professions Code. This chapter shall be known and may be cited as the Acupuncture Licensure Act. Whenever a reference is made to the Acupuncture Licensure Act by the provisions of any statute, it is to be construed as referring to the provisions of this chapter.

(b) Any reference in this chapter, or to the regulations pertaining thereto, to "certificate" or "certification" shall hereafter mean "license" or "licensure". Any reference to the term "certifying" means "licensing", and the term "certificate holder" means "licensee". Any reference to the "Acupuncture Committee" or "committee" means the "Acupuncture Board" or "board".

4926

In its concern with the need to eliminate the fundamental causes of illness, not simply to remove symptoms, and with the need to treat the whole person, the Legislature intends to establish in this article, a framework for the practice of the art and science of Asian medicine through acupuncture.

The purpose of this article is to encourage the more effective utilization of the skills of acupuncturists by California citizens desiring a holistic approach to health and to remove the existing legal constraints which are an unnecessary hindrance to the more effective provision of health care services. Also, as it effects the public health, safety, and welfare, there is a necessity that individuals practicing acupuncture be subject to regulation and control as a primary health care profession.

4927

As used in this chapter, unless the context otherwise requires:

(a) "Board" means the Acupuncture Board.

(b) "Person" means any individual, organization, or corporate body, except that only individuals may be licensed under this chapter.

(c) "Acupuncturist" means an individual to whom a license has been issued to practice acupuncture pursuant to this chapter, which is in effect and is not suspended or revoked.

(d) "Acupuncture" means the stimulation of a certain point or points on or near the surface of the body by the insertion of needles to prevent or modify the perception of pain or to normalize physiological functions, including pain control for the treatment of certain diseases or dysfunctions of the body, and includes the techniques of electroacupuncture, cupping, and moxibustion.

4927.5

(a) For purposes of this chapter, "approved educational and training program" means a school or college offering education and training in the practice of an acupuncturist that meets all of the following requirements:

(1) Offers curriculum that includes at least 3000 hours of which at least 2050 hours are didactic and laboratory training, and at least 950 hours are supervised clinical instruction. Has submitted that curriculum to the board, and has received board approval of the curriculum. Any school or college offering education and training in the practice of acupuncture that was approved by the board prior to January 1, 2017, has not had its approval revoked, and has not changed its curriculum since receiving board approval, is deemed to have had its curriculum approved by the board for the purposes of this section.

(2) Has received full institutional approval under Article 6 (commencing with Section 94885) of Chapter 8 of Part 59 of Division 10 of Title 3 of the Education Code in the field of traditional Asian medicine, or in the case of institutions located outside of this state, approval by the appropriate governmental educational authority using standards equivalent to those of Article 6(commencing with Section 94885) of Chapter 8 of Part 59 of Division 10 of Title 3 of the Education Code.

(3) Meets any of the following:

(A) Is accredited by the Accreditation Commission for Acupuncture and Oriental Medicine.

(B) Has been granted preaccreditation status by the Accreditation Commission for Acupuncture and Oriental Medicine. Has submitted a letter of intent to pursue accreditation to the Accreditation Commission for Acupuncture and Oriental Medicine within 30 days of receiving full institutional approval pursuant to paragraph, and is granted preaccreditation status within three years of the date that letter was submitted.

(b) Within 30 days after receiving curriculum pursuant to paragraph(1), the board shall review the curriculum, determine whether the curriculum satisfies the requirements established by the board, and notify the school or college, the Accreditation Commission for Acupuncture and Oriental Medicine, and the Bureau for Private and Postsecondary Education of whether the board has approved the curriculum.

4928

(a) The Acupuncture Board, which consists of seven members, shall enforce and administer this chapter.

(b) This section shall remain in effect only until January 1, 2023, and as of that date is repealed.

(c) Notwithstanding any other law, the repeal of this section renders the board subject to review by the appropriate policy committees of the Legislature.

4928.1

Protection of the public shall be the highest priority for the Acupuncture Board in exercising its licensing, regulatory, and disciplinary functions. Whenever the protection of the public is inconsistent with other interests sought to be promoted, the protection of the public shall be paramount.

4929

Three members of the board shall be acupuncturists with at least five years of experience in acupuncture and four members shall be public members who do not hold a license or certificate as a physician and surgeon or acupuncturist. The acupuncturist members shall be appointed to represent a cross section of the cultural backgrounds of licensed members of the acupuncturist profession.

The Governor shall appoint the three acupuncturist members and two of the public members. All members appointed to the board by the Governor shall be subject to confirmation by the Senate. The Senate Rules Committee and the Speaker of the Assembly shall each appoint a public member. Any member of the board may be removed by the appointing power for neglect of duty, misconduct, or malfeasance in office, after being provided with a written statement of the charges and an opportunity to be heard.

4930

Each member of the board shall be appointed for a term of four years.

4931

Each member of the board shall receive per diem and expenses as provided in Section 103.

4933

(a) The board shall administer this chapter.

(b) The board may adopt, amend, or repeal, in accordance with the Administrative Procedure Act[Chapter 3.5(commencing with Section 11340) of Part 1 of Division 3 of Title 2 of the Government Code], regulations as may be necessary to enable it to carry into effect the provisions of law relating to the practice of acupuncture.

(c) Four members of the board, including at least one acupuncturist, shall constitute a quorum to conduct business.

(d) It shall require an affirmative vote of a majority of those present at a meeting of the board to take any action or pass any motion.

4933.5

The board, by and with the approval of the director, may employ personnel necessary for the administration of this chapter.

4934

(a) The board, by and with the approval of the director, may appoint an executive officer who is exempt from the State Civil Service Act [Part 2 (commencing with Section 18500) of Division 5 of Title 2 of the Government Code].

(b) This section shall remain in effect only until January 1, 2023, and as of that date is repealed.

4934.1

(a) The Legislature requests the Milton Marks "Little Hoover" Commission on California State Government Organization and Economy to conduct a comprehensive analysis consisting of the following reviews and evaluations and shall report their findings and recommendations to the Legislature by September 1, 2004:

(1) Review and make recommendations on the scope of practice for acupuncturists.

(2) Review and make recommendations on the educational requirements for acupuncturists.

(3) Evaluate the national examination, administered by the National Certification Commission for Acupuncture and Oriental Medicine, and make recommendations as to whether or not the national examination should be offered in California in lieu of, or as part of, the state examination.

(4) Evaluate and make recommendations on the approval process of the Accreditation Commission of Acupuncture and Oriental Medicine, the approval process of the Bureau for Private Postsecondary Education, and the board's approval process.

(b) The board shall pay for all of the costs associated with the comprehensive analysis. An amount to pay for all of the costs associated with the comprehensive analysis, up to two hundred fifty thousand dollars ($250,000), is hereby appropriated to the board from the Acupuncture Fund.

4934.2

The board shall conduct the following studies and reviews, and shall report its findings and recommendations to the department and the Joint Committee on Boards, Commissions, and Consumer Protection no later that September 1, 2004:

(a) The board shall conduct a comprehensive study of the use of unlicensed acupuncture assistants and the need to license and regulate those assistants.

(b) The board shall study and recommend ways to improve the frequency and consistency of their auditing and the quality and relevance of their courses.

ARTICLE 2   CERTIFICATION REQUIREMENTS

4935

(a)(1) It is a misdemeanor, punishable by a fine of not less than one hundred dollars ($100) and not more than two thousand five hundred dollars($2,500), or by imprisonment in a county jail not exceeding one year, or by both that fine and imprisonment, for any person who does not hold a current and valid license to practice acupuncture under this chapter or to advertise or otherwise represent that he or she is practicing or engaging in the practice of acupuncture.

(2) It is a misdemeanor, punishable by a fine of not less than one hundred dollars($100) and not more than two thousand five hundred dollars($2,500), or by imprisonment in a county jail not exceeding one year, or by both that fine and imprisonment, for any person to fraudulently buy, sell, or obtain a license to practice acupuncture, or to violate the provisions of this chapter.

(b) Notwithstanding any other law, any person, other than a physician and surgeon, a dentist, or a podiatrist, who is not licensed under this article but is licensed under Division 2 (commencing with Section 500), who practices acupuncture involving the application of a needle to the human body, performs any acupuncture technique or method involving the application of a needle to the human body, or directs, manages, or supervises another person in performing acupuncture involving the application of a needle to the human body is guilty of a misdemeanor.

(c) A person advertises or otherwise represents that he or she is practicing or engaging in the practice of acupuncture by the use of any title or description of services incorporating the words "acupuncture", "acupuncturist", "certified acupuncturist", "licensed acupuncturist", "Asian medicine", "oriental medicine", or any combination of those words, phrases, or abbreviations of those words or phrases, or by representing that he or she is trained, experienced, an expert, or otherwise qualified to practice in the field of acupuncture, Asian medicine, oriental medicine, or any other complementary or integrative medicine that involves acupuncture and is associated with an Asian subgroup, including Chinese medicine, Japanese medicine, or Korean medicine.

(d) Subdivision(a) shall not prohibit a person from administering acupuncture treatment as part of his or her educational training if the person is either of the following:

(1) Engaged in a course or tutorial program in acupuncture, as provided in this chapter.

(2) A graduate of an approved educational and training program and participating in a postgraduate review course that does not exceed one year in duration at an approved educational and training program.

4936

(a) It is unprofessional conduct for an acupuncturist to use the title "Doctor" or the abbreviation "Dr." in connection with the practice of acupuncture unless he or she possesses a license that authorizes the use or possesses an earned doctorate degree from an accredited, approved, or authorized educational institution as set forth under Chapter 8 (commencing with Section 94800) of Part 59 of Division 10 of Title 3 of the Education Code, which is in acupuncture, oriental medicine, a biological science, or is otherwise related to the authorized practice of an acupuncturist as set forth in Sections 4927 and 4937.

(b) The use of the title "Doctor" or the abbreviation "Dr." by an acupuncturist as authorized in subdivision (a) without further indicating the type of license or degree which authorizes that use shall constitute unprofessional conduct.

4937

An acupuncturist's license authorizes the holder thereof:

(a) To engage in the practice of acupuncture.

(b) To perform or prescribe the use of Asian massage, acupressure, breathing techniques, exercise, heat, cold, magnets, nutrition, diet, herbs, plant, animal, and mineral products, and dietary supplements to promote, maintain, and restore health. Nothing in this section prohibits any person who does not possess an acupuncturist's license or another license as a healing arts practitioner from performing, or prescribing the use of any modality listed in this subdivision.

(c) For purposes of this section, a "magnet" means a mineral or metal that produces a magnetic field without the application of an electric current.

(d) For purposes of this section, "plant, animal, and mineral products" means naturally occurring substances of plant, animal, or mineral origin, except that it does not include synthetic compounds, controlled substances or dangerous drugs as defined in Sections 4021 and 4022, or a controlled substance listed in Chapter 2 (commencing with Section 11053) of Division 10 of the Health and Safety Code.

(e) For purposes of this section, "dietary supplement" has the same meaning as defined in subsection (ff) of Section 321 of Title 21 of the United States Code, except that dietary supplement does not include controlled substances or dangerous drugs as defined in Section 4021 or 4022, or a controlled substance listed in Chapter 2 (commencing with Section 11053) of Division 10 of the Health and Safety Code.

4938

(a) The board shall issue a license to practice acupuncture to any person who makes an application and meets the following requirements:

(1) Is at least 18 years of age.

(2) Furnishes satisfactory evidence of completion of one of the following:

(A)(i) An approved educational and training program.

(ii) If an applicant began an educational and training program at a school or college that submitted a letter of intent to pursue accreditation to, or attained candidacy status from, the Accreditation Commission for Acupuncture and Oriental Medicine, but the commission subsequently denied the school or college candidacy status or accreditation, respectively, the board may review and evaluate the educational training and clinical experience to determine whether to waive the requirements set forth in this subdivision with respect to that applicant.

(B) Satisfactory completion of a tutorial program in the practice of an acupuncturist that is approved by the board.

(C) In the case of an applicant who has completed education and training outside the United States, documented educational training and clinical experience that meets the standards established pursuant to Sections 4939 and 4941.

(3) Passes a written examination administered by the board that tests the applicant's ability, competency, and knowledge in the practice of an acupuncturist. The written examination shall be developed by the Office of Professional Examination Services of the Department of Consumer Affairs.

(4) Is not subject to denial pursuant to Division 1.5(commencing with Section 475).

(5) Completes a clinical internship training program approved by the board. The clinical internship training program shall not exceed nine months in duration and shall be located in a clinic in this state that is an approved educational and training program. The length of the clinical internship shall depend upon the grades received in the examination and the clinical training already satisfactorily completed by the individual prior to taking the examination. The purpose of the clinical internship training program shall be to ensure a minimum level of clinical competence.

(b) Each applicant who qualifies for a license shall pay, as a condition precedent to its issuance and in addition to other fees required, the initial licensure fee.

4939

(a) For purposes of this chapter, "approved credential evaluation service" means an agency or organization that is approved by the board to evaluate education completed outside the United States and identify the equivalency of that education to education completed within the United States.

(b) If an applicant completes education outside of the United States, the applicant shall do both of the following:

(1) Submit documentation of his or her education to a board-approved credential evaluation service for evaluation.

(2) Have the results of the evaluation sent directly from the credential evaluation service to the board.

(c) If the board receives the results of an applicant's evaluation pursuant to subdivision (b), the board shall examine the results and determine whether the applicant meets requirements for licensure. If the evaluated education is not sufficient to meet the requirements for licensure, the board may offer the applicant additional education, training, or standardized testing to satisfy the educational requirements. The board shall not require the applicant to complete education, training, or testing that is not otherwise required of applicants who complete education or training within the United States.

(d) The board shall establish, by regulation, an application process, criteria, and procedures for approval of credential evaluation services. The regulations shall, at a minimum, require the credential evaluation service to meet all of the following requirements:

(1) Furnish evaluations written in English directly to the board.

(2) Be a member of a nationally recognized foreign credential evaluation association, such as, but not limited to, the American Association of Collegiate Registrars and Admissions Officers or the National Association of Credential Evaluation Services.

(3) Undergo reevaluation by the board every five years.

(4) Certify to the board that the credential evaluation service maintains a complete set of reference materials as determined by the board.

(5) Base evaluations only upon verified authentic, official transcripts, and degrees.

(6) Have a written procedure for identifying fraudulent transcripts.

(7) Include in an evaluation report submitted to the board the specific method or methods of authentication for the transcripts, certification, degrees, and other education evaluated for the purposes of the report.

(8) Include in the evaluation report, for each degree held by the applicant, the equivalent degree offered in the United States, the date the degree was granted, the institution granting the degree, an English translation of the course titles, and the semester unit equivalence for each course.

(9) Have an appeal procedure for applicants.

(10) Provide information concerning the credential evaluation service to the board that includes, but is not limited to, resumes or curriculum vitae for each evaluator and translator, which includes biographical information, three letters of references from public or private agencies, statistical information on the number of applications processed annually for the past five years, and any other information the board may require to determine whether the credential evaluation service meets the standards under this subdivision and the board's regulations.

(11) Provide to the board all information required by the board, including, but not limited to, the following:

(A) Its credential evaluation policy.

(B) A complete list of terminology and evaluation terms used in producing its credential evaluations.

(C) A detailed description of the specific methods utilized for credential authentication.

4940

(a) The board shall establish standards for the approval of tutorial programs for education and training in the practice of acupuncture, that satisfy the requirements of Section 4938. The board shall also establish standards for the approved supervising acupuncturists.

(b) An acupuncturist shall be approved to supervise a trainee, provided the supervisor meets the following conditions:

(1) Is licensed to practice acupuncture in this state and that license is current, valid, and has not been suspended or revoked or otherwise subject to disciplinary action.

(2) Has filed an application with the board.

(3) Files with the board the name of each trainee to be trained or employed and a training program satisfactory to the board.

(4) Does not train or employ more than two acupuncture trainees at any one time.

(5) Has at least 10 years of experience practicing as an acupuncturist and has been licensed in this state for at least five years.

(6) Is found by the board to have the knowledge necessary to educate and train the trainee in the practice of an acupuncturist.

The amendments made to this section at the 1993 portion of the 1993 – 94 Regular Session of the Legislature shall not affect the approval of any supervising acupuncturist which has been issued prior to the effective date of those amendments.

4941

In reviewing applications for licensure based upon the completion of a tutorial program in acupuncture, the board may provide that credit is granted for relevant prior training and experience when that training or experience otherwise meets the standards set by the board.

4944

(a) The board shall have the authority to investigate and evaluate each and every applicant applying for a license to practice acupuncture and to make the final determination of the admission of the applicant to the examination, or for the issuance of a license, in conformance with the provisions of this chapter.

(b) The board shall investigate and evaluate each school or college applying for approval under Section 4939 and may utilize and contract with consultants to evaluate those training programs. This subdivision shall become inoperative on January 1, 2017.

(c) The board may delegate to the executive officer or other official of the board its authority under this section in routine matters.

4945

(a) The board shall establish standards for continuing education for acupuncturists.

(b) The board shall require each acupuncturist to complete 50 hours of continuing education every two years as a condition for renewal of his or her license. No more than five hours of continuing education in each two-year period may be spent on issues unrelated to clinical matters or the actual provision of health care to patients. A provider of continuing education shall apply to the board for approval to offer continuing education courses for credit toward this requirement on a form developed by the board, shall pay a fee covering the cost of approval and for the monitoring of the provider by the board and shall set forth the following information on the application:

(1) Course content.

(2) Test criteria.

(3) Hours of continuing education credit requested for the course.

(4) Experience and training of instructors.

(5) Other information as required by the board.

(6) That interpreters or bilingual instruction will be made available, when necessary.

(c) Licensees residing out of state or out of the country shall comply with the continuing education requirements.

(d) Providers of continuing education shall be monitored by the board as determined by the board.

(e) If the board determines that any acupuncturist has not obtained the required number of hours of continuing education, it may renew the acupuncturist's license and require that the deficient hours of continuing education be made up during the following renewal period in addition to the current continuing education required for that period. If any acupuncturist fails to make up the deficient hours and complete the current requirement of hours of continuing education during the subsequent renewal period, then his or her license to practice acupuncture shall not be renewed until all the required hours are completed and documented to the board.

4947

(a) Nothing in this chapter shall be construed to prevent the practice of acupuncture by a person licensed as a dentist or a podiatrist, within the scope of their respective licenses, if the licensee has received a course of instruction in acupuncture. This course material shall be approved by the licensing board having jurisdiction over the licensee. The board shall assist the licensing boards in providing information as requested by the individual licensing boards.

(b) The course requirement set forth in subdivision (a) shall not apply to a podiatrist or dentist who has completed a course in acupuncture, including a continuing education course, and has utilized acupuncture prior to July 1, 1982.

4948

The provisions of this chapter shall not be construed to make unlawful the activities of persons involved in research pursuant to Section 2075.

4949

The provisions of this chapter shall not prohibit an acupuncturist from another state or country, who is not a licensed acupuncturist in this state, who is the invited guest of a professional acupuncture association or scientific acupuncture foundation, an approved educational and training program, or a continuing education provider that is approved under Section 4945, solely from engaging in professional education through lectures, clinics, or demonstrations. The guest acupuncturist may engage in the practice of acupuncture in conjunction with these lectures, clinics, or demonstrations for a maximum of six months, but may not open an office or appoint a place to meet patients or receive calls from patients or otherwise engage in the practice of acupuncture.

ARTICLE 4 ENFORCEMENT

4955

The board may deny, suspend, or revoke, or impose probationary conditions upon, the license of any acupuncturist who is guilty of unprofessional conduct.

Unprofessional conduct shall include, but not be limited to, the following:

(a) Using or possessing any controlled substance, as defined in Division 10(commencing with Section 11000) of the Health and Safety Code, dangerous drug, or alcoholic beverage to an extent or in a manner dangerous to the acupuncturist, or to any other person, or to the public, and to an extent that the use impairs the acupuncturist's ability to engage in the practice of acupuncture with safety to the public.

(b) Conviction of a crime substantially related to the qualifications, functions, or duties of an acupuncturist, the record of conviction being conclusive evidence thereof.

(c) False or misleading advertising.

(d) Aiding or abetting in, or violating or conspiring in, directly or indirectly, the violation of the terms of this chapter or any regulation adopted by the board pursuant to this chapter.

(e) Except for good cause, the knowing failure to protect patients by failing to follow infection control guidelines of the board, thereby risking transmission of blood-borne infectious diseases from licensee to patient, from patient to patient, and from patient to licensee. In administering this subdivision, the board shall consider referencing the standards, regulations, and guidelines of the State Department of Public Health developed pursuant to Section 1250.11 of the Health and Safety Code and the standards, regulations, and guidelines pursuant to the California Occupational Safety and Health Act of 1973[Part 1(commencing with Section 6300) of Division 5 of the Labor Code] for preventing the transmission of HIV, hepatitis B, and other blood-borne pathogens in health care settings. As necessary, the board shall consult with healing arts boards within this division, including, but not limited to, the Medical Board of California, the California Board of Podiatric Medicine, the Dental Board of California, the Board of Registered Nursing, and the Board of Vocational Nursing and Psychiatric Technicians, to encourage appropriate consistency in the implementation of this subdivision.

The board shall seek to ensure that licensees are informed of the responsibility of licensees and others to follow infection control guidelines, and of the most recent scientifically recognized safeguards for minimizing the risk of transmission of blood-borne infectious diseases.

(f) The use of threats or harassment against any patient or licensee for providing evidence in a disciplinary action, other legal action, or in an investigation contemplating a disciplinary action or other legal action.

(g) Discharging an employee primarily for attempting to comply with the terms of this chapter.

(h) Disciplinary action taken by any public agency for any act substantially related to the qualifications, functions, or duties of an acupuncturist or any professional health care licensee.

(i) Any action or conduct that would have warranted the denial of the acupuncture license.

(j) The violation of any law or local ordinance on an acupuncturist's business premises by an acupuncturist's employee or a person who is working under the acupuncturist's professional license or business permit, that is substantially related to the qualifications, functions, or duties of an acupuncturist. These violations shall subject the acupuncturist who employed the individuals, or under whose acupuncturist license the employee is working, to disciplinary action.

(k) The abandonment of a patient by the licensee without written notice to the patient that treatment is to be discontinued and before the patient has had a reasonable opportunity to secure the services of another practitioner.

(l) The failure to notify the board of the use of any false, assumed, or fictitious name other than the name under which the licensee is licensed as an individual to practice acupuncture.

4955.1

The board may deny, suspend, revoke, or impose probationary conditions upon the license of any acupuncturist if he or she is guilty of committing a fraudulent act including, but not be limited to, any of the following:

(a) Securing a license by fraud or deceit.

(b) Committing a fraudulent or dishonest act as an acupuncturist.

(c) Committing any act involving dishonesty or corruption with respect to the qualifications, functions, or duties of an acupuncturist.

(d) Altering or modifying the medical record of any person, with fraudulent intent, or creating any false medical record.

(e) Failing to maintain adequate and accurate records relating to the provision of services to their patients.

4955.2

The board may deny, suspend, revoke, or impose probationary conditions upon the license of any acupuncturist if he or she is guilty of committing any one of the following:

(a) Gross negligence.

(b) Repeated negligent acts.

(c) Incompetence.

4956

A plea or verdict of guilty or a conviction following a plea of nolo contendere made to a charge which is substantially related to the qualifications, functions, or duties of an acupuncturist is deemed to be a conviction within the meaning of this chapter.

The board may order a license suspended or revoked, or may deny a license, or may impose probationary conditions upon a license, when the time for appeal has elapsed, or the judgment of conviction has been affirmed on appeal, or when an order granting probation is made suspending the imposition of sentence irrespective of a subsequent order under the provisions of Section 1203.4 of the Penal Code allowing the person to withdraw his or her pleas of guilty and to enter a plea of not guilty, or setting aside the verdict of guilty, or dismissing the accusation, complaint, information, or indictment.

4959

(a) The board may request the administrative law judge, under his or her proposed decision in resolution of a disciplinary proceeding before the board, to direct any licensee found guilty of unprofessional conduct to pay to the board a sum not to exceed actual and reasonable costs of the investigation and prosecution of the case.

(b) The costs to be assessed shall be fixed by the administrative law judge and shall not in any event be increased by the board. When the board does not adopt a proposed decision and remands the case to an administrative law judge, the administrative law judge shall not increase the amount of any costs assessed in the proposed decision.

(c) When the payment directed in the board's order for payment of costs is not made by the licensee, the board may enforce the order for payment in the superior court in the county where the administrative hearing was held. This right of enforcement shall be in addition to any other rights the board may have as to any licensee directed to pay costs.

(d) In any judicial action for the recovery of costs, proof of the board's decision shall be conclusive proof of the validity of the order of payment and the terms for payment.

(e) All costs recovered under this section shall be considered a reimbursement for costs incurred and shall be deposited in the Acupuncture Fund.

4960

Disciplinary proceedings under this article shall be conducted pursuant to the Administrative Procedure Act [Chapter 5 (commencing with Section 11500) of Part 1 of Division 3 of Title 2 of the Government Code].

4960.2

The board in all cases of revocation shall certify the fact of the revocation, under the seal of the board, to the business licensing entity of the cities or counties in which the license of the acupuncturist has been revoked. The record of the revocation made by the county or city clerk shall be sufficient evidence of the revocation, and of the regularity of all proceedings of the board in the matter of the revocation.

4960.5

(a) A person whose license or registration has been revoked, suspended, or surrendered, or who has been placed on probation, may petition the board for reinstatement or modification of penalty, including modification or termination of probation, after a period of not less than the following minimum periods has elapsed from the effective date of the decision ordering that disciplinary action:

(1) At least three years for reinstatement of a license revoked or surrendered.

(2) At least two years for early termination of probation of three years or more.

(3) At least two years for modification of a condition of probation.

(4) At least one year for early termination of probation of less than three years.

(b) The board may require an examination for that reinstatement.

(c) Notwithstanding Section 489, a person whose application for a license or registration has been denied by the board, for violations of Division 1.5(commencing with Section 475) of this chapter, may reapply to the board for a license or registration only after a period of three years has elapsed from the date of the denial.

4961

(a) Every person who is now or hereafter licensed to practice acupuncture in this state shall register, on forms prescribed by the Acupuncture Board, the licensee's place of practice, or, if the licensee has more than one place of practice, all of the places of practice. If the licensee has no place of practice, the licensee shall notify the board of that fact. A person licensed by the board shall register within 30 days after the date of licensure.

(b) An acupuncturist licensee shall post the wall license in a conspicuous location in the acupuncturist's place of practice at all times. If an acupuncturist licensee has more than one place of practice, the licensee shall obtain from the board a duplicate wall license for each additional location and post the duplicate wall license at each location.

(c) Any licensee that changes the location of their place of practice shall register each change within 30 days of making that change. In the event a licensee fails to notify the board of any change in the address of a place of practice within the time prescribed by this section, the board may deny renewal of licensure. An applicant for renewal of licensure shall specify in the application whether or not there has been a change in the location of the licensee's place of practice and, if so, the date of that change. The board may accept that statement as evidence of the change of address.

4962

(a) On and after July 1, 2019, except as otherwise provided in subdivision(c), the board shall require a licensee to provide a separate disclosure that includes the licensee's probation status, the length of the probation, the probation end date, all practice restrictions placed on the licensee by the board, the board's telephone number, and an explanation of how the patient can find further information on the licensee's probation on the licensee's profile page on the board's online license information Internet Web site, to a patient or the patient's guardian or health care surrogate before the patient's first visit following the probationary order while the licensee is on probation pursuant to a probationary order made on and after July 1, 2019.

(b) A licensee required to provide a disclosure pursuant to subdivision (a) shall obtain from the patient, or the patient's guardian or health care surrogate, a separate, signed copy of that disclosure.

(c) A licensee shall not be required to provide a disclosure pursuant to subdivision (a) if any of the following applies:

(1) The patient is unconscious or otherwise unable to comprehend the disclosure and sign the copy of the disclosure pursuant to subdivision (b) and a guardian or health care surrogate is unavailable to comprehend the disclosure and sign the copy.

(2) The visit occurs in an emergency room or an urgent care facility or the visit is unscheduled, including consultations in inpatient facilities.

(3) The licensee who will be treating the patient during the visit is not known to the patient until immediately prior to the start of the visit.

(4) The licensee does not have a direct treatment relationship with the patient.

(d) On and after July 1, 2019, the board shall provide the following information, with respect to licensees on probation and licensees practicing under probationary licenses, in plain view on the licensee's profile page on the board's online license information Internet Web site.

(1) For probation imposed pursuant to a stipulated settlement, the causes alleged in the operative accusation along with a designation identifying those causes by which the licensee has expressly admitted guilt and a statement that acceptance of the settlement is not an admission of guilt.

(2) For probation imposed by an adjudicated decision of the board, the causes for probation stated in the final probationary order.

(3) For a licensee granted a probationary license, the causes by which the probationary license was imposed.

(4) The length of the probation and end date.

(5) All practice restrictions placed on the license by the board.

(e) A violation of this section shall not be punishable as a crime.

4963

Whenever any person has engaged in an act or practice which constitutes an offense against this chapter, a superior court of a county on application of the board may issue an injunction or other appropriate order restraining that conduct. Proceedings under this section shall be governed by Chapter 3(commencing with Section 525) of Title 7 of Part 2 of the Code of Civil Procedure. The board may commence action in such superior court under the provisions of this section on its own motion and no undertaking shall be required in any action commenced by the board.

4964

The provisions of this article insofar as they are substantially the same as provisions relating to the same subject matter of any previous acupuncture licensure law shall be construed as a restatement and continuation thereof, and not as a new enactment.

ARTICLE 5 RENEWAL

4965

(a) Licenses issued pursuant to this chapter shall expire on the last day of the birth month of the licensee during the second year of a two-year term, if not renewed.

(b) The board shall establish and administer a birth date renewal program.

(c) To renew an unexpired license, the holder shall apply for renewal on a form provided by the board and pay the renewal fee fixed by the board.

4966

Except as provided in Section 4969, a license that has expired may be renewed at any time within three years after its expiration by filing of an application for renewal on a form provided by the board, paying all accrued and unpaid renewal fees, and providing proof of completing continuing education requirements. If the license is not renewed prior to its expiration, the acupuncturist, as a condition precedent to renewal, shall also pay the prescribed delinquency fee. Renewal under this section shall be effective on the date on which the application is filed, on the date on which the renewal fee is paid, or on the date the delinquency fee is paid, whichever occurs last. If so renewed, the license shall continue in effect through the expiration date provided in Section 4965, after the effective date of the renewal, when it shall expire and become invalid if it is not again renewed.

4967

A person who fails to renew his or her license within three years after its expiration may not renew it, and it may not be restored, reissued, or reinstated thereafter, but that person may apply for and obtain a new license if he or she meets all of the following requirements:

(a) Has not committed any acts or crimes constituting grounds for denial of licensure under Division 1.5(commencing with Section 475).

(b) Takes and passes the examination, if any, which would be required of him or her if an initial application for licensure was being made, or otherwise establishes to the satisfaction of the board that, with due regard for the public interest, he or she is qualified to practice as an acupuncturist.

(c) Pays all of the fees that would be required if an initial application for licensure was being made. The board may provide for the waiver or refund of all or any part of an examination fee in those cases in which a license is issued without an examination pursuant to this section.

4969

(a) A suspended license is subject to expiration and shall be renewed as provided in this article, but the renewal does not entitle the acupuncturist, while the license remains suspended, and until it is reinstated, to engage in the practice of acupuncture, or in any other activity or conduct in violation of the order or judgment by which the license was suspended.

(b) A revoked license is subject to expiration as provided in this article, but it may not be renewed. If it is reinstated after its expiration, the former licensee, as a condition to reinstatement, shall pay a reinstatement fee in an amount equal to the renewal fee in effect on the last regular renewal date before the date on which the license was reinstated, plus the delinquency fee, if any, accrued at the time of its expiration.

ARTICLE 6 REVENUE

4970

The amount of fees prescribed for licensed acupuncturists shall be those set forth in this section unless a lower fee is fixed by the board in accordance with Section 4972:

(a) The application fee shall be seventy-five dollars($75).

(b) The examination and reexamination fees shall be the actual cost to the Acupuncture Board for the development and writing of, grading, and administering of each examination.

(c) The initial license fee shall be three hundred twenty-five dollars($325), except that if the license will expire less than one year after its issuance, then the initial license fee shall be an amount equal to 50 percent of the initial license fee.

(d) The renewal fee shall be three hundred twenty-five dollars($325) and in the event a lower fee is fixed by the board, shall be an amount sufficient to support the functions of the board in the administration of this chapter. The renewal fee shall be assessed on an annual basis until January 1, 1996, and on and after that date the board shall assess the renewal fee biennially.

(e) The delinquency fee shall be set in accordance with Section 163.5.

(f) The application fee for the approval of a school or college under Section 4939 shall be three thousand dollars($3,000). This subdivision shall become inoperative on January 1, 2017.

(g) The duplicate wall license fee is an amount equal to the cost to the board for the issuance of the duplicate license.

(h) The duplicate renewal receipt fee is ten dollars($10).

(i) The endorsement fee is ten dollars($10).

(j) The fee for a duplicate license for an additional office location as required under Section 4961 shall be fifteen dollars($15).

(k) This section shall remain in effect only until January 1, 2021, and as of that date is repealed.

4971

The amount of fees prescribed for acupuncture tutorial programs shall be as follows:

(a) The application and registration fee to supervise an acupuncture trainee is two hundred dollars($200).

(b) The annual renewal fee for approval to supervise an acupuncture trainee is fifty dollars ($50).

(c) The application fee for an acupuncture trainee is twenty-five dollars($25).

(d) The annual renewal fee for an acupuncture trainee is ten dollars($10).

(e) The delinquency fee is 50 percent of the renewal fee.

4972

Fees fixed by the board shall be set forth in regulations duly adopted by the board.

4974

The board shall report to the Controller at the beginning of each month for the month preceding the amount and source of all revenue received by it pursuant to this chapter, and shall pay the entire amount thereof to the Treasurer for deposit in the Acupuncture Fund, which fund is created to carry out the provisions of this chapter, upon appropriation by the Legislature.

ARTICLE 7 ACUPUNCTURE CORPORATIONS

4975

An acupuncture corporation is a corporation which is authorized to render professional services, as defined in Section 13401 of the Corporations Code, so long as that corporation and its shareholders, officers, directors, and employees rendering professional services who are acupuncturists are in compliance with the Moscone-Knox Professional Corporation Act, this article and all other statutes and regulations now or hereafter enacted or adopted pertaining to that corporation and the conduct of its affairs.

With respect to an acupuncture corporation, the governmental agency referred to in the Moscone-Knox Professional Corporation Act is the Acupuncture Board.

4976

It shall constitute unprofessional conduct and a violation of this chapter for any person licensed under this chapter to violate, attempt to violate, directly or indirectly, or assist in or abet the violation of, or conspire to violate, any provision or term of this article, the Moscone-Knox Professional Corporation Act, or any regulations duly adopted under those laws.

4977

An acupuncture corporation shall not do or fail to do any act the doing of which or the failure to do which would constitute unprofessional conduct under Article 4(commencing with

Section 4955). In the conduct of its practice, it shall observe and be bound by statutes and regulations to the same extent as a person holding a license under this chapter.

4977.1

The income of an acupuncture corporation attributable to professional services rendered while a shareholder is a disqualified person (as defined in Section 13401 of the Corporations Code) shall not in any manner accrue to the benefit of such shareholder or his or her shares in the acupuncture corporation.

4977.2

Except as provided in Section 13403 of the Corporations Code, each director, shareholder, and officer of an acupuncture corporation, except an assistant secretary and an assistant treasurer, shall be a licensed person as defined by Section 13401 of the Corporations Code.

4978

The name of an acupuncture corporation and any name or names under which it may render professional services shall contain words "acupuncture" or "acupuncturist" and wording or abbreviations denoting corporate existence.

4979

The board may adopt and enforce regulations to carry out the purposes and objectives of this article, including, but not limited to, regulations requiring (a) that the bylaws of an acupuncture corporation shall include a provision whereby the capital stock of the corporation owned by a disqualified person (as defined in Section 13401 of the Corporations Code), or a deceased person, shall be sold to the corporation or to the remaining shareholders of the corporation within the time the regulations may provide, and (b) that an acupuncture corporation shall provide adequate security by insurance or otherwise for claims against it by its patients arising out of the rendering of professional services.

CALIFORNIA CODE OF REGULATIONS

16 CCR § 1399.400[1]

§ 1399.400   CITATION

This chapter may be cited and referred to as the "Acupuncture Regulations".

16 CCR § 1399.401

§ 1399.401   LOCATION OF OFFICES [REPEALED]

16 CCR § 1399.402

---

[1] California Code of Regulations, Title 16. Professional and Vocational Regulations Division 13. 7. Acupuncture Examining Committee of the Board of Medical Quality Assurance.

§ 1399.402   TENSES, GENDER AND NUMBER [REPEALED]

16 CCR § 1399.403

§ 1399.403   DEFINITIONS

For the purpose of the regulations contained in this chapter, the terms

(a) "Board" shall mean the Acupuncture Board.

(b) "Code" shall mean the Business and Professions Code.

16 CCR § 1399.404

§ 1399.404   ADMINISTRATION OF CHAPTER [REPEALED]

16 CCR § 1399.405

§ 1399.405   DELEGATION OF FUNCTIONS

Except for those powers reserved exclusively to the "agency itself" under the Administrative Procedure Act Section 11500, et seq. of the Government Code, the board delegates and confers upon the executive officer of the board, or in his or her absence, the designee of the executive officer, all functions necessary to the dispatch of business of the board in connection with investigative and administrative proceedings under the jurisdiction of the board, including, but not limited to, the ability to approve settlement agreements for the revocation, surrender or interim suspension of a license.

16 CCR § 1399.406

§ 1399.406   FILING OF ADDRESSES

Each person holding a license, registration, approval or any other authority issued under this chapter shall file his or her proper and current mailing address with the board, and shall notify the board, in writing, within thirty (30) days of any and all changes of mailing address, giving both the old and new address.

16 CCR § 1399.407

§ 1399.407   DEFINITIONS

(a) For the purposes of section 901 of the Code:

(1) "Community-based organization" means a public or private nonprofit organization that is representative of a community or a significant segment of a community, and is engaged in meeting human, educational, environmental, or public safety community needs.

(2) "Out-of-state practitioner" means a person who is not licensed in California to engage in the practice of acupuncture but who holds a current valid license or certificate in good standing in another state, district, or territory of the United States to practice acupuncture.

(3) "In good standing" means the person:

(A) Has not been charged with an offense for any act substantially related to the practice for which the applicant is licensed by any public agency; and

(B) Has not entered into any consent agreement or been subject to an administrative decision that contains conditions placed upon the applicant's professional conduct or practice, including any voluntary surrender of license; and

(C) Has not been the subject of an adverse judgment resulting from the practice for which the applicant is licensed that the board determines constitutes evidence of a pattern of negligence or incompetence.

16 CCR § 1399.407.1

§ 1399.407.1 SPONSORING ENTITY REGISTRATION AND RECORDKEEPING REQUIREMENTS

(a) Registration. A sponsoring entity that wishes to provide, or arrange for the provision of, health care services at a sponsored event under section 901 of the Code shall register with the board not later than 90 calendar days prior to the date on which the sponsored event is scheduled to begin. A sponsoring entity shall register with the board by submitting to the board a completed "Registration of Sponsoring Entity Under Business & Professions Code Section 901" Form 901 – A(DCA/2016 – revised), which is hereby incorporated by reference.

(b) Determination of Completeness of Form. The board may, by resolution, delegate to the Department of Consumer Affairs the authority to receive and process Form 901 – A on behalf of the board. The board or its delegatee shall inform the sponsoring entity within 15 calendar days of receipt of Form 901 – A in writing that the form is either complete and the sponsoring entity is registered or that the form is deficient and what specific information or documentation is required to complete the form and be registered. The board or its delegatee shall reject the registration if all of the identified deficiencies have not been corrected at least 30 days prior to the commencement of the sponsored event.

(c) Recordkeeping Requirements. Regardless of where it is located, a sponsoring entity shall maintain at a physical location in California a copy of all records required by section 901 as well as a copy of the authorization for participation issued by the board to an out-of-state practitioner. The sponsoring entity shall maintain these records for a period of at least five years after the date on which a sponsored event ended. The records may be maintained in either paper or electronic form. The sponsoring entity shall notify the board at the time of registration as to the form in which it will maintain the records. In addition, the sponsoring entity shall keep a copy of all records required by section 901(g) of the Code at the physical location of the sponsored event until that event has ended. These records shall be available for inspection and copying during the operating hours of the sponsored event upon request of any representative of the board.

(d) Requirement for Prior Board Approval of Out-of-State Practitioner. A sponsoring entity shall not permit an out-of-state practitioner to participate in a sponsored event unless and until the sponsoring entity has received written approval from the board.

(e) Report. Within 15 calendar days after a sponsored event has concluded, the sponsoring entity shall file a report with the board summarizing the details of the sponsored event. This report may be in a form of the sponsoring entity's choosing, but shall include, at a minimum, the following information:

(1) The date(s) of the sponsored event;

(2) The location(s) of the sponsored event;

(3) The type(s) and general description of all health care services provided at the sponsored event; and

(4) A list of each out-of-state practitioner granted authorization pursuant to this article who participated in the sponsored event, along with the license number of that practitioner.

16 CCR § 1399.407.2

§ 1399.407.2 OUT-OF-STATE PRACTITIONER AUTHORIZATION TO PARTICIPATE IN SPONSORED EVENTS

(a) Request for Authorization to Participate. An out-of-state practitioner ("applicant") may request authorization from the board to participate in a sponsored event and provide such health care services at the sponsored event as would be permitted if the applicant were licensed by the board to provide those services. An applicant shall request authorization by submitting to the board a completed "Request For Authorization To Practice Without a California License at a Registered Free Health Care Event" Form 901 - B(CAB/2016), which is hereby incorporated by reference, accompanied by a non-refundable processing fee of $25. The applicant shall also furnish either a full set of fingerprints or submit a Live Scan inquiry to establish the identity of the applicant and to permit the board to conduct a criminal history record check.

(b) Response to Request for Authorization to Participate. Within 20 calendar days of receiving a completed request for authorization, the board shall notify the sponsoring entity whether that request is approved or denied.

(c) Denial of Request for Authorization to Participate.

(1) The board shall deny a request for authorization to participate if:

(A) The submitted Form 901 - B is incomplete and the applicant has not responded within 7 calendar days to the board'S request for additional information; or

(B) The applicant has failed to comply with a requirement of this article or has committed any act that would constitute grounds for denial of an application for licensure by the board; or

(C) The applicant does not possess a current valid License in good standing as defined in Section 1399.407.

(2) The board may deny a request for authorization to participate if:

(A) The request is received less than 20 calendar days before the date on which the sponsored event will begin; or

(B) The applicant has been previously denied a request for authorization by the board to participate in a sponsored event; or

(C) The applicant has previously had an authorization to participate in a sponsored event terminated by the board; or

(D) The applicant has already participated in four(4) or more sponsored events during the 12 month period immediately preceding the date the current request for authorization is received by the board.

(d) Appeal of Denial. An applicant requesting authorization to participate in a sponsored event may appeal the denial of such request by following the procedures set forth in section 1399.407.3.

16 CCR § 1399.407.3

§ 1399.407.3 TERMINATION OF AUTHORIZATION AND APPEAL

(a) Grounds for Termination. The board may terminate an out-of-state practitioner's authorization to participate in a sponsored event for any of the following reasons:

(1) The out-of-state practitioner has failed to comply with any applicable provision of this article, or any applicable practice requirement or regulation of the board.

(2) The out-of-state practitioner has committed an act that would constitute grounds for discipline if done by a licensee of the board.

(3) The board has received a credible complaint indicating that the out-of-state practitioner is unfit to practice at the sponsored event or has otherwise endangered consumers of the practitioner's services.

(b) Notice of Termination. The board shall provide both the sponsoring entity and the out-of-state practitioner with a written notice of the termination, including the basis for the termination. If the written notice is provided during a sponsored event, the board may provide the notice to any representative of the sponsored event on the premises of the event.

(c) Consequences of Termination. An out-of-state practitioner shall immediately cease his or her participation in a sponsored event upon receipt of the written notice of termination. Termination of authority to participate in a sponsored event shall be deemed a disciplinary measure reportable to the national practitioner data banks. In addition, the board shall provide a copy of the written notice of termination to the licensing authority of each jurisdiction in which the out-of-state practitioner is licensed.

(d) Appeal of Termination. An out-of-state practitioner may appeal the board's decision to terminate an authorization in the manner provided by section 901(j)(2) of the Code. The request for an appeal shall be considered a request for an informal hearing under the Administrative Procedure Act pursuant to the provisions of Chapter 4.5(commencing with Section 11445.10) of Part 1 of Division 3 of Title 2 of the Government Code.

(e) Informal Conference Option. In addition to requesting a hearing, the out-of-state practitioner may request an informal conference with the Executive Officer regarding the reasons for the termination of authorization to participate. The Executive Officer shall, within 30 days from receipt of the request, hold an informal conference with the out-of-state practitioner. At the conclusion of the informal conference, the Executive Officer may affirm or dismiss the termination of authorization to participate. The Executive Officer shall state in writing the reasons for his or her action and mail a copy of his or her findings and decision to the out-of-state practitioner within ten days from the date of the informal conference. The out-of-state practitioner does not waive his or her request for a hearing to contest a termination of authorization by requesting an informal conference. If the termination is dismissed after the informal conference, the request for a hearing shall be deemed to be withdrawn.

16 CCR § 1399.410

§ 1399.410　VERIFICATION

All statements submitted by or on behalf of an applicant shall be made under penalty of perjury.

16 CCR § 1399.411

§ 1399.411　CERTIFICATION OF DOCUMENTATION

Documentation submitted by or on behalf of the applicant shall be certified by the appropriate official or governmental seal or authority. The board in its discretion may waive this requirement when it is determined that it cannot be obtained through the exercise of due diligence.

16 CCR § 1399.412

§ 1399.412　TRANSLATION REQUIRED

All documentation submitted in a language other than English shall be accompanied by a translation into English certified by a translator other than the applicant who shall attest to the accuracy of such translation under penalty of perjury.

This database is current through 10/9/20 Register 2020, No.41

16 CCR § 1399.412, 16 CA ADC § 1399.412

16 CCR § 1399.413

§ 1399.413　APPLICATION DEADLINE

(a) All new applications for examination shall be submitted on a form provided by the board, accompanied by such statements and documents as required. All such applications shall be received in the board's Sacramento office at least 120 calendar days prior to the date of the examination for which the application is made.

(b) All applications for re-examination shall be submitted on a form provided by the board ("Application Update for Examination/Licensure", revised 3/96), accompanied by such statements and documents as required. All such applications shall be received in the board's office at least 30 calendar days prior to the date of the examination for which the application is made.

(c) All transcripts and supporting documents from qualifying educational institutions or tutorial supervisors shall be received in the board's office at least 30 calendar days prior to the date of examination for which an application was made.

(d) The board may waive the foregoing filing dates if there are difficulties with the administration of the examination or other circumstances warrant.

16 CCR § 1399.414

§ 1399.414   DENIAL OF APPLICATIONS

(a) Any applicant whose application is denied, may submit within fifteen (15) calendar days from the date of rejection, a request in writing that his or her application be presented to the board for further evaluation.

(b) If the board determines that an applicant has met the requirements for acupuncture licensure, it shall schedule the applicant for examination.

(c) Nothing in this section shall be constructed to deprive an applicant of his or her rights of appeal as afforded by other provisions of law.

16 CCR § 1399.415

§ 1399.415   DOCUMENTATION OF TRAINING

(a) Each applicant shall have completed the education or tutorial requirements set forth in these regulations as documented by the registrar of each school from which the applicant attended or from the applicant's tutor, in the case of a tutorial program.

(b)(1) All applicants for examination who are enrolled in an approved acupuncture and Oriental medicine educational training program prior to January 1, 2005, shall have completed the coursework and training set forth in Section 1399.436.

(2) All applicants for examination who are enrolled in an approved acupuncture and Oriental medicine educational training program on or after January 1, 2005, shall have completed the coursework and training set forth in Section 1399.434.

(c) All applicants applying for examination shall meet the minimum educational or tutorial requirements set forth in these regulations at least thirty (30) days prior to the date of the examination for which the application has been made.

16 CCR § 1399.416

§ 1399.416   EQUIVALENT TRAINING AND CLINICAL EXPERIENCE QUALIFYING FOR LICENSURE

In order for documented educational training and clinical experience to qualify for licensure under Section 4938, subdivision (b)(3) of the Code, the applicant shall document that such education and experience meets the requirements of Section 1399.436, subsections (a), (b), and (c) or, if applicable, Section 1399. 434. All foreign trained applicants shall submit documentation of his or her education to a credentials evaluation service that is a member of the National Association of Credentials Evaluation Services, Inc. for review and a report to the board. This report shall be filed by the applicant with his or her application for examination.

16 CCR § 1399.417

§ 1399.417   ABANDONMENT OF APPLICATIONS

(a) An application for examination shall be deemed to have been abandoned and the applicant's fee forfeited in any of the following circumstances:

(1) The applicant fails to complete his or her application within 180 calendar days after it has been filed. An application shall be deemed complete when all documents and information required to determine eligibility for examination have been submitted to the board.

(2) The applicant fails to take the licensing examination within two years after the date that he or she is notified by the board of his/her eligibility to take the examination, unless prior to the application being deemed abandoned, the applicant submits a written explanation to the board, of his or her inability to appear for the examination. The board may extend the applicant's eligibility to take the examination for two more consecutive administrations of the examination.

(3) The applicant, after failing the examination, fails to take a re-examination within two years after the date the applicant was notified of such failure, unless prior to the application being deemed abandoned, the applicant submits a written explanation to the board, of his or her inability to appear for the examination. The board may extend the applicant's eligibility to take the examination for two more consecutive administrations of the examination.

(b) An application submitted after the abandonment of a former application for examination shall be treated as a new application.

(c) An applicant who, after passing the examination, fails to submit a complete application for licensure within three years after the date he or she is notified of his or her eligibility for licensure shall be deemed to have abandoned his or her application for licensure. An application submitted after the abandonment for a former application for licensure shall be treated as a new application and the applicant shall take and pass the examination, if any, which would be required of him or her if an initial application for licensure was being made.

16 CCR § 1399.418

§ 1399.418　FAILURE TO APPEAR FOR EXAMINATION-WITHDRAWAL OF APPLICATION [REPEALED]

16 CCR § 1399.419

§ 1399.419　REVIEW AND PROCESSING OF EXAM APPLICATIONS

(a) Within forty-five(45) calendar days after receipt of an application for examination, the board shall inform the applicant whether the application is complete and accepted for filing or that it is deficient and what specific information or documentation is required to complete the application.

(b) Within forty-five (45) calendar days of receipt of a completed application, the applicant will be notified as to his/her eligibility for the written examination.

(c) Within thirty(30) calendar days from the date the written examination is administered, candidates will be notified of their results, and if passed, will be offered, upon payment of the specified fee, a license to practice acupuncture.

(d) The minimum, median and maximum processing times for examination results from the time of receipt of a complete application until the board makes a decision is set forth below.

Minimum – 130 calendar days

Median – 155 calendar days

Maximum – 180 calendar days

These processing times apply to those candidates who take and pass the first available examination and who submit a complete application by the first available application deadline.

(e) In addition to any other requirements for licensure, whenever it appears that an applicant for a license may be unable to perform as an acupuncturist safely because the applicant's ability to perform may be impaired due to mental illness, or physical illness affecting competency, the board may require the applicant to be examined by one or more physicians and surgeons or psychologists designated by the board. The board shall pay the full cost of such examination. An applicant's failure to comply with the requirement shall render his or her application incomplete.

The report of the evaluation shall be made available to the applicant.

16 CCR § 1399.419.1

§ 1399.419.1　RESPONSE TO BOARD INQUIRY

If the board or its designee asks a licensee to provide criminal history information, a licensee shall respond to that request within 30 days. The licensee shall make available all documents and other records requested and shall respond with accurate information.

16 CCR § 1399.419.2

§ 1399.419.2　FINGERPRINT AND DISCLOSURE REQUIREMENTS FOR RENEWAL OF LICENSE

(a) As a condition of renewal for a license that expires on or after January 1, 2011, a licensee who was initially licensed prior to January 1, 2001, or for whom an electronic record of the submission of fingerprints no longer exists, shall furnish to the Department of Justice a full set of fingerprints for the purpose of conducting a criminal history record check and to undergo a state and federal level criminal offender record information search conducted through the Department of Justice.

(1) The licensee shall pay any costs for furnishing the fingerprints and conducting the searches.

(2) A licensee shall certify when applying for renewal whether his or her fingerprints have been furnished to the Department of Justice in compliance with this section.

(3) This requirement is waived if the licensee is renewed in an inactive status, or is actively serving in the military outside the United States.

(4) A licensee shall retain, for at least three years from the renewal date, either a receipt showing the electronic transmission of his or her fingerprints to the Department of Justice or a receipt evidencing that the licensee's fingerprints were taken.

(b) As a condition of renewal, a licensee shall disclose whether, since the licensee last applied for renewal, he or she has been convicted of any violation of the law of this or any other state, the United States, or other country, omitting traffic infractions under $300 not involving alcohol, dangerous drugs as defined in Section 4022 of the Code, or controlled substances.

(c) As a condition of renewal, a licensee shall disclose whether, since the licensee last applied for renewal, he or she has been denied a license or had a license disciplined by another licensing authority of this state, of another state, of any agency of the federal government, or of another country.

(d) Failure to comply with the requirements of this section renders any application for renewal incomplete and the license may not be renewed until the licensee demonstrates compliance with all requirements.

(e) Failure to furnish a full set of fingerprints to the Department of Justice as required by this section on or before the date required for renewal of a license is grounds for discipline by the Board.

(f) Before a license in inactive status may be activated, the licensee shall comply with this section. A licensee who is serving in the military outside of the United States shall immediately comply with this section upon his or her return to the United States unless the return is for less than thirty days.

16 CCR § 1399.420

§ 1399.420 CITATION AND REFERENCE

This article shall be cited and referred to as the "Acupuncture Tutorial Regulations."

16 CCR § 1399.421

§ 1399.421 DEFINITIONS

As used in these regulations:

(a) "Acupuncture tutorial" means an acupuncture tutorial program which is approved by the board pursuant to Sections 4939 and 4940 of the code which when successfully completed meets the requirements of Section 4938 of the code for licensure as an acupuncturist.

(b) "Supervising acupuncturist" or "supervisor" means a licensed acupuncturist who is approved by the board to provide an acupuncture tutorial to a trainee who is registered with the board pursuant to Section 4940 of the code and these regulations. Pursuant to Section 4940 no physician, podiatrist or dentist may be a supervising acupuncturist unless he or she is a licensed acupuncturist.

(c) "Trainee" means a person who is registered with the board in order to participate in an acupuncture tutorial under a supervising acupuncturist.

16 CCR § 1399.422

§ 1399.422 PRIOR APPROVAL TO PRACTICE AS AN ACUPUNCTURE TRAINEE

No person shall practice acupuncture in tutorial without the prior approval of the board.

16 CCR § 1399.423

§ 1399.423 PRIOR APPROVAL TO SUPERVISE AN ACUPUNCTURE TRAINEE

No acupuncturist shall supervise any person in an acupuncture tutorial without the prior approval of the board.

16 CCR § 1399.424

§ 1399.424 FILING OF APPLICATIONS; CREDIT FOR PRIOR TRAINING

(a) Applications for approval as an acupuncture trainee shall be filed on a form provided by the board at its Sacramento office and accompanied by the application fee required in Section 1399.461.

(b) Applications for approval to supervise an acupuncture trainee shall be filed on a form provided by the board at its Sacramento office and accompanied by any necessary documents, including the training agreement, and the application fee required in Section 1399.461.

(c) Any prior training and experience already obtained within ten(10) years of the date of the application by the trainee, which meets the standards of the board may be considered when developing a training plan between a supervisor and trainee, and specifically the required hours of theoretical and clinical training may be reduced on account of such prior training and experience. Evidence of such prior training and experience should be submitted to the board for its review with the applications for registration of the supervising acupuncturist and trainee.

16 CCR § 1399.425

§ 1399.425 REQUIREMENTS FOR APPROVAL OF AN ACUPUNCTURE TUTORIAL

(a) An acupuncture tutorial shall provide a trainee with a structured learning experience in all the basic skills and knowledge necessary for the independent practice of acupuncture.

(b) An acupuncture tutorial which is in the nature of on-the-job training may be full time or part time employment relationship, however, the training plan and proposed supervision shall be contained in a written agreement between the supervisor and trainee. There shall be no tuition fees charged to the trainee by the supervising acupuncturist.

(c) An acupuncture tutorial shall provide formal clinical training with supplemental theoretical and didactic instruction. The theoretical and didactic training required in subsections (e)(8) through(e)(20) shall be obtained in an approved acupuncture school or another postsecondary educational institution which is accredited or approved under Article 7(commencing with Section 94900) of Chapter 7 Part 59 of the Education Code or is accredited by a regional accrediting agency authorized by the U.S. Department of Education.

(d) The clinical training shall consist of a minimum of 2250 hours in the following areas:

(1) Practice observation

(2) History and physical examination

(3) Therapeutic treatment planning

(4) Preparation of the patient

(5) Sterilization, use and maintenance of equipment

(6) Moxibustion

(7) Electroacupuncture(AC and DC voltages)

(8) Body and auricular acupuncture

(9) Treatment of emergencies, including cardiopulmonary resuscitation

(10) Pre-and post-treatment instructions to the patient

(11) Contraindications and precautions

(e) The theoretical and didactic training shall consist of a minimum of 1548 hours (approximately 100 semester units) in the following areas:

Minimum Class Hours

(1) Traditional Oriental medicine-a survey of the theory and practice of traditional diagnostic and therapeutic procedures.

(2) Acupuncture anatomy and physiology-fundamentals of acupuncture, including the meridian system, special and extra loci, and auriculotherapy.

(3) Acupuncture techniques-instruction in the use of needling techniques, moxibustion, electroacupuncture, including contraindications and complications. Tutorial trainees shall either (1) successfully complete, at a board approved acupuncture school, a course which requires a student to pass an examination in clean needle technique that uses as its primary reference the most current edition of the "Clean Needle Technique Manual", published by the National Acupuncture Foundation, or (2) successfully complete a Clean Needle Technique course administered by the Council of Colleges of Acupuncture and Oriental Medicine.

(4) Acupressure.

(5) Breathing techniques-introductory course in Qi Gong.

(6) Traditional Oriental exercise-introductory course in Tai Chi Chuan.660

(7) Traditional Oriental herbology including botany.300

(8) Practice management-instruction in the legal and ethical aspects of maintaining a professional practice, including record keeping, professional liability, patient accounts, and referral procedures.

(9) Ethics relating to the practice of acupuncture.30 Minimum Class Hours

(10) Clinical medicine-a survey of the clinical practice of medicine, osteopathy, dentistry, psychology, nursing, chiropractic, podiatry, and homeopathy to familiarize practitioners with the practices of other health care practitioners.

(11) History of medicine-a survey of medical history, including transcultural healing practices.

(12) Medical terminology-fundamentals of English language medical terminology.

(13) General sciences-a survey of or courses in general biology, chemistry, and physics.

(14) Anatomy-a survey of microscopic and gross anatomy and neuroanatomy.

(15) General Psychology-including counseling skills.

(16) Physiology-a survey of basic physiology, including neurophysiology, endocrinology, and neurochemistry.

(17) Pathology-a survey of the nature of disease and illness, including microbiology, immunology, psychopathology, and epidemiology.

(18) Clinical sciences-a review of internal medicine, pharmacology, neurology, surgery, obstetrics/gynecology, urology, radiology, nutrition, vitamins, and public health.

(19) Western pharmacology.558

(20) A minimum of eight(8) hours in a certified course offering first-aid and adult/child cardiopulmonary resuscitation(CPR). Such course shall be taken from the American Red Cross, American Heart Association or other organization with an equivalent course work approved by the Board.

(f) The course work specified in this section shall extend over a minimum period of four (4) academic years, eight(8) semesters, twelve(12) quarters, nine(9) trimesters, or thirty-six(36) months. No more than 1500 hours of clinical training and/or theoretical and didactic training is to be completed per twelve(12) month period.

(g) The acupuncture services provided by the trainee shall be done so in a manner which does not endanger the health and welfare of patients receiving such services.

No trainee shall render acupuncture services to any patient unless the patient has been informed that such services will be rendered by that trainee. The patient on each occasion of treatment shall be informed of the procedure to be performed by the trainee under the supervision of the supervising acupuncturist and have consented in writing prior to performance to permit such rendering of the acupuncture procedure by the trainee. The foregoing requirements shall also be applied to those instances wherein the trainee is to assist the supervisor in the rendering of acupuncture services.

(h) The acupuncture tutorial training program shall be set forth in a written agreement signed by the supervisor and trainee which sets forth, but is not limited to, the training plan, length of training time, the method for providing the theoretical and didactic training and guidelines for supervision of the acupuncture services rendered by the trainee. A copy of such written agreement shall be submitted with the application for approval.

(i) As a condition of approval, or continued approval, all tutorial programs are subject to an on-site visit by representatives of the board to review and evaluate the status of the program. It will be the responsibility of the trainee and supervisor to reimburse the board for direct costs incurred in conducting such review and evaluation.

(j) Acupuncture trainees shall have met the following prerequisites prior to the approval of the tutorial program:

(1) Be at least 18 years of age.

(2) Successful completion of an approved high school course of study or have passed a standard equivalency test.

(k) An acupuncture tutorial shall be made available regardless of sex, race, religion, creed, color or physical handicap.

(1) The requirements of this section shall not apply to persons who commenced a tutorial and registered with the board as provided in Section 1399.424 prior to January 1, 1999. Such persons shall meet the curriculum and clinical training requirements in effect at the time that their application for a tutorial program was approved by the board.

16 CCR § 1399.426

§ 1399.426　SUPERVISING ACUPUNCTURIST'S RESPONSIBILITIES

Each supervising acupuncturist shall have the following duties and responsibilities:

(a) A supervisor shall at all times be responsible for and provide supervision of the work performed by the trainee as required in these regulations.

(b) The supervisor shall only assign those patient treatments which can be safely and effectively performed by the trainee and which are consistent with the level of training received by the trainee. The supervisor shall provide continuous direction and immediate supervision of the trainee when patient services are provided. The supervisor shall be in the same facility as and in proximity to the location where the trainee is rendering services and shall be readily available at all times to provide advice, instruction and assistance to the trainee.

(c) The supervisor shall insure that patient informed consent is obtained when necessary.

(d) The supervisor shall insure that the objectives of the training plan submitted are provided and met by the trainee, and that the required theoretical training is obtained in accordance with subsection(c) of Section 1399.425.

(e) The supervisor shall insure that the trainee complies with the standards of practice in Article 5 of the Acupuncture Regulations.

(f) The supervisor shall file quarterly with the board a progress report on a form provided by the board which sets forth the schedules for theoretic and didactic training and for clinical training of the trainee.

(g) The supervisor shall insure that when rendering services or otherwise engaging in professional activity the trainee always identifies himself or herself as an "acupuncture trainee" and wears at such times the identification badge required in Section 1399.427.

(h) There shall be no separate billing by the trainee.

(i) The supervisor shall comply with the provisions of the acupuncture law, the Acupuncture Regulations and applicable laws and regulations governing wages and compensation paid to employees or apprentices, maximum hours and working conditions. Any overtime worked by the trainee shall not interfere with or impair the training program and shall not be detrimental to the health and safety of the trainee or patients.

16 CCR § 1399.427

§ 1399.427　TRAINEE'S RESPONSIBILITIES

Each acupuncture trainee shall have the following duties and responsibilities.

(a) The trainee shall not provide acupuncture services without the required supervision or autonomously, and shall not provide any services for which he or she is not trained or competent to perform.

(b) The trainee shall satisfactorily meet the objectives of the training plan submitted to the board, including the necessary theoretical training.

(c) The trainee shall comply with the standards of practice in Article 5 of the Acupuncture Regulations.

(d) The trainee shall always identify himself or herself as an acupuncture trainee when rendering services or otherwise engaging in professional activity and shall wear at such times an identification badge on an outer garment and in plain view which states the trainee's name and the title "Acupuncture Trainee."

(e) The trainee shall report to the board any delay, interruption or termination of the acupuncture tutorial not reported by the supervisor.

(f) The trainee shall maintain a written log of the patients whom he or she has seen during the clinical training. The log shall contain the date and time of the patient visit and a description of the acupuncture services provided by the trainee to the patient. The log shall be made available to the committee upon request.

16 CCR § 1399.428

§ 1399.428 TERMINATION OR MODIFICATION OF TUTORIAL

(a) The board shall be notified in writing within ten(10) calendar days of the termination of any acupuncture tutorial for any reason. At the time of such notification the registration of both the supervisor and trainee shall be cancelled. If the supervisor or trainee subsequently participate in an acupuncture tutorial, a new application for registration shall be filed with the board as set forth in Section 1399.424.

(b) If the training plan of the acupuncture tutorial is substantially modified, then a report of such modifications shall be filed with the board. There shall be no charge for filing such a report.

16 CCR § 1399.429

§ 1399.429 APPLICATION FOR EXAMINATION

At the completion of the tutorial the trainee may file an application for examination.

16 CCR § 1399.430

§ 1399.430 DENIAL, SUSPENSION OR REVOCATION OF REGISTRATION AS A SUPERVISOR

The board may deny, issue subject to terms and conditions, suspend, revoke or place on probation a registration to supervise a trainee in an acupuncture tutorial for the following causes:

(a) Failure to comply with the provisions of Section 4940 of the code or the Acupuncture Tutorial Regulations for approval of an acupuncture tutorial.

(b) Violation of the Acupuncture Licensure Act or the Acupuncture Regulations.

(c) The supervisor is the subject of a successful disciplinary action or has had charges in a disciplinary action filed against him or her.

(d) The registration was obtained by fraud or misrepresentation or false or misleading information was presented to the division with respect to an acupuncture tutorial.

(e) Failure of the supervisor or the trainee to comply with the regulations relating to supervision, patient care or informed consent.

(f) The trainee has rendered acupuncture services in violation of this act within the setting of the acupuncture tutorial regardless of whether the supervising acupuncturist has knowledge of the acts performed.

16 CCR § 1399.431

§ 1399.431　DENIAL, SUSPENSION OR REVOCATION OF REGISTRATION AS A TRAINEE

The board may deny, issue, subject to terms and conditions, suspend, revoke or place on probation a registration as a trainee in an acupuncture tutorial for the following causes:

(a) Failure to comply with the Acupuncture Tutorial Regulations for approval and registration as a trainee.

(b) Violation of the Acupuncture Licensure Act or the Acupuncture Regulations.

(c) The registration was obtained by fraud or misrepresentation or false or misleading information was presented to the division with respect to the acupuncture tutorial.

(d) Failure to comply with the regulations relating to supervision, patient care or informed consent.

(e) The rendering of acupuncture services outside the approved acupuncture tutorial.

(f) Failure to identify oneself as an acupuncture trainee or failure to wear an appropriate identification badge when rendering acupuncture services.

(g) Rendering acupuncture services under a supervising acupuncturist who is not approved as a supervisor by the board or whose registration as a supervisor has been disciplined under Section 1399.430.

16 CCR § 1399.432

§ 1399.432　PROCEEDINGS

Any proceedings to suspend or revoke the registration of a supervising acupuncturist or trainee or to deny such registration on grounds of unprofessional conduct shall be conducted pursuant to the Administrative Procedure Act (Section 11500 et seq. of the Government Code).

16 CCR § 1399.434

§ 1399.434　CRITERIA FOR APPROVAL OF ACUPUNCTURE AND ORIENTAL MEDICINE CURRICULUM

To be approved by the Board, an acupuncture and Oriental medicine educational and training curriculum shall consist of at least 2,050 hours of didactic and laboratory training and at least 950 hours of supervised clinical instruction. The curriculum shall include the following coursework that contains the following criteria:

(a) Basic Sciences....................350 hours

The curriculum in basic sciences shall prepare students to enter postsecondary upper division biomedical and clinical science courses and shall consist of at least 350 hours of didactic and laboratory instruction in the following basic science courses:

(1) General biology;

(2) Chemistry, including organic and biochemistry;

(3) General physics, including a general survey of biophysics;

(4) General psychology, including counseling skills;

(5) Anatomy-a survey of microscopic, gross anatomy and neuroanatomy;

(6) Physiology-a survey of basic physiology, including neurophysiology, endocrinology, and neurochemistry;

(7) Pathology and Pathophysiology-a survey of the nature of disease and illness, including microbiology, immunology, psychopathology, and epidemiology;

(8) Nutrition and vitamins;

(b) Acupuncture and Oriental Medicine Principles, Theories and Treatment.................... 1,255 hours

The curriculum in acupuncture and Oriental medicine principles, theories and treatment shall consist of at least 1,255 hours of didactic instruction in the following principles, theories, prescription, and treatment procedures of acupuncture and Oriental medicine:

(1) Acupuncture and Oriental Medicine Principles and Theories

(A) Oriental Medicine Principles and Theory;

(B) Acupuncture Principles and Theory;

(C) Oriental Massage(e.g., Tui Na or Shiatsu) Principles and Theory;

(D) Chinese Herbal Medicine Principles and Theory, including relevant botany concepts (This subject area shall consist of at least 450 hours of instruction);

(E) Acupuncture and Oriental Medicine Diagnosis;

(F) Acupuncture and Oriental Medicine Specialties, including dermatology, gynecology, pediatrics, ophthalmology, orthopedics, internal medicine, geriatrics, family medicine, traumatology, and emergency care;

(G) Classical acupuncture and Oriental medicine literature, including Jin Gui, Wen Bing/ Shang Han, Nei Jing;

(H) Modern acupuncture and Oriental medicine literature.

(2) Acupuncture and Oriental Medicine Treatment

(A) Integrated acupuncture and Oriental medicine diagnostic and treatment procedures;

(B) Acupuncture techniques and treatment procedures, including electroacupuncture;

(C) Oriental massage (e.g., Tui Na or Shiatsu), acupressure, and other techniques utilizing manual therapy and mechanical devices;

(D) Exercise therapy, including breathing, qi gong and taiji quan;

(E) Herbal prescription, counseling and preparation;

(F) Oriental and Western clinical and medical nutrition, dietary and supplement prescription and counseling;

(G) Cold and heat therapy, including moxibustion and ultrasound;

(H) Lifestyle counseling, and self-care recommendations;

(I) Adjunctive acupuncture procedures, including bleeding, cupping, gua sha, and dermal tacks;

(J) Acupuncture micro therapies, including auricular and scalp therapy;

(K) Hygienic standards, including clean needle techniques. The clean needle technique portion of this subject shall use the "Clean Needle Technique Manual 7th edition" (rev. January 2016), published by the Council of Colleges of Acupuncture and Oriental Medicine, which is hereby incorporated by reference. Students shall successfully complete the clean needle technique portion of the hygienic standards subject prior to performing any needling techniques on human beings;

(L) Equipment maintenance and safety;

(M) Adjunctive acupoint stimulation devices, including magnets and beads.

(c) Clinical Medicine, Patient Assessment and Diagnosis....................240 hours

The curriculum in clinical medicine, patient assessment and diagnosis shall consist of at least 240 hours of didactic instruction and shall prepare the student to possess the knowledge, skills and abilities necessary to utilize standard physical examinations, laboratory and imaging studies, and International Classification of Diseases (ICD) diagnostic principles to improve treatment efficacy, patient safety, referral, and continuity of care; to improve communication and collaboration of care with all other medical providers; to assist in the evaluation and documentation of patient progress; and to improve the acupuncturists understanding of biochemical etiology and pathology. Clinical medicine, patient assessment, and diagnostic skills curriculum shall include the following:

(1) Comprehensive history taking;

(2) Standard physical examination and assessment, including neuromusculoskeletal, orthopedic, neurological, abdominal, and ear, nose and throat examinations, and functional assessment;

(3) Pharmacological assessment, emphasizing side-effects and herb-drug interactions;

(4) Patient/practitioner rapport, communication skills, including multicultural sensitivity;

(5) Procedures for ordering diagnostic imaging, radiological, and laboratory tests and incorporating the resulting data and reports;

(6) Clinical reasoning and problem solving;

(7) Clinical impressions and the formation of a working diagnosis, including acupuncture and Oriental medicine diagnoses, and the World Health Organization's International Classification of Diseases(ICD - 10);

(8) Awareness of at-risk populations, including gender, age, indigent, and disease specific patients;

(9) Standard medical terminology;

(10) Clinical sciences-a review of internal medicine, pharmacology, neurology, surgery, obstetrics/gynecology, urology, radiology, nutrition and public health;

(11) Clinical medicine-a survey of the clinical practice of medicine, osteopathy, dentistry, psychology, nursing, chiropractic, podiatry, naturopathy, and homeopathy to familiarize practitioners with the practices of other health care practitioners.

(d) Case Management....................90 hours

The curriculum in case management shall consist of at least 90 hours of didactic instruction and shall prepare the student to manage patient care as a primary health care professional, and shall include instruction in the following subject:

(1) Primary care responsibilities;

(2) Secondary and specialty care responsibilities;

(3) Psychosocial assessment;

(4) Treatment contraindications and complications, including drug and herb interactions;

(5) Treatment planning, continuity of care, referral, and collaboration;

(6) Follow-up care, final review, and functional outcome measurements;

(7) Prognosis and future medical care;

(8) Case management for injured workers and socialized medicine patients, including a knowledge of workers compensation/labor codes and procedures and qualified medical evaluations;

(9) Coding procedures for current procedural and diagnostic codes, including Current Procedural Terminology(CPT) and International Classification of Disease ICD - 10 diagnostic codes;

(10) Medical-legal report writing, expert medical testimony, and independent medical review;

(11) Special care/seriously ill patients;

(12) Emergency procedures.

(e) Practice Management....................45 hours

The curriculum in practice management shall consist of at least 45 hours of didactic instruction and shall include the following subjects:

(1) Record keeping, insurance billing and collection;

(2) Business written communication;

(3) Knowledge of regulatory compliance and jurisprudence [municipal, California, and federal laws, including OSHA, Labor Code, Health Insurance Portability and Accountability Act of 1996(HIPAA)];

(4) Front office procedures;

(5) Planning and establishing a professional office;

(6) Practice growth and development;

(7) Ability to practice in interdisciplinary medical settings including hospitals;

(8) Risk management and insurance issues;

(9) Ethics and peer review.

(f) Public Health....................40 hours

The curriculum in public health shall consist of at least 40 hours of didactic instruction and shall include training in the principles of public health, including the following subjects:

(1) Public and community health and disease prevention;

(2) Public health education;

(3) A minimum of eight(8) hours in first-aid and adult/child cardiopulmonary resuscitation (CPR) from the American Red Cross, American Heart Association or other organization with an equivalent course approved by the board;

(4) Treatment of chemical dependency;

(5) Communicable disease, public health alerts, and epidemiology.

(g) Professional Development....................30 hours

The curriculum in professional development shall consist of at least 30 hours of didactic instruction and shall prepare the student with the skills to continue to expand their knowledge, including instruction in the following subjects:

(1) Research and evidence based medicine;

(2) Knowledge of academic peer review process;

(3) Knowledge and critique of research methods;

(4) History of medicine.

(h) Clinical Practice....................950 hours

The curriculum in clinical practice shall consist of at least 950 hours in clinical instruction, 75% of which shall be in a clinic owned and operated by the school, which includes direct patient contact where appropriate in the following:

(1) Practice Observation (minimum 150 hours)-supervised observation of the clinical practice of acupuncture and Oriental medicine with case presentations and discussion;

(2) Diagnosis and evaluation(minimum 275 hours)-the application of Eastern and Western diagnostic procedures in evaluating patients;

(3) Supervised practice (minimum 275 hours)-the clinical treatment of patients with acupuncture and oriental medicine treatment modalities listed in the Business and Professions

Code sections 4927(d) and 4937(b).

(4) During the initial 275 hours of diagnosis, evaluation and clinical practice, the clinic supervisor shall be physically present at all times during the diagnosis and treatment of the patient. Thereafter, for a second period of 275 hours the clinic supervisor shall be physically present at the needling of the patient. The clinic supervisor shall otherwise be in close proximity to the location at which the patient is being treated during the clinical instruction. The student shall also consult with the clinic supervisor before and after each treatment.

16 CCR § 1399.435

§ 1399.435 CRITERIA FOR ACUPUNCTURE AND ORIENTAL MEDICINE TRAINING PROGRAMS

An acupuncture and Oriental medicine training program approved by the board shall adopt the following procedures for its program effective January 1, 2005:

(a) Candidates for admission shall have successfully completed at least two(2) academic years(60 semester credits/90 quarter credits) of education at the baccalaureate level that is appropriate preparation for graduate level work, or the equivalent from an institution accredited by an agency recognized by the U.S. Secretary of Education.

(b) The training program should be located in an educational institution approved under Article 4(commencing with Section 94770) of Chapter 7 of Part 59 of the Education Code, or in the case of training programs located outside California, in an institution which is approved by the appropriate governmental accrediting authority or an accrediting agency recognized by the U.S. Department of Education.

(c) The training program shall develop self study evaluation process to determine the effectiveness of its theoretical and clinical program.

(d) Coursework shall carry academic credit.

(e) The director and supervisor(s) of the clinical portion of the training program shall be a licensed acupuncturist in the state where the educational institution is located and with at least 5 years of licensed clinical experience in the practice of acupuncture and Oriental medicine.

(f) All instructors shall be competent to teach their designated courses by virtue of their education, training and experience. All faculty credentials shall be equivalent to the course and degree level being taught.

(g) Each training program shall develop policies and procedures to evaluate and award transfer credit to students for coursework and experience which is equivalent to current coursework and clinical instruction required. Such policies and procedures shall be defined in the school's catalog and shall include the following.

(1) Credit shall only be awarded for actual coursework.

(2) Where the coursework and clinical instruction were completed at an acupuncture school not approved by the board, the evaluation shall include an examination administered and retained

by the school in the subject area(s) in which transfer credit may be awarded.

(3) Up to 100% transfer credit may be awarded for coursework and clinical instruction completed successfully at another acupuncture school or college which is approved by the board.

(4) Up to 100% transfer credit may be awarded for courses completed successfully in basic sciences, clinical medicine, case management, practice management, public health, and professional development at a school which is approved under Article 4(commencing with Section 94770) of Chapter 7 of Part 59 of the Education Code or by an accrediting agency recognized by the U.S. Department of Education.

(5) Up to fifty percent(50%) credit, by transfer or challenge exam, for clinical practice coursework and instruction in acupuncture and Oriental medicine principles, theories and treatment procedures completed successfully at a school which is not approved by the board may be awarded by a school approved by the board, provided that at least 50% of the course hours in individual subjects are completed successfully at a school approved by the board.

(6) The entire record of the evaluation and award of the student's transfer credit shall be included in the student's academic file and shall be made an official part of the student's transcript which shall be filed with the board upon request.

(7) All students shall receive upon matriculation a copy of the school's policies and procedures for evaluating and awarding transfer credit.

16 CCR § 1399.436

§ 1399.436 CRITERIA FOR APPROVAL OF ACUPUNCTURE AND ORIENTAL MEDICINE TRAINING PROGRAMS [REPEALED]

16 CCR § 1399.437

§ 1399.437 REQUIREMENTS FOR BOARD APPROVAL OF CURRICULUM

(a) Each educational and training program seeking board approval of its curriculum shall submit an "Application for Board Approval of Curriculum" (rev 4/15), hereby incorporated by reference. The application shall be accompanied by the following information and documentation:

(1) Educational and training program legal name, current address, phone number, website, contact person, and program(s) requested for board curriculum approval;

(2) A completed course-by-course list for each course that meets the board required coursework with course number, clock hour, and course unit to document that the curriculum meets the requirements for Section 1399.434;

(3) A list of all courses in the program requested for board approval of curriculum with course hours, course units, course number and course title;

(4) A copy of all course syllabi for program(s) requested for board curriculum approval; and

(5) A copy of the current course catalog.

All information and documentation submitted under this section shall be in English.

(b) An "Application for Board Approval of Curriculum" shall be deemed received and complete pursuant to Business and Professions Code Section 4927.5, subdivision(b), when the board has received a complete application, including the form and all information and documentation, as defined in subdivision(a) of this regulation.

(c) An educational and training program whose "Application for Board Approval of Curriculum" is incomplete shall be notified, in writing, that the application is incomplete, and of the reasons the application is incomplete and instructions for how to address the incomplete application. An educational and training program's incomplete application shall be deemed abandoned if the educational and training program does not submit a complete application to the board within 30 days of the mailing of the written notification that the application is incomplete.

(d) An "Application for Board Approval of Curriculum" submitted subsequent to the abandonment of a prior application shall be treated as a new application.

(e) Any changes to coursework as listed in Section 1399.434 after Board approval constitutes a new curriculum and requires Board approval pursuant to Business and Professions Code Section 4927.5. The approval shall be attained prior to implementing the new curriculum.

16 CCR § 1399.438
§ 1399.438 SUSPENSION OR REVOCATION OF APPROVAL

The board may deny, place on probation, suspend or revoke the approval granted to any acupuncture training program for any failure to comply with the regulations in this article, the Acupuncture Regulations or the Acupuncture Licensure Act.

16 CCR § 1399.439
§ 1399.439 SCHOOL MONITORING; RECORDS; REPORTING

(a) Every approved acupuncture school shall be required to submit to the board within sixty(60) days after the close of the school's fiscal year a current course calalog with a letter outlining the following: 1) any courses added/deleted or significantly changed from the previous year's curriculum; 2) any changes in faculty, administration, or governing body; 3) any major changes in the school facility; and 4) a statement regarding the school's financial condition, which enables the board to evaluate whether the school has sufficient resources to ensure the capability of the program for enrolled students.

(b) If determined necessary an on-site visit by representatives of the board will be made to the school to review and evaluate the status of the school. The school will be required to reimburse the board for direct costs incurred in conducting such review and evaluation.

(c) All student records shall be maintained in at least English.

(d) Each approved acupuncture school shall report to the board within 30 days any substantial changes to the facility and/or clinic(s), and curriculum required in this section.

16 CCR § 1399.440
§ 1399.440 LOCATION

Examinations shall be administered at times and locations to be determined by the board. If the same examination is administered in more than one location, it shall be administered concurrently in each location.

16 CCR § 1399.441

§ 1399.441　LANGUAGES

Examinations shall be administered in English, Chinese, and Korean. An applicant shall notify the committee of the desired language where provided for in the Application for Examination/Licensure. Translations and translators, when necessary for other languages, shall be provided in any language for which a translation is formally requested as provided above by a minimum of five percent(5) of the total number of approved applications. Otherwise, such applicants shall take the examination in one of the languages listed above.

16 CCR § 1399.442

§ 1399.442　EXAMINATION COMMISSIONERS

16 CCR § 1399.443

§ 1399.443　EXAMINATION CONTENT

(a) The examination shall test the applicant's knowledge and competency in the practice of oriental medicine through acupuncture.

(b) In order to pass an examination an applicant shall be required to obtain a passing score as determined by a criterion-referenced method of establishing the passing point on each part of the examination.

16 CCR § 1399.444

§ 1399.444　LAPSED LICENSES; EXAMINATION

Any acupuncturist whose license has been expired for more than three years and who is applying for a new license under Section 4967 of the code shall be required to take and pass the written examination before a new license may be issued.

16 CCR § 1399.445

§ 1399.445　RECONSIDERATION OF CLINICAL EXAMINATION

16 CCR § 1399.450

§ 1399.450　CONDITION OF OFFICE

Every acupuncture office shall be maintained in a clean and sanitary condition at all times, and shall have a readily accessible bathroom facility in accordance with Title 24, Part 2, Building Standards Code Sections 494A.1 and 1994 Uniform Building Code Section 2902.3.

16 CCR § 1399.451

§ 1399.451　TREATMENT PROCEDURES

In treating a patient, an acupuncturist shall adhere to the following procedures:

(a) The acupuncturist's hands shall be brush-scrubbed with soap and warm water immediately before examining patients or handling acupuncture needles and other instruments, and between patients.

(b) All instruments shall be sterilized before and between uses in a manner which will destroy all microorganisms. All needle trays which contain sterile needles shall also be sterile. Each time instruments are sterilized, the acupuncturist shall use a tape or strip indicator which shows that sterilization is complete.

(c) Acupuncture points, where needles are to be inserted, shall be cleaned with an appropriate antiseptic before insertion of the needle.

(d) In the event an acupuncture needle inserted in a patient breaks subcutaneously, the treating acupuncturist shall immediately consult a physician. An acupuncturist shall not sever or penetrate the tissues in order to excise such a needle.

(e) Any complication, including but not limited to, hematoma, peritonitis or pneumothorax arising out of acupuncture treatment shall be referred immediately to a physician or dentist or podiatrist, if appropriate, if immediate medical treatment is required.

(f) Acupuncture shall not be performed using hypodermic needles.

(g) All instruments to be discarded shall be disposed of safely.

(h) Needles shall be disposed of by placing them in a sealed, unbreakable container marked "Hazardous Waste" and disposed of in accordance with state and local law.

16 CCR § 1399.452

§ 1399.452   TREATMENTS OUTSIDE THE OFFICE

(a) Any acupuncturist who provides acupuncture treatment outside the office shall carry the required sterile needles and other instruments in a sterile airtight container.

(b) All standards of practice applicable to treatment outside the office shall be adhered to by the acupuncturist providing such treatment.

16 CCR § 1399.453

§ 1399.453   RECORDKEEPING

An acupuncturist shall keep complete and accurate records on each patient who is given acupuncture treatment, including but not limited to, treatments given and progress made as a result of the acupuncture treatments.

16 CCR § 1399.454

§ 1399.454   SINGLE USE NEEDLES

An acupuncturist shall use needles labeled for single use only that meet the requirements of federal regulations 21 CFR Part 880.5580(61 FR 64617, December 6, 1996). It shall constitute unprofessional conduct for an acupuncturist to use a needle more than once.

16 CCR § 1399.455

§ 1399.455   ADVERTISING

(a) A licensed acupuncturist may advertise the provision of any acupuncture services authorized to be provided by such licensure in a manner authorized by Section 651 of the code so long as such advertising does not promote the excessive or unnecessary use of such services.

(b) It is improper advertising as provided in Section 4955 of the code to disseminate any advertising which represents in any manner that the acupuncturist can cure any type of disease, condition or symptom.

(c) It is improper advertising as provided in Section 4955 of the code to disseminate any advertising of a practice, technique or procedure which is not within the scope of the practice of acupuncture as defined in Sections 4927 and 4937 of the code and which is the unlawful practice of medicine.

16 CCR § 1399.456

§ 1399.456　USE OF TITLE "DOCTOR".

It is unprofessional conduct for an acupuncturist to use the title "Doctor" or the abbreviation "Dr." in connection with the practice of acupuncture unless he or she possesses a license or certificate which authorizes such use or possesses an earned doctorate degree from an accredited, approved or authorized educational institution as set forth under Article 4 (commencing with Section 94760) of Chapter 7 of Part 59 which is in acupuncture, Oriental medicine, a biological science, or is otherwise related to the authorized practice of an acupuncturist as set forth in Sections 4927 and 4937 of the Code.

The use of the title "Doctor" or the abbreviation "Dr." by an acupuncturist as authorized above without further indicating the type of license, certificate or degree which authorizes such use, constitutes unprofessional conduct.

16 CCR § 1399.460

§ 1399.460　FEES

(a) The application fee shall be seventy-five dollars($75).

(b) The examination and reexamination fee shall be five hundred, fifty dollars($550), plus the applicable fingerprint processing fee in effect at the time the application is submitted.

(c) In order to establish and administer a birthdate renewal program, the initial license fee for an acupuncture license will be based on the date the license is issued and the birthmonth of the applicant. No license will be issued for less than twelve(12) months. The fee for an initial license shall be in accordance with the following schedule:

Effective January 1, 1996, the biennial renewal fee for a licensed acupuncturist shall be three hundred twenty-five dollars($325).

(d) An expired license may be renewed at any time within three years after its expiration. The licensee will be required to pay all accrued and unpaid renewal fees, plus any delinquency fee.

(e) The delinquency fee is twenty-five dollars($25).

(f) The application fee for the approval of a school or college shall be one thousand and five hundred dollars($1,500).

(g) The fee for a duplicate or replacement engraved wall license shall be fifteen dollars($15).

CALIFORNIA

<<arrow>>Birth   Month Fee Received

	January	February	March	April	May	June	July	August	September	October	November	December
January	$176	$325	$312	$298	$285	$271	$257	$244	$230	$217	$203	$190
February	$190	$176	$325	$312	$298	$285	$271	$257	$244	$230	$217	$203
March	$203	$190	$176	$325	$312	$298	$285	$271	$257	$244	$230	$217
April	$217	$203	$190	$176	$325	$312	$298	$285	$271	$257	$244	$230
May	$230	$217	$203	$190	$176	$325	$312	$298	$285	$271	$257	$244
June	$244	$230	$217	$203	$190	$176	$325	$312	$298	$285	$271	$257
July	$257	$244	$230	$217	$203	$190	$176	$325	$312	$298	$285	$271
August	$271	$257	$244	$230	$217	$203	$190	$176	$325	$312	$298	$285
September	$285	$271	$257	$244	$230	$217	$203	$190	$176	$325	$312	$298
October	$298	$285	$271	$257	$244	$230	$217	$203	$190	$176	$325	$312
November	$312	$298	$285	$271	$257	$244	$230	$217	$203	$190	$176	$325
December	$325	$312	$298	$285	$271	$257	$244	$230	$217	$203	$190	$176

(h) The fee for a duplicate or replacement renewal receipt/pocket license shall be ten dollars($10).

(i) The fee for a letter of endorsement shall be ten dollars($10).

16 CCR § 1399.461

§ 1399.461 ACUPUNCTURE TUTORIALS

The annual renewal fees shall be due within 30 days of completion of one(1) year of an approved acupuncture tutorial.

16 CCR § 1399.462

§ 1399.462 CONTINUING EDUCATION FEE

The approval fee for each provider of continuing education shall be $150.00.

16 CCR § 1399.463

§ 1399.463 AUTHORITY TO ISSUE CITATIONS AND FINES

(a) The executive officer of the board is authorized to issue a citation which may contain an order of abatement or an administrative fine for violations by a licensee of the statutes contained in the Acupuncture Licensure Act(commencing with Business and Professions Code Section 4925 et seq.) or the regulations adopted by the board. For purposes of this Section and Sections 1399.464, 1399.466, 1399.467, and 1399.468, the term "licensee" refers to either a California licensed acupuncturist or a board approved continuing education provider.

(b) Each citation shall be in writing and shall describe with particularity the nature and facts of the violation, including a reference to the statute or regulation alleged to have been violated. The citation shall be served upon the licensee personally or by certified mail.

16 CCR § 1399.464

§ 1399.464 EXCEPTIONS

A citation shall not be issued in any of the following circumstances:

(a) The violation is of such a nature and/or severity that revocation of the license or restrictions on the license are necessary in order to ensure consumer protection.

(b) The licensee's conduct displayed a disregard for the patient and/or patient's rights. This includes, but is not limited to, physical abuse, neglect; abandonment; fiduciary abuse(as defined in Welfare and Institution Code Section 15610).

(c) The licensee failed to comply with any requirement of any previous citation, including any order of abatement or fine.

(d) The violation involves unprofessional conduct related to controlled substances or dangerous drugs.

(e) The violation involves unprofessional conduct related to sexual abuse, misconduct or relations with a patient.

(f) The licensee was convicted of an offense substantially related to the qualifications, functions and duties of an acupuncturist and there is insufficient evidence of rehabilitation.

16 CCR § 1399.465

§ 1399.465   CITATION; ASSESSMENT OF FINE

(a) The amount of any administrative fine to be levied by the executive officer shall be no less than $100 nor more than $2500.

In assessing the amount of the fine, the executive officer will consider the following factors in determining the amount of the fine:

(1) Gravity of the violation.

(2) The good or bad faith exhibited by the cited person.

(3) Evidence that the violation was willful.

(4) The extent to which the cited person cooperated with the board's investigation.

(5) The extent to which the cited person has mitigated or attempted to mitigate any damage caused by his or her violation.

(6) Such other factors as justice may require.

(b) Notwithstanding the administrative fine amounts specified in subsection(a), a citation may include a fine between $2,501 and $5,000 if one or more of the following circumstances apply:

(1) The citation involves a violation that has an immediate relationship to the health and safety of another person.

(2) The cited person has a history of two or more prior citations of the same or similar violations.

(3) The citation involves multiple violations that demonstrate a willful disregard of the law.

(4) The citation involves a violation or violations perpetrated against a senior citizen or person with disabilities.

16 CCR § 1399.466

§ 1399.466   COMPLIANCE WITH ORDERS OF ABATEMENT

(a) If a cited person who has been issued an order of abatement is unable to complete the abatement within the time set forth in the citation because of conditions beyond his or her control after the exercise of reasonable diligence, the person cited may request an extension of time from the executive officer in which to complete the correction. Such a request shall be in writing and shall be made within the time set forth for abatement.

(b) When an order of abatement is not contested or if the order is appealed and the person cited does not prevail, failure to abate the violation charged in the citation within the time allowed shall constitute a violation and failure to comply with the order of abatement. Such failure may result in disciplinary action being taken by the board or other appropriate judicial relief being taken against the person cited.

16 CCR § 1399.467

§ 1399.467   CITATIONS FOR UNLICENSED PRACTICE

The executive officer of the board is authorized to determine when and against whom a citation will be issued and to issue citations containing orders of abatement and fines against persons who are performing or who have performed services for which license as an acupuncturist is required under the Acupuncture Licensure Act. Each citation issued for unlicensed activity shall contain either an order of abatement, or, where appropriate, the executive officer shall levy a fine for such unlicensed activity in accordance with section 1399.465 of these regulations. The provisions of sections 1399.463, 1399.465, 1399.466, and 1399.468 apply to the issuance of citations for unlicensed activity under this section. The citation issued under this section shall be separate from and in addition to any other civil or criminal remedies.

16 CCR § 1399.468

§ 1399.468　CONTEST OF CITATIONS

(a) In addition to requesting a hearing provided for in subdivision(b)(4) of section 125.9 of the code, the person cited may, within ten(10) days after service or receipt of the citation, notify the executive officer in writing of his or her request for an informal conference with the executive officer regarding the acts charged in the citation.

(b) The executive officer shall hold, within 60 days from the receipt of the request, an informal conference with the person cited. At the conclusion of the informal conference, the executive officer may affirm, modify or dismiss the citation, including any fine levied or order of abatement issued. The executive officer shall state in writing the reasons for his or her action and serve or mail, as provided in subsection(b) of section 1399.463, a copy of his or her findings and decision to the person cited within ten days from the date of the informal conference. This decision shall be deemed to be a final order with regard to the citation issued, including the fine levied and the order of abatement.

(c) The person cited does not waive his or her request for a hearing to contest a citation by requesting an informal conference after which the citation is affirmed by the executive officer. If the citation is dismissed after the informal conference, the request for a hearing on the matter of the citation shall be deemed to be withdrawn. If the citation, including any fine levied or order of abatement, is modified, the citation originally issued shall be considered withdrawn and new citation issued. If a hearing is requested for the subsequent citation, it shall be requested within 30 days in accordance with subdivision(b)(4) of section 125.9.

16 CCR § 1399.469

§ 1399.469　DISCIPLINARY GUIDELINES

In reaching a decision on a disciplinary action under the Administrative Procedure Act (Government Code Section 11400 et seq.), the Acupuncture Board shall consider the disciplinary guidelines entitled "Department of Consumer Affairs, Acupuncture Board 'Disciplinary Guidelines' 1996" which are hereby incorporated by reference. Deviation from these guidelines and orders, including the standard terms of probation is appropriate where the Acupuncture Board in its sole discretion determines that the facts of the particular case warrant such a deviation-for example:

the presence of mitigating factors; the age of the case; evidentiary problems.

16 CCR § 1399.469.1

§ 1399.469.1   REQUIRED ACTIONS AGAINST REGISTERED SEX OFFENDERS

(a) Except as otherwise provided, if an individual is required to register as a sex offender pursuant to Section 290 of the Penal Code, or the equivalent in another state or territory, or military or federal law, the board shall:

(1) Deny an application by the individual for licensure, in accordance with the procedures set forth in Chapter 5(commencing with Section 11500) of Part 1 of Division 3 of Title 2 of the Government Code.

(2) Promptly revoke the license of the individual, in accordance with the procedures set forth in Chapter 5(commencing with Section 11500) of Part 1 of Division 3 of Title 2 of the Government Code, and shall not stay the revocation nor place the license on probation.

(3) Deny any petition to reinstate or reissue the individual's license.

(b) This section shall not apply to any of the following:

(1) An individual who has been relieved under Section 290.5 of the Penal Code of his or her duty to register as a sex offender, or whose duty to register has otherwise been formally terminated under California law or the law of the jurisdiction that required registration.

(2) An individual who is required to register as a sex offender pursuant to Section 290 of the Penal Code solely because of a misdemeanor conviction under Section 314 of the Penal Code, provided, however, that nothing in this paragraph shall prohibit the board from exercising its discretion to discipline a licensee under any other provision of state law based upon the licensee's conviction under section 314 of the Penal Code.

(3) Any administrative proceeding that is fully adjudicated prior to the effective date of this regulation. A petition for reinstatement of a revoked or surrendered license shall be considered a new proceeding for purposes of this paragraph, and the prohibition in subsection(a) against reinstating a license shall govern.

16 CCR § 1399.469.2

§ 1399.469.2   UNPROFESSIONAL CONDUCT

In addition to the conduct described in Section 4955 of the Business and Professions Code, "unprofessional conduct" also includes but is not limited to the following:

(a) Including or permitting to be included any of the following provisions in an agreement to settle a civil dispute arising from the licensee's practice to which the licensee is or expects to be named as a party, whether the agreement is made before or after the filing of an action:

(1) A provision that prohibits another party to the dispute from contacting, cooperating, or filing a complaint with the board.

(2) A provision that requires another party to the dispute to attempt to withdraw a complaint the party has filed with the board.

(b) Failure to provide to the board, as directed, lawfully requested copies of documents within 15 days of receipt of the request or within the time specified in the request, whichever is later, unless the licensee is unable to provide the documents within this time period for good cause, including but not limited to, physical inability to access the records in the time allowed due to illness or travel. This subsection shall not apply to a licensee who does not have access to, and control over, medical records.

(c) Failure to cooperate and participate in any board investigation pending against the licensee. This subsection shall not be construed to deprive a licensee of any privilege guaranteed by the Fifth Amendment to the Constitution of the United States, or any other constitutional or statutory privileges. This subsection shall not be construed to require a licensee to cooperate with a request that would require the licensee to waive any constitutional or statutory privilege or to comply with a request for information or other matters within an unreasonable period of time in light of the time constraints of the licensee's practice. Any exercise by a licensee of any constitutional or statutory privilege shall not be used against the licensee in a regulatory or disciplinary proceeding against the licensee.

(d) Failure to report to the board within 30 days any of the following:

(1) The bringing of an indictment or information charging a felony against the licensee.

(2) The arrest of the licensee.

(3) The conviction of the licensee, including any verdict of guilty, or pleas of guilty or no contest, of any felony or misdemeanor.

(4) Any disciplinary action taken by another licensing entity or authority of this state or of another state or an agency of the federal government or the United States military.

(e) Failure or refusal to comply with a court order, issued in the enforcement of a subpoena, mandating the release of records to the board.

16 CCR § 1399.469.3

§ 1399.469.3 NOTICE TO CONSUMERS OF LICENSURE BY THE ACUPUNCTURE BOARD

(a) A licensed acupuncturist engaged in the practice of acupuncture shall provide notice to each patient of the fact that the acupuncturist is licensed and regulated by the California Acupuncture Board. This notice must be posted at each of the practice locations the licensee provides services. The notice shall include the following statement and information:

"NOTICE TO CONSUMERS

Acupuncturists are licensed and regulated by the California Acupuncture Board

(916) 515-5200

http://www.acupuncture.ca.gov/"

(b) The notice required by this section shall be provided by prominently posting the notice in a conspicuous location accessible to public view on the premises where the acupuncturist provides the licensed services, in which case the notice shall be at least 48 - point type font.

16 CCR § 1399.470

§ 1399.470   CITATION AND AUTHORITY

These regulations may be cited and referred to as the "Acupuncture Corporation Regulations".

16 CCR § 1399.471

§ 1399.471   PROFESSIONAL RELATIONSHIPS AND RESPONSIBILITIES NOT AFFECTED [REPEALED]

16 CCR § 1399.472

§ 1399.472   OFFICE FOR FILING [REPEALED]

16 CCR § 1399.473

§ 1399.473   APPLICATION [REPEALED]

16 CCR § 1399.474

§ 1399.474   APPROVAL AND ISSUANCE OF CERTIFICATES [REPEALED]

16 CCR § 1399.475

§ 1399.475   REQUIREMENTS FOR ACUPUNCTURE CORPORATIONS

An acupuncture corporation shall comply with the following provisions:

(a) The corporation is organized and exists pursuant to the general corporation law and is a professional corporation within the meaning of Part 4, Division 3, Title 1 of the Corporations Code.

(b) Each shareholder, director, and officer (except as provided in Section 13403 of the Corporations Code and Section 4977.2 of the code) holds a valid acupuncture certificate. An acupuncturist may be a shareholder in more than one acupuncture corporation.

(c) Each professional employee of the corporation who will practice acupuncture, whether or not a director, officer, or shareholder, holds a valid acupuncture certificate.

16 CCR § 1399.476

§ 1399.476   NAMESTYLE

The name of the corporation and any name or names under which it may render professional services shall include words or abbreviations denoting corporate existence limited to the following: "Professional Corporation", "Prof. Corp.", "Corporation", "Corp.", "Incorporated", or "Inc."

16 CCR § 1399.477

§ 1399.477   SHARES: OWNERSHIP AND TRANSFER

(a) Where there are two or more shareholders in an acupuncture corporation and one of the shareholders:

(1) Dies or

(2) Becomes a disqualified person as defined in Section 13401(d) of the Corporations Code, his or her shares shall be sold and transferred to the corporation, its shareholders, or

other eligible licensed persons on such terms as are agreed upon. Such sale or transfer shall not be later than six(6) months after any such death and not later than ninety(90) days after the date the shareholder becomes a disqualified person. The requirements of this subsection shall be set forth in the acupuncture corporation's articles of incorporation or bylaws.

(b) A corporation and its shareholders may, but need not, agree that shares sold to it by a person who becomes a disqualified person may be resold to such person if and when he or she again becomes an eligible shareholder.

(c) The share certificates of an acupuncture corporation shall contain an appropriate legend setting forth the restrictions of subsection(a).

(d) Nothing in these regulations shall be construed to prohibit an acupuncture corporation from owning shares in a nonprofessional corporation.

16 CCR § 1399.478

§ 1399.478 TRUSTS

The restrictions on the ownership of the shares of professional corporations shall apply to both the legal and equitable title to such shares.

16 CCR § 1399.479

§ 1399.479 CORPORATE ACTIVITIES

(a) An acupuncture corporation may perform any act authorized in its articles of incorporation or bylaws so long as that act is not in conflict with or prohibited by these regulations, the Acupuncture Certification Act or the regulations adopted pursuant thereto.

(b) An acupuncture corporation may enter into partnership agreements with other acupuncturists practicing individually or in a group or with other acupuncture corporations.

16 CCR § 1399.480

§ 1399.480 DEFINITIONS

(a) For purposes of this article:

(1) "Provider" means those persons or organizations approved by the board to offer continuing education.

(2) "Course" means a systematic learning experience, at least one hour in length, which deals with and is designed for the acquisition of knowledge, skills and information relevant to the practice of acupuncture.

(3) "Hour" means at least fifty(50) minutes of participation in an organized learning experience.

16 CCR § 1399.481

§ 1399.481 CRITERIA FOR PROVIDER APPROVAL

(a) In order to be a provider, those persons, organizations, schools or other entities seeking approval shall submit to the board a Continuing Education Provider Application, (Rev.5/08), that is hereby incorporated by reference, accompanied by the fee set forth in Section 1399.462.

All provider applications and documentation submitted to the Board shall be typewritten and in English.

(b) The approval of the provider shall expire two(2) years after it is issued by the Board and may be renewed upon the filing of the required application and fee.

16 CCR § 1399.482

§ 1399.482 APPROVED PROVIDERS

(a) For the purpose of this Article, the title "provider" can only be used when a person or organization has submitted a provider application, remitted the appropriate fee, received approval by the board and has been issued a provider number.

(b) A person or organization may be issued only one provider number. When two or more providers co-sponsor a course, the course shall be identified by only one provider number and that provider shall assume responsibility for recordkeeping, advertising, issuance of certificates, instructor(s) qualifications, and any other requirements.

(c) A provider shall keep the following records for a period of four years in one identified location:

(1) Course outlines of each approved course given.

(2) Record of time and places of each approved course given.

(3) Course instructor curriculum vitaes or resumes.

(4) The attendance record for each approved course that shows the name, signature and license number of the acupuncturists who took the course and a record of any certificates issued to them.

(5) Participant evaluation forms for each approved course given.

(d) Providers shall issue, within 60 days of the conclusion of an approved course, to each participant who has completed the course, a typewritten or printed certificate of completion that contains the following information:

(1) Provider's name and number.

(2) Course title.

(3) Participant's name and, if applicable, his or her acupuncture license number.

(4) Date and location of course.

(5) Number of continuing education hours completed.

(6) Statement directing the acupuncturist to retain the certificate for at least four(4) years from the date of completion of the course.

(e) Providers shall notify the board within 30 days of any changes in organizational structure of a provider or the person(s) responsible for the provider's continuing education course, including name, address, or telephone number changes.

(f) Provider approval is non-transferable.

(g) The board retains the right and authority to audit or monitor courses given by any provider.

(h) Upon request, providers shall submit to the board attendance records for an approved course that includes name, signature and license number of the acupuncturists taking the course and course evaluation forms completed by the participant on the quality and usefulness of the course.

16 CCR § 1399.483

§ 1399.483 APPROVAL OF CONTINUING EDUCATION COURSES

(a) Only a provider may obtain approval to offer continuing education courses.

(b) The content of all courses of continuing education submitted for board approval shall be relevant to the practice of acupuncture and Asian medicine and shall fall within the following two(2) categories:

(1) Category 1 courses are those courses related to clinical matters or the actual provision of health care to patients. Examples of Category 1 courses include, but are not limited to, the following:

(A) Acupuncture and Asian Medicine

(B) Western biomedicine and biological sciences.

(C) Scientific or clinical content with a direct bearing on the quality of patient care, community or public health, or preventive medicine.

(D) Courses concerning law and ethics and health facility standards.

(E) Courses designed to develop a licensee's patient education skills, including, but not limited to, patient education in therapeutic exercise techniques, nutritional counseling, and biomechanical education.

(F) Courses designed to enhance a licensee's ability to communicate effectively with other medical practitioners.

(G) Courses in acupuncture's role in individual and public health, such as emergencies and disasters.

(H) Courses in the behavioral sciences, patient counseling, and patient management and motivation when such courses are specifically oriented to the improvement of patient health.

(I) Research and evidence-based medicine as related to acupuncture and Asian medicine.

(2) Category 2 courses are those courses unrelated to clinical matters or the actual provision of health care to patients. Examples of Category 2 courses include, but are not limited to, the following:

(A) Practice management courses unrelated to clinical matters and direct patient care, including, but not limited to administrative record keeping, laws and regulations unrelated to clinical medicine, insurance billing and coding, and general business organization and management.

(B) Breathing and other exercises, i.e. qi gong and taiji quan that are for the benefit of the licensee and not the patient.

(C) Each provider shall include, for each course offered, a method by which the course participants evaluate the following:

(I) The extent to which the course met its stated objectives.

(II) The adequacy of the instructor's knowledge of the course subject.

(III) The utilization of appropriate teaching methods.

(IV) The applicability or usefulness of the course information.

(V) Other relevant comments.

(c) Courses designed to be completed by an individual on an independent or home study basis shall not exceed 50% of the required continuing education hours.

(1) Courses that require practical or hands on techniques may not be approved for independent or home study.

(2) Courses approved for independent or home study shall include a self-assessment by the licensee upon completion of the course that tests the participants mastery of the course material.

(d) A provider is prohibited from selling, advertising or promoting any named brand product or service during a course. A provider shall ensure that any discussion of name product or service is objectively selected and presented with favorable and unfavorable information and balanced discussion of prevailing information on the product, competing products, alternative treatments or services. A provider shall ensure written disclosure to the audience, at the time of the program, of any relationship between any named product(s) or services discussed and the provider or between any such products or service and any individuals instructor, presenter, panelist, or moderator. However, a provider may offer for sale products or services after the course has been completed as long as it is made clear to all participants that they are under no obligation whatsoever to stay for the sales presentation or purchase any products. Nothing in this subdivision shall be interpreted as restricting a provider from discussing generic products during a course.

16 CCR § 1399.484

§ 1399.484 APPLICATION FOR COURSE APPROVAL

(a) Providers may not offer a course for continuing education hours without prior approval from the board. To obtain approval for a course, a provider shall submit to the board, at least 45 days before the course is first offered, a request for course approval, in English, on the "Request for Continuing Education(CE) Course Approval Form" (Rev.5/08) that is hereby incorporated by reference.

(b) When a previously approved course is to be repeated, the provider shall notify the board in writing of the new date and location at least 30 days before the new course date.

(c) Providers shall notify the board of any changes to the date or location of an approved course. A change to the date of an approved course may not be prior to the date for which the course was originally approved.

(d) Providers shall notify the board within 48 hours of a course date if the approved course is postponed. The provider shall notify the board in writing of the new date and location of the postponed course. If a postponed course is not taught within three (3) months of the original course date, the provider must reapply for approval.

(e) Any changes in the content of or instructor(s) for an approved course shall require the submittal of a new course application at least 45 days before the course begins.

16 CCR § 1399.485

§ 1399.485 INSTRUCTORS

(a) It shall be the responsibility of each provider to use qualified instructors.

(b) Instructors teaching approved continuing education courses shall have the following minimum qualifications:

(1) An acupuncturist instructor, shall

(A) hold a current valid license to practice acupuncture or is otherwise authorized to act as a guest acupuncturist in accordance with section 4949 of the code. A "current valid license" is one that has not been revoked, suspended, placed on probation, voluntarily surrendered or otherwise disciplined by the board, and

(B) be knowledgeable, current and skillful in the subject matter of the course as evidenced through:

1. holding a baccalaureate or higher degree from a college or university and written documentation of experience in the subject matter or

2. have at least two years's experience in teaching similar subject matter content within the five years preceding the course; or

3. have at least two years's experience within the last five years in the specialized area in which he or she is teaching.

(2) A non-acupuncturist instructor shall

(A) be currently licensed or certified in his or her area of expertise if appropriate, and

(B) show written evidence of specialized training, that may include, but not be limited to, a certificate of training or an advanced degree in given subject area, and

(C) have at least two years's teaching experience within the last five years in the specialized area in which he or she teaches.

16 CCR § 1399.486

§ 1399.486 ADVERTISEMENTS

(a) Information disseminated by providers publicizing continuing education shall be true and not misleading and shall include the following:

(1) Course titles shall reflect course content and may not contain marketing language.

(2) A clear, concise description of the course content and objectives.

(3) Whether the course has been approved as a Category 1 or Category 2 course.

(4) The date and location of the course.

(5) The provider's name, provider's number and telephone number.

(6) The statement "This course has been approved by the California Acupuncture Board, Provider Number ____, for ____ hours of continuing education in Category _____."

(7) Provider's policy on refunds for cases of non-attendance or cancellations.

(8) A written disclosure of all products that will be for sale after completion of the course.

(b) A provider may not describe a course as being board approved until written confirmation of approval by the board has been received by the provider. Where a provider is waiting for a determination by the board on a request for course approval, the provider may advertise that the course is "pending" approval. A provider that advertises that its course is pending approval shall assume all responsibility if the course is subsequently denied by the board.

16 CCR § 1399.487

§ 1399.487 DENIAL, WITHDRAWAL AND APPEAL OF APPROVAL

(a) The board may deny a provider application or withdraw its approval of a provider for causes that include, but are not limited to, the following:

(1) the provider or applicant has been convicted of a crime substantially related to the activities of a provider or licensee;

(2) the provider or applicant has failed to comply with any provision of Chapter 12, Division 2 of the Business and Professions Code or Division 13.7 of Title 16 of the California Code of Regulations;

(3) the provider or applicant has had a license revoked, suspended, placed on probation, voluntarily surrendered or otherwise disciplined by the board;

(4) the board may suspend review and approval of an application if an administrative action is pending against an applicant's license.

(b) Any material misrepresentation of fact by a provider or applicant in any information required to be submitted to the board is grounds for withdrawal or denial of an application.

(c) The board may withdraw its approval of a provider or a course after giving the provider written notice setting forth its reasons for withdrawal and after giving the provider a reasonable opportunity to be heard by the board or its designee.

(d) Should the board deny approval of a provider or a course request, the applicant may appeal the action by submitting to the board, a letter stating the reason(s) for the appeal. The letter of appeal shall be filed with the board within ten(10) days of the mailing of the applicant's notification of the board's denial. The appeal shall be considered by the board or its designee. In the event that the board or its designee grants the appeal after the date of the course for which the appeal is being made, the board will accept continuing education hours from its licensees who completed the course.

16 CCR § 1399.488

§ 1399.488　PROCESSING TIMES FOR PROVIDER AND COURSE REQUEST APPLICATIONS

(a) The board shall inform a provider seeking approval within thirty(30) days after receipt of a completed application and required fees of its decision whether the application has been approved.

(b) The board shall inform a provider seeking course approval within thirty(30) days after receipt of a completed application form together with all required information and documentation whether the course is approved.

(c) If a provider seeking approval submits a request for a course approval along with the initial provider application, the course request will not be considered for approval until the provider application is approved. In such cases, the board's processing time for the course request will be in accordance with Section 1399.488(b).

16 CCR § 1399.489

§ 1399.489　CONTINUING EDUCATION COMPLIANCE

(a) With the exception of those holding an inactive license, when renewing an initial license that has been issued for less than two years, licensees shall complete the following hours of board-approved continuing education:

Period of Required Continuing Initial Licensure Education Hours

13 – 16 Months, 35

17 – 20 Months, 40

21 – 23 Months, 45

Thereafter, all licensees shall complete 50 hours every two years as a condition of renewal. No more than five(5) hours of continuing education in each two-year period may be obtained in Category 2.

(b) Licensees are limited to fifty percent(50%) of the required continuing education hours every two(2) years for independent or home study courses.

(c) Each licensee at the time of license renewal shall sign a statement under penalty of perjury that he or she has or has not complied with the continuing education requirements. It shall constitute unprofessional conduct for any licensee to misrepresent completion of the required continuing education.

(d) The board may audit a random sample of licensees who have reported compliance with the continuing education requirement.

(e) Any licensee selected for audit shall be required to submit documentation or records of continuing education coursework that he or she has taken and completed.

(f) Each licensee shall retain for a minimum of four(4) years records of all continuing education programs that he or she has attended that indicate the provider's name, title of the course or program, date(s) and location of course, and number of continuing education hours awarded.

(g) Instructors of approved continuing education courses may receive one hour of continuing education credit for each classroom hour completed as an instructor, up to a maximum of six(6) hours of continuing education credit per year, regardless of how many hours or courses are taught. Participation as a member of a panel presentation for an approved course shall not entitle the participant to earn continuing education hours equal to the actual panel presentation time within the appropriate category.

(h) Any licensee who participates in the development of an occupational analysis, an examination development session, item review session or a passing score workshop, shall receive one(1) hour of continuing education for every two(2) hours of participation.

16 CCR § 1399.489.1

§ 1399.489.1   INACTIVE LICENSE

(a) Any licensee who is not actively engaged in the practice of acupuncture desiring an inactive license under the provisions of Article 9(commencing with Section 700) Chapter 1 of Division 2 of the code or to restore an inactive license to active status shall submit a completed "Active/Inactive License Application" (Rev.5/08), that is hereby incorporated by reference, to the board. The applicant need not submit his or her certificate or a copy thereof to the board with the application.

(b) To restore an inactive license to active status, the licensee shall have completed a minimum of 50 hours of approved continuing education within the last two (2) years in compliance with this article. At least 45 hours of continuing education must be in coursework approved as Category 1. In the event a license has been inactive less than one (1) year, a minimum of 25 hours of continuing education is required, with at least 22 hours of coursework approved as Category 1.

(c) The inactive status of any licensee shall not deprive the board of its authority to institute or continue a disciplinary proceeding against a licensee upon any ground provided by law or to enter an order suspending or revoking a license or otherwise taking disciplinary action against the licensee on any such ground.

16 CCR § 1399.489.2

§ 1399.489.2   CONTINUING EDUCATION: COURSES IN PRACTICE MANAGEMENT AND MEDICAL ETHICS

COLORADO

COLORADO REVISED STATUTES ANNOTATED

12 – 200 – 101 LEGISLATIVE DECLARATION

While recognizing that the rendering of acupuncture services is not part of the traditional practice of western medicine, it is the intent of the general assembly that those citizens who wish to obtain acupuncture services be allowed to do so and, in addition, that those citizens have available certain information to assist them in making informed choices when seeking acupuncture services. It is also the intent of the general assembly that the providers or practitioners of acupuncture should not misrepresent their qualifications, harm their clients, practice in an unhealthy manner, or otherwise deceive insurers or the recipients of acupuncture services.

12 – 200 – 102 APPLICABILITY OF COMMON PROVISIONS

Articles 1, 20, and 30 of this title 12 apply, according to their terms, to this article 200.

12 – 200 – 103 DEFINITIONS

As used in this article 200, unless the context otherwise requires:

(1) "Acupuncture" means a system of health care based upon traditional and modern oriental medical concepts that employs oriental methods of diagnosis, treatment, and adjunctive therapies for the promotion, maintenance, and restoration of health and the prevention of disease.

(2) "Acupuncturist" means any person who provides for compensation, or holds himself or herself out to the public as providing, acupuncture services.

(3) "Guest acupuncturist" means an acupuncturist who is:

(a) Licensed, registered, certified, or regulated as an acupuncturist in another jurisdiction;

(b) In this state for the purpose of instruction or education for not more than seven days within a three-month period; and

(c) Under the direct supervision of a Colorado licensed acupuncturist or licensed chiropractor while performing instruction or education.

(4) "Injection therapy" means the injection of sterile herbs, vitamins, minerals, homeopathic

substances, or other similar substances specifically manufactured for nonintravenous injection into acupuncture points by means of hypodermic needles used primarily for the treatment of musculoskeletal pain. Permissible substances include saline, glucose, lidocaine, procaine, oriental herbs, vitamin B-12, traumeel, sarapin, and homeopathic substances. "Injection therapy" includes the use of epinephrine and oxygen as necessary for patient care and safety, including for the purpose of addressing any risk of allergic reactions when using injection substances.

(5)(a) "Practice of acupuncture" means the insertion and removal of acupuncture needles, injection therapy, the application of heat therapies to specific areas of the human body, and adjunctive therapies. Adjunctive therapies within the scope of acupuncture may include manual, mechanical, thermal, electrical, and electromagnetic treatment; the recommendation of therapeutic exercises; and, subject to federal law, the recommendation of herbs and dietary guidelines. The "practice of acupuncture" is based upon traditional and modern oriental medical concepts and does not include the utilization of western medical diagnostic tests and procedures, such as magnetic resonance imaging, radiographs (X rays), computerized tomography scans, and ultrasound.

(b) Nothing in this article 200 authorizes an acupuncturist to perform the practice of medicine; surgery; spinal adjustment, manipulation, or mobilization; or any other form of healing except as authorized by this article 200.

12 - 200 - 104 INJECTION THERAPY-TRAINING-SUBSTANCES-RULES

(1) A licensee shall obtain the necessary training as determined by the director prior to practicing injection therapy.

(2) Notwithstanding section 12 - 280 - 305, a licensee who has received the necessary training to practice injection therapy may obtain substances for injection therapy from a registered prescription drug outlet, registered manufacturer, or registered wholesaler. An entity that provides a substance to a licensee in accordance with this section, and who relies in good faith upon the license information provided by the licensee, is not liable for providing the substance.

(3) The director shall promulgate rules to implement this section that include the necessary training for a licensee to practice injection therapy and a list of substances that a licensee may obtain for injection therapy. In promulgating the rules, the director shall consult with knowledgeable medical professionals and pharmacists.

12 - 200 - 105 MANDATORY DISCLOSURE OF INFORMATION TO PATIENTS-RETENTION OF RECORDS OF DISCLOSURE

(1) Every acupuncturist shall provide the following information in writing to each patient during the initial patient contact:

(a) The name, business address, and business phone number of the acupuncturist;

(b) A fee schedule;

(c) A statement indicating that: (I) The patient is entitled to receive information about the methods of therapy, the techniques used, and the duration of therapy, if known; (II) The patient may seek a second opinion from another health care professional or may terminate therapy at any time; (Ⅲ) In a professional relationship, sexual intimacy is never appropriate and should be reported to the director;

(d) A listing of the acupuncturist's education, experience, degrees, membership in a professional organization whose membership includes not less than one-third of the persons licensed pursuant to this article 200, certificates or credentials related to acupuncture awarded by the organizations, the length of time required to obtain the degrees or credentials, and experience;

(e) A statement indicating any license, certificate, or registration in acupuncture or any other health care profession that was issued to the acupuncturist by any local, state, or national health care agency, and indicating whether any such license, certificate, or registration was suspended or revoked;

(f) A statement that the acupuncturist is complying with any rules promulgated by the department of public health and environment with respect to this article 200, including those related to the proper cleaning and sterilization of needles used in the practice of acupuncture and the sanitation of acupuncture offices;

(g) A statement indicating that the practice of acupuncture is regulated by the department of regulatory agencies and the address and phone number of the director; and

(h) A statement indicating the acupuncturist's training and experience in the recommendation and application of adjunctive therapies and herbs as defined by traditional oriental medical concepts.

(2) Any changes in the information required by subsections (1)(a) to (1)(f) of this section shall be made in the mandatory disclosure within five days of the change.

(3) The acupuncturist shall retain a copy of the written information specified in subsection (1) of this section, dated and signed by the patient, from the time of the initial evaluation until at least three years after the termination of treatment.

12 – 200 – 106 REQUIREMENT FOR LICENSURE WITH THE DIVISION-ANNUAL FEE-REQUIRED DISCLOSURES

(1) Every acupuncturist shall apply for licensure with the division by providing an application to the director in the form the director shall require. The application shall include the information specified in section 12 – 200 – 105 (1)(a) and (1)(d) to (1)(g) and shall include the disclosure of any act that would be grounds for disciplinary action against a licensed acupuncturist under this article 200.

(2) Any changes in the information required by subsection (1) of this section shall be reported within thirty days of the change to the division in the manner prescribed by the director.

(3) In order to qualify for licensure, an acupuncturist shall have:

(a) Successfully completed an education program for acupuncturists that conforms to standards approved by the director, which standards may be established by utilizing the assistance of any professional organization whose membership includes not less than one-third of the persons licensed pursuant to this article 200; or

(b) Qualifications based on education, experience, or training that are substantially similar to those provided by subsection (3)(a) of this section, which are documented in the form required by the director and accepted by the director in lieu of the education program.

(4) Every applicant for licensure shall pay license, renewal, and reinstatement fees to be established by the director as authorized by section 12-20-105. Licenses issued pursuant to this article 200 are subject to the renewal, expiration, reinstatement, and delinquency fee provisions specified in section 12-20-202 (1) and (2). Any person whose license has expired shall be subject to the penalties provided in this article 200 or section 12-20-202 (1).

(5) Every acupuncturist shall report to the director every judgment or administrative action, as well as the terms of any settlement or other disposition of any judgment or action, against the acupuncturist involving malpractice or improper practice of acupuncture, whether occurring in Colorado or in any other jurisdiction. The acupuncturist shall make the report either within thirty days after the judgment or action or upon application for licensure or reinstatement, whichever occurs earlier.

(6) As a condition of licensure, every acupuncturist shall purchase and maintain commercial professional liability insurance with an insurance company authorized to do business in this state in a minimum indemnity amount of:

(a) Fifty thousand dollars per incident and fifty thousand dollars per year, if practicing as a sole proprietor or general partnership;

(b) Three hundred thousand dollars per incident and three hundred thousand dollars per year, if practicing as a limited liability company or a corporation.

12-200-107 LICENSURE BY ENDORSEMENT-RULES-DEFINITION

(1) The director shall issue a license by endorsement to engage in the practice of acupuncture in this state to any applicant who has a license in good standing as an acupuncturist under the laws of another jurisdiction if the applicant presents satisfactory proof to the director that, at the time of application for a license by endorsement, the applicant possesses substantially equivalent credentials and qualifications to those required for licensure pursuant to this article 200.

(2) The director shall specify by rule what shall constitute "substantially equivalent credentials and qualifications" for the purposes of this section. (3) For the purposes of this section, "in good standing" means a license that has not been revoked or suspended, or against which there are no disciplinary or adverse actions.

12-200-108 UNLAWFUL ACTS-EXCEPTIONS-DEFINITION

(1) Nothing in this article 200 shall interfere with, or be interpreted to interfere with or prevent, any other licensed health care professional from practicing within the scope of his or her practice, as defined in this title 12.

(2)(a) It is unlawful for any person to practice acupuncture without a valid and current license on file with the division, unless the acupuncturist is practicing pursuant to section 12-240-107 (3)(1) or has met the requirements of subsection (3) of this section.

(b) It is unlawful for any person to:

(Ⅰ) Engage in the practice of acupuncture without being licensed; or

(Ⅱ) Use the title "licensed acupuncturist", "registered acupuncturist", or "diplomate of acupuncture", or use the designation "L. Ac.", "R. Ac.", or "Dipl. Ac.", unless the person is practicing pursuant to section 12-240-107 (3).

(3) Notwithstanding any provision of this section to the contrary, a person in training may practice acupuncture without a valid and current license issued by the division if the practice takes place in the course of a bona fide training program and the person performs all acupuncture acts and services under the direct, on-site supervision of a licensed acupuncturist, who is responsible for all such acts and services as though the licensed acupuncturist had personally performed them.

(4)(a) Notwithstanding any provision of this article 200 to the contrary, a mental health care professional who has provided documentation that he or she has been trained to perform auricular acudetox in compliance with subsection (4)(d) of this section may perform auricular acudetox if the auricular acudetox is performed under the mental health care professional's current scope of practice, and the mental health care professional is:

(Ⅰ) Licensed pursuant to article 245 of this title 12;

(Ⅱ) Certified as a level Ⅲ addiction counselor pursuant to part 8 of article 245 of this title 12; or

(Ⅲ) Registered as a psychotherapist pursuant to part 7 of article 245 of this title 12.

(b) A mental health professional performing auricular acudetox pursuant to this subsection (4) shall not use the title "acupuncturist" or otherwise claim to be a person qualified to perform acupuncture beyond the scope of this subsection (4).

(c) As used in this subsection (4), "auricular acudetox" means the subcutaneous insertion of sterile, disposable acupuncture needles in the following five consistent, predetermined bilateral locations:

(Ⅰ) Sympathetic;

(Ⅱ) Shen men;

(Ⅲ) Kidney;

(Ⅳ) Liver; and

(Ⅴ) Lung.

(d) In order to perform auricular acudetox pursuant to this subsection (4), a mental health care professional must successfully complete a training program in auricular acudetox for the treatment of substance use disorders that meets or exceeds standards of training established by the

National Acupuncture Detoxification Association or another organization approved by the director.

12 - 200 - 109   GROUNDS FOR DISCIPLINARY ACTION

(1) The director may deny licensure to or take disciplinary action against an acupuncturist pursuant to sections 12 - 20 - 403, 12 - 20 - 404, and 24 - 4 - 105 if the director finds that the acupuncturist has committed any of the following acts:

(a) Violated the provisions of section 12 - 200 - 108;

(b) Failed to provide the mandatory disclosure required by section 12 - 200 - 105 or provided false, deceptive, or misleading information to patients in the disclosure;

(c) Failed to provide the information required by section 12 - 200 - 106 (1) or provided false, deceptive, or misleading information to the division;

(d) Committed, or advertised in any manner that he or she will commit, any act constituting an abuse of health insurance as prohibited by section 18 - 13 - 119 or a fraudulent insurance act as defined in section 10 - 1 - 128;

(e) Failed to refer a patient to an appropriate practitioner when the problem of the patient is beyond the training, experience, or competence of the acupuncturist;

(f) Accepted commissions or rebates or other forms of remuneration for referring clients to other professional persons;

(g) Offered or gave commissions, rebates, or other forms of remuneration for the referral of clients; except that, notwithstanding the provisions of this subsection (1)(g), an acupuncturist may pay an independent advertising or marketing agent compensation for advertising or marketing services rendered on his or her behalf by the agent, including compensation that is paid for the results of performance of the services, on a per patient basis;

(h) Failed to comply with, or aided or abetted a failure to comply with, the requirements of this article 200 or any lawful rules adopted by the executive director of the department of public health and environment, including those rules governing the proper cleaning and sterilization of acupuncture needles or the sanitary conditions of acupuncture offices, or any lawful orders of the department of public health and environment or of a court;

(i) Failed to comply with, or aided or abetted a failure to comply with, the requirements of this article 200 or any lawful rules governing the practice of acupuncture adopted by the director, an applicable provision of article 20 or 30 of this title 12, or any lawful orders of the director or of a court;

(j) Engaged in sexual contact, sexual intrusion, or sexual penetration, as defined in section 18 - 3 - 401, with a patient during the period of time beginning with the initial patient evaluation and ending with the termination of treatment;

(k) Departed from, or failed to conform to, minimal standards of care of similar practitioners under the same or similar circumstances, whether or not actual injury to a patient is established;

(I) Failed to notify the director of a physical illness, physical condition, or behavioral, mental health, or substance use disorder that impacts the licensee's ability to practice acupuncture with reasonable skill and safety to patients;

(Ⅱ) Failed to act within the limitations created by a physical illness, physical condition, or behavioral, mental health, or substance use disorder that renders the licensee unable to perform acupuncture with reasonable skill and safety to the patient; or

(Ⅲ) Failed to comply with the limitations agreed to under a confidential agreement;

(1) Continued in the practice of acupuncture while abusing or habitually or excessively using alcohol, a habit-forming drug, or controlled substance as defined in section 18-18-102 (5);

(m) Committed and been convicted of a felony or entered a plea of guilty or nolo contendere to a felony; and

(n) Published or circulated, directly or indirectly, any fraudulent, false, deceitful, or misleading claims or statements relating to acupuncture or to the acupuncturist's practice, capabilities, services, methods, or qualifications.

(2) The director may accept, as prima facie evidence of the commission of any act enumerated in subsection (1) of this section, evidence of disciplinary action taken by another jurisdiction against an acupuncturist's license or other authorization to practice if the disciplinary action was based upon acts or practices substantially similar to those enumerated in subsection (1) of this section.

12-200-110 DISCIPLINARY AUTHORITY AND PROCEEDINGS

(1) A proceeding for discipline of a licensee may be commenced by the director when the director has reasonable grounds to believe that a licensee has committed any act prohibited by section 12-200-109 (1).

(2) Disciplinary actions may consist of the following:

(a) Revocation or suspension of licensure;

(b) Placement of the licensee on probation and setting the terms of that probation; and

(c) Issuing and sending a letter of admonition by first-class mail to the licensee under the circumstances specified in and in accordance with section 12-20-404 (4).

(3) The director may issue and send a confidential letter of concern to a licensee under the circumstances specified in section 12-20-404 (5).

(4) Complaints of record on file with the director and the results of investigations shall be closed to public inspection during the investigatory period and until dismissed or until notice of hearing and charges are served on a licensee. The director's records and papers shall be subject to the provisions of sections 24-72-203 and 24-72-204.

(5) The director may issue cease-and-desist orders under the circumstances and in accordance with the procedures specified in section 12-20-405.

12-200-111 UNAUTHORIZED PRACTICE-PENALTIES

(1) Any person who practices or offers or attempts to practice acupuncture without an

active license issued under this article 200 is subject to penalties pursuant to section 12 – 20 – 407 (1)(a).

(2) Any person who violates the provisions of section 12 – 200 – 109 (1)(j) by engaging in sexual contact with a patient during the course of patient care commits a class 1 misdemeanor and shall be referred for criminal prosecution.

(3) Any person who violates the provisions of section 12 – 200 – 109 (1)(j) by engaging in sexual intrusion or sexual penetration with a patient during the course of patient care commits a class 4 felony and shall be referred for criminal prosecution.

12 – 200 – 112   CONFIDENTIAL AGREEMENT TO LIMIT PRACTICE

(1) Except as specified in subsection (2) of this section, section 12 – 30 – 108 concerning confidential agreements to limit practice applies to this article 200.

(2) This section and section 12 – 30 – 108 do not apply to a licensee subject to discipline under section 12 – 200 – 109 (1)(m).

12 – 200 – 113   CIVIL PENALTIES

(1) No action may be maintained against a recipient of acupuncture services for breach of a contract involving the rendering of acupuncture services provided under the contract by an acupuncturist who has committed, with respect to the recipient, any act prohibited by section 12 – 200 – 109 (1).

(2) When a patient, a patient's insurer, or a patient's legal guardian or representative has paid for acupuncture services rendered by an acupuncturist who has committed, with respect to the patient, any act prohibited by section 12 – 200 – 109 (1), whether or not the patient knew that the act or acts were illegal, the patient, the patient's insurer, or the patient's legal guardianor representative may recover, in an action at law, the amount of any fees paid for the acupuncture services and reasonable attorney fees.

(3) The criminal and civil penalties specified under this article 200 are not exclusive but cumulative and in addition to any other causes of action, rights, or remedies a patient may have under law.

12 – 200 – 114   DIRECTOR-POWERS AND DUTIES-RULES

(1) In addition to any other powers and duties conferred by this article 200, the director shall have the following powers and duties:

(a) To adopt rules pursuant to section 12 – 20 – 204;

(b) To accept or deny applications for licensure and to collect the annual license fees authorized by this article 200;

(c) To inspect on a complaint basis any premises where acupuncture services are provided to ensure compliance with this article 200 and the rules adopted pursuant thereto;

(d) To contract with the department of public health and environment or others to provide appropriate services as needed to carry out the inspections authorized with respect to the proper cleaning and sterilization of needles and the sanitation of acupuncture offices;

(e) To make investigations, hold hearings, and take evidence in accordance with section 12 - 20 - 403 with respect to any complaint against any licensee when the director has reasonable cause to believe that the licensee is violating any of the provisions of this article 200;

(f) To conduct any other meetings or hearings necessary to carry out the provisions of this article 200;

(g) Through the department of regulatory agencies, and subject to appropriations made to the department of regulatory agencies, to employ administrative law judges on a full-time or part-time basis to conduct any hearings required by this article 200;

(h) To seek an injunction in accordance with section 12 - 20 - 406 to enjoin any person from committing any act prohibited by this article 200;

(i) To order the physical or mental examination of an acupuncturist if the director has reasonable cause to believe that the acupuncturist is subject to a physical or mental disability that renders the acupuncturist unable to treat patients with reasonable skill and safety or that may endanger a patient's health or safety; and the director may order an examination whether or not actual injury to a patient is established;

(j) To report to the United States department of health and human services, pursuant to applicable federal law and regulations, any adverse action taken against the license of any acupuncturist.

12 - 200 - 115　POWERS AND DUTIES OF THE EXECUTIVE DIRECTOR OF THE DEPARTMENT OF PUBLIC HEALTH AND ENVIRONMENT-RULES

The executive director of the department of public health and environment shall promulgate rules relating to the proper cleaning and sterilization of needles to be used in the practice of acupuncture and the sanitation of acupuncture offices.

12 - 200 - 116　INSURANCE COVERAGE-NOT AFFECTED

Nothing in this article 200 shall be construed to affect any present or future provision of law or contract or other agreement concerning insurance or insurance coverage with respect to the provision of acupuncture services.

12 - 200 - 117　SCOPE OF ARTICLE

The provisions of this article 200 shall not apply to those persons who are otherwise licensed by the state of Colorado under this title 12 if the provision of acupuncture services is within the scope of the licensure. It is not intended nor shall it be interpreted that the practice of acupuncture constitutes the practice of medicine within the scope of the "Colorado Medical Practice Act", article 240 of this title 12.

12 - 200 - 118　REPEAL OF ARTICLE-REVIEW OF FUNCTIONS

This article 200 is repealed, effective September 1, 2022. Before the repeal, the licensing functions of the director are scheduled for review in accordance with section 24 - 34 - 104.

COLORADO ADMINISTRATIVE CODE

RULE 1 REQUIREMENT FOR LICENSURE

The purpose of this Rule is to establish the qualifications for an acupuncturist license as required in sections 12 – 200 – 106(3) and 12 – 20 – 202(4), C.R.S.

A. In order to qualify for licensure, section 12 – 200 – 106(3), C.R.S., requires an applicant to either successfully complete an education program that conforms to the standards approved by the Director of the Division of Professions and Occupations (Director) or provide documentation of qualifications that are substantially similar to an approved education program. The Director approved education program includes any diploma program in acupuncture and Oriental medicine accredited by the Accreditation Commission for Acupuncture and Oriental Medicine (ACAOM) or a successor organization.

B. To satisfy the licensure requirement in section 12 – 200 – 106(3), C.R.S., the Director requires an applicant to have a current certification at the time of initial license application by the National Certification Commission for Acupuncture and Oriental Medicine ("NCCAOM") or a successor organization. The applicant shall provide verification of this current certification in a manner prescribed by the Director.

C. Education, training, or service gained in military services outlined in section 12 – 20 – 202(4), C.R.S., to be accepted and applied towards receiving a license, must be substantially equivalent, as determined by the Director, to the qualifications otherwise applicable at the time of receipt of application. It is the applicant's responsibility to provide timely and complete evidence for review and consideration. Satisfactory evidence of such education, training, or service will be assessed on a case by case basis.

RULE 2 LICENSURE BY ENDORSEMENT

The purpose of this Rule is to establish the qualifications that are substantially equivalent for an acupuncturist license by endorsement pursuant to section 12 – 200 – 107(2), C.R.S.

A. For an applicant to establish "substantially equivalent credentials and qualifications" under section 12 – 200 – 107(2), C.R.S., the Director requires the applicant to submit a certification by NCCAOM or a successor organization. Verification of the certification shall be provided directly from NCCAOM or its successor in a manner prescribed by the Director; and

B. Verification of licensure in another state shall be provided in a manner prescribed by the Director.

RULE 3 REQUIREMENTS FOR REINSTATEMENT

The purpose of this Rule is to state the requirements for reinstatement of a license that has expired, pursuant to section 12 – 200 – 106(4), C.R.S.

A. An applicant seeking reinstatement of an expired license shall complete a reinstatement application, pay a reinstatement fee, and attest to malpractice insurance in the amount required by statute.

B. If the license has been expired for more than two years from the date of receipt of the reinstatement application, but less than five years an applicant shall establish competency to practice under sections 12 - 20 - 202(2)(c)(II), C.R.S., and 12 - 20 - 105, C.R.S., by demonstrating one of the following:

1. Licensure in good standing from another state along with proof of active practice in that state for two years of the previous five years from the date of application for reinstatement.

2. Completion of thirty hours of continuing education courses related to the practice of acupuncture during the two years immediately preceding the application for reinstatement. The continuing education must meet the approval of and shall be attested to in a manner prescribed by the Director.

3. Active certification by NCCAOM or a successor organization.

4. Competency to practice by any other means approved by the Director.

C. An applicant seeking to reinstate a license that has been expired for more than five years shall establish competency to practice as required in section 12 - 20 - 202(2)(c)(II), C.R.S. by demonstrating one of the following:

1. Licensure in good standing from another state along with proof of active practice for two years of the previous five years from the date of application for reinstatement.

2. Completion of supervised practice for a period no less than six months subject to the terms established by the Director.

3. Competency to practice by any other means approved by the Director.

RULE 4   UNLICENSED PERSONS IN ACUPUNCTURE TRAINING PROGRAMS

The purpose of this Rule is to identify the circumstances and conditions under which a person in training may practice acupuncture without a valid and current license on file with the Division of Professions and Occupations pursuant to section 12 - 200 - 108(3), C.R.S.

A. A person in training may practice acupuncture without a valid and current license issued by the Division of Professions and Occupations if such practice takes place in the course of a bona fide training program. A bona fide training program is a training or apprenticeship program with an accredited school of acupuncture.

B. A person in training shall be supervised by an acupuncturist licensed in Colorado who holds an active and unrestricted license to practice acupuncture in Colorado.

C. Section 12 - 200 - 108(3), C.R.S., requires a supervising acupuncturist to provide direct, on-site supervision of persons in training. Direct supervision shall mean supervision that is on the premises and in the same building where any such persons in training are practicing.

D. A person in training may engage in the full scope of the practice of acupuncture as defined in section 12 – 200 – 103(5)(a), C.R.S.

E. The supervising acupuncturist is responsible for maintaining documentation detailing the beginning and ending dates of the bona fide training program and for ensuring that, the names and current addresses of all supervised persons in training are maintained by the supervising acupuncturist and are readily available for inspection at the request of the Director or designee.

RULE 5   USE OF TITLE AND RESTRICTIONS

The purpose of this Rule is to clarify the use of title "licensed acupuncturist" and "diplomat of acupuncture", and use of the designations "L. Ac." and "Dipl. Ac." under section 12 – 200 – 108(2)(b)(II), C.R.S.

A. Obtaining an acupuncturist license does not automatically entitle or confer upon the licensee the right to use the title "Dr." or "Doctor."

B. A licensed acupuncturist can use the title "Doctor" or Dr.only when such licensee has, in fact, been awarded a doctorate degree from an acupuncture or oriental medicine academic/educational institution and satisfies the requirements of section 6 – 1 – 707, C.R.S.

C. In such instances where a licensee qualifies to use the title "Doctor" or "Dr.", an acupuncturist can use the title "Doctor" or "Dr." only when accompanied by the words "Doctor of Acupuncture" or letters "D. Ac.", "Oriental Medicine Doctor" or "OMD", "Doctor of Acupuncture and Oriental Medicine" or "D. Ac. OM", "Doctor of Traditional Chinese Medicine" or "DTCM", "Doctor of Acupuncture and Oriental Medicine" or "DAOM", or any other doctoral degree recognized and approved by the Director.

RULE 6   DECLARATORY ORDERS

The purpose of this Rule is to establish procedures for the handling of requests for declaratory orders filed pursuant to the Colorado Administrative Procedures Act at section 24 – 4 – 105(11), C.R.S.

A. Any person or entity may petition the Director for a declaratory order to terminate controversies or remove uncertainties as to the applicability of any statutory provision or of any rule or order of the Director.

B. The Director will determine, at her discretion and without notice to petitioner, whether to rule upon such petition. If the Director determines that the Director will not rule upon such a petition, the Director shall promptly notify the petitioner of the action and state the reasons for such decision.

C. In determining whether to rule upon a petition filed pursuant to this rule, the Director will consider the following matters, among others:

1. Whether a ruling on the petition will terminate a controversy or remove uncertainties as to the applicability to petitioner of any statutory provisions or rule or order of the Director.

2. Whether the petition involves any subject, question or issue that is the subject of a formal or informal matter or investigation currently pending before the Director or a court involving one

or more petitioners.

3. Whether the petition involves any subject, question or issue that is the subject of a formal or informal matter or investigation currently pending before the Director or a court but not involving any petitioner.

4. Whether the petition seeks a ruling on a moot or hypothetical question or will result in an advisory ruling or opinion.

5. Whether the petitioner has some other adequate legal remedy, other than an action for declaratory relief pursuant to Colorado Rules of Civil Procedure 57, which will terminate the controversy or remove any uncertainty as to the applicability to the petitioner of the statute, rule, or order in question.

D. Any petition filed pursuant to this rule shall set forth the following:

1. The name and address of the petitioner and whether the petitioner is licensed pursuant to Title 12, Article 200.

2. The statute, rule, or order to which the petition relates.

3. A concise statement of all of the facts necessary to show the nature of the controversy or uncertainty and the manner in which the statute, rule, or order in question applies or potentially applies to the petitioner.

E. If the Director decides to rule on the petition, the following procedures shall apply:

1. The Director may rule upon the petition based solely upon the facts presented in the petition. In such a case:

a. Any ruling of the Director will apply only to the extent of the facts presented in the petition and any amendment to the petition.

b. The Director may order the petitioner to file a written brief, memorandum, or statement of position.

c. The Director may set the petition, upon due notice to petitioner, for a non-evidentiary hearing.

d. The Director may dispose of the petition on the sole basis of the matters set forth in the petition.

e. The Director may request the petitioner to submit additional facts in writing. In such event, such additional facts will be considered as an amendment to the petition.

f. The Director may take administrative notice of facts pursuant to the Colorado Administrative Procedures Act at section 24-4-105(8), C.R.S., and may utilize the Director's experience, technical competence, and specialized knowledge in the disposition of the petition.

2. If the Director rules upon the petition without a hearing, the Director shall promptly notify the petitioner of her decision.

3. The Director may, at the Director's discretion, set the petition for hearing, upon due notice to petitioner, for the purpose of obtaining additional facts or information or to determine

the truth of any facts set forth in the petition or to hear oral argument on the petition. The hearing notice to the petitioner shall set forth, to the extent known, the factual or other matters that the Director intends to inquire.

For the purpose of such a hearing, to the extent necessary, the petitioner shall have the burden of proving all the facts stated in the petition; all of the facts necessary to show the nature of the controversy or uncertainty; and the manner in which the statute, rule, or order in question applies or potentially applies to the petitioner and any other facts the petitioner desires the Director to consider.

F. The parties to any proceeding pursuant to this rule shall be the Director and the petitioner. Any other person may seek leave of the Director to intervene in such a proceeding, and leave to intervene will be granted at the sole discretion of the Director. A petition to intervene shall set forth the same matters as are required by Section D of this Rule. Any reference to a "petitioner" in this rule also refers to any person who has been granted leave to intervene by the Director.

G. Any declaratory order or other order disposing of a petition pursuant to this rule shall constitute agency action subject to judicial review pursuant to the Colorado Administrative Procedures Act at section 24 – 4 – 106, C.R.S.

RULE 7 REPORTING CONVICTIONS, JUDGMENTS AND ADMINISTRATIVE PROCEEDINGS

The purpose of the Rule is to clarify the procedures for reporting convictions, and other adverse actions to include judgments and administrative proceedings pursuant to sections 12 – 200 – 105, 12 – 200 – 106, and 12 – 200 – 109, C.R.S.

A licensee as defined in section 12 – 200 – 103, C.R.S., shall inform the Director, in a manner set forth by the Director, within thirty days of any of the following events:

A. The conviction of the licensee of a felony under the laws of any state or of the United States, which would be a violation of section 12 – 200 – 109(1)(n), C.R.S. A guilty verdict, a plea of guilty or a plea of nolo contendere (no contest) accepted by the court is considered a conviction;

B. A disciplinary action imposed upon the licensee by another jurisdiction that licenses acupuncturists, which would be a violation of section 12 – 200 – 109, C.R.S., including, but not limited to, a citation, sanction, probation, civil penalty, or a denial, suspension, revocation, or modification of a license whether it is imposed by consent decree, order, or other decision, for any cause other than failure to pay a license fee by the due date or failure to meet continuing professional education requirements;

C. Revocation or suspension by another state board, municipality, federal or state agency of any health services related license, other than a lapsed license for acupuncture as described in Section 12 – 200 – 109, C.R.S.;

D. Any judgment, award or settlement of a civil action or arbitration in which there was a final judgment or settlement against the licensee for malpractice of acupuncture.

E. The notice to the Director shall include the following information:

1. If the event is an action by a governmental agency(as described above), the name of the agency, its jurisdiction, the case name, court docket, proceeding or case number by which the event is designated, and a copy of the consent decree, order or decision;

2. If the event is a felony conviction, the court, its jurisdiction, the case name, the case number, a description of the matter or a copy of the indictment or charges, and any plea or verdict entered by the court. The licensee shall also provide to the Director a copy of the imposition of sentence or judgment, whether deferred or immediate, related to the felony conviction and the completion of all terms of the sentence or judgment with thirty(30) days of such action;

3. If the event concerns a civil action or arbitration proceeding, the court or arbiter, the jurisdiction, the case name, the case number, court docket, a description of the matter or a copy of the complaint, and a copy of the verdict, the court or arbitration decision, or, if settled, the settlement agreement and court's order of dismissal;

F. The licensee notifying the Director may submit a written statement with the notice to be included with the licensee records.

RULE 8 REPEALED

RULE 9 DUTY TO SELF-REPORT CERTAIN MEDICAL CONDITIONS

A. No later than thirty days from the date a physical or mental illness or condition that affects a licensee's ability to perform acupuncture services with reasonable skill and safety, the licensee shall provide the Director, in writing, the following information:

1. The diagnosis and a description of the illness or condition;

2. The date that the illness or condition was first diagnosed;

3. The name of the current treatment provider and documentation from the current treatment provider confirming the diagnosis, date of onset, and treatment plan; and

4. A description of the acupuncturist's practice and any modifications, limitations or restrictions to that practice that have been made as a result of the illness or condition.

B. The licensee shall notify the Director of any worsening of any worsening of the illness or condition, or any significant change in the illness or condition that affects the licensee's ability to practice with reasonable skill and safety, within thirty days of the change of the illness or condition. The acupuncturist shall provide to the Director, in writing, the following information:

1. The name of the current treatment provider, documentation from the current treatment provider confirming the change of the illness or condition, the date that the illness or condition changed, the nature of the change of the illness or condition, and the current treatment plan; and

2. A description of the licensee's practice, and any modifications, limitations, or restrictions

to that practice that have been made as a result of the change of condition.

C. Compliance with this Rule is a prerequisite for eligibility to enter into a Confidential Agreement with the Director pursuant to section 12－200－112(1), C.R.S. However, mere compliance with this rule does not require the Director to enter into a Confidential Agreement. Rather, the Director will evaluate all facts and circumstances to determine whether a Confidential Agreement is appropriate.

D. If the Director discovers that a licensee has a mental or physical illness or condition that affects the licensee's ability to practice with reasonable skill and safety, and the licensee has not timely notified the Director of such illness or condition, the licensee may be subject to disciplinary action pursuant to section 12－200－109(1)(1), C.R.S.

RULE 10 INJECTION THERAPY

A. Definitions. For purposes of this Rule only:

1. The Director recognizes that "Injection therapy" is the stimulation of acupuncture points, including trigger points (historically known as "AHSHI" points), by the injection of saline, sterile herbs, vitamins, minerals, homeopathic substances, glucose, lidocaine, procaine, and sarapin, or other similar substances specifically manufactured for nonintravenous injection by means of hypodermic needles.

B. Except as restricted by paragraph (C) of this Rule, an acupuncturist with an active license may practice injection therapy in the treatment of patients in his or her care.

C. Requirements to Practice Injection Therapy. The acupuncturist shall:

1. Possess a Colorado acupuncture license in good standing;

2. Hold a current Clean Needle Technique Certificate through the NCCAOM (or successor organization); and

3. Be current in basic life support (BLS) or cardiopulmonary resuscitation (CPR) approved by the American Heart Association or American Red Cross;

4. Complete educational coursework covered in subsection D.

D. Acupuncturists employing injection therapy shall use only those substances and techniques for which they have received training. Required Educational Coursework shall include:

1. Anatomy and Physiology;

2. Acupuncture physical exam and differential diagnosis;

3. Acupuncture point location, including underlying anatomy;

4. Acupuncture needling technique;

5. General injection safety;

6. [FN1] Acupuncture point injection therapy;

7. Pharmacology; and

8. Clean Needle Technique.

9. For the use of injectable substances prepared from oriental herbs, completion of training

in Chinese herbology and injection of Chinese herbal injectables is required.

To demonstrate satisfying the training requirements in Chinese herbology and injection of Chinese herbal injectables the Director will accept NCCAOM, or a successor organization's, certification in Chinese herbology and/or certification in Oriental Medicine.

10. For the use of substances listed in (E)(3)(a)(12 – 17), instruction on the use of inhaled O2 and IM epinephrine for emergency use is required.

E. Permissible Substances

1. An acupuncturist shall comply with all federal and state laws that pertain to obtaining, possessing and administering any drug;

2. A substance shall only be approved for use if procured in compliance with all federal and state laws;

3. The following drugs are authorized in the modes of administration that are specified except as limited or restricted by federal or state law:

a. Permissible substances that an acupuncturist may obtain for injection therapy as permitted per section 12 – 200 – 103(4), C.R.S and as permitted by the Director:

(1) Dextrose;

(2) d-glucose;

(3) Enzymes except urokinase;

(4) Glucose;

(5) [FN2]Homeopathic Substances(to only include those that are within the US Pharmacopia);

(6) Hyaluronic Acid;

(7) Minerals;

(8) Saline;

(9) Sarapin;

(10) Sodium chloride;

(11) Sterile water;

(12) Traumeel;

(13) Vitamins;

(14) Cyanocobalamin;

(15) Lidocaine;

(16) Marcaine(Bupivacaine Hydrochloride) with or without epinephrine;

(17) Oriental Herbs;

(18) Procaine; and

(19) Vitamin B – 12.

F. Patient safety.

1. Acupuncturists shall have an adverse event/emergency plan in place.

2. An acupuncturist practicing injection therapy of substances listed in (E)(3)(a)(14) –

(19) shall be equipped and trained to treat patients with oxygen and epinephrine. The oxygen and emergency epinephrine kit shall be on site where injection therapy utilizing substances with potential allergic side effects are being rendered.

3. An acupuncturist authorized to practice injection therapy shall not inject any substance intravenously.

G. Acupuncturists shall show current medical malpractice coverage for this procedure and maintain coverage.

1. It is the acupuncturist's responsibility to only inject substances that are listed in subsection E and are explicitly covered by the acupuncturist's insurance policy obtained in compliance with section 12-200-106(6), C.R.S.

RULE 11 CONCERNING HEALTH CARE PROVIDER DISCLOSURES TO CONSUMERS ABOUT THE POTENTIAL EFFECTS OF RECEIVING EMERGENCY OR NONEMERGENCY SERVICES FROM AN OUT-OF-NETWORK PROVIDER

This Rule is promulgated and adopted by the Director of the Division of Professions and Occupations ("Director"), pursuant to the rulemaking authority in sections 12-20-204, 12-200-114(1)(a), and 24-34-113(3), C.R.S., in consultation with the Commissioner of Insurance and the State Board of Health under the authority of section 24-34-113(2), C.R.S.

The purpose of this Rule is to establish requirements for health care providers to provide disclosures to consumers about the potential effects of receiving emergency or non-emergency services from an out-of-network provider as required by section 24-34-113(2), C.R.S.

This Rule applies to health care providers as defined in sections 24-34-113(1)(f) and 10-16-102(56), C.R.S.

A. Disclosure requirements. Pursuant to section 24-34-113, C.R.S., health care providers shall provide the disclosure contained in Appendix A to all clients about the potential effects of receiving emergency or nonemergency services from an out-of-network facility or agency or an out-of-network provider who provides services at an in-network facility or agency. The health care provider shall provide the disclosure contained in Appendix A at all of the following occasions:

1. For emergency services: after performing an appropriate screening examination and after determining that a client does not have an emergency medical condition or after treatment has been provided to stabilize an emergency medical condition. The disclosure shall be signed by the client or their designated representative prior to discharge;

2. At the time the client consents to care or treatment by the health care provider for nonemergency services. The disclosure shall be signed by the client or their designated representative before the start of services;

3. On billing statements and billing notices issued by the health care provider; and

4. On other forms or communications related to the services being provided pursuant to

insurance coverage.

B. Noncompliance with this Rule may result in the imposition of any of discipline made available by sections 12－200－109(1)(i) and 12－200－110, C.R.S.

APPENDIX A
SURPRISE BILLING—KNOW YOUR RIGHTS

Beginning January 1, 2020, Colorado state law protects you [FN*] from "surprise billing," also known as "balance billing." These protections apply when:

• You receive covered emergency services, other than ambulance services, from an out-of-network provider in Colorado, and/or

• You unintentionally receive covered services from an out-of-network provider at an in-network facility in Colorado.

WHAT IS SURPRISE/BALANCE BILLING, AND WHEN DOES IT HAPPEN?

If you are seen by a health care provider or use services in a facility or agency that is not in your health insurance plan's provider network, sometimes referred to as "out-of-network," you may receive a bill for additional costs associated with that care. Out-of-network health care providers often bill you for the difference between what your insurer decides is the eligible charge and what the out-of-network provider bills as the total charge. This is called "surprise" or "balance" billing.

WHEN YOU CANNOT BE BALANCE-BILLED:
EMERGENCY SERVICES

If you are receiving emergency services, the most you can be billed for is your plan's in-network cost-sharing amounts, which are copayments, deductibles, and/or coinsurance. You cannot be balance-billed for any other amount. This includes both the emergency facility where you receive emergency services and any providers that see you for emergency care.

NONEMERGENCY SERVICES AT AN IN-NETWORK OR OUT-OF-NETWORK HEALTH CARE PROVIDER

The health care provider must tell you if you are at an out-of-network location or at an in-network location that is using out-of-network providers. They must also tell you what types of services that you will be using may be provided by any out-of-network provider.

You have the right to request that in-network providers perform all covered medical services. However, you may have to receive medical services from an out-of-network provider if an in-network provider is not available. In this case, the most you can be billed for covered services is your in-network cost-sharing amount, which are copayments, deductibles, and/or coinsurance. These providers cannot balance bill you for additional costs.

ADDITIONAL PROTECTIONS

• Your insurer will pay out-of-network providers and facilities directly.

COLORADO

- Your insurer must count any amount you pay for emergency services or certain out-of-network services(described above) toward your in-network deductible and out-of-pocket limit.
- Your provider, facility, hospital, or agency must refund any amount you overpay within sixty days of being notified.
- No one, including a provider, hospital, or insurer can ask you to limit or give up these rights.

If you receive services from an out-of-network provider or facility or agency OTHER situation, you may still be balance billed, or you may be responsible for the entire bill. If you intentionally receive nonemergency services from an out-of-network provider or facility, you may also be balance billed.

If you want to file a complaint against your health care provider, you can submit an online complaint by visiting this website: https://www.colorado.gov/pacific/dora/DPO_File_Complaint.

If you think you have received a bill for amounts other than your copayments, deductible, and/or coinsurance, please contact the billing department, or the Colorado Division of Insurance at 303-894-7490 or 1-800-930-3745.

Please contact your health insurance plan at the number on your health insurance ID card or the Colorado Division of Insurance with questions.

MONTANA

MONTANA CODE ANNOTATED

PART 1   GENERAL

37 – 13 – 101   CITATION OF CHAPTER

This chapter shall be known and may be cited as the "Acupuncture Practice Act of 1974".

37 – 13 – 102   LEGISLATIVE FINDING AND PURPOSE

The legislature finds and declares that the practice of acupuncture in Montana affects the public health, safety, and welfare and should therefore be subject to regulation and control in the public interest in order to protect the public from the unauthorized and unqualified practice of acupuncture and from unprofessional conduct by persons licensed to practice acupuncture.

37 – 13 – 103   DEFINITIONS

As used in this chapter, the following definitions apply:

(1) "Acupuncture" means the diagnosis, treatment, or correction of human conditions, ailments, diseases, injuries, or infirmities by means of mechanical, thermal, or electrical stimulation effected by the insertion of solid needles. The term includes the use of acupressure and the use of oriental food remedies and herbs.

(2) "Acupuncturist" means a natural person licensed by the board of medical examiners to practice acupuncture.

(3) "Board" means the Montana state board of medical examiners.

(4) "School of acupuncture" means a school in which acupuncture is taught that has been recognized and designated by the board of medical examiners.

37 – 13 – 104   PARTIAL EXEMPTIONS

(1)(a) This chapter may not be construed to require doctors of medicine, osteopathy, chiropractic, dentistry, and podiatry who are licensed in Montana to take further examinations in anatomy, physiology, chemistry, dermatology, diagnosis, bacteriology, materia medica, or other subjects that are or may be required for licensure in their respective professions.

(b) A doctor of medicine, osteopathy, chiropractic, dentistry, or podiatry may not practice acupuncture in this state unless that doctor has completed a course and passed an examination in acupuncture as required by this chapter.

(2) Except as provided in 37-13-301 and with particular regard to the insertion of solid needles used to perform acupuncture, this chapter is not intended to limit, interfere with, or prevent a licensed health professional from practicing within the scope of the health professional's license.

(3) This chapter does not affect the practice of an occupation by an individual who does not represent to the public that the individual is licensed under this chapter.

PART 2   BOARD OF MEDICAL EXAMINERS

37-13-201   POWERS AND DUTIES

In addition to all other powers and duties conferred and imposed upon the board by this chapter, the board shall have and exercise the following powers and duties:

(1) To promulgate, under the applicable provisions of the Montana Administrative Procedure Act, rules which it determines to be necessary to carry out the provisions of this chapter;

(2) To adopt a schedule of minimum educational requirements, not inconsistent with the provisions of this chapter;

(3) To prescribe forms for application for examination and license;

(4) To prepare and supervise examination of applicants for license to practice acupuncture;

(5) To obtain the services of professional examination agencies in lieu of its own preparation of the examinations;

(6) To issue, revoke, and suspend licenses as hereinafter provided;

(7) To hold hearings, issue subpoenas, administer oaths, and take testimony and proofs concerning all matters within its jurisdiction;

(8) To issue commissions to take depositions of witnesses who are sick or absent from the state; and

(9) To adopt a seal, which shall be affixed to all licenses issued by the board and other official papers.

PART 3   LICENSING

37-13-301   LICENSE REQUIRED FOR PRACTICE

(1) A person may not engage in the practice of acupuncture in this state unless the person is licensed under the provisions of this chapter.

(2) A person may not purport to practice acupuncture or use the title "acupuncturist" or any similar title unless the person is licensed under the provisions of this chapter.

37 – 13 – 302 APPLICATION FOR LICENSURE-FEE-QUALIFICATIONS

(1) Each person desiring to practice acupuncture in this state shall apply to the board for licensure. A fee prescribed by the board must accompany the application.

(2) An applicant shall furnish to the board evidence that the applicant is:

(a) At least 18 years of age;

(b) Of good moral character as determined by the board;

(c) A graduate of a school of acupuncture that is approved by the national accreditation commission for schools and colleges of acupuncture and oriental medicine and offers a course of at least 1,000 hours of entry-level training in recognized branches of acupuncture or an equivalent curriculum approved by theboard; and

(d) Has passed an examination prepared and administered by the national commission for the certification of acupuncturists or its successor.

37 – 13 – 303 REPEALED. SEC.2, CH.307, L.1987

37 – 13 – 304 ISSUANCE OF CERTIFICATE OF LICENSE-LICENSE FEE

All applicants successfully passing the examination required by this chapter shall be registered as licensed acupuncturists in the board register and, upon the payment of a license fee prescribed by the board, shall be issued a certificate of license in such form as prescribed by the board. The certificate shall bear the official seal of the board.

37 – 13 – 305 REPEALED. SEC.128, CH.429, L.1995

37 – 13 – 306 REPEALED. SEC.127, CH.467, L.2005

37 – 13 – 307 REPEALED. SEC.127, CH.467, L.2005

PART 3 LICENSING

THROUGH 37 – 13 – 310 RESERVED

37 – 13 – 308 THROUGH 37 – 13 – 310 RESERVED

37 – 13 – 311 REPEALED. SEC.128, CH.429, L.1995

37 – 13 – 312 REPEALED. SEC.128, CH.429, L.1995

37 – 13 – 313 REPEALED. SEC.128, CH.429, L.1995

37 – 13 – 314 REPEALED. SEC.128, CH.429, L.1995

37 – 13 – 315 ENJOINING UNLAWFUL PRACTICE

The practice of acupuncture in any way other than as defined in this chapter may be enjoined by the district court on petition by the board. In the proceeding, it is not necessary to show that any person is individually injured by the actions complained of. If the respondent is found to have practiced improperly, the court shall enjoin the respondent from practicing until the respondent has been licensed. Procedure in these cases is the same as in any other injunction suit. The remedy by injunction is in addition to criminal prosecution and punishment.

37-13-316 PENALTY

A person who violates any of the provisions of this chapter or the rules of the Montana state board of medical examiners is guilty of a misdemeanor punishable by imprisonment in the county jail not exceeding 6 months or by a fine not exceeding $500, or both.

ADMINISTRATIVE RULES OF MONTANA

24.156.1401 DEFINITIONS

(1) "Examinations" means the examinations required for certification in acupuncture as granted by the National Commission for the Certification of Acupuncture and Oriental Medicine, or its successor.

(2) "National Commission for the Certification of Acupuncture and Oriental Medicine" is the organization known before 1997 as the National Commission for the Certification of Acupuncturists.

(3) "Council of Colleges for Acupuncture and Oriental Medicine" means the organization responsible for administering the clean needle technique examination.

(4) "Accreditation Commission for Acupuncture and Oriental Medicine" is the organization known before 1997 as the National Accreditation Commission for Schools and Colleges of Acupuncture and Oriental Medicine.

24.156.1402 FEES

(1) An applicant for licensure shall remit a license fee of $65 with his or her application.

(2) The renewal fee to practice acupuncture will be: $100

(3) Additional standardized fees are specified in ARM[①]24.101.403.

24.156.1403 REQUIREMENTS FOR LICENSURE

(1) Applicants for licensure must meet the prerequisites for and pass the examinations required for certification in acupuncture by the National Commission for the Certification of Acupuncture and Oriental Medicine, or its successor.

(2) Applicants for licensure must pass the examination in clean needle technique administered by the Council of Colleges for Acupuncture and Oriental Medicine, or its successor.

24.156.1404 APPLICATION FOR LICENSURE

(1) An applicant for an acupuncture license shall submit an application, the appropriate fees, and:

(a) Applicant's official transcript from a school accredited by the Accreditation Commission for Acupuncture and Oriental Medicine;

[①] Administrative Rules of Montana.

(b) Applicant's clean needle exam results from the Council of Colleges of Acupuncture and Oriental Medicine or its successor; and

(c) Acupuncture certification examination results provided by the National Commission for the Certification of Acupuncture and Oriental Medicine.

(2) The board or its designee will obtain a query from the National Practitioner Data Bank for each applicant.

(3) Applicants licensed in another state or jurisdiction shall cause all states and jurisdictions in which the applicant holds or has ever held a license to submit a current verification of licensure directly to the board on behalf of the applicant.

(4) The applicant may voluntarily withdraw the application prior to being placed on a board agenda by submitting a written request to the board.

24.156.1405　APPROVAL OF SCHOOLS(REPEALED)

(See the Transfer and Repeal Table)

Action	From	To	Effective Date
Repeal	2.21.1401		3/16/1984
Repeal	2.21.1402		2/16/1984
Repeal	2.21.1403		3/16/1984
Repeal	2.21.1404		3/16/1984
Repeal	2.21.1405		3/16/1984
Repeal	2.21.1406		3/16/1984
Repeal	2.21.1407		3/16/1984
Repeal	2.21.1408		3/16/1984
Repeal	2.21.1411		3/16/1984

24.156.1406　CURRICULUM

(1) The board will review any equivalent curriculum as provided for in 37 - 13 - 302, MCA, on an individual basis, using acceptable curriculum existing at the time of the individual's study as a guide for evaluation.

24.156.1407　OBLIGATION TO REPORT TO THE BOARD

(1) Within three months from the date of a final judgment, final order, or final disciplinary action, an acupuncturist licensed under this chapter shall report to the board all information related to the malpractice, misconduct, criminal, or disciplinary action in which the acupuncturist

is a named party.

(2) An acupuncturist with suspected or known impairment shall self-report to the board. In lieu of reporting to the board, the acupuncturist may self-report to the board-endorsed professional assistance program.

(3) An acupuncturist is obligated to report suspected or known impairment of other health care providers to the appropriate licensing board, agency, or in lieu of the board or agency, may report to the endorsed professional assistance program.

24.156.1408 CONTINUING EDUCATION FOR ACUPUNCTURISTS

(1) Each acupuncture licensee of the Board of Medical Examiners shall earn 15 clock hours of accredited continuing acupuncture education each year. Clock hours or contact hours shall be the actual number of hours during which instruction was given.

(2) A maximum of eight clock hours may be given for the first-time preparation of a new course, in-service training workshop, or seminar which is related to the enhancement of acupuncture practice, values, skills, and knowledge; or a maximum of eight clock hours credit may be given for the preparation by the author or authors of a professional acupuncture paper published for the first time in a recognized professional journal; or given for the first time at a statewide or national professional meeting.

(3) If a licensee completes more than 30 hours of continuing education in a two-year licensing period, excess hours in an amount not to exceed 15 hours may be carried forward to the next two-year licensing period.

(4) Any licensee may apply for a hardship exemption from the continuing acupuncture education requirements of these rules by filing a statement with the board setting forth good faith reasons why he or she is unable to comply with these rules and an exemption may be granted by the board.

(5) Continuing education is not required for licensees renewing their license for the first time.

24.156.1409 ACCREDITATION, APPROVAL, AND STANDARDS

(1) The board shall appoint a continuing education review committee which shall assist the board in approving courses, papers, workshops, and other activities designed to meet the continuing education requirements of licensed acupuncturists.

(2) The continuing education review committee shall approve continuing acupuncture education courses, papers, workshops, and other activities that meet the following standards:

(a) They shall have significant intellectual or practical content, and the primary objective shall be to increase the participant's professional competence as an acupuncturist.

(b) They shall constitute an organized program of learning dealing with matters directly related to the practice of acupuncture, professional responsibility, or ethical obligations of acupuncturists.

(c) Providers of continuing acupuncture education and authors of published papers shall apply to the board for course or publication approval by submitting an application on a form prescribed by the department. The application must be complete and accompanied by the appropriate documents.

(d) Applicants shall demonstrate that the offered course complies with the standards.

(e) The board, in its discretion, may determine the number of hours acceptable for any continuing education credit.

(f) Courses accredited by the National Commission for the Certification of Acupuncture and Oriental Medicine shall be preapproved by the board.

(g) Courses sponsored by a state acupuncture association or an acupuncture school shall be preapproved by the board.

(h) Teaching acupuncture in an accredited academic or continuing education program shall be accepted as continuing education.

(3) Licensees may claim five hours of self-study toward meeting the requirements of ARM 24.156.1408.

24.156.1410 REPORTING REQUIREMENTS

(1) Each licensee shall maintain a record of courses attended on a form approved by the board, attesting to the number of accredited continuing education hours completed each year.

24.156.1411 RENEWALS(Repealed)

24.156.1412 UNPROFESSIONAL CONDUCT

(1) In addition to those forms of unprofessional conduct defined in 37-1-316, MCA, the following is unprofessional conduct for a licensee or license applicant under Title 37, chapter 13, MCA:

(a) Commission of an act of sexual abuse, sexual misconduct, or sexual exploitation, whether or not related to the licensee's practice of acupuncture;

(b) Failure to utilize clean needle technique, as required by the National Commission for the Certification of Acupuncture and Oriental Medicine, or its successor;

(c) Conduct likely to deceive, defraud, or harm the public;

(d) Making a false or misleading statement regarding the licensee's skill or the effectiveness or value of the medicine, treatment, or remedy prescribed by the licensee or at the licensee's direction, in the treatment of a disease or other condition of the body or mind;

(e) Resorting to fraud, misrepresentation, or deception in the examination or treatment of a person; or in billing, giving, or receiving a fee related to professional services; or reporting to a person, company, institution, or organization, including fraud, misrepresentation, or deception with regard to a claim for benefits under Title 39, chapter 71 or 72, MCA;

(f) Use of a false, fraudulent, or deceptive statement in any document connected with the practice of acupuncture;

(g) Having been subject to disciplinary action of another state or jurisdiction against a license or other authorization to practice acupuncture, based upon acts or conduct by the licensee similar to acts or conduct that would constitute grounds for disciplinary action under Title 37, chapter 13, MCA, or these rules. A certified copy of the record of the action taken by the other state or jurisdiction is evidence of unprofessional conduct;

(h) Willful disobedience of a rule adopted by the board, or an order of the board regarding enforcement of discipline of a licensee;

(i) Failing to furnish to the board or its investigators or representatives information legally requested by the board;

(j) Failing to cooperate with a lawful investigation conducted by the board;

(k) Obtaining a fee or other compensation, either directly or indirectly, by the misrepresentation that a manifestly incurable disease, injury, or condition of a person can be cured;

(l) Abusive billing practices;

(m) Testifying in court on a contingency basis;

(n) Conspiring to misrepresent or willfully misrepresenting a medical condition improperly to increase or decrease a settlement, award, verdict, or judgment;

(o) Except as provided in this subsection, practicing acupuncture as the partner, agent, or employee of, or in joint venture with, a person who does not hold a license to practice acupuncture within this state; however, this does not prohibit:

(i) The incorporation of an individual licensee or group of licensees as a professional service corporation under Title 35, chapter 4, MCA;

(ii) The organization of a professional limited liability company under Title 35, chapter 8, MCA, for the providing of professional services as defined in Title 35, chapter 8, MCA;

(iii) Practicing acupuncture as the partner, agent or employee of, or in joint venture with, a hospital, medical assistance facility or other licensed health care provider; however,

(A) The partnership, agency, employment or joint venture must be evidenced by a written agreement containing language to the effect that the relationship created by the agreement may not affect the exercise of the acupuncturist's independent judgment in the practice of acupuncture;

(B) The acupuncturist's independent judgment in the practice of acupuncture must in fact be unaffected by the relationship; and

(C) The acupuncturist may not be required to refer any patient to a particular provider or supplier or take any other action that the acupuncturist determines not to be in the patient's best interest;

(p) Failing to transfer pertinent and necessary patient records to another licensed health care provider, the patient or the patient's representative when requested to do so by the patient or the patient's legally designated representative;

(q) Misrepresenting professional credentials (i.e. education, training, experience, level of competence, skills, and/or certification status);

(s) Engaging in conduct that demonstrates a lack of knowledge of, or lack of ability in, or failure to apply the prevailing principles and/or skills of the profession in which the individual has been certified;

(t) Failing to place patient medical records in a secure location preceding, during, or following a change in practice location or termination of a patient relationship or an acupuncture practice; or knowingly breaching confidentiality of patient medical records with an individual unauthorized to receive medical records; or

(u) Any other act, whether specifically enumerated or not, that in fact constitutes unprofessional conduct.

24.156.1413 MANAGEMENT OF INFECTIOUS WASTES

(1) Each acupuncturist licensed by the board shall store, transport off the premises, and dispose of infectious wastes, as defined in 75 – 10 – 1003, MCA, in accordance with the requirements set forth in 75 – 10 – 1005, MCA.

(2) Used sharps are properly packaged and labeled within the meaning of 75 – 10 – 1005, MCA, when this is done as required by the Occupational Safety and Health Administration (OSHA).

24.156.1414 CONTINUING EDUCATION AUDIT

(1) The board shall conduct a random audit of continuing education following each renewal period.

(2) Licensees selected for the audit shall submit documentation as required in Rule Reporting Requirements that attests to completion of the continuing education hours.

(3) Failure to comply with continuing education requirements may be grounds for discipline.

NEVADA

NEVADA REVISED STATUTES ANNOTATED

GENERAL PROVISIONS

NRS 634A.010 LEGISLATIVE DECLARATION

The practice of Oriental medicine and any branch thereof is hereby declared to be a learned profession, affecting public safety and welfare and charged with the public interest, and therefore subject to protection and regulation by the State.

NRS 634A.020 DEFINITIONS

As used in this chapter, unless the context otherwise requires:

1. "Acupuncture" means the insertion of needles into the human body by piercing the skin of the body to control and regulatethe flow and balance of energy in the body and to cure, relieve or palliate the body for therapeutic purposes, including, without limitation:

(a) Any ailment or disease of the mind or body; or

(b) Any wound, bodily injury or deformity.

2. "Board" means the State Board of Oriental Medicine.

3. "Doctor of Oriental medicine" means a person who is licensed under the provisions of this chapter to practice as a doctor of Oriental medicine.

4. "Dry needling":

(a) Means an advanced needling skill or technique limited to the treatment of myofascial pain, using a single-use, single-insertion, sterile needle without the use of heat, cold or any other added modality or medication, which is inserted into the skin or underlying tissue to stimulate a trigger point.

(b) Does not include:

(1) The stimulation of an auricular point;

(2) Utilization of a distal point or nonlocal point;

(3) Needle retention;

(4) Application of a retained electrical stimulation lead; or

(5) The teaching or application of other acupuncture theory.

5. "Herbal medicine" and "practice of herbal medicine" mean suggesting, recommending, prescribing or directing the use of herbs for the cure, relief or palliation of any ailment or disease of the mind or body, or for the cure or relief of any wound, bodily injury or deformity.

6. "Herbs" means any plant or part of a plant which is not prohibited by the laws of the United States or this State and is used in tests or examinations in the practice of Oriental medicine.

7. "Oriental medicine" means a system of the healing art which places the chief emphasis on the flow and balance of energy in the body mechanism as being the most important single factor in maintaining the well-being of the organism in health and disease. The term includes, without limitation, the practice of acupuncture, herbal medicine, moxibustion, dry needling and other services approved by the Board.

NRS 634A.025 APPLICABILITY OF CHAPTER

1. This chapter does not apply to Oriental physicians who are:

(a) Called into this State for consultation; or

(b) Temporarily exempt from licensure pursuant to NRS 634A.163 and are practicing Oriental medicine within the scope of the exemption.

2. This chapter does not apply to a practitioner of acupuncture:

(a) Who is employed by an accredited school of Oriental medicine located in this State;

(b) Who is licensed to practice acupuncture in another state or jurisdiction; and

(c) Whose practice of acupuncture in this State:

(1) Is limited to teaching, supervising or demonstrating the methods and practices of acupuncture to students in a clinical setting; and

(2) Does not involve the acceptance of payment from any patient for services relating to his or her practice of acupuncture.

3. This chapter does not apply to a physician who is licensed pursuant to chapter 630 or 633 of NRS.

4. This chapter does not prohibit:

(a) Gratuitous services of druggists or other persons in cases of emergency.

(b) The domestic administration of family remedies.

(c) Any person from assisting any person in the practice of the healing arts licensed under this chapter, except that such person may not insert needles into the skin or prescribe herbal medicine.

5. For the purposes of this section, "accredited school of Oriental medicine" means a school that has received at least candidacy status for institutional accreditation from the Accreditation Commission for Acupuncture and Oriental Medicine, or its successor organization.

STATE BOARD OF ORIENTAL MEDICINE

NRS 634A.030 CREATION; NUMBER AND APPOINTMENT OF MEMBERS; OATHS

1. The State Board of Oriental Medicine, consisting of seven members appointed by the Governor, is hereby created.

2. Each member of the Board shall, before entering upon the duties of office, take the oath of office prescribed by the Constitution before someone qualified to administer oaths.

3. The members of the Board serve at the pleasure of the Governor.

NRS 634A.040 QUALIFICATIONS OF MEMBERS

1. The Governor shall appoint four members to the Board who:

(a) Have a license issued pursuant to this chapter;

(b) Currently engage in the practice of Oriental medicine in this State, and have engaged in the practice of Oriental medicine in this State for at least 3 years preceding appointment to the Board;

(c) Are citizens of the United States; and

(d) Are residents of the State of Nevada and have been for at least 1 year preceding appointment to the Board.

2. The Governor shall appoint one member to the Board who:

(a) Is licensed pursuant to chapter 630 of NRS by the Board of Medical Examiners as a physician;

(b) Does not engage in the administration of a facility for Oriental medicine or a school for Oriental medicine;

(c) Does not have a pecuniary interest in any matter pertaining to Oriental medicine, except as a patient or potential patient;

(d) Is a citizen of the United States; and

(e) Is a resident of the State of Nevada and has been for at least 1 year preceding appointment to the Board.

3. The Governor shall appoint one member to the Board who:

(a) Does not engage in the administration of a facility for Oriental medicine or a school for Oriental medicine;

(b) Does not have a pecuniary interest in any matter pertaining to Oriental medicine, except as a patient or potential patient;

(c) Is a citizen of the United States; and

(d) Is a resident of the State of Nevada and has been for at least 1 year preceding appointment to the Board.

4. The Governor shall appoint one member to the Board who represents a school or college of Oriental medicine whose establishment has been approved by the Board pursuant to NRS 634A.090.

NRS 634A.050 SALARY OF MEMBERS; PER DIEM ALLOWANCE AND TRAVEL EXPENSES OF MEMBERS AND EMPLOYEES

1. Each member of the Board is entitled to receive:

(a) A salary of not more than $150 per day, as fixed by the Board, while engaged in the business of the Board; and

(b) A per diem allowance and travel expenses at a rate fixed by the Board, while engaged in the business of the Board. The rate must not exceed the rate provided for state officers and employees generally.

2. While engaged in the business of the Board, each employee of the Board is entitled to receive a per diem allowance and travel expenses at a rate fixed by the Board. The rate must not exceed the rate provided for state officers and employees generally.

NRS 634A.060 OFFICERS

The Board shall annually elect from its members a President, Vice President and Secretary-Treasurer.

NRS 634A.070 EMPLOYEES; OFFICES; REGULATIONS; SUBPOENAS

The Board may:

1. Employ attorneys, investigators and other professional consultants and clerical personnel necessary to discharge its duties. To conduct its examinations, the Board may call to its aid persons of established reputation and known ability in Oriental medicine.

2. Maintain offices in as many localities in the State as it finds necessary to carry out the provisions of this chapter.

3. Adopt regulations not inconsistent with the provisions of this chapter. The regulations may include a code of ethics regulating the professional conduct of licensees.

4. Compel the attendance of witnesses and the production of evidence by subpoena.

NRS 634A.080 MEETINGS; SEAL; DEPOSIT AND USE OF MONEY RECEIVED BY BOARD; FISCAL YEAR; RECORDS

The Board shall:

1. Hold meetings at least once a year and at any other time at the request of the President or the majority of the members;

2. Have and use a common seal;

3. Deposit in interest-bearing accounts in the State of Nevada all money received under the provisions of this chapter, which must be used to defray the expenses of the Board;

4. Operate on the basis of the fiscal year beginning July 1 and ending June 30; and

5. Keep a record of its proceedings which must be open to the public at all times and which must contain the name and business address of every registered licensee in this State.

NRS 634A.083 INSPECTION OF PREMISES BY BOARD

Any member or agent of the Board may enter any premises in this State where a person who holds a license issued pursuant to the provisions of this chapter practices Oriental medicine and inspect it to determine whether a violation of any provision of this chapter has occurred, including, without limitation, an inspection to determine whether any person at the premises is practicing Oriental medicine without a license issued pursuant to the provisions of this chapter.

NRS 634A.085 DUTIES OF BOARD CONCERNING WRITTEN COMPLAINTS; ATTORNEY GENERAL MAY BE RETAINED BY BOARD TO CONDUCT INVESTIGATION OF NONFRIVOLOUS COMPLAINT; PROMPT DETERMINATION REQUIRED BY BOARD; RETENTION OF COMPLAINTS; ATTORNEY GENERAL MAY CHARGE FOR SERVICES

1. If a written complaint regarding a person who practices Oriental medicine is filed with the Board, the Board shall review the complaint. A complaint may be filed anonymously. If a complaint is filed anonymously, the Board may accept the complaint but may refuse to consider the complaint if anonymity of the complainant makes processing the complaint impossible or unfair to the person who is the subject of the complaint. If, from the complaint or from other records, it appears that the complaint is not frivolous, the Board may:

(a) Retain the Attorney General to investigate the complaint; and

(b) If the Board retains the Attorney General, transmit the original complaint and any facts or information obtained from the review to the Attorney General.

2. If the Board retains the Attorney General, the Attorney General shall conduct an investigation of the complaint transmitted to the Attorney General to determine whether it warrants proceedings for the modification, suspension or revocation of the license. If the Attorney General determines that further proceedings are warranted, the Attorney General shall report the results of the investigation and any recommendation to the Board.

3. The Board shall promptly make a determination with respect to each complaint reported to it by the Attorney General. The Board shall:

(a) Dismiss the complaint; or

(b) Proceed with appropriate disciplinary action.

4. The Board shall retain all complaints received by the Board pursuant to this section for at least 10 years, including, without limitation, any complaints not acted upon.

5. If the Board retains the Attorney General, the Attorney General may, in accordance with the provisions of NRS 228.113, charge the Board for all services relating to the investigation of a complaint pursuant to subsection 2.

NRS 634A.090 REQUIREMENTS FOR ESTABLISHMENT AND MAINTENANCE OF SCHOOLS AND COLLEGES OF ORIENTAL MEDICINE IN STATE; AUTHORITY OF BOARD TO PRESCRIBE COURSE OF STUDY REQUIRED FOR DEGREE

1. A school or college of Oriental medicine may be established and maintained in this State only if:

(a) Its establishment is approved by the Board;

(b) It is accredited by or has received at least candidacy status for institutional accreditation from the Accreditation Commission for Acupuncture and Oriental Medicine or its successor organization; and

(c) It holds a current license issued by the Commission on Postsecondary Education.

2. The Board may prescribe the course of study required for the degree of doctor of Oriental medicine.

LICENSES

NRS 634A.110　APPLICATION; FINGERPRINTS; FEES

1. An applicant for examination for a license to practice Oriental medicine, or any branch thereof, shall:

(a) Submit an application to the Board on forms provided by the Board;

(b) Submit satisfactory evidence that he or she is 21 years or older and meets the appropriate educational requirements;

(c) Submit with the application a complete set of fingerprints which the Board may forward to the Central Repository for Nevada Records of Criminal History for submission to the Federal Bureau of Investigation for its report;

(d) Pay a fee established by the Board of not more than $1,000; and

(e) Pay any fees required by the Board for an investigation of the applicant or for the services of a translator, if the translator is required to enable the applicant to take the examination.

2. An application submitted to the Board pursuant to subsection 1 must include all information required to complete the application.

NRS 634A.115　PAYMENT OF CHILD SUPPORT: SUBMISSION OF CERTAIN INFORMATION BY APPLICANT; GROUNDS FOR DENIAL OF LICENSE; DUTY OF BOARD

1. In addition to any other requirements set forth in this chapter:

(a) An applicant for the issuance of a license issued pursuant to this chapter shall include the social security number of the applicant in the application submitted to the Board.

(b) An applicant for the issuance or renewal of a license issued pursuant to this chapter shall submit to the Board the statement prescribed by the Division of Welfare and Supportive Services of the Department of Health and Human Services pursuant to NRS 425.520. The statement must be completed and signed by the applicant.

2. The Board shall include the statement required pursuant to subsection 1 in:

(a) The application or any other forms that must be submitted for the issuance or renewal of the license; or

(b) A separate form prescribed by the Board.

3. A license may not be issued or renewed by the Board pursuant to this chapter if the applicant:

(a) Fails to submit the statement required pursuant to subsection 1; or

(b) Indicates on the statement submitted pursuant to subsection 1 that the applicant is subject to a court order for the support of a child and is not in compliance with the order or a plan approved by the district attorney or other public agency enforcing the order for the repayment of the amount owed pursuant to the order.

4. If an applicant indicates on the statement submitted pursuant to subsection 1 that the applicant is subject to a court order for the support of a child and is not in compliance with the order or a plan approved by the district attorney or other public agency enforcing the order for the repayment of the amount owed pursuant to the order, the Board shall advise the applicant to contact the district attorney or other public agency enforcing the order to determine the actions that the applicant may take to satisfy the arrearage.

NRS 634A.120 EXAMINATIONS: NATIONAL EXAMINATION; EXAMINATION APPROVED BY BOARD; REGULATIONS

1. Each applicant for a license to practice as a doctor of Oriental medicine must pass:

(a) Each examination required and administered by the National Certification Commission for Acupuncture and Oriental Medicine or its successor organization for certification in Oriental medicine; and

(b) An examination approved by the Board that tests the applicant's knowledge and understanding of the laws and regulations of this State relating to health and safety in the practice of Oriental medicine.

2. The Board may establish by regulation for the examination required by paragraph(b) of subsection 1:

(a) Additional subject areas to be included in the examination; and

(b) Specific methods for the administration of the examination, including, but not limited to, written, oral, demonstrative, practical or any combination thereof.

3. The Board shall contract for the preparation, administration and grading of the examination required by paragraph(b) of subsection 1.

4. Except as otherwise provided in subsection 5, the Board shall offer the examination required by paragraph(b) of subsection 1 at least two times each year at a time and place established by the Board.

5. The Board may cancel a scheduled examination required by paragraph(b) of subsection 1 if, within 60 days before the examination, the Board has not received a request to take the examination.

6. A person who fails the examination required by paragraph(b) of subsection 1 may retake the examination.

NRS 634A.140 ISSUANCE OF LICENSE TO PRACTICE AS DOCTOR OF ORIENTAL MEDICINE

1. The Board shall issue a license to practice as a doctor of Oriental medicine to an applicant who:

(a) Has:

(1) Successfully completed an accredited 4 - year program of study, or its equivalent, in Oriental medicine at a school or college of Oriental medicine accredited by the Accreditation Commission for Acupuncture and Oriental Medicine or its successor organization that meets any requirements prescribed by the Board pursuant to NRS 634A.090, including, without limitation, requirements concerning clinical and didactic components;

(2) Earned a bachelor's degree, or completed a combined bachelor's and master's degree program in Oriental medicine, from an accredited college or university in the United States;

(3) Passed an investigation of his or her background and personal history conducted by the Board; and

(4) Passed the examinations required by NRS 634A.120; and

(b) Holds a current certification in Oriental medicine issued by the National Certification Commission for Acupuncture and Oriental Medicine or its successor organization.

2. Except as otherwise provided in subsection 3, the Board may issue a license to practice as a doctor of Oriental medicine to an applicant who:

(a) Has:

(1) Successfully completed a 4 - year program of study, or its equivalent, in Oriental medicine at a school or college of Oriental medicine that is approved by the Board and meets any requirements prescribed by the Board pursuant to NRS 634A.090, including, without limitation, requirements concerning clinical and didactic components;

(2) Lawfully practiced Oriental medicine in another state or foreign country for at least 4 years;

(3) Passed an investigation of his or her background and personal history conducted by the Board; and

(4) Passed the examinations required by NRS 634A.120; and

(b) Holds a current certification in Oriental medicine issued by the National Certification Commission for Acupuncture and Oriental Medicine or its successor organization.

3. The Board may issue a license to practice as a doctor of Oriental medicine to an applicant who:

(a) Has:

(1) Successfully completed a program in Oriental medicine from a school or college of Oriental medicine accredited by the Accreditation Commission for Acupuncture and Oriental Medicine or its successor organization before January 1 2008, that included the study of herbology;

(2) Practiced Oriental medicine pursuant to the laws of another state or territory of the

United States, the District of Columbia, or foreign country for at least 6 of the 8 years immediately preceding the date of the application;

(3) Passed an investigation of his or her background and personal history conducted by the Board; and

(4) Passed the examinations required by NRS 634A.120; and

(b) Holds a current certification in Oriental medicine issued by the National Certification Commission for Acupuncture and Oriental Medicine or its successor organization.

NRS 634A.142 ENDORSEMENT TO PRACTICE ACUPUNCTURE POINT INJECTION THERAPY

1. A doctor of Oriental medicine licensed pursuant to this chapter may apply to the Board for an endorsement to practice acupuncture point injection therapy. The applicant must submit with his or her application proof that the applicant has:

(a) Successfully completed postgraduate coursework approved by the National Certification Commission for Acupuncture and Oriental Medicine or a successor organization which provides at least 24 hours of instruction provided in person, including, without limitation, at least 8 hours of instruction received by practicum and 2 hours of training in the administration of intramuscular epinephrine; and

(b) Obtained or otherwise carries a policy of professional liability insurance which insures the applicant against any liability arising from the provision of acupuncture point injection therapy by the applicant.

2. The Board shall issue an endorsement to practice acupuncture point injection therapy to an applicant who meets the requirements of subsection 1.

3. A licensee who is issued an endorsement to practice acupuncture point injection therapy may only inject substances for which the licensee has received training which may include, without limitation, nutritional, homeopathic and herbal substances.

4. As used in this section, "acupuncture point injection therapy" means the subcutaneous, intramuscular and intradermal injection of substances to stimulate acupuncture points, ashi points and trigger points to relieve pain and prevent illness.

NRS 634A.144 REPEALED

NRS 634A.160 DISPLAY OF LICENSES

Every license must be displayed in the office, place of business or place of employment of the holder thereof.

NRS 634A.163 TEMPORARY EXEMPTION FROM LICENSURE TO PRACTICE ORIENTAL MEDICINE FOR DOCTOR OF ORIENTAL MEDICINE TO PROVIDE SERVICES TO VISITING ATHLETIC TEAM OR ATHLETIC EVENT IN THIS STATE; EXTENSION OF EXEMPTION; CONDITIONS AND LIMITATIONS

1. Except as otherwise provided in subsection 5, if a doctor of Oriental medicine who holds

a valid and unrestricted license to practice Oriental medicine in another state or territory of the United States or another country has entered into a written or oral agreement to provide services to members of a visiting athletic team or organization, the doctor of Oriental medicine is temporarily exempt from licensure and may practice Oriental medicine in this State while providing services pursuant to the agreement to members of the visiting athletic team or organization who are present in this State for the purpose of engaging in competition or training.

2. Except as otherwise provided in subsection 5, if a doctor of Oriental medicine who holds a valid and unrestricted license to practice Oriental medicine in another state or territory of the United States or another country has been invited by the governing body of a national organization to provide services to persons participating in an athletic event or training sanctioned or operated by the organization, the doctor of Oriental medicine is temporarily exempt from licensure and may practice Oriental medicine in this State while providing services to such persons.

3. Except as otherwise provided in this subsection and subsection 4, an exemption described in this section is valid for a period of not more than 10 days for each competition or training session. Upon the application of a doctor of Oriental medicine, the Board may grant an exemption of not more than 20 additional days for each competition or training session.

4. A doctor of Oriental medicine who is practicing Oriental medicine under an exemption described in this section shall not:

(a) Practice Oriental medicine at a medical facility;

(b) Provide services to persons who are not described in subsection 1 or 2, as applicable; or

(c) Practice Oriental medicine under such an exemption for more than 60 days in a calendar year.

5. The provisions of this section do not apply to any contest or exhibition of unarmed combat conducted pursuant to chapter 467 of NRS.

6. As used in this section, "visiting athletic team or organization" means an athletic team or organization which is primarily based at a location outside of this State.

NRS 634A.165 TEMPORARY CERTIFICATES FOR LECTURING OR EDUCATIONAL SEMINARS: ISSUANCE; FEE; REGULATIONS

1. The Board may adopt regulations for the issuance of temporary certificates to persons not licensed pursuant to this chapter. A temporary certificate may be issued:

(a) In connection with a bona fide educational seminar concerning Oriental medicine or acupuncture; or

(b) For the purpose of authorizing a person to engage in lecturing on or teaching Oriental medicine or acupuncture in this State on a short-term basis.

2. The Board may charge a fee for the issuance of a temporary certificate. The fee must not exceed an amount which adequately reimburses the Board for costs incurred in:

(a) Investigating an applicant under this section; and

(b) Monitoring a seminar, if the Board deems that action necessary.

NRS 634A. 167 REQUIREMENTS FOR RENEWAL; DUTY OF BOARD TO REQUIRE CONTINUING EDUCATION FOR RENEWAL OR REINSTATEMENT; AUTOMATIC EXPIRATION AND REINSTATEMENT

1. To renew a license issued pursuant to this chapter, each person must, on or before February 1 of each year:

(a) Apply to the Board for renewal;

(b) Pay the annual fee for a license prescribed by the Board, which must not exceed $1000;

(c) Submit evidence to the Board of completion of the requirements for continuing education; and

(d) Submit all information required to complete the renewal.

2. The Board shall, as a prerequisite for the renewal or reinstatement of a license, require each holder of a license to comply with the requirements for continuing education adopted by the Board.

3. If the holder of a license fails to pay the fee or submit all required information by February 1 of each year, the license expires automatically. The license may be reinstated by payment of the required fee and submission of all required information within 90 days after the expiration of the license pursuant to this subsection.

DISCIPLINARY AND OTHER ACTIONS

NRS 634A.170 SUSPENSION, REVOCATION OR REFUSAL OF LICENSE: GROUNDS

The Board may refuse to issue or may suspend or revoke any license for any one or any combination of the following causes:

1. Conviction of:

(a) A felony relating to the practice of Oriental medicine;

(b) Any offense involving moral turpitude;

(c) A violation of any state or federal law regulating the possession, distribution or use of any controlled substance, as shown by a certified copy of the record of the court; or

(d) A violation of any of the provisions of NRS 616D.200, 6 16D.220, 6 16D.240 or 6 16D.300 to 6 16D.440, inclusive;

2. The obtaining of or any attempt to obtain a license or practice in the profession for money or any other thing of value, by fraudulent misrepresentations;

3. Gross or repeated malpractice, which may be evidenced by claims of malpractice settled against a practitioner;

4. Advertising by means of a knowingly false or deceptive statement;

5. Advertising, practicing or attempting to practice under a name other than one's own;

6. Habitual drunkenness or habitual addiction to the use of a controlled substance;

7. Using any false, fraudulent or forged statement or document, or engaging in any fraudulent, deceitful, dishonest or immoral practice in connection with the licensing requirements of this chapter;

8. Sustaining a physical or mental disability which renders further practice dangerous;

9. Engaging in any dishonorable, unethical or unprofessional conduct which may deceive, defraud or harm the public, or which is unbecoming a person licensed to practice under this chapter;

10. Using any false or fraudulent statement in connection with the practice of Oriental medicine or any branch thereof;

11. Violating or attempting to violate, or assisting or abetting the violation of, or conspiring to violate any provision of this chapter;

12. Being adjudicated incompetent or insane;

13. Advertising in an unethical or unprofessional manner;

14. Obtaining a fee or financial benefit for any person by the use of fraudulent diagnosis, therapy or treatment;

15. Willful disclosure of a privileged communication;

16. Failure of a licensee to designate the nature of his or her practice in the professional use of his or her name by the term doctor of Oriental medicine;

17. Willful violation of the law relating to the health, safety or welfare of the public or of the regulations adopted by the State Board of Health;

18. Administering, dispensing or prescribing any controlled substance, except for the prevention, alleviation or cure of disease or for relief from suffering;

19. Performing, assisting or advising in the injection of any liquid silicone substance into the human body; and

20. Performing or supervising the performance of a pelvic examination in violation of section 1 of this act; and

21. Operation of a medical facility, as defined in NRS 449.0151, at any time during which:

(a) The license of the facility is suspended or revoked; or

(b) An act or omission occurs which results in the suspension or revocation of the license pursuant to NRS 449.160.

This subsection applies to an owner or other principal responsible for the operation of the facility.

NRS 634A.175 SUSPENSION OF LICENSE FOR FAILURE TO PAY CHILD SUPPORT OR COMPLY WITH CERTAIN SUBPOENAS OR WARRANTS; REINSTATEMENT OF LICENSE

1. If the Board receives a copy of a court order issued pursuant to NRS 425.540 that provides for the suspension of all professional, occupational and recreational licenses, certificates and

permits issued to a person who is the holder of a license issued pursuant to this chapter, the Board shall deem the license issued to that person to be suspended at the end of the 30th day after the date on which the court order was issued unless the Board receives a letter issued to the holder of the license by the district attorney or other public agency pursuant to NRS 425.550 stating that the holder of the license has complied with the subpoena or warrant or has satisfied the arrearage pursuant to NRS 425.560.

2. The Board shall reinstate a license issued pursuant to this chapter that has been suspended by a district court pursuant to NRS 425.540 if the Board receives a letter issued by the district attorney or other public agency pursuant to NRS 425.550 to the person whose license was suspended stating that the person whose license was suspended has complied with the subpoena or warrant or has satisfied the arrearage pursuant to NRS 425.560.

NRS 634A.180 COMMENCEMENT OF DISCIPLINARY PROCEEDINGS REQUIRED FOR CERTAIN VIOLATIONS OF INDUSTRIAL INSURANCE ACT

Notwithstanding the provisions of chapter 622A of NRS, if the Board receives a report pursuant to subsection 5 of NRS 228.420, a disciplinary proceeding regarding the report must be commenced within 30 days after the Board receives the report.

NRS 634A.185 CONFIDENTIALITY OF CERTAIN RECORDS OF BOARD; EXCEPTIONS

1. Except as otherwise provided in this section and NRS 239.0115, a complaint filed with the Board, all documents and other information filed with the complaint and all documents and other information compiled as a result of an investigation conducted to determine whether to initiate disciplinary action against a person are confidential, unless the person submits a written statement to the Board requesting that such documents and information be made public records.

2. The charging documents filed with the Board to initiate disciplinary action pursuant to chapter 622A of NRS and all documents and information considered by the Board when determining whether to impose discipline are public records.

3. An order that imposes discipline and the findings of fact and conclusions of law supporting that order are public records.

4. The Board shall, to the extent feasible, communicate or cooperate with or provide any documents or other information to any other licensing board or any other agency that is investigating a person, including, without limitation, a law enforcement agency.

MISCELLANEOUS PROVISIONS

NRS 634A.190 LICENSEES NOT SUBJECT TO CHAPTER 630 OF NRS; REFERENCE TO LICENSEE AS PHYSICIAN OF ORIENTAL MEDICINE

1. Persons licensed pursuant to this chapter are not subject to the provisions of chapter 630 of NRS.

2. A person who is licensed pursuant to this chapter to practice as a doctor of Oriental medicine may refer to himself or herself as a physician of Oriental medicine.

NRS 634A.200   634A.025 SUBSTITUTED IN REVISION FOR 634A.200
NRS 634A.210   REPORTING VITAL STATISTICS

Doctors of Oriental medicine shall observe and are subject to all state and municipal regulations relative to reporting all births and deaths in all matters pertaining to the public health.

PROHIBITED ACTS; PENALTIES; ENFORCEMENT

NRS 634A.225   SEMINARS NOT IN ACCORDANCE WITH BOARD'S REGULATIONS PROHIBITED; PENALTY

1. No seminar concerning Oriental medicine or acupuncture may be conducted in this State except in accordance with regulations prescribed by the Board for bona fide educational seminars.

2. Any person who violates subsection 1 is guilty of a misdemeanor.

NRS 634A.226   634A.083 SUBSTITUTED IN REVISION FOR 634A.226
NRS 634A.228   PRACTICING OR OFFERING TO PRACTICE WITHOUT LICENSE: REPORTING REQUIREMENTS OF BOARD

Unless the Board determines that extenuating circumstances exist, the Board shall forward to the appropriate law enforcement agency any substantiated information submitted to the Board concerning a person who practices or offers to practice Oriental medicine without a license issued pursuant to the provisions of this chapter.

NRS 634A.230   PRACTICE WITHOUT LICENSE PROHIBITED; PENALTIES

1. Any person who represents himself or herself as a practitioner of Oriental medicine, or any branch thereof, or who engages in the practice of Oriental medicine, or any branch thereof, in this State without holding a valid license issued by the Board is guilty of a gross misdemeanor, unless a greater penalty is provided pursuant to NRS 200.830 or 200.840.

2. In addition to any other penalty prescribed by law, if the Board determines that a person has committed any act described in subsection 1, the Board may:

(a) Issue and serve on the person an order to cease and desist until the person obtains from the Board the proper license or otherwise demonstrates that he or she is no longer in violation of subsection 1. An order to cease and desist must include a telephone number with which the person may contact the Board.

(b) Issue a citation to the person. A citation issued pursuant to this paragraph must be in writing, describe with particularity the nature of the violation and inform the person of the provisions of this paragraph. Each activity in which the person is engaged constitutes a separate offense for which a separate citation may be issued. To appeal a citation, the person must submit a written request for a hearing to the Board not later than 30 days after the date of issuance of the citation.

(c) Assess against the person an administrative fine as provided in NRS 634A.250.

(d) Impose any combination of the penalties set forth in paragraphs(a),(b) and(c).

NRS 634A.240　Injunctive relief.

1. The Board may maintain in any court of competent jurisdiction a suit for an injunction against any person who violates any provision of this chapter.

2. Such an injunction:

(a) May be issued without proof of actual damage sustained by any person, this provision being understood to be a preventive as well as a punitive measure.

(b) Shall not relieve such person from any criminal prosecution for the violation.

NRS 634A.250　ADMINISTRATIVE FINES

In addition to any other penalties prescribed by law, the Board may, after notice and a hearing, as required by law, impose upon any person who violates any provision of this chapter or the regulations adopted pursuant thereto an administrative fine of not more than $2500.

NEVADA ADMINISTRATIVE CODE

NAC 634A.001

634A.001　DEFINITIONS

As used in this chapter, unless the context otherwise requires, the words and terms defined in NAC 634A.002 to 634A.008, inclusive, have the meanings ascribed to them in those sections.

NAC 634A.002

634A.002　"BOARD" DEFINED

"Board" means the State Board of Oriental Medicine.

NAC 634A.003

634A.003　"DOCTOR OF ORIENTAL MEDICINE" DEFINED

"Doctor of Oriental medicine" means a person who is licensed pursuant to chapter 634A of NRS to practice as a doctor of Oriental medicine.

NAC 634A.004

634A.004　"EXECUTIVE DIRECTOR" DEFINED

"Executive Director" means the Executive Director of the Board.

NAC 634A.007

634A.007　"Licensee" defined

"Licensee" means a doctor of Oriental medicine.

NAC 634A.008

634A.008　"ORIENTAL MEDICINE" DEFINED

"Oriental medicine" has the meaning ascribed to it in NRS 634A.020.

NAC 634A.010

634A.010 EXECUTIVE DIRECTOR; PRINCIPAL OFFICE

1. The Board will designate a person to act as Executive Director of the Board.

2. The principal office of the Board is the office of that person designated as the Executive Director.

NAC 634A.020

634A.020 MEETINGS

Regular meetings of the Board will be held at its principal office or such other place as the Board may specify, and at such times as the Board may designate.

NAC 634A.025

634A.025 RESTRICTIONS ON SALARIES OF OFFICERS

The President, Vice President and Secretary-Treasurer of the Board are not entitled to receive a salary other than, or in addition to, that which is authorized and fixed by the Board for each member thereof pursuant to NRS 634A.050. The Board will not pay any salary pursuant to NRS 634A.060.

NAC 634A.035

634A.035 APPROVAL OF CURRICULUM OF PROGRAM OF STUDY OF SCHOOL OR COLLEGE OF ORIENTAL MEDICINE

For the purposes of paragraph (b) of subsection 1 of NRS 634A.090, the Board will approve the curriculum of a program of study of a school or college of Oriental medicine if the school or college submits to the Board proof of payment of annual sustaining accreditation or pre-accreditation dues for that program of study to the Accreditation Commission for Acupuncture and Oriental Medicine or its successor organization. No other review of the curriculum by the Board will be deemed necessary.

NAC 634A.071

634A.071 APPLICATION: GENERAL REQUIREMENTS

1. A person who desires to be licensed by the Board as a doctor of Oriental medicine must, at least 3 months before the date of the practical examination in which the person wishes to participate:

(a) File an application with the Executive Director;

(b) Pay to the Board at the time of filing his or her application any applicable fees set forth in NAC 634A.165; and

(c) Submit any other documentation or proof that the Board may require.

2. The application must be:

(a) Made on the form provided by the Board; and

(b) Typed or written in English.

3. The application must include:

(a) The social security number of the applicant;

(b) A set of the fingerprints of the applicant, together with written consent for the Board to submit the fingerprints to any law enforcement agency in connection with his or her application;

(c) Written consent of the applicant to an investigation of his or her personal background, professional training and experience by the Board or any person acting on its behalf; and

(d) Evidence that the applicant possesses the qualifications required pursuant to this chapter and chapter 634A of NRS for licensure as a doctor of Oriental medicine.

NAC 634A.075

634A.075 APPLICATION: REJECTION BY BOARD

1. The Board may reject an application for licensure as a doctor of Oriental medicine if it appears that:

(a) The applicant is not qualified for licensure or is not of good moral character or reputation;

(b) Any credential submitted is false;

(c) The application is not made in proper form or other deficiencies appear in it; or

(d) The application is not completed within 6 months.

2. The Board will reject an application if the applicant's check to pay any applicable fees is returned for insufficient funds.

NAC 634A.080

634A.080 EVIDENCE OF QUALIFICATIONS OF APPLICANT; APPROVAL OF PROGRAM OF STUDY

1. An applicant for a license to practice Oriental medicine must submit, together with his or her application, evidence that he or she has successfully completed a 4 – year program of study, or its equivalent, in Oriental medicine at a school or college of Oriental medicine which is approved by the Board.

2. If the application is submitted pursuant to subsection 1 of NRS 634A.140, the applicant must submit evidence showing that he or she has earned a bachelor's degree from an accredited college or university in the United States.

3. If the application for licensure by endorsement is submitted pursuant to subsection 2 of NRS 634A.140, the applicant must submit evidence that he or she:

(a) Has lawfully practiced Oriental medicine in another state or foreign country for at least 4 years; and

(b) Holds Oriental Medicine Certification by the National Certification Commission for Acupuncture and Oriental Medicine or its successor organization.

4. For the purposes of subsection 1, the Board may approve a 4 – year program of study, or its equivalent, in Oriental medicine at a school or college of Oriental medicine if the Board finds that:

(a) The school or college of Oriental medicine is:

(1) Accredited by the Accreditation Commission for Acupuncture and Oriental Medicine or its successor organization; or

(2) In pre-accreditation status with the Accreditation Commission for Acupuncture and Oriental Medicine or its successor organization and satisfies the requirements of paragraph(b).

(b) The program of study includes training or instruction in the subjects of acupuncture, moxibustion, herbology, Oriental physiology, Oriental pathology, Oriental diagnosis, tuina or qigong, biology, chemistry or biochemistry, anatomy, Western physiology, Western pathology, Western diagnosis, pharmacology, laboratory and radiology.

(c) The program of study:

(1) Required the completion of at least 2,800 hours of instruction, including not less than 2,500 didactic hours, for a student to have graduated before November 25, 2002; or

(2) Requires the completion of at least 3,000 hours of instruction, including not less than 2,500 didactic hours, for a student to graduate on or after November 25, 2002.

5. For the purposes of subsection 1, the Board will deem a master's degree to be the equivalent of a 4 - year program of study if the program of study for the degree conforms to the requirements of paragraphs (b) and (c) of subsection 4.

6. For the purposes of subsections 2 and 3, evidence that the applicant is qualified for licensure as a doctor of Oriental medicine must include certified copies of any diplomas, transcripts, licenses and certificates issued to the applicant. If possible, all certified copies of official diplomas, transcripts, licenses or certificates must be forwarded directly to the Executive Director from the issuing entity rather than from the applicant.

NAC 634A.085

634A.085 COMPLIANCE WITH REQUIREMENT OF PASSING EXAMINATION ADMINISTERED BY NATIONAL ORGANIZATION

To comply with the requirement of passing an examination in Oriental medicine that is administered by a national organization approved by the Board pursuant to NRS 634A.120, an applicant for licensure as a doctor of Oriental medicine must:

1. Have passed the examinations for Oriental Medicine Certification administered by the National Certification Commission for Acupuncture and Oriental Medicine or its successor organization within the 12 months preceding the date of application for licensure; or

2. Be certified by the National Certification Commission for Acupuncture and Oriental Medicine or its successor organization.

NAC 634A.090

634A.090 INVESTIGATION OF APPLICANT: PREREQUISITE TO PRACTICAL EXAMINATION

1. An investigation of an applicant's background and training by the Board or any person acting on its behalf must include:

(a) Verification of a report from the Federal Bureau of Investigation showing no prior convictions;

(b) Verification of graduation from a school or college approved by the Board;

(c) Verification of licensure in another state or country, if applicable;

(d) Verification that questions on the application relating to the applicant's background have been answered correctly; and

(e) Further investigation of an applicant who attended a foreign school or college or practiced Oriental medicine in another state or country as the circumstances warrant.

2. An applicant may not take the practical examination for which he or she has applied before the investigation of his or her background and training has been completed.

NAC 634A.095

634A.095 PROFICIENCY OF APPLICANT IN ENGLISH LANGUAGE

1. Except as otherwise provided in subsection 2, an applicant for a license to practice Oriental medicine must:

(a) Before taking the practical examination:

(1) Pass the Test of English as a Foreign Language Paper-Based Test with a score of at least 550; or

(2) Pass the Test of English as a Foreign Language Internet-Based Test with a total score of at least 80; and

(b) At the time of the practical examination, demonstrate a reasonable proficiency in the English language through an oral interview.

2. Subsection 1 does not apply to an applicant who graduated from a high school or college in the United States.

NAC 634A.100

634A.100 PRACTICAL EXAMINATION OF APPLICANT; SUBJECTS INCLUDED IN EXAMINATION

1. Until such time as the Board implements a process for administering a practical examination online:

(a) The practical examination will be given in June and December of each year.

(b) An applicant may not take the practical examination unless the applicant has first passed the examinations required pursuant to NAC 634A.085. The Executive Director shall notify an applicant of the time and place of the practical examination not later than 20 days before the date on which the practical examination is scheduled.

(c) During the practical examination, only the testing consultant and the applicants will be allowed in the examination rooms.

2. Upon the implementation of a process for administering the practical examination online:

(a) Examinations will be offered at times and places established by the Board but at least two times each year in accordance with NRS 634A.120.

(b) The Board will notify an applicant of his or her eligibility to take the practical examination online. Not later than 90 days after notification by the Board, the applicant must take the examination online at the facility that is designated by the Board.

3. As a part of the practical examination, the Board may examine an applicant as to his or her basic knowledge of the following subjects:

(a) Basic medical science concerning anatomy, physiology, pathology, bacteriology and communicable diseases.

(b) The Clean Needle Technique, as presented in the current guidelines of the Clean Needle Technique course administered by the Council of Colleges of Acupuncture and Oriental Medicine.

(c) Oriental medicine theory, herbology and acupuncture.

(d) Oriental herb safety and herb-drug interactions.

(e) Applicable laws and regulations pertaining to health and safety.

4. The practical examination will be given in written form. Each applicant shall take the examination in the English language.

5. An applicant must receive an overall score of 70 percent on the practical examination and 65 percent on each of its sections or subparts to pass the examination.

NAC 634A.105

634A.105 DISCLOSURE OF CERTAIN RELATIONSHIPS BETWEEN MEMBER OF BOARD AND APPLICANT

No member of the Board may participate in preparing, examining or grading an examination or in any other decision made with respect to an applicant to whom the member is related within the third degree of consanguinity or affinity or with whom the member has a significant pecuniary relationship. Information regarding such a relationship must be disclosed by the Board member and applicant at the time of application.

NAC 634A.110

634A.110 REEXAMINATION OF APPLICANT WHO FAILS PRACTICAL EXAMINATION

1. An applicant for a license to practice Oriental medicine who fails the practical examination may retake the examination on the next scheduled examination date. A person seeking reexamination must notify the Executive Director by completing a form prescribed by the Board and submitting the fee set forth in NAC 634A.165.

2. If an applicant who has failed the practical examination failed only one section of the practical examination, the applicant will be reexamined only with respect to the section that he or she failed. If the applicant failed two or more sections of the practical examination, he or she must repeat the entire practical examination at the time of reexamination.

NAC 634A.116

634A.116 LICENSE ISSUED TO ALIEN: INACTIVE STATUS; REQUIRED STATEMENT

1. A license issued to an alien automatically transfers to inactive status if he or she loses his or her entitlement to remain and work in the United States.

2. A license issued to an alien after June 17, 2008, must state in a conspicuous manner:

This license is issued subject to any limitations imposed by the United States Citizenship and Immigration Services of the Department of Homeland Security. This license becomes inactive immediately upon the termination of the right of the person named herein to remain and work in the United States lawfully.

NAC 634A.121

634A.121 PRACTICE UNDER FICTITIOUS NAME; PROHIBITION AGAINST MULTIPLE LICENSES AND REGISTRATION UNDER SAME NAME

1. A licensee shall not operate under a fictitious name unless the licensee complies with chapter 602 of NRS and files with the Board a certified copy of the certificates issued by the county clerk.

2. Any licensee who wishes to practice under a fictitious name must submit to the Board an application, on a form provided by the Board, accompanied by a fee of $50.

3. The Board will not issue more than one license or register more than one licensee under the same name.

NAC 634A.125

634A.125 ISSUANCE OF TEMPORARY CERTIFICATE FOR SEMINAR, LECTURE OR TEACHING

A person who is not a licensee may be issued a temporary certificate pursuant to NRS 634A.165 if:

1. The person submits an application to the Board, on a form provided by the Board, that includes:

(a) The curriculum vitae of the applicant;

(b) The specific topic concerning Oriental medicine or acupuncture which is the subject of the seminar, lecture or teaching;

(c) The specific dates for which the temporary certificate is requested; and

(d) Evidence that the person is competent with respect to the specific topic concerning Oriental medicine or acupuncture which is the subject of the seminar, lecture or teaching;

2. The person submits the appropriate fee for issuance of a temporary certificate pursuant to NAC 634A.165; and

3. The Board approves the application at a meeting of the Board.

NAC 634A.130

634A.130 POCKET LICENSE

1. At the time a license is issued and on each renewal thereof, a pocket license bearing the expiration date of the license or renewal will be issued to each licensee, and the licensee shall keep the pocket license in his or her possession at all times during the performance of his or her professional services.

2. At the request of any patient or prospective patient, any member of the Board or any peace officer, the licensee shall permit the pocket license to be inspected for the purpose of identification and as proof that all current fees have been paid.

NAC 634A.133

634A.133 HOLDER OF LICENSE ISSUED AFTER DECEMBER 31, 2018, REQUIRED TO MAINTAIN NATIONAL CERTIFICATION; PROOF OF CERTIFICATION

Each holder of a new license that is first issued after December 31, 2018, including, without limitation, a holder of a license by endorsement issued pursuant to subsection 2 of NRS 634A.140, shall:

1. Maintain Oriental Medicine Certification by the National Certification Commission for Acupuncture and Oriental Medicine or its successor organization; and

2. Provide proof of that certification to the Executive Director upon:

(a) Certification;

(b) Recertification; and

(c) The change of classification of his or her license from inactive status to active status.

NAC 634A.135

634A.135 CONTINUING EDUCATION; PLACEMENT OF LICENSE ON INACTIVE STATUS; REINSTATEMENT TO ACTIVE STATUS

1. Except as otherwise provided in this section, a licensee shall complete, during each calendar year, at least 10 hours of continuing education.

2. A licensee may only receive credit for hours of continuing education in courses that have been approved by the Board pursuant to NAC 634A.137.

3. Beginning with the 2003 calendar year, a licensee who earns more than 10 hours of credit for continuing education in any calendar year may carry forward up to 10 hours of excess credit and apply such excess credit to the educational requirements for the next calendar year if the licensee indicates in writing, at the time he or she submits the form for renewal of his or her license pursuant to NRS 634A.167, that the licensee intends to carry forward such excess credit.

4. A licensee who is not practicing in this State may request the Board to classify his or her license as inactive. A person who holds an inactive license is exempt from the requirements set forth in this section regarding continuing education.

5. A person who is requesting the Board to change the classification of his or her license

from inactive to active must:

(a) Satisfy the requirements of continuing education for the year in which the person seeks to reclassify his or her license;

(b) Submit proof to the Board that the person has satisfied the applicable requirements; and

(c) Submit the fee set forth in NAC 634A.165.

NAC 634A.137

634A.137 APPROVAL OF COURSES OF CONTINUING EDUCATION; APPLICATION; EXCEPTION FROM APPROVAL AND EXEMPTION FROM FEES FOR CERTAIN COURSES; EXPIRATION OF APPROVAL

1. Except as otherwise provided in subsection 2, a person or entity shall not offer a course of continuing education for licensees in this State unless the person or entity has first obtained approval for the course from the Board pursuant to this section.

2. Courses in the core competency of Acupuncture and Oriental Medicine and Biomedicine (AOM-BIO) which are approved for recertification by the National Certification Commission for Acupuncture and Oriental Medicine may be offered as courses of continuing education for licensees in this State without approval from the Board and are exempt from the imposition of fees for approval of courses of continuing education pursuant to NAC 634A.165.

3. A person or entity may apply for approval of a course of continuing education by submitting to the Board:

(a) An application, on a form provided by the Board, which must include information indicating the specific subject or topics to be presented and the name of each proposed instructor;

(b) All material relating to the course, including, without limitation, written material to be provided to a licensee attending the course; and

(c) The fee required pursuant to NAC 634A.165.

4. If the Board approves a course of continuing education pursuant to this section, the Board will determine the number of hours of continuing education that a licensee may receive for attending the course.

5. Board approval of a course of continuing education other than a course described in subsection 2 expires 4 years after that approval.

NAC 634A.140

634A.140 PAYMENT OF ANNUAL RENEWAL FEE; PRORATION OF FEE FOR FIRST RENEWAL

Except as otherwise provided in this section, each person who holds an active or inactive license to practice Oriental medicine shall pay to the Board an annual fee for the renewal of the license as required by NAC 634A.165. The Board will prorate by month the annual fee for the first renewal of an active or inactive license to practice Oriental medicine.

NAC 634A.150

634A.150 REINSTATEMENT OF LICENSE CANCELLED FOR FAILURE TO PAY ANNUAL FEE; REAPPLICATION FOR NEW LICENSE

1. Any person whose license has been cancelled pursuant to NRS 634A.160 and who desires to reinstate his or her license may have the license reinstated if:

(a) Not later than 1 year after the date on which the license was cancelled:

(1) The person submits to the Board all required fees for the period during which his or her license was cancelled, plus any late fee set forth in NAC 634A.165; and

(2) The person submits proof of compliance with the applicable requirements concerning continuing education; and

(b) The Board reinstates the license of the person at a regularly scheduled meeting.

2. Any person whose license has been cancelled pursuant to NRS 634A.160, who fails to comply with the requirements of paragraph(a) of subsection 1 and who desires a license must reapply for a new license.

NAC 634A.160

634A.160 SURRENDER OF LICENSE AND POCKET LICENSE WHEN SUSPENDED OR REVOKED; REPLACEMENT OF LOST, STOLEN OR DESTROYED LICENSE OR POCKET LICENSE

1. If a license is revoked, the license and the pocket license previously issued by the Board must be surrendered by the licensee to the Executive Director within 5 days after receipt of a notice of revocation.

2. If a license is suspended for a fixed period, the license and pocket license previously issued by the Board must be surrendered by the licensee to the Executive Director within 5 days after receipt of a notice of suspension.

3. If a license or pocket license must be surrendered pursuant to subsection 1 or 2 but has been lost, stolen or destroyed, the licensee must complete and file an affidavit with the Board stating that the license or pocket license has been lost, stolen or destroyed and that the licensee will immediately return the license or pocket license if it is later recovered by the licensee.

4. If the license or pocket license of a licensee is lost, stolen or destroyed, the licensee must:

(a) Complete and file an affidavit with the Board stating that the license or pocket license has been lost, stolen or destroyed and that the licensee will immediately return the license or pocket license if it is later recovered by the licensee; and

(b) Pay the fee set forth in NAC 634A.165 for replacement of the license or pocket license.

NAC 634A.165

634A.165 FEES OF BOARD

The Board will charge and collect the following fees:

Original application for licensure as a doctor of Oriental medicine	$1,000.00
Renewal of active license before February 1	700.00
Renewal of inactive license before February 1	500.00
Penalty for late renewal of license within 90 days after February 1	100.00
Penalty for late renewal of license more than 90 days after February 1	200.00
Penalty for reinstatement of cancelled license	200.00
Original application for use of fictitious name	100.00
Replacement of pocket license	100.00
Replacement of license	200.00
Original fee for practical examination	1,000.00
Reexamination fee for practical examination	500.00
Transfer of license from active status to inactive status	200.00
Transfer of license from inactive status to active status	500.00
Approval of course of continuing education	100.00
Temporary certificate for lecturing or training	100.00
Check returned for insufficient funds	25.00
For copies of this chapter and chapter 634A of NRS	10.00
For other copies, per page	0.25
For other copies, per compact disc or tape recording	20.00
Original application fee for a school or college of Oriental medicine	2,000.00
Annual fee for approval of curriculum before February 1	1,000.00

NAC 634A.170

634A.170 GROUNDS FOR DISCIPLINARY ACTION

The Board considers the following acts to be unethical and unprofessional conduct warranting appropriate disciplinary action:

1. The division or "splitting" of fees with another licensee, unless the other licensee has actually rendered services, other than referral, to the first licensee in connection with one or more of his or her patients. A person licensed by this Board shall not:

(a) Employ another to solicit or obtain, or remunerate another for soliciting or obtaining, professional employment for the licensee.

(b) Directly or indirectly share with an unlicensed person any compensation arising out of or incidental to professional employment.

(c) Directly or indirectly aid or abet an unlicensed person to practice Oriental medicine, acupuncture or herbal medicine or to receive compensation therefrom.

2. The use of any paid testimonial to solicit or encourage use of the licensee's services by members of the public.

3. The making or publishing, or causing to be made or published, any advertisement, offer,

statement or other form of representation, oral or written, which directly or by implication is false, misleading or deceptive. It is sufficient in bringing any proceeding for violation of this subsection that any advertising of the type referred to has a tendency to deceive, mislead or be harmful to the public even though no member of the public is actually deceived, misled or harmed by the advertising. As used in this subsection, "advertisement" includes, without limitation:

(a) Any calling card, indoor or outdoor sign, stationery, or listing in a telephone directory or other directory;

(b) Any advertisement in a newspaper or magazine; and

(c) Any advertisement made through electronic means, including, without limitation, an advertisement placed on the Internet.

4. The use of any fictitious name that has not been approved by the Board.

NAC 634A.210

634A.210 SCOPE, CONSTRUCTION AND APPLICATION OF REGULATIONS

1. The provisions of NAC 634A.210 to 634A.570, inclusive, govern all practice and procedure before the Board unless otherwise directed by the Board.

2. The provisions of NAC 634A.210 to 634A.570, inclusive, will be liberally construed to secure a just, speedy and economical determination of all issues presented to the Board.

3. If any provision of NAC 634A.210 to 634A.570, inclusive, or any application thereof to any person, thing or circumstance is held invalid, the Board intends that such invalidity will not affect the remaining provisions, or their application, that may be given effect without the invalid provision or application.

NAC 634A.220

634A.220 COMMUNICATIONS

All formal written communications and documents must be addressed to the State Board of Oriental Medicine and not to individual members of the Board or its staff.

NAC 634A.230

634A.230 PAYMENT OF FEES AND REMITTANCES; REFUND OF APPLICATION FEE

1. Fees and remittances must be paid to the Board by money order, bank draft or check payable to "State Board of Oriental Medicine." Remittances in currency or coin are wholly at the risk of the remitter and the Board assumes no responsibility for their loss. Postage stamps will not be remitted.

2. The Board will not refund any part of the application fee to an applicant if the applicant:

(a) Does not complete his or her application by providing all the documentation required by the form for application within 6 months after the actual date of filing of the form by the applicant;

(b) Withdraws his or her application; or

(c) Dies before he or she is issued a license by the Board.

NAC 634A.240

634A.240 COMPUTATION OF TIME

The time within which any act must be done, as authorized by NAC 634A.210 to 634A.570, inclusive, will be computed by excluding the first day and including the last day unless it is Saturday, Sunday or a legal holiday, and then it is excluded and the time is extended to the next regular business day.

NAC 634A.245

634A.245 REQUEST FOR BOARD TO CONSIDER OR TAKE ACTION UPON MATTER AT MEETING

A request for the Board to consider or take action upon a matter at a meeting must be received by the Board at least 15 business days before the date of the meeting.

NAC 634A.250

634A.250 REQUEST FOR ADDITIONAL INFORMATION FROM BOARD

Additional information with reference to proceedings before the Board or the status of any matter may be secured by applying to the Executive Director at the principal office of the Board.

NAC 634A.260

634A.260 CLASSIFICATION OF PARTIES

1. A party to a proceeding before the Board must be styled an applicant, petitioner, complainant, respondent, intervener or interested party according to the nature of the proceeding and the relationship of the party thereto.

2. Persons applying or petitioning for any right or authority from the Board must be styled the "applicants".

3. Persons petitioning for affirmative relief (other than complainants) must be styled the "petitioners".

4. Persons who complain to the Board of any act or of any persons must be styled the "complainants". In any proceeding which the Board brings on its own motion, it will be styled the "complainant".

5. Persons against whom any complaint is filed or investigation initiated must be styled the "respondents".

6. Persons, other than the original parties to the proceeding, who may be directly and substantially affected by the proceeding, must, upon securing an order from the Board or the presiding officer granting leave to intervene, be styled the "interveners". The granting of leave to intervene, or otherwise appear, in any matter or proceeding is not a finding or determination of the Board that the party will or may be a party aggrieved by any ruling, order or decision of the Board, for the purposes of court review or appeal.

7. Persons who believe they may be affected by a proceeding, but who do not seek to

participate in the proceeding, must be styled the "interested parties".

NAC 634A.270
634A.270 STAFF OF BOARD MAY BE PARTY TO PROCEEDING

The Board's staff may appear at any hearing and has the right to participate as a party to the proceeding.

NAC 634A.280
634A.280 RIGHTS OF PARTIES

At any hearing, all parties named in NAC 634A.260, except interested parties, may enter an appearance, introduce evidence, examine and cross-examine witnesses, make arguments and generally participate in the conduct of the proceeding. Interested parties may be acknowledged to state their possible interest.

NAC 634A.290
634A.290 APPEARANCES

Parties shall enter their appearances at the beginning of a hearing, or at any time as may be designated by the presiding officer, by giving their names and addresses and stating their positions or interests to the presiding officer. This information will be recorded in the transcript of the hearing.

NAC 634A.300
634A.300 REPRESENTATION OF PARTIES; QUALIFICATIONS OF ATTORNEYS

1. A party may be heard in person or by his or her designated attorney or other representative.

2. An attorney appearing as counsel in any proceeding must be an attorney at law, admitted to practice and in good standing before the highest court of any state. If the attorney is not admitted and entitled to practice before the Supreme Court of Nevada, an attorney so admitted and entitled to practice must be associated.

NAC 634A.310
634A.310 SERVICE OF PROCESS ON ATTORNEY

Following the entry of an appearance by an attorney for a party, all notices, pleadings and orders thereafter served must be served upon the attorney. The service will be considered a valid service for all purposes upon the party represented.

NAC 634A.320
634A.320 WITHDRAWAL OF ATTORNEY

Any attorney of record wishing to withdraw from a proceeding before the Board must, in writing, immediately notify the Board or the presiding officer, the party whom he or she represented, and any other parties to the proceeding.

NAC 634A.330
634A.330 CONDUCT REQUIRED

A person appearing at any proceeding before the Board shall conform to the recognized standards of ethical and courteous conduct.

NAC 634A.340

634A.340 CAPTIONS, AMENDMENTS AND CONSTRUCTION OF PLEADINGS

1. Pleadings before the Board must be styled applications, petitions, complaints and answers.

2. All pleadings, except complaints brought on the Board's own motion, must be verified.

3. The Board may, when substantial rights of the parties are not violated thereby, allow any pleading to be amended or corrected or any omission therein to be supplied.

4. All pleadings will be liberally construed to effect justice between the parties, and the Board or the presiding officer will, at every stage of any proceeding, disregard errors or defects in the pleadings or proceedings which do not affect the substantial rights of the parties.

NAC 634A.350

634A.350 APPLICATIONS

1. All pleadings requesting a privilege, license or authority from the Board must be styled "Applications".

2. An application must set forth the full name and address of the applicant and must be signed by the applicant.

NAC 634A.360

634A.360 PETITIONS

1. All pleadings praying for affirmative relief (other than applications, complaints, or answers), including requests for declaratory orders, advisory opinions, and requests for the adoption, filing, amendment or repeal of any regulation, must be styled "Petitions".

2. All petitions must set forth the full name and address of the petitioner and must be signed by the petitioner.

NAC 634A.370

634A.370 COMPLAINTS; NOTIFICATION OF RESPONDENTS; USE OF EVIDENCE OBTAINED AFTER NOTIFICATION

1. Upon the initiative of any interested person, or upon the initiative of any member of the Board, a complaint may be made alleging one or more causes of action based on chapter 634A of NRS.

2. Two or more complainants may join in one complaint if their respective causes of action are against the same person and deal with substantially the same violation of a law, regulation or order of the Board.

3. Every complaint must be in writing and must be filed with the Executive Director of the Board.

4. Complaints will be set for hearing at the earliest convenience of the Board, unless notice of satisfaction of the complaint, by answer or otherwise, is received by the Board.

5. At least 30 days before the date set for the hearing, the Board will notify the respondent

of the date, time and place of the hearing and, together with the notice, provide the respondent with a copy of the complaint and copies of all communications, reports, affidavits or depositions in possession of the Board relevant to the complaint. Evidence obtained after the date on which the notice and copies of relevant material were provided to the respondent pursuant to this subsection may not be presented to the Board unless it is shown that the evidence was not available upon diligent investigation before that date and that the evidence was given or communicated to the respondent immediately after it was obtained.

NAC 634A.380

634A.380 ANSWERS; ENTRY OF DEFAULT UPON FAILURE TO FILE

1. The respondent shall file an answer within 20 days after service of the notice and relevant material pursuant to subsection 5 of NAC 634A.370. The answer must contain an admission or denial of each of the averments contained in the complaint and any defenses upon which the respondent will rely.

2. The answer may be served by personal delivery to the Board at its principal office or by certified mail to the principal office of the Board.

3. Upon the presentation of evidence that the respondent received notice of the complaint and hearing and has not filed an answer within the time prescribed pursuant to this section, the respondent's default may be entered and a decision may be issued based upon the allegations of the complaint.

NAC 634A.390

634A.390 MOTIONS: CONTENTS; OPPOSITION; REPLY; ORAL ARGUMENT

1. A motion is a proceeding directed at the Board's authority to act on a given subject.

2. All motions, unless made during a hearing, must be in writing.

3. All written motions must set forth the nature of the relief which is sought, and the grounds therefor.

4. A party desiring to oppose a motion may serve and file a written response to the motion within 10 days of receipt of the motion.

5. The moving party may serve and file a written reply within 5 days only if an opposition to the motion has been served and filed.

6. A decision on a motion will be rendered without oral argument unless oral argument is requested by the Board. If so requested, the Board will set a date and time for a hearing.

NAC 634A.400

634A.400 FILING

An original and two legible copies of all pleadings, motions or other papers must be filed with the Board. The Board may direct that a copy of a pleading be made available by the party filing it to any other person whom the Board determines may be affected by the proceeding and who desires a copy of the pleading.

NAC 634A.410

634A.410 SERVICE OF PROCESS

Except as otherwise provided by specific statute or regulation, all notices, opinions and documents required to be served by the Board, other than decisions or orders, and all documents filed by any party must be served in accordance with the provisions of Rule 4 of the Nevada Rules of Civil Procedure.

NAC 634A.430

634A.430 HEARINGS HELD BEFORE BOARD: LOCATION; NOTICE

1. Hearings will be held at such place in the State as is designated by the Board in the notice of the hearing.

2. A hearing which has previously been continued may be reset on notice of at least 10 days.

NAC 634A.440

634A.440 CONTINUANCES

1. The Board may, before a hearing or during a hearing, on a proper showing of good faith, grant a request for a continuance for the submission of further or additional proof of any subject that is relevant to the hearing.

2. A request for a continuance before a hearing must be received within 7 business days before the date scheduled for the hearing.

NAC 634A.450

634A.450 FAILURE OF PARTY TO APPEAR

1. If a party fails to appear at a hearing scheduled by the Board and no continuance has been requested or granted, the Board may hear the evidence of such witnesses as may have appeared and the Board may proceed to consider the matter and dispose of it on the basis of the evidence before it.

2. If, because of accident, sickness or other reasonable cause, a person fails to appear for a hearing scheduled by the Board or fails to request a continuance thereof, the person may, within a reasonable period of time not to exceed 15 days, apply to the Executive Director to reopen the proceedings, and the Board, upon finding such cause sufficient and reasonable, will immediately fix a time and place for a hearing and give the person notice thereof. At the time and place fixed, the person may testify in his or her own behalf or present such other evidence as may be beneficial to his or her cause. Witnesses who have previously testified are not required to appear at the second hearing unless so directed by the Board.

NAC 634A.460

634A.460 SUBPOENAS

1. Subpoenas requiring the attendance of a witness at a hearing may be issued by the Board upon application in writing.

2. Subpoenas for the production of documents, books or other records, unless issued by the Board on its own motion, will be issued only upon application in writing. The application must specify, as clearly as possible, the documents, books or other records desired.

3. The Board, at or before the time specified in the subpoena for compliance therewith, may:

(a) Quash the subpoena if it is unreasonable or oppressive; or

(b) Condition denial of a motion upon the advancement by the person in whose behalf the subpoena is issued of the reasonable cost of producing the documents, books or other records desired.

NAC 634A.470

634A.470　TESTIMONY MUST BE UNDER OATH

All testimony to be considered by the Board in a formal hearing, except matters noticed officially or entered by stipulation, must be sworn testimony. Before taking the witness stand, each person shall swear(or affirm) that the testimony he or she is about to give in the hearing is the truth, the whole truth and nothing but the truth.

NAC 634A.480

634A.480　PRELIMINARY PROCEDURE

The presiding member of the Board shall call the proceeding or hearing to order and proceed to take the appearances and act upon any pending motions. The parties may then make opening statements.

NAC 634A.490

634A.490　PRESENTATION OF EVIDENCE

1. Applicants, petitioners or complainants may present their evidence and then such parties as may be opposing the application, petition or complaint, may submit their proof. The presiding member of the Board shall determine the order in which any intervener may introduce his or her evidence. Evidence will ordinarily be received from the parties in the following order:

(a) Upon applications and petitions:

(1) Applicant or petitioner;

(2) Board's staff;

(3) Intervener; and

(4) Rebuttal by the applicant or the petitioner.

(b) Upon complaints:

(1) Complainant;

(2) Respondent;

(3) Board's staff; and

(4) Rebuttal by the complainant.

(c) Upon complaints by the Board:

(1) Board;

(2) Respondent; and

(3) Rebuttal by the Board's staff.

2. This procedure may be modified at the discretion of the Board or the presiding member.

3. Closing statements by the parties may be allowed at the discretion of the Board or the presiding member.

NAC 634A.500

634A.500 CONSOLIDATION

1. The Board may consolidate two or more proceedings in any one hearing when it appears that the issues are substantially the same and that the interests of the parties will not be prejudiced by the consolidation.

2. At any consolidated hearing, the presiding member of the Board shall determine the order in which all the parties may introduce their evidence and which party or parties may open and close.

NAC 634A.510

634A.510 STIPULATIONS

1. With the approval of the presiding member of the Board, the parties may stipulate as to any fact at issue, either by written stipulation introduced in evidence as an exhibit or by oral statements shown upon the record.

2. Any stipulation is binding upon all parties so stipulating and may be regarded by the Board as evidence at the hearing. The Board may require proof by evidence of the facts stipulated to, notwithstanding the stipulation of the parties.

NAC 634A.520

634A.520 OFFICIAL NOTICE OF BOARD

The Board may take official notice of judicially cognizable facts and of recognized technical or scientific facts within the Board's specialized knowledge, including:

1. Regulations, official reports, decisions and orders of the Board or any other regulatory agency of this State.

2. The Nevada Revised Statutes.

3. Certificates and permits issued by the Board.

4. Matters of common knowledge and technical or scientific facts of established character.

5. Official documents, if:

(a) The documents are pertinent and properly introduced into the record by reference;

(b) Proper and definite reference to the documents is made by the party offering them; and

(c) The documents are published and generally circulated so that an opportunity is given to all the parties of interest to the hearing to examine them and present rebuttal evidence.

NAC 634A.530

634A.530 BRIEFS

1. In any hearing, the Board may order briefs to be filed within such time as may be allowed

by the Board.

2. Three copies of any requested brief must be filed with the Board and must be accompanied by an acknowledgment of service or a certificate of mailing on other parties of record.

3. The Board may, following the filing of briefs or upon contested motions, set the matter for oral argument. Ten days notice thereof, unless the Board deems a shorter time advisable, will be given to all parties of record.

NAC 634A.540

634A.540   DECISIONS AND ORDERS

1. A proceeding is submitted for decision by the Board after the taking of evidence, the filing of briefs or the presentation of such oral argument as may have been permitted by the Board.

2. Orders or decisions will be rendered within 90 days of the completion of the hearing.

3. Additional copies of orders may be obtained upon written request.

NAC 634A.550

634A.550   RECORDS OF HEARINGS

1. A record of a hearing will be kept by either a mechanical or electronic device.

2. A copy of the record will be made available to any person upon his or her request and at his or her expense.

NAC 634A.560

634A.560   PETITION; ISSUANCE OF ORDER OR OPINION

1. A petition for a declaratory order or an advisory opinion may be filed only by a holder of or applicant for a license or certificate.

2. The original and seven copies of the petition must be filed with the Executive Director not less than 10 days before the next regularly scheduled meeting of the Board. The petition must be submitted to the Board at that meeting. Within 30 days after the meeting, the Board will issue its declaratory order or advisory opinion.

NAC 634A.570

634A.570   PETITION

1. A petition requesting the adoption, filing, amendment or repeal of any regulation must be in writing.

2. The original and seven copies of the petition must be filed with the Board.

UTAH

UTAH ACUPUNCTURE LICENSING ACT

PART 1 GENERAL PROVISIONS

58-72-101 TITLE

This chapter shall be known as the "Acupuncture Licensing Act".

58-72-102 ACUPUNCTURE LICENSING-DEFINITIONS

In addition to the definitions in Section 58-1-102, as used in this chapter:

(1) "Board" means the Acupuncture Licensing Board created in Section 58-72-201.

(2)(a) "Injection therapy" means the use of a hypodermic needle, by a licensed acupuncturist who has obtained a clean needle technique certificate from the National Commission for the Certification of Acupuncture and Oriental Medicine (NCCAOM), to inject any of the following sterile substances in liquid form into acupuncture points on the body subcutaneously or intramuscularly:

(i) A nutritional substance;

(ii) A local anesthetic;

(iii) Autologous blood, if the licensee holds a current phlebotomy certification to draw blood;

(iv) Sterile water;

(v) Dextrose;

(vi) Sodium bicarbonate; and

(vii) Sterile saline.

(b) "Injection therapy" includes using ultrasound guidance to ensure that an injection is only a subcutaneous injection or an intramuscular injection.

(c) "Injection therapy" does not include injecting a substance into a vein, joint, artery, blood vessel, nerve, tendon, deep organ, or the spine.

(d) "Injection therapy" may not be performed on a pregnant woman or a child under the age of eight.

(3) "Licensed acupuncturist," designated as "L. Ac.," means a person who has been licensed under this chapter to practice acupuncture.

(4) "Moxibustion" means a heat therapy that uses the herb moxa to heat acupuncture points of the body.

(5)(a) "Practice of acupuncture" means the insertion of acupuncture needles, the use of injection therapy, and the application of moxibustion to specific areas of the body based on traditional oriental medical diagnosis and modern research as a primary mode of therapy.

(b) Adjunctive therapies within the scope of the practice of acupuncture may include:

(i) Manual, mechanical, thermal, electrical, light, and electromagnetic treatments based on traditional oriental medical diagnosis and modern research;

(ii) The recommendation, administration, or provision of dietary guidelines, herbs, supplements, homeopathics, and therapeutic exercise based on traditional oriental medical diagnosis and modern research according to practitioner training; and

(iii) the practice described in Subsections (5)(a) and (b) on an animal to the extent permitted by: (A) Subsection 58-28-307(12);

(B) the provisions of this chapter; and

(C) division rule.

(c) "Practice of acupuncture" does not include:

(i) the manual manipulation or adjustment of the joints of the body beyond the elastic barrier; or

(ii) the "manipulation of the articulation of the spinal column" as defined in Section 58-73-102.

(6) "Unprofessional conduct" is as defined in Sections 58-1-501 and 58-72-503, and as may be further defined by division rule.

58-72-103 RULEMAKING

When exercising rulemaking authority under this chapter, the division shall comply with the requirements of Title 63G, Chapter 3, Utah Administrative Rulemaking Act.

PART 2 BOARD

58-72-201 ACUPUNCTURE LICENSING BOARD

(1) There is created an Acupuncture Licensing Board consisting of:

(a) four licensed acupuncturists; and

(b) One member from the general public.

(2) The board shall be appointed and serve in accordance with Section 58-1-201. (3)

(a) The duties and responsibilities of the board shall be in accordance with Sections 58-1-202 and 58-1-203.

(b) In addition, the board shall designate one of its members on a permanent rotating basis to:

(i) Assist the division in reviewing complaints concerning the unlawful or unprofessional conduct of a licensee; and

(ii) Advise the division in its investigation of these complaints.

(4) A board member who has, under Subsection (3), reviewed a complaint or advised in its investigation may be disqualified from participating with the board when the board serves as a presiding officer in an adjudicative proceeding concerning the complaint.

PART 3 LICENSURE

58-72-301 LICENSE REQUIRED-LICENSE CLASSIFICATION

(1) A license is required to engage in the practice of acupuncture, except as specifically provided in Section 58-1-307 or 58-72-304.

(2) The division shall issue to a person who qualifies under this chapter a license in the classification of licensed acupuncturist.

58-72-302 QUALIFICATIONS FOR LICENSURE

An applicant for licensure as a licensed acupuncturist shall:

(1) Submit an application in a form prescribed by the division;

(2) Pay a fee determined by the department under Section 63J-1-504;

(3) Meet the requirements for current active certification in acupuncture under guidelines established by the National Commission for the Certification of Acupuncture and Oriental Medicine (NCCAOM) as demonstrated through a current certificate or other appropriate documentation;

(4) Pass the examination required by the division by rule;

(5) Establish procedures, as defined by rule, which shall enable patients to give informed consent to treatment; and

(6) Meet with the board, if requested, for the purpose of evaluating the applicant's qualifications for licensure.

58-72-303 TERMS OF LICENSE-EXPIRATION-RENEWAL

(1)(a) Each license issued under this chapter shall be issued in accordance with a two-year renewal cycle established by rule.

(b) A renewal period may be extended or shortened by as much as one year to maintain established renewal cycles or to change an established renewal cycle.

(2) Each license automatically expires on the expiration date shown on the license unless renewed by the licensee in accordance with Section 58-1-308.

(3) Renewal qualifications shall include:

(a) Either documentation of current and active NCCAOM certification; or

(b) Meeting the same professional development requirements as those licensed under this chapter.

58-72-304　EXCEPTIONS FROM LICENSURE

In addition to the exemptions from licensure set forth in Section 58-1-307, the following persons may engage in the practice of acupuncture subject to the stated circumstances and limitations without being licensed under this chapter:

(1) An individual licensed as a physician and surgeon or osteopathic physician and surgeon under Chapter 67, Utah Medical Practice Act, and Chapter 68, Utah Osteopathic Medical Practice Act;

(2) A commissioned physician or surgeon serving in the armed forces of the United States or other federal agency; and

(3) A chiropractic physician licensed under Chapter 73, Chiropractic Physician Practice Act. A chiropractic physician may not claim to be a licensed acupuncturist without acupuncturist licensure.

PART 4　LICENSE DENIAL AND DISCIPLINE

58-72-401　GROUNDS FOR DENIAL OF LICENSE-DISCIPLINARY PROCEEDINGS-RESUMPTION OF PRACTICE

Grounds for refusal to issue a license to an applicant, for refusal to renew the license of a licensee, to revoke, suspend, restrict, or place on probation the license of a licensee, to issue a public or private reprimand to a licensee, and to issue cease and desist orders shall be in accordance with Section 58-1-401.

PART 5　UNLAWFUL AND UNPROFESSIONAL CONDUCT-PENALTIES

58-72-501　ACUPUNCTURE LICENSEE-RESTRICTION ON TITLES USED

(1)(a) A person practicing as a licensed acupuncturist may not display or in any way use any title, words, or insignia in conjunction with the person's name or practice except the words "licensed acupuncturist" or "L. Ac.".

(b) When used in conjunction with the person's practice, the term "licensed acupuncturist" or "L. Ac." shall be displayed next to the name of the licensed acupuncturist.

(2)(a) A licensed acupuncturist may not use the term "physician," "physician or surgeon," or "doctor" in conjunction with the acupuncturist's name or practice.

(b) "Doctor of acupuncture" or "oriental medical doctor" may be used if the term is commensurate with the degree in acupuncture received by the practitioner.

(3) Medical doctors or chiropractic physicians who choose to practice acupuncture shall represent themselves as medical doctors or chiropractic physicians practicing acupuncture and not as licensed acupuncturists.

58-72-502　PENALTY FOR UNLAWFUL CONDUCT

(1) Any person who violates the unlawful conduct provision defined in Subsection 58-1-501(1)(a) is guilty of a third degree felony.

(2) Any person who violates any of the unlawful conduct provisions defined in Subsections 58-1-501(1)(b) through (e) is guilty of a class A misdemeanor.

58-72-503　UNPROFESSIONAL CONDUCT

Unprofessional conduct includes the failure to transmit records in the English language to the division, the patient's practitioner, or a third party insurance payor upon request.

PART 6　ACUPUNCTURIST PRACTICE-INSURANCE PAYMENTS

58-72-601　ACUPUNCTURE LICENSE NOT AUTHORIZING MEDICAL PRACTICE-INSURANCE PAYMENTS

Nothing in this chapter may be construed to permit the practice of medicine nor require direct payment from third party insurers directly to a person engaged in the practice of acupuncture.

PART 7　PROCUREMENT AND ADMINISTRATION AUTHORITY

58-72-701　PROCUREMENT AND ADMINISTRATION AUTHORITY

(1) A licensee who has received the necessary training to practice injection therapy, including having obtained a clean needle technique certificate from the National Commission for the Certification of Acupuncture and Oriental Medicine (NCCAOM):

(a) Has authority to procure and administer prescriptive substances described in Subsections 58-72-102(2)(a) and (b) for in-office administration only; and

(b) May obtain substances described in Subsection 58-72-102(2) from a registered prescription drug outlet, registered manufacturer, or registered wholesaler.

(2) An entity that provides any substance to a licensee in accordance with this chapter, and relies in good faith on license information provided by the licensee, is not liable for providing the substance.

UTAH ADMINISTRATIVE CODE

R156-72-101　TITLE

This rule is known as the "Acupuncture Licensing Act Rule".

R156-72-102　DEFINITIONS

In addition to the definitions in Title 58, Chapter 1, Division of Occupational and Professional

Licensing Act, and Title 58, Chapter 72, Acupuncture Licensing Act, the following rule definitions supplement the statutory definitions:

(1) "ACAOM" means the Accreditation Commission for Acupuncture and Oriental Medicine.

(2) "According to practitioner training" in Subsection 58-72-102(5)(b)(ii) means that the licensee has completed education and training from an educational program accredited or recognized by ACAOM regarding the recommendation, administration, or provision of dietary guidelines, herbs, supplements, homeopathics, and therapeutic exercise.

(3) "Administration" in Subsection 58-72-102(5)(b)(ii) means the direct application of an herb, homeopathic, or supplement to the body of a patient by:

(a) Ingestion;

(b) Topical application;

(c) Inhalation; or

(d) Point injection therapy (PIT).

(4) "Herbs" and "homeopathics", as used in Subsection 58-72-102(5)(b)(ii), may include:

(a) Vitamins;

(b) Minerals;

(c) Amino acids;

(d) Proteins; and

(e) Enzymes.

(5) "Insertion of acupuncture needles" in Subsection 58-72-102(5)(a) means a procedure of acupuncture and oriental medicine including myofascial trigger point therapy, intramuscular therapy, perineural injection therapy (PIT), prolotherapy, proprioceptive stimulation, Ashi points, or dry needling techniques.

(6) "Modern research" in Subsection 58-72-102(5)(b)(ii) means practicing according to acupuncture and oriental medicine education and training as recognized through NCCAOM.

(7) "NCCAOM" means the National Commission for the Certification of Acupuncture and Oriental Medicine, formerly known as the National Commission for the Certification of Acupuncturists (NCCA).

R156-72-103 AUTHORITY—PURPOSE

This rule is adopted by the Division under the authority of Subsection 58-1-106(1)(a) to enable the Division to administer Title 58, Chapter 72.

R156-72-104 ORGANIZATION—RELATIONSHIP TO RULE R156-1

The organization of this rule and its relationship to Rule R156-1 is as described in Section R156-1-107.

R156-72-302A QUALIFICATIONS FOR LICENSURE—CERTIFICATION AND EXAM REQUIREMENTS.

In accordance with Subsections 58-72-302(3) and (4), to meet the requirements for current active certification in acupuncture under guidelines established by NCCAOM, and the requirements for passing the examination required by the Division, an applicant for licensure as a licensed acupuncturist shall submit documentation of:

(1) Current and active NCCAOM certification; or

(2) Pursuant to Subsection 58-1-302(1), licensure in good standing as an acupuncturist in any state, district, or territory of the United States, for at least one year immediately preceding the application.

R156-72-302B QUALIFICATIONS FOR LICENSURE—ANIMAL ACUPUNCTURE

In accordance with Subsections 58-28-307(12)(d) and 58-72-102(5)(b)(iii), to engage in the practice of animal acupuncture, a licensed acupuncturist shall complete 100 hours of animal acupuncture training and education that includes:

(1) Fifty hours of on the job training under the indirect supervision of a licensed veterinarian;

(2) Animal anatomy training; and

(3) The remaining hours in animal specific continuing education.

R156-72-302C INFORMED CONSENT

(1) In accordance with Subsection 58-72-302(5), to enable patients to give informed consent to treatment, a licensed acupuncturist shall have a patient chart for each patient that includes:

(a) A written review of symptoms;

(b) A statement signed by the patient consenting to acupuncture treatment; and

(c) If the patient is receiving an adjunctive therapy as defined in Subsection 58-72-102(5), a written disclosure signed by the patient regarding the licensed acupuncturist's education and training to perform that therapy.

(2) In accordance with Section 58-72-503, patient records, including records documenting informed consent, shall be maintained for seven years.

R156-72-302D RENUMBERED

Formerly cited as UT ADC R156-72

R156-72-303 RENEWAL CYCLE—PROCEDURES

(1) In accordance with Subsection 58-1-308(1), the renewal date for the two-year renewal cycle applicable to licensees under Title 58, Chapter 72 is established by rule in Section R156-1-308a.

(2) Renewal procedures shall be in accordance with Section R156-1-308b through R156-1-308l.

(3) In accordance with Subsections 58-1-308(3)(b) and 58-72-303(3), a licensee

who does not maintain current and active NCCAOM certification shall:

(a) Complete at least 30 continuing education units (CEU) or 30 professional didactic activity (PDA) points within the two-year renewal period; and

(b) Maintain current BLS-CPR certification.

R156 - 72 - 503 UNPROFESSIONAL CONDUCT

In accordance with Subsection 58 - 72 - 102(6), "unprofessional conduct" includes:

(1) Failing to maintain office, instruments, equipment, appliances, or supplies in a safe and sanitary condition;

(2) Violating Subsection 58 - 72 - 303(3) regarding renewal qualifications by:

(a) Failing to maintain current and active NCCAOM certification;

(b) Failing to complete all CEUs required under Subsection R156 - 72 - 303(3); or

(c) Failing to maintain current BLS-CPR certification;

(3) Failing to abide by the NCCAOM Code of Ethics revised January 1, 2016, that is hereby incorporated by reference;

(4) Failing to maintain patient records for a seven-year period;

(5) Recommending, administering, or providing dietary guidelines, herbs, supplements, homeopathics, or therapeutic exercise without having completed the required practitioner training pursuant to Subsection 58 - 72 - 102(5)(b)(ii) and Subsection R156 - 72 - 102(2); or

(6) Administering venous injections, immunizations, or controlled substances.